PENGUIN BOOKS
THE NEPAL NEXUS

Sudheer Sharma is a leading Nepali journalist and editor-in-chief of *Kantipur Daily*, Nepal's highest-selling daily.

PRAISE FOR THE BOOK

'As Nepal's leading editor, Sudheer Sharma is deeply knowledgeable about the country's political goings-on. In *The Nepal Nexus*, he generously shares his knowledge so that readers can grasp the intricate, personality-driven events of the recent past, and glean an understanding of the difficult path that lies ahead for Nepal. Sharma has a command of his material that lets him render even the most obscure details lucid and comprehensible. He has done Nepal a great service by writing *The Nepal Nexus*.'—Manjushree Thapa, author of *Forget Kathmandu*

'Sudheer Sharma's *The Nepal Nexus* is a factually sound and analytically insightful narrative of Nepal's complex and radical political transition from a traditional monarchy to a republican polity. It holds King Gyanendra largely responsible for the collapse of monarchy; blames the Maoists for being driven more by the lure of power than their vision of "New Nepal" and exposes India's role as being ad-hocist and shaped largely by its intelligence agencies than a sound political assessment and strategy. It's a must-read for all those who love Nepal and want to understand its contemporary politics.'—Sukh Deo Muni, professor emeritus, Jawaharlal Nehru University, and former Indian ambassador and special envoy

'A politically stable democratic Nepal will not only reap prosperity for its citizens but usher dividends for the contiguous, densely populated plains of India. The telescoped interlude since Nepal achieved democracy in 1990, as detailed in this work by Sudheer Sharma—including a Maoist-state conflict, a palace massacre, several identity movements, a royal coup, foreign interventionism, a massive earthquake and an economic blockade—ended in the promulgation of a Constitution that made Nepal federal, secular and republican. A key requirement for nurturing Nepal's stable and democratic future under the new Constitution, as the author concludes after recording Nepal's intense three-decade journey, is for New Delhi to end the unaccountable adventurism of its intelligence apparatchiks and to restore the bilateral relationship back to the level of politicians and diplomats.'—Kanak Mani Dixit, founding editor, *Himal Southasian*

'This is a leading journalist's remarkable account of the conspiratorial tradition in Nepali politics. Sharma reveals the secret meetings, the improbable alliances, the fixes and the double-crosses that the Maoist war provoked. Anyone trying to understand what goes down in the salons and hotel suites of power will need to read this book.'—Thomas Bell, author of *Kathmandu*

The
NEPAL
NEXUS

*An Inside Account of the Maoists,
the Durbar and New Delhi*

Sudheer Sharma

Translated from the Nepali by Sanjay Dhakal

PENGUIN BOOKS

An imprint of Penguin Random House

PENGUIN BOOKS

USA | Canada | UK | Ireland | Australia
New Zealand | India | South Africa | China

Penguin Books is part of the Penguin Random House group of companies
whose addresses can be found at global.penguinrandomhouse.com

Published by Penguin Random House India Pvt. Ltd
4th Floor, Capital Tower 1, MG Road,
Gurugram 122 002, Haryana, India

Penguin
Random House
India

First published in Viking by Penguin Random House India 2019
Published in paperback in Penguin Books in 2021

10 9 8 7 6 5 4 3 2 1

The views and opinions expressed in this book are the author's own and the
facts are as reported by him which have been verified to the extent possible,
and the publishers are not in any way liable for the same.

ISBN 9780143456193

Typeset in Adobe Caslon Pro by Manipal Technologies Limited, Manipal
Printed at Replika Press Pvt. Ltd, India

www.penguin.co.in

Contents

Introduction

Witness to change

On 17 May 2018, Prachanda, the communist leader who had spearheaded the decade-long Maoist people's war, turned towards a completely different path. That day he not only announced the dissolution of his party, the Communist Party of Nepal (Maoist Centre), but, more significantly, also gave up his love for Maoism. He unified his party with the Communist Party of Nepal (Unified Marxist–Leninist) which had been in the parliamentary mainstream since the 1990s. The new party was called the Nepal Communist Party or NCP, which was the original name of the party when it was first established in Nepal in 1949.

The NCP adopted Marxism–Leninism as its guiding principle. It abandoned the Maoist road map of grabbing power forcibly. And, it expressly committed itself to peaceful multiparty competition. This was a radical departure for Prachanda, who had till the recent past been dedicated to the cause of armed revolution.

Prachanda—his real name was Pushpa Kamal Dahal—started people's war in 1996 and joined the peace process ten years later in 2006. But the complexities of the subsequent decade-long political transition made him a disillusioned man. In this interregnum, his party led the government thrice. He himself became prime minister twice. During this process he and his comrades had handed over their arms to the state, his People's Liberation Army had merged with the Nepali Army and the cadres had integrated with Nepali society. The UN political mission, the United Nations Mission in Nepal (UNMIN), that had come to facilitate the peace process in Nepal, had returned once these tasks were complete. But the party that had remained intact during the painful insurgency years, had split many times after it joined the political mainstream. His key stalwarts of the war days including Baburam Bhattarai, Mohan Baidhya and Netra Bikram Chand, had parted ways and floated their own separate outfits.

Consequently, the Maoist party was not only weakened organizationally in the open political space, it was also forced to share the same leftist constituency as another big communist party, the CPN–UML. It was clear that only one communist party could survive prominently in the long run.

This objective reality could not have escaped a politician as shrewd as Prachanda. Hence, in the first election for province and centre under the new Constitution, he was keen to join hands with the CPN–UML. When the UML and the Maoists declared their electoral alliance on 3 October 2017, they also announced their intention to unite. Initially, many saw it as a strategic electoral ploy, but within eight months, they created a single party. Having fought together, the communist alliance bagged a clear majority. The election results acted as catalyst to cement the Maoist–UML unity.

These were the objective circumstances under which Maoist Chairman Prachanda and UML Chairman K.P. Sharma Oli— who had had an antagonistic relationship till recently—agreed to jointly chair the new unified party. As a result, Oli got to head the government with a clear majority and Prachanda became convinced that his political future would be secured by supporting Oli. Prachanda, in fact, decided to unify with the UML based on his calculation that he would get to head the unified party and the government after Oli.

This was a new direction that Prachanda took after he abandoned the people's war. Where did this direction take him? Did it do justice to his political past? It is still too early to say but the answers would be of great interest not just to commentators and political scientists, but to the people of Nepal as a whole.

* * *

Prachanda had launched the 'People's War' in Nepal in February 1996, a time the communist movement was on its back foot elsewhere in the world. Initially none of the actors–the government, political parties, security forces, civil society, media and international community–took it seriously. The Nepal Police claimed it would bring the insurgency under control quickly, but singularly failed to do so. Six years after the revolt the Nepali Army came into the picture. The army did not win but it prevented the Maoists from winning. That stalemate forced both sides to explore the middle path to restore peace. Hence, the peace process that started from 2006.

The previous decade (1996–2006) had witnessed major upheavals in the Nepali body politic. The subsequent decade was usurped by the uncertainties of protracted political transition. This book covers both periods. It is focused on the origin and expansion of Maoist revolt, but is not a history that covers all the aspects of the Maoist movement. It merely places them at the centre and analyses their chaotic relations with the monarchy (termed 'Durbar' in this book) and the Indian establishment (called 'Delhi'). In other words, this book is an account of a three-way interplay between Delhi, the Durbar and the Maoists which has had a profound impact on the present.

In the two and a half centuries since the establishment of the modern Nepali state, the ten-year people's war posed its

greatest internal challenge. Thousands of people took part in
that armed movement risking their lives in pursuit of the dream
of communist revolution. It was during this people's war that
the country could take great strides towards a progressive social
agenda, such as the republic, a Constituent Assembly, social
awareness of inequality, and inclusion. The Maoist revolt played
a decisive role in the socio-political transformation of this feudal
unitary Hindu state.

Certainly, that revolt was born in the hills of Nepal, and not in
Delhi or the Durbar. But to fulfil their own interests the latter two
played indirect roles in its expansion. Initially, the Durbar took a
soft approach towards Maoists in the belief that it would lead to the
failure of the parliamentary system restored in the early 1990s and
pave the way for the return of an assertive monarchy. Therefore,
the Durbar did not allow the army, which had remained under its
control, to venture out of their barracks for the first six years of
the insurgency. The lack of support from the army meant that the
police was forced to confront the guerrillas alone and, in the end,
was decisively defeated by the latter.

How did the conflict between the government and the Durbar
flare up when the latter did not allow the army to be deployed
against the Maoists? How did the rebels take advantage of such
fissures within the state? How did they establish relations with
the Durbar? How and why did the king's brother have a secret
dialogue with the Maoists? How did the palace massacre push
Nepal's politics towards a new phase? This book attempts to
examine these questions.

King Gyanendra who was enthroned following the palace
massacre, first tried dialogue with the Maoists, then opted
for a military solution. He failed on both fronts. It led him to
stage a coup to take over executive authority. His move created
a situation whereby the two conflicting sides—the Maoists and
the parliamentary parties—came together. The historic people's
movement was launched at their behest in 2006. It ended the

240-year-old monarchy and established the republican system. This book chronicles that political transformation.

The other aspect of this book is to track the role of the Indian government. Since the start of the people's war, some top Maoist leaders were based in India, albeit underground. The Indian government seemed interested in the Maoist movement from its inception. After the palace massacre, it became a strategic concern for them. India did not wish to control the activities of Nepali Maoists on its soil; instead it began to develop a relationship with them. India even encouraged the joint action by the parliamentary parties and the Maoists against the monarchy. The 12-point understanding reached in Delhi, which became the starting-point for the republic, was the result of this facilitation.

The existing poverty, inequality, exploitation, discrimination, unemployment and government repression were the main causes behind the origin and expansion of the Maoist revolt in Nepal. Maoist leaders had started a political project to lure Nepali youth into the armed campaign by identifying these issues, and by creating initial bases in the then Mid-Western Development Region of the country with a Magar ethnic majority. They had accurately diagnosed the problems and contradictions within Nepali society. Their conclusions and plans regarding public discontent and ways to channelize it towards revolt, also turned out to be correct. They even attempted to manipulate strong power centres like Delhi and the Durbar. But whether they managed to take advantage of them or were themselves taken for a ride is a question that future historians will have to answer.

One simple fact is that the Maoists failed in their declared objective to establish a people's republic. When they realized that they could not attain this objective, they switched goals and agreed to join the middle path of the Constituent Assembly and the peace process. From the perspective of conservative communism, they may have seemed to be revisionist; but it was due to their movement that Nepali society embraced big changes like the republic, federalism, secularism, inclusion, etc. The roles played by the parliamentary parties and the subsequent Madhesi uprising, too, were important in effecting these changes, but the start of the Maoist movement was the decisive factor. Therefore, it is my view that the major credit for restructuring the state should go to the Maoists.

* * *

I have filed numerous field reports for *Himal Khabarpatrika* and *Kathmandu Today* magazines since the Maoists started the people's war in 1996. In subsequent years when I worked as editor of the *Kantipur* daily and of *Nepal* magazine, I have had a ringside view of the various dimensions of the transition that Nepal was going through and I was witness to many political and geopolitical machinations. As a journalist, the informal access that I received to the palace and the President, ministers and prime ministers, political leaders, bureaucrats, security officials, experts and diplomats, helped me get closer to the truth and facts.

It was against this background that my book *Prayogshala* was written. Nepali readers loved the book, which remained on the bestseller list for a long time. I still encounter readers who are looking for the book, and ones who keep on pushing me to write '*Prayogshala-2*'. There were also quite a few well-wishers who asked me to bring out an English edition of the book. This book is the modified, updated and translated version of *Prayogshala*. It is different from the original Nepali edition. Some chapters have been removed, new ones have been added, and updates of recent events have been included.

This book is mainly based on primary sources. The facts I gathered from direct interviews, discussions with sources and details compiled during reporting from the main bases of my story. Apart from where I have attributed the sources, other conversations, quotes and information were gathered from the concerned individuals themselves. I have included a list of interviews and discussions at the end of this book. Alongside, the important information and insights received from anonymous sources also helped in the writing of this book. Although their full identity cannot be disclosed, I have tried to describe the types of sources in the endnotes as far as possible.

I have made use of my diary, email, phone conversations and recollections as and when necessary. Original documents and unpublished reports that I came across during research also helped a lot. Other resources for the book include books, newspapers, websites, journals, radio and television materials. I have mentioned them in the endnotes as well.

This book is a description of the recent past and the present of Nepali politics and geopolitics as I saw, felt, heard, read and analysed during the course of my job as a journalist. But it was not easy to write about the present. Our generation has witnessed a lot during a short time—the Maoist revolt, the palace massacre, the state of emergency, army mobilization, the royal coup, the people's movement, the republic, the Madhesi uprising, the Constituent Assembly, federalism, the new Constitution and so on. Too many questions emerged as I tried to write about them. I did not have answers to all of them. Therefore, I have refrained from trying to reach conclusions in this book. I have merely brought to the fore the facts, details and analyses, and left it to the readers to arrive at their own.

Lalitpur, Nepal   Sudheer Sharma
August 2019

Part I

The Beginning

1

The Revolt

'. . . External causes are the condition of change and internal causes are the basis of change, and that external causes become operative through internal causes. In a suitable temperature an egg changes into a chicken, but no temperature can change a stone into a chicken, because each has a different basis.'

—Mao Tse Tung, on political changes[1]

The year was 1971. Having just received membership of the Communist Party from Ruplal Bishwakarma of the Pushpa Lal faction, Pushpa Kamal Dahal was in two minds. Should he join the Royal Nepali Army and become a second lieutenant? Or should he take the plunge into the communist movement? At first, he thought becoming an army officer would be better. Then he joined the National Cadet Corps (NCC).

He had been brought up in the central Nepali district of Chitwan, and around that period, he was studying intermediate-level science (ISc) at Patan Multiple Campus. 'They used to recruit those qualified in ISc as second lieutenants. Besides that, anyone doing a course at NCC would also get preference,' Prachanda recounted. 'I don't know where my interest in joining the army had come from. I fervently wanted to become an army officer.'

But he changed his mind. He decided to become a revolutionary communist instead. He had completed the one-year NCC course, but did not sit for the examination for second lieutenant. Why?

'As I completed my courses at the NCC and the ISc, I was increasingly attracted to politics. I decided not to pursue a career in uniform,' he said.

Had he joined the army, perhaps he would have one day fought against the Maoists. Or perhaps Nepal would never have seen the Maoists' People's War.

'Well, I don't know what I would have become!' he laughed. He went on to lead a decade-long armed struggle and became the commander of the 'People's Liberation Army', which he founded. He pointed a gun at the very institution that he'd wanted to join. Pushpa Kamal Dahal metamorphosed into the famous 'Prachanda'.[2]

Gorkha trial

Established in 1949, the Communist Party of Nepal (CPN) was wracked by internal divisions and splits.[3] There were several factions operating at that time. Prachanda had become a regional bureau member of the CPN (Fourth Convention). In line with party policy, he was active in the boycott of the 1981 election of the National Panchayat. After that, the police began harassing his family; his father was assaulted, but Prachanda somehow managed to escape. Police seized all his academic certificates and his citizenship card. Prachanda was left without a Nepali *nagarikata* (citizenship). It never mattered. In 1981, he abandoned the identity of Pushpa Kamal Dahal and was subsumed into underground politics.

The same year, he had the opportunity to take part in the plenum meeting of the party central committee, which was organized in Ayodhya, India. But his meeting with two leaders of the old guard, whom he had greatly admired as 'true revolutionaries', Mohan Bikram Singh and Nirmal Lama, was 'disappointing'.

'My faith in the leadership crumbled. I decided that there was no alternative to coming forward myself.' So he readied himself for the revolution. In 1983, the party split. He chose to side with CPN–Masal under Singh's leadership. A year later, he became a central committee (CC) member. But at the very first CC meeting, he clashed with Singh. Prachanda wanted the party to immediately take up arms; Singh did not. In 1984, the party split again. Singh kept the leadership of CPN–Masal and Prachanda left to join the other faction, confusingly named CPN–Mashal (with an 'sh'), which was led by Mohan Baidya 'Kiran'.

Kiran hailed from the western district of Pyuthan. Although lacking charisma, he was well known for his encouragement to youth organizers in the party. Among those youths was Prachanda, the rising star.

'Right from the start, I found Prachanda to be an affable, easygoing and energetic young talent,' Kiran has written. 'In his future, I saw an able communist who could carry the torch of revolution forward.'[4] Having parted ways with Mohan Bikram with the objective of launching a revolution, the Prachanda–Kiran group then busied themselves with drawing up plans for the struggle. They started by studying other insurgencies. Between 1985 and 1989, they soaked up every available document on insurgencies, from the Jhapa revolt inspired by Naxalbari to international revolutionary struggles. They also immersed themselves in fierce debates on those struggles.

Then something happened on 28 April 1986 that put Prachanda on a rapidly rising trajectory. The party had decided to actively boycott the National Panchayat elections scheduled for that month. They attacked police posts in nine sectors of Kathmandu. Known as the 'sector episode', the action resulted in no casualties, but invited fierce retaliation from the police. The ensuing raids and arrests completely destroyed the Kathmandu Valley network of the CPN–Mashal.

At the central committee meeting held in Chitwan in October 1989, the party accepted that the episode was a grave mistake. Among the central leaders, it was only Prachanda who was not linked to the episode. Prachanda was known as Comrade Bishwas then, and Kiran proposed him as the new party general secretary. He was only thirty-five years old.

Prachanda had already recognized his party's weakness in launching the sector episode. As the attack was carried out in a city, and that too in the capital, the government was able to go decisively on the offensive. This incident reinforced his belief that armed struggle should be initiated from rural areas. The protracted people's war launched by Mao in China offered similar lessons.

Prachanda planned to launch a peasants' movement by raising local issues and, subsequently, politicizing those issues to fan the movement. 'The government is certain to intervene during such struggle. Therefore, it is necessary to secretly collect the names of local goons, tyrants, informers and feudal lords so that we can take action at the right time. Efforts should be made to transform the peasants' movement into a force of combatants': such was Prachanda's plan seven years before he finally launched the Maoists' People's War.[5]

But the party that was planning to launch a war did not have even a single gun. Prachanda and Ram Bahadur Thapa 'Badal' were, after much hard work, able to purchase just two rifles at NRs. 10,000 from one Ganesh Gurung of Manang district. They organized a ten-day-long arms training at Siranchowk in Gorkha, which included training in using guns and making bombs.

That was the first guerrilla training Prachanda and his comrades had ever taken. Subsequently, Prachanda and another leader, C.P. Gajurel 'Gaurav', contacted the Maoist Communist Centre (MCC) active across the border in Bihar. They received another fifteen days of guerrilla training from the MCC in the jungles of Palamu village, then in Bihar.[6] Armed with this training and experience, Prachanda decided to start the 'trial' of the People's War from Gorkha district soon after he became party general secretary.

Another training camp was organized in Siranchowk, Gorkha. This time, Prachanda and Badal were the trainers. Most of the sixteen youths who received firearms training from them later went on to become central committee members. But just as Prachanda was preparing for 'guerrilla action' by mobilizing these youths, the country became embroiled in the first People's Movement against the Panchayat system. This pushed the party to change its tactics.

The party decided to join the People's Movement, shelving their plans of a people's war. To support the Nepali Congress, which led the movement, the then CPN–Marxist Leninist had formed a 'Unified Leftist Front.' Parties such as the CPN–Mashal, which followed Mao's thought, formed a separate 'Unified National People's Movement' committee. The Leftist Front supported the slogan of multiparty democracy, whereas the more radical movement called for the establishment of a republic. When the movement ended after the dissolution of the Panchayat, and restoration of multiparty democracy, Prachanda et al. termed the agreement as a 'betrayal, since their goal was to make Nepal a People's Republic.' But they were not in a position to continue the movement, so they decided to take a roundabout path towards armed struggle.

The first task before them was building an organization and its capability. In 1990, Prachanda united his party with the Nirmal Lama-led CPN (Fourth Convention) and the Proletarian Labour Organization led by Ruplal Bishwakarma (the new party was named CPN–Unity Centre). The same year, the Baburam Bhattarai group, which had split from Mohan Bikram's party, came to join the Unity Centre. After completing his PhD in architectural engineering in India, Baburam had returned to join the communist movement. In Kathmandu, he engaged briefly in his profession, but soon became a full-time member of the communist cadre. He was fond of writing and holding intellectual debates. The meeting between the underground leader Prachanda and academic-cum-communist Baburam, who had exercised mostly open politics, gave new energy to the party.

The CPN–Unity Centre also had leaders who wanted to try parliamentary politics. Even Prachanda wanted to experiment with parliamentary politics as it would shorten their path. So, despite opposing the Constitution of 1990, they took part in the parliamentary election held under that Constitution the following year. Around sixty-nine candidates were fielded under the banner of the United People's Front (UPF) and the leadership of Baburam Bhattarai. Of them, nine were elected. With 4.39 per cent of popular votes, the UPF was the third force in the Parliament after Congress and the UML. It also received two seats in the National Assembly, the upper house.

Prachanda's team concluded that it was difficult to reach the centre of power through the parliamentary path. Therefore, although they had joined Parliament, they were still preparing for the armed struggle. In November 1991, the fifteen-day national unity convention of CPN–Unity Centre was held in Madi, Chitwan, and passed Prachanda's proposal for launching a 'protracted people's war with the idea of establishing base areas' in what was called the 'Chinese model' of revolution. It stated, 'Our political strategy is to establish a new people's republic of Nepal under the dictatorship of the proletariat, through the unity of proletarians and peasants-workers against feudalism and imperialism.'[7]

Preparations for war then gathered pace. However, internal dissent intensified and the party split in 1994, when another young leader, Narayan Kaji Shrestha 'Prakash', gained leadership of the Unity Centre by gathering the dissenters. Prachanda's group changed the name of their party to the Communist Party of

Nepal–Maoist. The new name was the ultimate indication of how close to the 'Maoist war' they were.

Champagne time

Prachanda was at ease after the split in the party. Now he had around him only those comrades who were committed to the people's war. So the third plenum of the CPN–Maoist, held in February 1995 in Gorkha district, passed the military action plan for the people's war. The party received support from the CPI–ML (People's War) and the MCC in India, particularly in technical preparations. These groups helped in selecting strategic vantage points in the Mahabharat range, which had been identified by the Nepali Maoists as the backbone of their struggle.

Physical training was the main aspect of technical preparation. The traditional baton play of the Magars of Rolpa–Rukum was employed. Training was provided in the use of *khukuris*, country-made guns and rifles. Martial arts were taught. The collection of arms and ammunition began. Retired soldiers of the Indian Gorkha regiments were the main trainers. In October 1995, just before they declared the People's War, selected combatants were gathered in Siranchowk, Gorkha. They were provided training in the use of rifles, bomb-making and the use of explosives, as well as given ideological briefing on the art of war.

In the course of preparation for the struggle, they were taught how and where to launch the people's war. In urban centres, public assemblies and campaigns were carried out by the party's legitimate political wing, the United People's Front (UPF). In rural areas, action including sabotage, propaganda operations and 'cleansing' of class enemies. In the villages of districts such as Rolpa, Rukum, Gorkha, Ramechhap, Sindhuli, Kavre and Sindhupalchowk, the plan was to push the people into direct confrontation with the local administration and the ruling Congress party. It was intended to incite the police administration into carrying out oppressive action, and to take advantage of the feeling of vengeance that this would trigger among the wider populace. The most successful implementation of this plan was seen in Rolpa–Rukum. The state did not understand the Maoist plan and, instead, pushed a wide segment of the innocent population into the Maoist fold by resorting to indiscriminate oppression.

As the Maoist leader Biplav remembers, 'We could do nothing then apart from holding meetings in our rooms. But in the course of such discussions, we came up with a bold method—sacrifice. We thought that if we were ready to sacrifice our lives, then we could achieve a lot. And we accordingly prepared our leaders and cadres, politically and ideologically.' The aim of this organizational preparation was to create an 'elite force' of leaders and cadres who were unafraid of fighting a war. Everyone was taught to be ready to go underground. Those harbouring any doubt were removed from party committees. 'We had estimated that once the people's war began, up to 80 per cent of party organization could get decimated (due to mass arrests, killings and escapes), and the remaining 20 per cent would be left to carry the struggle forward,' Biplav recalls.

In September of 1995, the central committee made a comprehensive review of the four areas of preparation, and concluded that the time was ripe to launch the people's war. Following the meeting, Baburam Bhattarai began a public campaign across the country through the UPF, while Prachanda provided politico-military training to leading cadres underground. Baburam was the public face of the Maoists, whereas Prachanda pulled the strings from behind.

The public leaders of the party, Baburam Bhattarai and Pampha Bhusal, went to Singha Durbar, the seat of the Nepali government, and to the then prime minister, Sher Bahadur Deuba, of the Nepali Congress party. Deuba was handed the list of 'forty-point demands.'[8]

They handed the list on 4 February 1996 with a stern warning that they would launch a 'forceful struggle' if no positive initiative was taken to address those demands by 17 February. Deuba saw this as no more than a political stunt. So he went to visit India days after receiving the demands, as if nothing had happened. The Maoists themselves were not serious about their deadline either. Five days *before* it expired, they started the war by launching simultaneous attacks on police posts in Rolpa, Rukum, Sindhuli and Gorkha on 13 February 1996.

At that very moment, Prime Minister Deuba was on a special plane, en route to Chennai from Delhi. Liquors were banned on domestic airlines, but the ban could not affect Deuba's entourage. As the then Indian Ambassador K.V. Rajan remembers, somebody mentioned that a group in Nepal, armed with crude weapons and calling itself 'Maoists', had attacked police posts. But nobody took the news seriously as it was already 'champagne time'.[9]

Delhi and the Durbar

Looking back, the first Maoist attacks were not especially violent. Nobody was killed. But it was the beginning of a campaign, an unprecedented campaign, in Nepal's history. The communist leaders of Nepal had been raising slogans of armed struggle since the communist party was founded in 1949. But the credit for actually launching the planned armed struggle went to the CPN–Maoists, forty-six years later. When they started the war, the CPN–Maoists had just seventy-two 'whole-time' cadres, from central to local level. Those six dozen experimented with Mao's war in Nepal.

The strategy formulated by the Maoists was successful probably because, in the initial phase, they concentrated on collecting books and documents more than arms and ammunition. They read about everything from history, ethnicity, geography and politics to culture. They looked like political scientists and sociologists. What was the speciality of a particular region? What were the characteristics and attitudes of a specific ethnic group? What was the relationship between the various ethnic groups, and between the state and such groups? How could a particular community be pushed to fight the state? Why did past struggles fail? What was the scope for implementing the strategy of a protracted people's war in Nepal? They laboriously searched for answers to these questions.

Although they followed Marx to Mao ideologically, for all practical purposes, they looked inward to learn the lessons of armed struggle. They distilled the thousand-year history of Nepali society and came to some unique conclusions. For example: Nepal is not a yam between two boulders, but a piece of dynamite; or that the people of this land of Buddha were not peaceful, but violent. Some of the deductions were:

- The reactionary propaganda that the Nepali people are peace-loving and that they don't like violence is absolutely false. It is an incontrovertible fact that the Nepali people have been waging violent struggle for their rights throughout history.
- Whatever general reforms have been achieved by the Nepali people so far have been driven by the force of violent and illegal struggle by the people.
- The anti-establishment feeling among Nepali people has always been very strong.
- The Nepali people are the greatest warriors in the world, known for their ability to bear severe material and bodily hardship while fighting.

Prachanda's plan was to employ this fighting spirit, this anti-establishment feeling, and initiate violence to destroy the 250-year-old monarchy. He took up the strategy of surrounding the cities from the villages, since a large segment of the army was located in urban centres and the villages had minimal government presence. Among the rural areas, he identified the hilly range from east to west as the backbone for the struggle, with the Rapti hills at their centre. There were enough reasons why a guerrilla campaign could be sustained in these areas: remoteness, dense jungles, acute underdevelopment, the warrior Magar community, and the pent-up frustration of decades-long indifference from the state. Most importantly, they had a long-established communist tradition. But if he started the war from Rapti alone, there was a danger that the government could concentrate its response there. So the Maoists prepared to launch the war simultaneously from different parts of the country, hoping that the government's attention would be scattered.

There were enough political, economic and social factors in Nepali society to let the armed revolt fester: poverty, unemployment, the lack of improvement in people's living standards despite the 1990 political change; the shameless lust for power demonstrated during the hung Parliament elected in 1994; corruption scandals; opposition to the 1990 Constitution in some quarters; discontent over Nepal's identity as a Hindu kingdom; the issues of Dalits and ethno-regional discord. These apart, there was a significant group of leftist intellectuals and writers who had considered revolution a romantic outcome ever since the formation of the Communist Party of Nepal in 1949.

The Maoists prepared for their people's war fully alert to these objective and subjective considerations. 'Strike your blow at one target at one time. When doing so, if possible, work in temporary coordination with other enemies. If not, at least, isolate them . . .' The Maoist headquarters sent such circulars to its cadres, adding, 'For example, if we want to target a particular feudal/murderer of a village, it may be necessary to make use of or neutralize others from the same class who are inimical to him.'[10]

When the Maoists launched their people's war, the three major forces of Nepali politics—Congress, CPN–UML and the royal palace—were busy trying to weaken each other. The royal palace was still not able to reconcile itself to the 1990 Constitution, which had curtailed the powers of the monarchy.

The CPN–UML had written a twenty-seven-point list of objections to the Constitution, while the Nepali Congress treated it as one of the best Constitutions in the world. In day-to-day politics, the Nepali Congress was pitted against the CPN–UML. The royal palace was against them both. It was looking for a good opportunity to seize power again by fomenting discord between them. Therefore, when the Maoists targeted the Congress, the UML and the royal palace were unconcerned. It seemed that they were sympathetic to the people's war as it could provide them with the opportunity to seize power.

In the forty-point list of demands that the Maoists had submitted to the government before launching the people's war, most points were related to the monarchy and to ending special relations with India. This indicated that they would adopt aggressive policies against both Delhi and the Durbar. However, in practice, they could be seen employing the policy of using Delhi and the Durbar, turn by turn—even when it turned out that they themselves were the ones who were being used at times.

2

Police a Foe, but Army a Friend!

'The people's liberation force that played a historic role in the revolution of 1950 was turned into *Raksha Dal* and became Nepal Police. In this way, the army was gradually being displaced and losing its identity . . . The feeling that this was the force that defeated the national army caught hold and the feeling of animosity became entrenched, with the army on the lookout for a chance for revenge.'

—Shyam Kumar Tamang, tracing the
background of army–police bitterness[1]

The Maoist People's War was intensifying. The Rapti Hills were the flashpoint. A series of attacks and clashes pushed the names of various villages of that area into national headlines. Khara village of Rukum was among those that became 'famous'. On 22 February 2000, fifteen innocents were killed in a police operation there. The police had entered the village in search of Maoist insurgents. But those killed were not insurgents. In fact, some of them were workers of the ruling Nepali Congress party.

When I reached the village a few days later, I could see remnants of houses burnt by the police, who had thought they were being used as shelters by insurgents. Everybody there was eager to share the pain of losing their relatives. The police had already returned to district headquarters; there was no presence of any other government agency. Except one—the Royal Nepali Army was moving around freely.

Lieutenant Colonel Jaga Bahadur Gurung was at a local tea stall along with his troops. He was telling the villagers who had gathered around him, 'We were three kilometres away when the Khara incident occurred. Perhaps the police might not have dared to commit such atrocities had we been closer.'

It had been fourteen months since Lt Col. Gurung had been stationed there, leading a troop of 400 soldiers in building a road linking the Rukum headquarters of Musikot with Salyan district. Yet, they never encountered the rebels, despite the rapid expansion of the Maoist movement. In fact, the army blamed the police, rather than the insurgents, for the intensification of the insurgency. The local army barracks provided relief materials to the families of those killed in Khara. Police officers were understandably angry at the army's behaviour. One officer could hold it in no longer. He told Lt Col. Gurung, 'You guys are giving medicines to those who deserve cyanide.'

However, the army not only distributed medicines, but also copybooks to students, building materials to schools, drinking water to locals and shoes to porters. This was part of the army headquarters' psychological campaign, to win the hearts and minds of local people while refraining from direct encounters with the insurgents, a campaign that Lt Col. Gurung and his troops were carrying out.[2]

The army activity in Khara was just an example. I found friendly behaviour between the army and the insurgents in the course of my reporting work in various districts. At many places, the soldiers and insurgents used to come face to face. But, surprisingly, they did not fight. They would converse with each other and disperse. Such scenes were common before the army was mobilized against the rebels in November 2001.

The Maoists, on their part, were in no mood to provoke the army. In 1998, when the government entrusted the army with the responsibility of securing the telephone towers in fifty-six places, the Maoists stopped attacking communication towers—earlier, such towers used to be their favourite targets. In 1999, they killed police personnel mobilized for the general election, but left the soldiers untouched. Prachanda declared in an interview, 'While they are limited to providing security to the election, we will not do anything to provoke the army.'[3]

The ministers and police officers at the time tried to portray a grave picture of conspiracy by making claims such as that of the discovery of army grenades when the Maoists attacked the police in Ghartigaon, Rolpa; or that of thousands of rounds of ammunition from the Swayambhu arsenal reaching the Maoists; or of the Maoists getting hold of cartridges that were 'lost' from the Rasuwa barracks. Yet, there is no hard evidence to support such claims.

But one thing is pretty clear: during a certain period there was, indeed, an undeclared cooperation between the two forces. In fact, while the army was confined to the barracks for six years (1996–2001), the Maoists were allowed enough space to spread and strengthen themselves. Had the army been mobilized earlier, they may not have got that space.

An operation that never took off

Whether it was the armed struggle launched by the Nepali Congress after 1961, or the Jhapa revolt (1971) by the Naxalite communists, the royal palace would nip dissent in the bud. The palace had also planned to mobilize the army against the Maoist insurgency since the beginning of 1997. The environment was also right when a person loyal to the palace, the leader of the RPP, Lokendra Bahadur Chand, became the prime minister with the support of the CPN–UML.

In August 1997, the army headquarters dispatched a team of 102 of its best officers to undertake a ground study in Rolpa, Rukum, Salyan and Jajarkot districts. But before they could complete their study, the Chand government was brought down in Kathmandu. As it happened, another pro-palace leader, Surya Bahadur Thapa, became the prime minister. This time, the Nepali Congress was his ruling ally. But the plan for army mobilization was still on. Based on a report from his team, in November 1997, the army chief, Gen. Dharmapal Barsingh Thapa, presented the prime minister with a detailed action plan for army mobilization. It stated that action must be taken before the struggle reached the scale of an all-out insurgency; before it spread out beyond the current four districts (Rukum, Rolpa, Salyan and Jajarkot) and became harder to control.

Number four brigade of Surkhet was ordered to look after all the four districts. There were around 3500 troops in the Surkhet brigade, and a reinforcement of 2200 from Pokhara and Kathmandu was approved. C.B. Gurung was named the western operation commander. The army also decided to mobilize a temporary brigade under the command of Sadip Bahadur Shah to look after four districts in the east—Sindhuli, Ramechhap, Kavre and Sindhupalchok—where Maoist activities were rapidly increasing.

Two days after it took the decision to mobilize the army, the Surya Bahadur Thapa-led government collapsed after failing to win a no-confidence motion. Nepali Congress President Girija Prasad Koirala returned as the new prime minister. However, he did not overturn the previous government's decision to mobilize the army. Therefore, in the third week of April 1998, Lt Gen. C.B. Gurung left for Surkhet to take up operational command. Immediately, he contacted the deputy inspector general of police (DIG), Sahabir Thapa, who was in charge of the midwest regional police office. 'We will now start our operation. We will command it. You guys should help us. Please provide whatever information you have,' Gurung told him. The police naturally had more field information, since they had been fighting for the last three years. Gurung got some information from Sahabir, but he got much more information from the previous DIG, Ram Bahadur Thapa.

'Ram Bahadur provided us with a document titled 'Lessons Learnt'. That was very good.' Gurung prepared a preliminary framework for the operation based on that document. He prepared to add 2000 soldiers from the local population by opening up on-the-spot recruitment. In order to prevent Maoists from taking advantage of unemployed youths, the army had tried to open up recruitment much earlier. 'I communicated my idea to chief Dharmapal sir,' Gurung said. 'He briefed the prime minister (Girija Prasad Koirala).'

The prime minister also gave the green signal. 'That is a positive plan. Unemployment has caused this problem; go ahead and open up recruitment.' Accordingly, they were all ready to publicly advertise for recruitment on the state-owned Radio Nepal and in the *Gorkhapatra Daily* on 29 May 1998. Then the operation was halted at the last minute by the prime minister himself after a briefing by the police, much to the army's fury. A few days after he returned to Kathmandu, the prime minister ordered the police to start a centralized operation that was named 'Kilo Sierra-2'.[4]

Koirala didn't normally listen to others, but when he was convinced, he waited for no one. Many in the know say there were three reasons the lobbying for the police operation was successful.

The first was financial. The army had initially asked for NRs. 44 crore to purchase arms, helicopters and 'logistics' for their operation. Of that, NRs. 5 crore had already been released during the term of Prime Minister Surya Bahadur Thapa. But the police said that they would perform their operation for half of that budget. In the end, the police operation was not at all cheap.

In four years (1996–2000), they spent NRs. 27 crore to pay for the lease of helicopters alone—a sum for which they could have bought three helicopters.

Secondly, the feeling that the internal conflict should be kept 'low-profile' had also prevailed. Since the police's .303 rifles would result in fewer casualties compared to the army's automatic weapons, it was felt that keeping the police in the front line of defence made sense. In addition to that, the police itself was claiming that it could do the job. Remembering the suffering that the police had meted out to them pre-democracy, and how the police had controlled the underground democracy movement during the thirty-year long autocratic Panchayat system, the Congress party leaders believed that the police were capable of keeping a lid on the revolt.

The third and most important reason was political. In particular, the ruling Congress party leaders harboured deep suspicions that once the army was ordered out of their barracks, they would never return, and the royal palace would take advantage of the ensuing situation to usurp democracy. They recalled how, in 1960, the then king, Mahendra, had used the army to overthrow the elected government of Congress leader B.P. Koirala and imposed the Panchayat regime. There was no way his brother G.P. Koirala was going to forget that.

Amid these visible and invisible reasons, the police, instead of the army, was sent to conduct operations against the Maoists. The army had to return to their barracks without a fight. The army headquarters was not amused. It considered the move a betrayal. Meanwhile, bitterness also grew between Koirala and the army's traditional guardian, the royal palace.

Police pushed back

The police formally implemented Operation Kilo Sierra-2 from 26 May 1998 onwards. The 'search and kill operation' seemed very aggressive for the first six months. It created such fear among the insurgents that even a patrol of fifteen policemen (or a 'striking force', as it was called) would be enough to scatter them. The most substantial achievement of the operation was the successfully conducted general election of 1999. Despite the Maoists' boycott, the election went ahead, thanks, largely, to police security.

In fact, the Maoists were quite alarmed by the operation. They actually called the fourth plenum of the central committee in August of 1998 to forge a strategy to counter it. This was the largest gathering of Maoists since they had launched their people's war three years previously. The plenum concluded that the party would get nowhere with hit-and-run tactics, but only end up going around in endless circles like the Indian Naxalite movement, which has been continuing since the 1960s. Therefore, the Nepali Maoists made a strategic decision to centralize their combatant force and use it to conduct big attacks. In order to counter the 'encircle and eliminate' strategy of the police operation, they adopted a tactic of 'break the circle and resist'. Accordingly, they carried out intensely concentrated simultaneous attacks at various places in the country on 27 October 1998. They proceeded with the aim of creating base areas by flushing out all government agencies, including the police.

The Maoists then seized the offensive position. The police, on the other hand, developed a tendency to simply abandon any post after an attack. There was no hot pursuit of the attackers. They were more concerned about saving their skins. The centre adopted the policy of removing outposts in villages and merging them with the *ilaka* or striking force base camp instead of leaving them in isolated places where they would be killed. When the Maoists began attacking the ilaka and base camps, they, too, were removed.

The general election of 1999 was the turning point, after which the police retreat was complete. Gradually, they became limited only to district headquarters. The election was held in two phases. After conducting the first phase of polls on 3 May in thirty-six districts of the west, 10,000 policemen were transported to the east for the second phase of elections on 17 May. In the middle of the election period, Maoists carried out a fierce attack at Jelbang in Rolpa district. The police presence was never reinstated there after that. The police retreated from wherever they faced a Maoist attack.

There was also a tendency to buy protection from the Maoists. Many policemen simply surrendered their arms when the Maoists attacked. In March 2001, fourteen policemen stationed at the Darkha post in Dhading surrendered their weapons without putting up a fight. They were later detained by the police themselves. A few weeks later, sixty-nine policemen surrendered en masse before the Maoists. This incident was symbolic of the total defeat of the police. By that time, 745 policemen had already lost their lives in the insurgency. Half of the 2000 police units had already been displaced.[5]

One reason why the same police force that had shown impressive effectiveness in the initial phase of the operation had now become totally defensive was that they lacked motivation to continue the fight. The police had received training in only maintaining law and order, not in fighting an insurgency. Most of them had joined the police force because it offered a secure government job. They found themselves face to face with ideologically committed, fierce guerrillas. Besides, the strategic blunder of the police was that they had tried to wipe the Maoists out. Their actions backfired when many innocents were pushed into the Maoist fold by police atrocities.

The police leadership, however, laid the blame squarely on the army. They concluded that they were unable to fight effectively because of the ban imposed by the army on modern weapons and resources for the police. The police were forced to fight the insurgency with Second World War-vintage .303 rifles. The guerrillas, on the other hand, wielded SMGs, SLRs and AK-47s.

Army–police shadow war

The cold war between the police and the army can be traced way back to the 1950s.[6] At that time, the Nepali Congress had fielded a 'liberation force' of 10,000 troops and toppled the Rana regime after one hundred days of war. That force was turned into the paramilitary 'Raksha Dal' three weeks after the success of the revolution. It was basically from that force that the Nepal Police was built in 1955.

In contrast, the post-revolution government clipped the wings of the army. A standing force of 40,000 men was brought down to 9000. However, despite being toppled from power, the domination of the Ranas in the army continued. King Mahendra later dissolved the elected Congress government in 1960 with the help of this army. He ushered in the party-less Panchayat regime. When the Panchayat was again replaced by democracy in 1990, and the Congress came back to power, it easily re-established its influence over the police. But the same was not true for the army. Whatever the law and the Constitution said, the army was still loyal to the palace.

The political parties, including the Congress, which considered the army a private force of the palace, had worked to create a parallel force within the police. In 1990, the army had 39,000 troops. That number stopped there, whereas the police force expanded over the next ten years to reach a strength of 48,000. The budget for the police increased gradually. In the fiscal year 1998–99, the budget for the army was just around NRs. 2 billion, while that for the police was nearly NRs. 3 billion. Senior policemen like DIGs roamed around the city in Japanese Prado SUVs, while even generals of the army were given Indian Maruti jeeps. The army felt insulted at every step.

The only area in which the army could top the police was in the supply of arms. There was a tradition of seeking the army's approval for arms supplies to the police. When the police wanted modern rifles instead of .303s to fight the Maoists, the army intervened, citing the reason that the Maoists would easily 'lay their hands on' (loot) the modern weapons if that happened.

Prime Minister G.P. Koirala too had an inkling of a brewing conspiracy because whenever he wanted to bring in the army to help hold elections amid the growing Maoist attacks, the palace refused. Nor did the generals agree. One reason for their refusal was their feeling of betrayal in 1998. 'He didn't listen to us then. And now he is coming to us', was how many generals felt.

The palace calculated that letting the Maoist movement spread to a certain extent would be in its interest. Koirala felt that the palace was conspiring to push the parliamentary system to the precipice by foiling the 1999 general election.

Prime Minister Koirala held the 1999 general election in two phases, depending mainly on the police. The army's role was limited to holding 'flag marches'. The army was accused of inaction even when a police inspector, Chudamani Ale, was killed by the Maoists on 2 May 1999 while he was transporting ballot papers in Bafukhola, Salyan district. This heightened the bitterness between the two forces.

After winning a majority in the election, the Congress party's leader, Krishna Prasad Bhattarai, became the new prime minister. He wanted to either arm the police or mobilize the army against the Maoists. Even before taking the oath of office, he described the Maoists as 'terrorists' in an interview and said, 'This criminal problem will be dealt with by the police and the army.'[7]

Then he met King Birendra and told him, 'The Maoists are spreading chaos across the country. The police lack training and firepower. They should be better armed; they should be provided SLRs, your majesty!'

King Birendra, who preferred speaking in English, responded with another question, 'Prime minister, are you going to war against them?'[8]

The prime minister returned, speechless. Later, Deputy Prime Minister Ram Chandra Poudel made this incident public.

The army had started making public accusations against the government and the political parties. In his farewell speech at the army headquarters on 19 May 1999, the outgoing chief, Gen. Dharmapal Barsingh Thapa, said, 'With the rise in untoward activities in the country, the people of Nepal are looking up to the institution of monarchy and the Royal Nepali Army, with the hope that they will bring a new dawn in their lives.' With these words, the general revealed what many had already conjectured: that the army and the palace perceived political benefits for themselves in these 'untoward incidents'.[9]

The army, under the leadership of the new chief, General Prajwalla Shumsher Rana, became even more aggressive towards the political parties.

It was around this time that King Birendra addressed a letter, ostensibly about the Maoist problem, to ten senior leaders including Prime Minister Bhattarai, speaker Taranath Ranabhat, and opposition leader Madhav Kumar Nepal. In the name of discussing the Maoist problem, the letter rebuked the multiparty system itself. 'How did the Maoist insurgency, which started from Rolpa and Rukum, spread to fifty-six districts of the country?' the king demanded.

Another question he asked was, 'What is the Maoist problem? Is it political or is it terrorism?' He also listed thirty-four recommendations to resolve the problem. He suggested the parties come up with a public commitment to resolve the crisis, carry out reforms in the judiciary, keep administration free from party politics, maintain law and order without political prejudice, and clarify the role of the police, the army and the intelligence agencies. These 'recommendations' were perceived less as constructive advice and more as royal pressure against the parliamentary system itself.[10]

First attempt at talks

The government was in an impossible position. The palace was not permitting the mobilization of the army, but it had despatched letters to pressurize the government. Against this backdrop, Prime Minister Bhattarai started exploring the possibility of holding talks with the rebels. And there was one name that he had in mind for this purpose—Durga Subedi.

An old Congress hand from Biratnagar, Subedi had a long-standing friendship with the Maoist leader Baburam Bhattarai and Congress politician Pradeep Giri, dating back to their time together in Delhi's Jawaharlal Nehru University. Subedi had become 'famous' when he and a few others hijacked a state-owned Royal Nepal Airlines Corporation (RNAC) plane in 1975 during the Nepali Congress's armed struggle against the autocratic Panchayat system. He had spent one-and-a-half years in an Indian jail in connection with that hijacking case. Prime Minister Bhattarai asked Subedi to find out if the Maoists were willing to talk. Entrusted with this responsibility, Durga Subedi became active.

His contact was Mumaram Khanal, who was engaged in Maoist politics under the cover of being a magazine editor. He worked for the monthly *Disabodh* magazine published from Kathmandu. He took Subedi to Patna to meet Baburam Bhattarai. Subedi recounts, 'After a long discussion, I found that he was in favour of talks. I returned after agreeing that we should meet again and discuss this with Prachanda.'

From the Maoist perspective, compared to G.P. Koirala, who had unleashed operation Kilo Sierra-2 against them, Prime Minister Bhattarai was relatively moderate. They also saw an opportunity to exploit the intra-Congress contradictions by holding talks with the Bhattarai government. The central committee meeting, held in January 2000, formally decided to 'isolate the Girija (Prasad Koirala) clique' and 'build relations with Bhattarai'.

Prime Minister Bhattarai was pondering on how Delhi would react to his initiative for talks with the Maoists. He again proposed to Subedi, '*Punditji*, you should go to Delhi. Try to sniff out what they are thinking. And also meet your friends there.'

Before he left for Delhi, Subedi's friend, Congress leader Pradeep Giri, introduced him to the Indian embassy's minister (consular), P.K. Hormis Tharakan. Operating under the cover of a diplomatic assignment, Tharakan was actually the station chief of India's external intelligence agency RAW (Research & Analysis Wing) in Nepal. Subedi assumed that the prime minister himself may have asked Giri to arrange that meeting.

'Why are you going to Delhi?' Hormis asked him as if he knew nothing, and added, 'If it is for some medical reason, we might be able to help you.' Hormis had not sounded awkward in making such a proposal because many Nepali leaders took such 'assistance' without batting an eyelid. Subedi told him it was for 'personal meetings'.

'But I later felt that Hormis knew about it all. He had also given me a phone number, asking me to call if I needed any assistance,' Subedi recalled. 'Once I landed at Delhi airport, I faced a difficulty. The immigration guys detained me. I had the number of our ambassador in Delhi, Bhesh Bahadur Thapa, but I could not contact him. So I was forced to call the number that Hormis had given me. Immediately, a call came to the officer who was holding me up. They released me. Later, I understood—the whole plan was set up to trail me from there onwards.'

Subedi had arranged to meet Prachanda in Delhi, so the RAW sprang to attention. Whether for that reason or another, Prachanda was unavailable. 'He sent word that he would meet me later,' Subedi said. He did, however, have a long talk with the Maoist leader Ram Karki. He concluded that the Maoists were ready for peace talks.

Subedi returned to Kathmandu and briefed the prime minister. Next, they planned to have direct talks with Prachanda himself. Two months later, Mumaram Khanal escorted Subedi across the

Mechi border to Siliguri in India, where the Maoist headquarters was located at that time. At the house of Ram Karki's wife, Subedi met Prachanda for the first time. Baburam was also there. The conversation they had was positive, but they faced a technical problem. Prachanda said, 'Durgaji, we have faith in you. But how do we know the government's intention? We must have some basis to believe the authenticity of the government's intention to hold a dialogue.'

Subedi replied, 'You will get it. But I will also need some guarantee from you.' The Maoists promised to arrange it.

The government formally appointed Subedi as its negotiator on 21 July 1999. A letter, handwritten by Home Minister Purna Bahadur Khadka on the ministry's official letterhead, said that Subedi would 'act in a most secret manner in view of the risks and sensitivities involved'. Subedi faxed a copy of that letter to the Maoist leadership. Within two to three hours, he got a reply from Prachanda acknowledging his position. The prime minister had wanted a handwritten letter from Prachanda, and that was what he sent.

Meanwhile, a politburo member of the Maoists, Suresh Wagle, was killed in police action in Gorkha on 8 September 1999. This halted the momentum towards talks. In revenge, the Maoists mounted a series of attacks across the country on 22 September. In an attack in Rukum, they abducted the deputy superintendent of police (DSP), Thule Rai. One hundred and fifty of their cadres having just received month-long training from the Indian Maoist politburo member Balaji and central member 'DK', at Darbot of Rolpa (in August 1999), the Maoists were clearly in an aggressive mood.[11]

The kidnapping of a senior policeman, a DSP, seriously demoralized the security forces. Prime Minister Bhattarai, Home Minister Khadka, Subedi and Giri decided that it was better to pursue the path of talks than to intensify the conflict. Accordingly, Home Minister Khadka himself wrote a letter addressed to

Prachanda on 27 September 1999. The government thus made the initial formal proposal for talks. It was agreed that the government would release Maoist leader Dev Gurung from detention, and the Maoists would release DSP Rai. After three months in Maoist detention, Rai was freed on 18 December 1999. And after spending three years in a government jail, Gurung was released on 13 January 2000. In its efforts to create a positive mood, the government also released two other Maoist leaders, Suresh Ale Magar and Pawan Man Shrestha.

On 25 February, the home minister handed over another letter to Durga Subedi, in which he had asked the Maoists to set a time and a date and appoint negotiators for talks. Prachanda immediately faxed his handwritten reply. He expressed his willingness to designate negotiators, provided some pre-conditions, such as the release of Maoist leaders and cadres, were fulfilled.[12]

But just as the government–Maoist effort was beginning to take formal shape, a political conspiracy was hatched that completely derailed the one-year-long preparation for talks.

Ganging up behind the PM's back

Initially, Prime Minister Bhattarai had kept his efforts at dialogue with the Maoists under wraps. When the preparations were complete, he went to Pokhara and briefed King Birendra, who was staying there at that time. The Congress party president, G.P. Koirala, also came to know about it from the palace the same day. The following day (12 March 2000), at Koirala's instruction, sixty-nine Congress members of Parliament registered a no-trust motion against the prime minister. Facing certain defeat at the hands of his fellow *Kangressis*, Prime Minister Bhattarai resigned on 16 March. Three days later, Koirala returned to Singha Durbar as the new prime minister.

Bhattarai was scheduled to fly to Paris a week later, the second official visit to France by a Nepali prime minister 150 years after the first such visit by Jung Bahadur Rana. Although the diplomatic arrangements had been completed, Bhattarai was prevented from embarking on that tour. His visit had to be cancelled because he was planning to hold talks with Maoist leaders somewhere in Europe during the tour. Neither Koirala nor the palace wanted the talks to take place under his leadership.

Forced to resign, Prime Minister Bhattarai made an emotional farewell speech at Parliament on 16 March 2000. 'Since 1996, the so-called "people's war" of the Maoists has become everyone's concern. But just when they are preparing to resolve the problem through talks, and are assigning their negotiators, the plots begin to be hatched to derail the process. Why?'

In a written statement, he further asked, 'When will we, Nepali, be free from the so-called curse on our patriots? The curse whose spell has not even spared the likes of Bhim Malla and Bhimsen Thapa in our history? Isn't democracy all about abandoning such political trickery and embracing transparency?'

Bhattarai had been a victim of double design, by his Party President Koirala and by the royal palace. The irony was that Koirala pulled the rug from under him on the pretext of his inability 'to control Maoist terror', whereas it was because of him that Bhattarai's efforts to end the 'terror' were being derailed. The very day that a no-trust motion was registered against Bhattarai, a Maoist leader named Ashok arrived in Kathmandu with the intention of holding talks with the government. As Prachanda later said, 'Before comrade Ashok could talk to anyone, the game to change the government was put in motion, bringing the whole talks episode to an automatic end.'[13]

As the new prime minister, Koirala imposed a condition for talks, stating, 'The Maoists should first cease violence.' Prachanda made an equally strong reply. He called Bhattarai's ouster 'a plot against negotiation' and said there was little chance of talking to the new government. Had the talks been successful, Bhattarai's stature would have grown—something Koirala shuddered to think about.[14] Perhaps the palace, too, was against the government–Maoist talks. It felt that if something like that were to happen, then it should happen under its patronage. Moreover, the palace was examining the possibility of taking advantage of the Maoist situation to explore an alternative to the whole multiparty system itself. Koirala and King Birendra had thus come together, driven to the same goal by their agenda against Bhattarai.[15]

Backed by the palace, Koirala had gone on a countrywide tour making tall claims that he had 'a medicine', a cure for the Maoist problem. In fact, the medicine was nothing but the same old 'military mobilization'. He had joined hands with the king with the intention of mobilizing the army to take care of the Maoists once he came to power.

Quick to read the new PM's intention, his trusted police chief, IGP Achyut Krishna Kharel called a conference of senior police officers on 11 and 12 April 2000. The conference proposed that the government should mobilize the army in Rolpa, Rukum, Salyan, Jajarkot, Pyuthan and Kalikot districts. Yet, the palace again showed its unwillingness to bring the army out of the barracks. The Koirala–palace alliance was only effective up to the point of Bhattarai's departure. So Koirala found himself banging his head at the palace walls. He was neither able to mobilize the army, nor hold talks.

The previous government negotiator, Durga Subedi, was already inactive. It was the Congress leader Sher Bahadur Deuba who continued to make efforts towards dialogue in his capacity as the convener of the 'High Level Committee to Resolve the Maoist Problem'. The committee had been formed on 6 January 2000 during the tenure of PM Bhattarai.

Dunai attack

Unable to conduct army operations, Koirala fell back on the police for security. However, on 3 April 2000, he was able to pass the following decisions through the National Defence Council, in the presence of the army chief, Prajwalla Shumsher Rana:

- The Nepal Police to take responsibility for the day-to-day maintenance of law and order.
- The Royal Nepali Army to provide training in modern weapons and guerrilla warfare to officers and personnel of the Nepal Police.
- The police to buy 9000 SLRs from the army.
- The army to provide necessary support to the police as a 'back-up' in situations where mass casualties were feared.[16]

As per this decision, the army provided forty-five days of training to 100 officers and constables of the Nepal Police at its Counter-insurgency and Jungle Warfare Training School in Amlekhgunj in August and September of 2000. It also conducted similar courses at five training academies of the police.[17]

A few policemen learned about guerrilla warfare this way, but they did not have suitable weapons.[18] So the government released NRs. 170 million for the police to purchase 9000 SLRs from the army. The home ministry was already making plans to deploy commando units of the police, armed with SLRs, to Rolpa, Rukum, Jajarkot, Salyan, Kalikot, Pyuthan, Dolpa, Dailekh and Achham districts from 17 September 2000. Yet, the army refused to sell the SLRs. It said that since no new weapons had been bought for the army, it could not sell 9000 SLRs from its stock of 40,000. The plan was derailed yet again.

Meanwhile, Singha Durbar learnt on 19 September 2000 that the Maoists were planning to launch a massive attack on Dunai, the district headquarters of Dolpa. Prime Minister Koirala ordered the army chief, Rana, to immediately give 500 SLRs to the police. The army chief again refused, saying on 22 September, 'The weapons cannot be given to the police since they have to be given to the proposed Armed Police Force (APF), which has not been set up yet.' Two days later, on 24 September, the Maoists attacked Dunai.

Following the army's refusal to give the SLRs, a reinforcement of forty-eight policemen had been despatched to Dunai a mere eight hours before the attack. Before they could get a sense of the area, the Maoists launched their offensive. Apart from a few who were in 'outposts,' all 118 policemen in Dunai were sleeping in the same barracks. When the Maoists threw bombs at night, the startled policemen resorted to indiscriminate firing, which is said to have caused casualties among themselves. Fifteen policemen died in that attack and forty-eight were injured. The insurgents withdrew with forty-seven captured weapons, nearly 50 million rupees in cash, and NRs. 1.3 million worth of gold from the local bank.

Even as the police fought the attackers for seven hours, the army, posted some half an hour away at Suligadh village, made no attempt to help them. This was despite the fact that it was the commander at the army camp who had provided information about the impending Maoist attack. He had informed the district administration office that he had seen 'groups of Maoists gathering in a jungle above Samratara nearby'.[19]

So why didn't the army come to the police's rescue despite knowing all about the attack? It was argued that the insurgents had cut off access to the barracks by destroying a local bridge and a ropeway (*tuin*). It was also said that of the 155 soldiers posted there, most had been deployed to guard the local wildlife reserve. It was technically impossible to pursue the insurgents with such a scattered force. But those were not the only reasons. The palace was not in the mood to deploy the army before it had ensured a favourable political situation. For public consumption, however, they said that the insurgents had fled too far, and it was impossible to seal their escape routes.[20]

The then home minister, Govinda Raj Joshi, publicly accused the army of refusing to cooperate in the government's effort to control the insurgency. He also revealed that despite receiving NRs. 170 million, the army had not given SLRs to the police, and said this was the reason police commandos could not be sent to Dunai earlier.

The fire that the Maoists had lit in remote Dunai had engulfed Kathmandu. Such was the pressure mounted on Prime Minister Koirala by the army and the palace that Home Minister Joshi was forced to resign on 29 September. Joshi was not alone on their blacklist. IGP Achyut Krishna Kharel was forced to take two months' leave, and subsequently retired. Home Secretary Padam Prasad Pokharel was transferred. Even Defence Secretary Chakra Bandhu Aryal was removed.

Army Chief Prajwalla Shumsher Rana later confided, 'We were not invited (into the fight) in a legitimate and clearly defined manner. A pre-study was needed even to launch a pursuit. When we completed the area study, it was already too late for any such pursuit. Despite knowing about these realities, Kharel tried to sow confusion. And Govinda Raj Joshi spoke against the nation despite his oath. So it was normal for him to resign.'[21]

Prime Minister Koirala knew that he had again been duped by the army–palace combine, but he was so helpless that he had to compromise. It was not only the Maoist onslaught that he was facing; even the main opposition, CPN–UML, was becoming increasingly belligerent towards him. He did not want to jeopardize his position by taking on the army and the palace. So he simply sacrificed a home minister and an IGP who were loyal to him.[22]

Pradeep Shumsher Rana, a distant cousin of the army chief, became the new IGP. The police were totally demoralized. 'In many places, the police themselves have collected donations and handed them over to the Maoists to buy their own protection,' IGP Rana told CPN–UML leaders on 12 April 2001. 'The police could face internal revolt if the situation is not improved.'[23]

In fact, the army, too, had been taken aback by the sheer audacity exhibited by the insurgents in the Dunai attack. For the first time, the insurgents had attacked a district headquarters. The army concluded that sooner rather than later, it would have to take up command. It took up the responsibility of security in sixteen district headquarters. It established division-level units. It began monitoring border points in the name of 'revenue patrolling'. A separate defence minister, Mahesh Acharya, was appointed. And it, finally, gave 350 SLRs to the police.

Formation of Armed Police Force

The Dunai debacle accelerated the establishment of the APF, which had long been under discussion. The government was furious with what was happening: neither was it allowed to mobilize the army, nor was it allowed to give automatic weapons to the police. And then the blame for inaction was laid squarely on its shoulders! So it agreed in principle to form a paramilitary force, the APF, which would be separate from the army and would be loyal to the government.[24]

The palace understood things differently. The number of members and budget for the police was already greater than that for the army. It was only automatic weapons and war training that the police lacked, compared to the army. And by demanding that the proposed APF be kept under its command, the police caused the army–palace combine to suspect its intentions. The latter two wanted to clip the spreading wings of the police, by allowing the formation of a totally new force.

Although the interests of the government and the palace seemed to be matched in the formation of the APF, they actually had divergent objectives. The government wanted the APF because it could not mobilize the army and could not arm the police with modern weapons. It thought the APF would be helpful in keeping the army-palace combine in check. The palace, on the other hand, believed that the formation of the APF would check the growing ambitions of the police and also create a useful paramilitary force, preventing the direct mobilization of the army in an internal conflict.

Therefore, the APF was established on 22 January 2001. Only a few officers from the army joined the APF. The main force came from the Nepal Police. A provision was included according to which, it would automatically come under army command if the army launched an operation. In any case, the APF was a paramilitary and not a military force. So the government's old yearning for military mobilization soon resurfaced.

3

Royal Cooperation

'Through you, we want to assure Prachanda that the military will not be mobilized, at any cost.'

—Former prince Dhirendra Shah, delivering
the palace's message to Maoist emissaries, Krishna
Dhwaj Khadka and Mohan Bahadur Karki, in April 2001[1]

Sharad Chandra Shah was the son of the former army chief, Field Marshal Surendra Bahadur Shah. Rarely seen in public, he was an influential palace hand. During the Panchayat regime, he was considered one of the leaders of the 'underground clique', which pulled the strings from behind the scenes. During the demise of the Panchayat regime in 1990, the Dillibazar residence of this hardliner royalist became the target of enraged demonstrators. They set fire to it. This forced him to live in self-imposed exile in Singapore. He had been running his own business in the city-state before he suddenly reappeared in Kathmandu in 1997, just when the Maoist conflict was beginning to grow.

I sought an interview immediately. Surprisingly, he turned out to be quite a supporter of the Maoists. 'We are hearing that the

people feel they will get justice only after the Maoists are successful,'
he told me. 'Their success shows that Nepal is fertile ground for
Maoists.' He even predicted, 'I see a new cycle of change coming
up. Let's hope for the best . . . but one doesn't know what sort of
changes will emerge.'[2]

He had probably come to Kathmandu to gauge which 'political
changes' could be manufactured. Just like him, several pro-palace
elements thought that the Maoists could become a means for such
changes. Therefore, in the initial years of the conflict, one could
hear all the pro-palace elements—from the palace officials at the
centre to the former *panchas* in villages—singing the Maoists'
praises.

A Panchayat-era former minister and a royal lineage of the
Jajarkot principality, Tej Bikram Shah publicly said, 'The Maoists
have not attacked ordinary people. I have heard that they have
targeted only village goons and local oppressors.' His interview
was published in the Maoist mouthpiece *Janadesh*.[3]

In Rukum, the *Bafikote raja* (a titular princeling), Dhruba
Bikram Shah, and the *Rukumkote raja* Lokendra Bahadur Shah,
had had cordial relations with the Maoists since the Panchayat era.
These *Thakuri rajauta* (petty rulers) had been providing protection
to Maoist cadres for their own political interests. Dhruba Bikram's
son, Bibek Kumar Shah, went on to become chief military secretary
at the royal palace in Kathmandu. Years later, Bibek ended up
playing the key role in facilitating talks between the Maoists and
King Gyanendra.

The palace was so taken by the 'romance' of Maoist violence
that King Birendra assigned his younger brother Dhirendra to
exchange letters with the Maoist leadership. A military officer,
Dilip Jung Rayamajhi, who happened to be the son of communist-
turned-monarchist leader, Dr Keshar Jung Rayamajhi, was also
asked to talk to the Maoist leaders.

The Maoists, too, had an interest in building relations with the
royals, from Rukum to Kathmandu. Their main and initial interest

was in preventing the government from mobilizing the military against them. When, in 1997–98, efforts to mobilize the military were intensified, the Maoists also increased their propaganda against the army and the palace. But after the government implemented the Kilo Sierra-2 police operation against them in June 1998, they shifted their target to the Congress–UML, the government and the police. They also raised anti-India and nationalist slogans during that period. And then they extended a hand of friendship toward the army and the palace. For a brief period, they even tempered their republican slogans, limiting them to their written documents alone.

The common target of both the Maoists and the palace was the 1990 Constitution. The Maoists wanted to tear apart that document and usher in a regime of their liking. The palace was also dissatisfied with the Constitution since it had turned the monarchy into what it perceived as a mere 'rubber stamp.' They had different objectives, but their target was the same. That is why the pro-palace elements that were sidelined by the 1990 movement were salivating at the prospect of winning back power by riding on the Maoist conflict.

On the ground, the Maoists adopted a policy of praising the army, of not touching the former panchas, and of targeting the Congress–UML workers and the police. This helped to push the palace and the army to one corner and the political parties, the police and the government to the other. This was the polarization that the Maoists had always wanted, so that the political parties and the palace would not gang up against them.

Formula of nationalism

The apparently softer line the Maoists took towards the palace was born of cold military and strategic calculations. But if one looks back at the history of the communist movement in Nepal, one can find a 'pro-monarchy tendency' being a key feature. That was reflected within the Maoists. A few Maoist leaders believed that monarchists were nationalists, and therefore they should join hands. Former King Mahendra is widely considered the fountainhead of such thinking.

When he ascended the throne in 1955, King Mahendra had expanded Nepal's relations with communist China in an attempt to curtail the growing Indian influence. The two countries established diplomatic relations on 1 August that year, and he used that relationship to cement the Panchayat regime he founded in 1960 after overthrowing the elected government. Mahendra easily attracted Chinese support because, in the words of Mao Tse Tung, Mahendra was a 'patriotic and nationalist king unlike Marcos of the Philippines' (whom Tung regarded as a foreign stooge).[4] Likewise, in Mahendra's eyes, Mao was a 'great leader'. In 1962, after meeting Mao in Beijing, Mahendra made a public address in which he said, 'We are impressed with his statesmanship and intellect.'[5]

Those Nepali communists who considered Mao their ideal were also impressed with Mahendra's anti-India nationalism. Mahendra himself wanted to use the communists to counter the Nepali Congress, whom he had ousted from power in his coup in 1960. He was quite heavily influenced by the then general secretary of the Communist Party of Nepal, Dr Keshar Jung Rayamajhi. When Rayamajhi supported his coup, it led to serious debates within his party. The party ultimately split, and Rayamajhi ended up leading the royalist faction while Pushpa Lal Shrestha led the republican faction.

Even at the height of the Panchayat regime, Rayamajhi continued to lead a communist faction by remaining close to the palace. Later, he gave up communist politics altogether and became Chairman of the Standing Committee of the Royal Council. Pushpa Lal passed away in 1978, but his successors continued to be engaged in anti-monarchy campaigns. A large chunk of his faction ultimately became the CPN–UML.

For a long time, the Nepali communist movement had exhibited an interesting tendency: to come close to the monarchy when adopting the line of nationalism, and to move close to India when adopting the line of *janabad* (people's democracy). The Maoists were adept at utilizing both these tendencies, turn by turn, as and when it suited them. Their first choice was the royal palace. The common agenda of nationalism and/or 'anti-Indianism' was a thread that bound them together. The Nepali Congress, which had come to power after 1990, was their common target. Both of them found Congress to be 'India-leaning'. The Maoists went to the extent of claiming that no one could surpass G.P. Koirala as the worst 'fascist, murderer and traitor'.[6]

Koirala was at the helm of government for the greater part of the period after 1990, and was often a target of attacks by the palace.[7] The Maoists understood that very well. At the meeting of their central committee on July 1999, they coined a new slogan: 'Topple the anti-national and fascist government. Form a united revolutionary government of patriots, democrats and communists.' It was a policy decision to move closer to the palace.

So Prachanda and his comrades would accuse the Koirala government of being 'anti-national and fascist' and of inviting Indian intervention. According to them, in order to resist such Indian intervention, it was necessary to form an alliance between *janabadis* or 'democrats' (themselves) and *rashtrabadis* or 'nationalists' (the royalists). They abandoned their old slogan of 'form a government of *janabadis*' and replaced it with 'form a united government of *janabadis* and *rashtrabadis*'. The Maoist central committee meeting held six months later formally decided to pursue the aim of 'forming a working alliance, forging cooperation and pursuing talks with all political groups outside of the Congress sphere'.

By 'non-Congress' groups, did they mean the opposition party of the Parliament, the CPN–UML? No, they meant the king and his coterie. Maoist leader Baburam Bhattarai wrote, 'Shouldn't the King and the patriots who have always called themselves nationalists come closer to communists who have always struggled against imperialism and, particularly, Indian expansionism—rather than Girija (Prasad Koirala) and *Kangressis* who are synonymous with foreign stooges?'[8]

That was an open invitation for cooperation to the monarchists. The monarchists, too, thought that their wings were clipped in 1990 at the behest of Delhi, and that Delhi had been continuously interfering in Nepal ever since. A few incidents that came to the fore during that period had also scared them.

The seventy-eight-page-long document titled *Pakistan's anti-India activities in Nepal*, prepared by the Indian intelligence agency RAW, is one such example. The document (made public through *India Today* magazine on 12 June 2000) heaped indiscriminate blame on various leaders, officials and even ordinary Nepalis of being agents of the Pakistani intelligence agency, the ISI, and of engaging in anti-India activities. It advocated 'intervention' to control them.[9] In fact, the then National Security Advisor to the Indian prime minister, Brajesh Mishra, had leaked the report to the magazine on the eve of a visit to Kathmandu, to portray extensive Pakistani activities in Nepal, and to push the Nepali side on to the defensive.[10]

A few months later, in December 2000, a startling incident occurred that was linked to India. In what appeared to be reaction to Bollywood actor Hrithik Roshan allegedly telling the channel Star Plus that he 'does not like Nepal and Nepalis', anti-India rioting shook the capital. Six people, including a young girl, died in police firing. Delhi sat up and took serious note of rioting against it in the capital of a neighbouring country.[11]

Though the monarchists were seen to be at the forefront in inciting the mob, the Maoists were equally active in doing so. The pressure was on Prime Minister Koirala. King Birendra summoned him. 'The situation is going out of hand. You should impose a state of emergency,' he told the prime minister.

The king's proposal was unacceptable to Koirala. He replied, 'The situation will come under control, your Majesty. The police will control it. There is no need to panic.'

According to Koirala, 'The king was trying to curtail the people's rights by imposing an emergency. He was plotting to seize power. I also told my ministers after that meeting, "I don't see good signs from the king."'[12]

By that time, the monarchists were openly advocating an alliance with the Maoists. Ramesh Nath Pandey, a royal nominee in the upper house, gave an interview to the Maoist mouthpiece in which he said, 'The ordinary Nepali feels that the possibility of foreigners interfering on the pretext of this domestic conflict must be ended.'[13]

By 'foreigners', Pandey had indicated India. And he was already on the Maoist list of 'patriots'. Initially, Maoist leader Rabindra Shrestha met with him at his residence in Kathmandu. Later, a Maoist cadre, Chandraman Shrestha, even escorted him to Delhi, where he went to a place near Noida and met with both Prachanda and Baburam.

The Maoist leaders were in the ironic situation of orchestrating an anti-India alliance while basing themselves in India. Their second national convention, held in January or February of 2001 in Punjab, India, passed a proposal calling for an all-party conference (which would make their alliance with the palace possible), the formation of an interim government through such a conference, and then the promulgation of a people's Constitution. The intention was to share power with the palace by sidelining the parliamentary parties such as the Congress and CPN–UML. The Maoists also believed that even if such an alliance did not come to fruition, their proposal would surely deepen the wedge between the palace and the parties.

Even though he saw the possibility of taking political advantage of the Maoists' violent activities, King Birendra harboured deep suspicions about the top Maoist leaders, who were operating from

India. In order to learn more about them, he called for Colonel Dilip Jung Rayamajhi, who was then working at the Directorate of Military Operations (DMO) of the Royal Nepali Army. The king wanted to understand: 'what is the relationship of the Maoists with India? Are they operated *by* India?'

There were other questions he wanted answers to, such as: What was the participation of ordinary people in the Maoist movement? Were they motivated by political ideology? Or did they take up arms simply due to dissatisfaction with the government? Or did they become Maoists out of vengeance due to indiscriminate police operations? Or was the public coerced into raising arms, under pressure from the Maoists?

'I tried to learn the answers from close quarters,' said Rayamajhi in an interview with me many years later, when he had retired as a brigadier general. 'What I found was: the midwestern hills of Rolpa and Rukum were a traditional communist bastion, so the ideological impression was quite deep there. The police oppression had also contributed a lot to the resentment among the public. As far as the eastern region was concerned, it was only a temporary wave of sorts there.'

It was around March of 2001 that Rayamajhi had his first contact with the Maoists. Through a teacher named Madhav Marhatta, he opened up a channel of communication with a Maoist leader, Krishna Dhwaj Khadka, who was active in Kathmandu.

A communist old-timer, D.R. Lamichhane, was another contact. Lamichhane used to come to Rayamajhi's house to meet Keshar Jung Rayamajhi, an old friend. He also had access to Prachanda. Soon, Rayamajhi got a chance to meet another Maoist leader, Hari Bhakta Kandel. Rayamajhi was curious when he saw the portrait of King Birendra hanging on a wall in the house in Boudha where they met. Nearby was a photo of the Tibetan spiritual leader the Dalai Lama, along with an Indian 500-rupee note as an offering. 'The meeting there was not very productive. We had just a general chat,' Rayamajhi said.

Working 'under cover', Rayamajhi was holding a series of such meetings. Just days before the palace massacre, on 1 June 2001, he was supposed to meet Prachanda and Baburam in Butwal. But Prachanda and Baburam were not in the house in the Sundarnagar area that D.R. Lamichhane took him to. He was told that they could not come due to 'technical reasons'. Instead, there was the Maoist leader Top Bahadur Rayamajhi and another man. Years later, he saw that second man on television and remembered meeting him in Butwal—he was a deputy commander of the Maoists' PLA, Chakrapani Khanal aka Baldev.

These talks were taking place at a time when the police was retreating in the face of the Maoist onslaught, and preparations were on to send the army into the field. 'The mission was to find out their thinking, their plan. It was pure military diplomacy. We call it the bamboo approach—whether you fight or not, it is necessary to learn about your adversary by becoming as flexible as bamboo shoots,' Rayamajhi said.

On behalf of King Birendra, Rayamajhi gave a clear message to the Maoists—they would be treated fairly if they abandoned war and chose peaceful protest instead, and they would also be helped in managing their combatants. The condition was that they should accept constitutional monarchy. He remembers how, at the end of one such long meeting, Top Bahadur Rayamajhi excitedly told him, 'OK, we will accept constitutional monarchy. But please create the (right) environment.'

It was around this time that some Maoist leaders, in their series of contacts with various monarchists, came in contact with the ex-prince Dhirendra himself. He was the younger brother of King Birendra.

Meeting with Dhirendra

As the leader of the so-called 'underground clique', Dhirendra was at the pinnacle of power during the Panchayat era, but after he fell out with his sister-in-law Queen Aishwarya, he left Nepal for good in 1988. Giving up his royal title, he settled in Britain and remarried. But as a Nepali saying goes, '*Barha barsama kholo pani pharkanchha* (even streams change course after twelve years).' He suddenly reappeared in Nepal twelve years later, in 2000.

His return amid the growing internal conflict was quite meaningful. Right after he came back, Dhirendra started making political remarks. 'Dissatisfaction has grown because of the administration's high-handedness in the name of resisting the Maoists,' he said in an interview. 'Although they have raised the slogan of republic, they are, after all, Nepali nationalists. Therefore, it would be better to take initiative for talks with them.'[14]

On 10 October 2000, he made his return public by attending a programme in Kathmandu hosted by a little-known pro-monarchy organization called the Rastrabadi Yuba Morcha, as its chief guest. It was in that programme that a film artist, Mohan Niraula, made a highly controversial statement, saying he was willing to kill Girija Prasad Koirala—or any other political leader—in order to improve the country's condition. Congress and UML parliamentarians took strong exception to that statement, made in the presence of Dhirendra. They demanded action. But, in an astonishing move, the Maoists came to the royalists' defence. Baburam wrote, 'What is the rationale for them to vent their anger at Dhirendra, who already has been stripped of the title of prince, when they themselves had respectfully made Achyut Krishna Kharel, a *murderer* of April 6 1990 [while attempting to suppress the first people's movement] the police chief?'[15]

Dhirendra's description of the Maoists as 'nationalists' in an interview, and Baburam coming to his defence in this way, suggested that something was cooking between them. Subsequently, Prachanda received a long letter from Dhirendra. According to Prachanda, it proposed a framework for what the Maoists and the monarchy could do together. Although a lot was written about society and the economy, not much was mentioned regarding political questions. But the message was clear: the king, through his brother, had invited the insurgents to a dialogue.

Dhirendra had contacted them. Therefore the Maoists, too, nominated Krishna Dhwaj Khadka, the Kathmandu-in-charge of their intellectual front, for the purpose. According to Khadka, he was then a newly appointed central committee member and had been assigned the task of political mobilization for such secret talks. Khadka's team also included another regional bureau member working in the intellectual front, Mohan Bahadur Karki a.k.a. Jibanta.

Khadka and Jibanta talked to Dhirendra for two hours at a private house in Kathmandu on 29 April 2001. The meeting between the emissaries of Prachanda and the king was kept secret. Even those Maoist leaders posted in Kathmandu who were senior to Khadka were kept in the dark. According to Prachanda, King Birendra had summoned his younger brother from Britain solely to hold talks with the Maoists. As he was no longer a prince, it was easy to meet Dhirendra.

To Khadka and Jibanta, Dhirendra posed many questions. He inquired what the Maoists wanted, what their goals were, how this conflict could be resolved and so on. Jibanta recalls how Dhirendra immediately fired questions upon meeting them: 'What is the viewpoint of Chairman Prachanda on contemporary politics? What is his idea of taking the country forward? What does he say about *thuldai* (King Birendra)? Is there a meeting point between the Maoists and the monarchy?'[16]

At the meeting, Khadka presented views that were in accordance with his party's approach. He talked about the 'need for the monarchy to take initiatives to end oppression and tyranny in rural villages'—something that was sure to bring the two forces together. He also spoke about their socioeconomic programmes.

Dhirendra was not opposed to the Maoists' checklist of transformational land reforms or to their left-leaning socio-economic policies. What he was most interested in, however,

was 'the power'. 'You guys implement your socio-economic
programmes, but let's share the power,' he said. Dhirendra wanted
to hold discussions on how such 'sharing' could be brought about.

The Maoist negotiators had given ample indication that they
would not be opposed to some form of monarchy if there was an
understanding on cooperation among nationalists. Jibanta clearly
remembers Dhirendra's last words before they left the meeting
venue: '*Thuldai* (King Birendra), *maldai* (then Prince Gyanendra)
and myself, we all agree that the Maoists are a nationalist force
and should be utilized for bringing about national prosperity. We
are totally against the autocratic steps taken by the government.
Through you, we want to assure Prachanda that the military will
not be mobilized at any cost.'[17]

At the end, he said that it would be good to document the
'points of understanding'. On 22 May 2001, the palace dispatched
a letter addressed to Prachanda, mentioning nine 'points of
understanding'. This handwritten letter was not written by
Dhirendra himself, but by somebody on his behalf, summarizing
points that had been in the first letter also. A Maoist leader who
saw the letter later said, 'It talked about such and such socio-
economic programmes that could be implemented'.

The main theme of Dhirendra's letter was simple: to sideline
the political parties and to enter into a power-sharing agreement
with the Maoists. 'They wanted to keep the chain of army
command under themselves while giving the position of prime
minister to us,' a Maoist source involved in the negotiations
confided. Dhirendra told them, 'Present what your party thinks.'

Implementing Dhirendra's blueprint would have required
some sort of a coup against the parliamentary system. A conclusion
on whether a power alliance between the palace and the Maoists
was possible may, perhaps, have been reached through one-on-
one talks between King Birendra and Prachanda. Preparations
were underway for such a meeting. Prachanda was already putting
together the points he would present before the king. And

Dhirendra was telling them to come up with their replies within a fortnight.

According to Prachanda, Dhirendra had said, during his talks with Maoist emissary Krishna Dhwaj Khadka, that *thuldai* also wanted to meet him. 'This is only hindered by the technical difficulty of him of coming out of the palace to meet,' he had said. Naturally, it was difficult for the king to evade the security cover, the government administration and the palace secretary to meet the 'terrorist leader' Prachanda.

Dhirendra had also said this to Khadka: 'First, the meeting should take place with *maldai*. Then with *thuldai*.' Shortly afterwards, he sent a different message: '*Thuldai* is still not convinced, but he can be convinced. (I have) talked with *maldai* and Dipendra (the then crown prince) too, and they have agreed.'

In other words, Crown Prince Dipendra and Prince Gyanendra were on board. But in the middle of preparations for this summit meeting, calamity struck—and it took the lives of the king who wanted to meet Prachanda, a prince who was arranging such a meeting, and the crown prince who was in the loop. That happened just a month after the Maoist emissary and Dhirendra met; just a week after the palace had sent a nine-point letter to the Maoist chief.

The royal massacre left only the *maldai* unharmed. And he became the new king.

Imagining Cambodia

Soon after he was crowned in 1971, King Birendra confronted a Maoist revolt in the eastern Jhapa district. He was able to crush it. But he did not allow the government to mobilize the army to douse the flame of another Maoist rebellion that later started from the west. No wonder there is a saying in some quarters: Prachanda started the people's war, but it was King Birendra who nurtured and helped spread it.

'So what was your relationship with King Birendra like?' When Prachanda was asked this question in 2006 by this author, his answer was: 'Whether because he felt that army mobilization would result in more bloodshed, or whether he felt the time was still not ripe for such action, he (Birendra) was surely not in favour of bringing the army into the picture. We also did not want to confront the army just then. We felt that if the army mobilization could be stopped by approaching Birendra and Dhirendra, then so be it. Because we had not become strong. Our army was not very strong. We did not have good weapons. So we felt it would be a bad idea to fight the army. That is the point where our interests met. That's what we called "undeclared unity in action".'[18]

'What was the reason for such unity in action with King Birendra, and not others?' I asked.

Prachanda said, 'Birendra became a king in the natural course of events, so he had a natural tendency to be concerned about his country and countrymen. Though he belonged to the feudal class, he did not have any appetite to see people being killed. Take, for instance, the events of 1979 (when an anti-monarchy agitation was heightened). There had not been too many casualties, but he quickly declared a referendum. Similarly, had 1000 people been killed in 1990, the People's Movement would have been finished. But instead of taking that course, he restored the multiparty system. So it seems that he wanted options besides resorting to bloodshed. That is why we saw liberal feudal characteristics in him.'

Prachanda added, 'Besides, he was also exploring a peaceful resolution of our movement. He sent Dhirendra. He also wanted to meet us himself. Maybe it was because of his own interests that he wanted to meet us, to take advantage of the situation. But I feel that was not the sole reason. I don't think he just wanted to squeeze us. Perhaps he thought that the country could be saved by some compromises.'

In the words of the former Maoist leader Rabindra Shrestha, who was quite close to Prachanda back then: 'Prachanda-Baburam imagined convincing King Birendra to turn into a president, or, if that was not possible, to let him continue as a ceremonial monarch while taking over control of the army.' But would King Birendra have agreed to this? That is something that could not be confirmed from any source. But one thing is certain, though. King Birendra did not like the government policy of trying to control the Maoists through police action, and the ensuing bloodshed among his people, and he felt that there should be a peaceful resolution to Maoist insurgency.

It was for this reason he was in talks with the Maoists through his brother Dhirendra. On the other hand, Prime Minister Girija Prasad Koirala had reached the opposite conclusion—that the insurgents must be crushed through army mobilization.

The prime minister and his legion

Towards the middle of 2001, the Maoist insurgency was already beginning to take the shape of a civil war. Dozens of policemen were being killed in single incidents. The army was still unwilling to take part. Prime Minister Koirala was a frustrated man. So he took a 'legion' of officials to the palace to put pressure on King Birendra.

The 'legion' contained seventeen members including ministers, secretaries, the army chief, the police chief and police officers.[19] The goal was to provide a decisive push for army mobilization. They even did a 'rehearsal' at the prime minister's residence in Baluwatar of the presentation they would give the king.

The programme was conducted at a large hall in Narayanhity palace. King Birendra, accompanied by Crown Prince Dipendra, gave a patient hearing to the three-hour-long briefing. At the end, the king spoke. He said the army could be mobilized, but he wanted a clear plan of action. He also inquired about the consequences of such action. He repeatedly asked for how long the army would be deployed.

The prime minister was surprised by the king's response. 'There was nothing in the plan for the king to speak, in fact,' Koirala later said. 'It was the first time such a thing had happened (at such a briefing). I was really surprised.'

Deputy Prime Minister and Home Minister Ram Chandra Poudel spoke after the king. Then the king asked, 'Prime minister, why don't you say something?'

'Your Majesty, I am not here to speak. I am here to give orders. I am not here for a speech,' Koirala replied. Army Chief Prajwalla Shumsher Rana tried to open his mouth after that, but the PM cut him short. 'I am not going to talk to you. Please be quiet.'[20]

This extraordinary meeting at the palace proceeded extraordinarily. According to the then Information and Communication Minister Jaya Prakash Gupta, who was present, the king presented a few conditions for the deployment of the army. For instance: the government should hold talks with the Maoists at least once before taking this step; all the parties in the Parliament should give their consent to the deployment; the budget should be immediately redrawn to bear the huge cost that would accompany any army mobilization; and nobody should call the army back midway, without letting it complete its mission.[21]

The prime minister simply could not meet those conditions. For example, it would be impossible for him to get the consent of all of the parties in Parliament. The opposition CPN–UML was already demanding his resignation over an alleged scam involving the lease of a Lauda Air aircraft for what was then known as the RNAC.

The army chief, Rana, was aware of the PM's predicament, so he repeated the king's conditions. 'If the Royal Nepali Army is to be involved in internal security and development plans, it would be essential that it receives sustained support from the political parties as well as from the general public,' he said.[22]

Till 12 April 2001, Rana believed that the Maoists were not out of control. That day, he told CPN–UML leaders at the army headquarters, 'So far, they are in a state of strategic defence.'[23] In other words, he believed that they could be tamed as and when desired through the use of the army. Maybe that is why the palace-army combine did not feel a sense of urgency.

However, the prime minister applying pressure, and taking a legion of officials to the palace, resulted in the army coming out of the barracks with a limited mandate. The army was not directly targeting the Maoists at this stage; it was deployed in development work under the Internal Security and Development Plan (ISDP). From mid-April 2001 onwards, the army was involved in development and social service under the ISDP in seven districts (Rolpa, Rukum, Jajarkot, Salyan, Kalikot, Pyuthan and Gorkha). The government wanted to push the army further, to fight the Maoists, but the army headquarters demanded a separate mandate from the National Security Council for that purpose. So, although the army had come out of the barracks, it had not yet become involved in the fight.

Prime Minister Koirala had a nagging doubt: whether the Maoists had protection from the palace, and whether the army had not been fully mobilized for that reason. Koirala described the talks he had with King Birendra on these issues in early 2001 to the BBC five years later:

I asked His Majesty: What is this Maoist phenomenon, Your Majesty? We can't resolve it without the answer. I have been in the government on and off, but Your Majesty has been there throughout, so Your Majesty may know about this phenomenon.' Koirala added, 'His Majesty indicated India. I then asked him, how can that be? Indians are themselves trapped in problems on their northern borders, such as in Assam, Mizoram, and they are embroiled in the Kashmir issue with Pakistan. So why would they want to take up another headache by raising a problem in this relatively peaceful part? The king was silent.[24]

One must believe that the king had spoken his mind—his perspective towards the Maoists was perhaps different from how it had been portrayed. He saw an Indian hand behind the rise of the Maoists. He understood that it would be counterproductive to start military operations without taking the Indians into confidence. So he was planning to hold a meeting at the top level with the Indians.

Meanwhile, he was searching for ways to end the Maoists' people's war peacefully. For this reason, he had asked his brother to hold talks with Maoist leaders. He felt that the army mustn't be used in a crude fashion. He saw the dangers of a military operation igniting wider bloodshed and forcing the country down the path of endless civil war. He thought of the army as the final weapon, which must be deployed only under conditions where victory was assured. Otherwise, he felt, it would invite external intervention.

But then, a wholly unanticipated incident struck the country and pushed Nepal's history in an entirely different direction.

4

A 'Coup' That Never Happened

'He sent emissaries out to London, Washington DC, New Delhi and Beijing to seek the concurrence of these capitals to interventionism of some kind with the democratic process in order to curb the growing Maoist threat. All the capitals except Beijing strongly discouraged adventurism of the kind contemplated.'

—K.V. Rajan on King Birendra's planned action[1]

By the middle of 2001, Nepali politics was a thorough wreck. The Maoists, in one of the most daring attacks, had killed thirty-two policemen, including an inspector, in Rukumkot. Five days later, a similar number of policemen, including another inspector, were killed in Naumule of Dailekh. Dozens of weapons were looted. These events clearly showed that the police were on the back foot. But the palace was dithering on army mobilization.

King Birendra wanted to take a decisive step, but he was in no hurry to do so, as then Prime Minister Girija Prasad Koirala described later: 'The way Gyanendra effected his coup against democracy, I think, sooner or later, Birendra would have gone down the same path. There are people who say that even when he was prince, Gyanendra would put pressure on King Birendra to act. But Birendra himself wanted to go slow.'[2]

Based on the course of events and facts gathered from various sources, one may conclude that King Birendra did, indeed, want to intervene on the pretext of controlling the Maoists. But when he made his move, the king wanted to kill three birds with a single stone:

- A resolution of the Maoist problem
- Winning back powers lost in 1990 by taking charge himself
- Reducing Nepal's external dependence (particularly upon India)

King Birendra had kept both options open: peaceful resolution and military mobilization. The only condition was that the palace should take the initiative and get the political reward. A former palace military secretary, and son of *Bafikote raja* (a titular princeling) Dhruba Bikram Shah as we mentioned about him earlier, Lt Gen. (Retd) Bibek Kumar Shah, revealed, 'It was his plan to dissolve the House of Representatives once there was an understanding with the Maoists. Then he planned to hold a roundtable conference involving political leaders to form a national government. He also wanted a general election after two years, and was working on the amendment of the Constitution without changing its preamble.'[3]

The name given to King Birendra's plan was 'Operation *Baaj* (Hawk)'. Towards the end of 2000, the king gave Bibek Kumar Shah a text of the plan to read. The king was in the process of forming a 'special task force' of retired senior administrators and security officials. He was to assign the task of coordinating all the security agencies to the former army chief, Dharmapal Barsingh Thapa. For this purpose, preparations to make Thapa a field marshal were in their final stage.[4]

Royal massacre

Just as King Birendra was planning a decisive step, the unimaginable palace massacre occurred. It was almost as if somebody knew about Birendra's plan and wanted to stop him.

Ten members of the royal family, including the king and the queen, were killed on 1 June 2001. The committee formed to probe the massacre concluded that it was carried out by Crown Prince Dipendra. If one were to believe the conclusion of the committee, which included Chief Justice Keshab Prasad Upadhyaya and Speaker Taranath Ranabhat, the crown prince, apparently enraged by his parents' objection to his choice of bride, his lover, Devyani Rana, had single-handedly slaughtered his parents, siblings and other relatives at a family gathering in Tribhuwan Sadan of the palace, before killing himself.[5] But many did not buy its conclusion.

There were many unanswered questions. Could any son simply kill his parents just because he was not allowed to marry his choice of bride? Could he kill his dear sister? Could he carry four weapons and hit the targets when he was apparently in an intoxicated state? The descendants of the king were totally obliterated, but the same incident left the family of the king-to-be unharmed. How could that be? Why was Gyanendra away from Kathmandu at that time? And why did the 'murderer' kill himself after the massacre? And that too by firing shots into his left side of the head, when he was right-handed? The committee was unable to provide answers to these questions.

The committee simply gathered witness accounts of the incident of 1 June. Neither did it carry out a full investigation, nor did it reach any independent conclusion, leaving many crucial questions unanswered. Was the incident purely a consequence of family conflict, or was it part of a wider political conspiracy? Was Dipendra being incited by anybody? Who was responsible for pushing Dipendra towards drug addiction, as mentioned in the report? These queries, too, were left hanging in the air.

There were also other incidents that added fuel to the fire of conspiracy theories. Post-mortems were not conducted on the bodies. Their funeral took place amid a curfew. After the death of Birendra, the comatose Crown Prince Dipendra was declared king for a brief period and Prince Gyanendra was declared his regent. In his first public statement, Gyanendra made a false and ludicrous claim that the incident occurred because of the 'accidental firing of automatic weapon'. That significantly eroded the public's faith in him. Gyanendra was proclaimed king after Dipendra was pronounced dead. This added to people's suspicions. In fact, five years later, at a press conference held before he left the Narayanhity Royal Palace for good, Gyanendra felt the need to issue a public clarification of his innocence.

The lack of a credible investigation into the massacre has created a situation in which people will dispute the truth even if it were to be uncovered. Like the assassination of American President John F. Kennedy, and the death of Indian Prime Minister Lal Bahadur Shastri, like the death of Princess Diana or that of Madan Bhandari, the palace massacre has entered history as an unsolved mystery, surrounded by numerous conspiracy theories.

The prime minister's suspicion

Even the prime minister, Girija Prasad Koirala, expressed great suspicions about the massacre. He treated it as part of a 'grand design' In fact, his statement on the massacre is itself mysterious. When, on the night of 1 June, he received a phone call from the chairman of the Raj Sabha (Royal Council) Standing Committee, Keshar Jung Rayamajhi, and when later, the king's chief secretary, Pashupati Bhakta Maharjan, came to Baluwatar to inform him about the massacre, Koirala first went to inspect the site of the massacre in the palace before visiting the army hospital in Chhauni, where the bodies were taken. When he reached the site of the killings with Maharjan at 11.30 p.m., it was almost deserted.

'I just saw one soldier there. Nobody else. Totally quiet,' he said. 'When I reached the place, there were no signs of blood. It had been cleaned up. I didn't see anything there. So then I went to the hospital.'[6]

Koirala's statement raises several questions. What is the meaning of cleaning up the site of such a horrendous massacre within two hours of the incident? Who had ordered the clean-up?

In fact, Koirala was also to be invited to the party in the palace that evening. He later said, 'The king said not to invite me, so I did not have to go there that night, and I was saved.'[7] A question arises: Was there a plot to kill both the king and the prime minister? Was that the reason he was to be invited there? Who had proposed inviting him?

The following day, when the funeral procession of the king and the queen took place, an attack was made on the vehicle carrying the prime minister. His bullet-proof car was seriously damaged. The attack was carried out amid a crowd which was enraged over the palace massacre. His bodyguard fired blank shots to save him. When the PM finally made his way to Baluwatar, his coat was covered with shards of glass. There were also wounds in his body caused by the sharp fragments.

'I have been attacked several times in my lifetime, but have never confronted such a grave attack. It was not something spontaneous. It was a planned attack. That was the plan to kill me,' Koirala has claimed.[8]

However, as a prime minister, Koirala demonstrated glaring weaknesses during the massacre. He did not call an emergency meeting of the sovereign Parliament to inform it about the incident and let the parties attempt a common response. Though he often muttered 'grand design', he never clarified what he meant by it. Three years after the incident, Koirala pointed his finger at King Gyanendra by saying that the latter's activities had made the massacre more mysterious.[9]

Bibek's details

Lt Gen. (Retd) Bibek Kumar Shah was the chief of palace security at the time of the massacre. He had a different version. According to his conclusion, the killings were carried out by Dipendra, but it was not merely a matter of family conflict. He smells a wider political plot in which the massacre was achieved by inciting Dipendra.

Born into the former princely family of Rukum, Shah had first come to Kathmandu for his education. He ended up spending thirty-five years in military service. He spent around thirty years in the palace. He watched Birendra's transformation from crown prince to king from close quarters. Talking to this author one evening at his residence in Gyaneshwor, Kathmandu in December 2007, Shah made a sensational claim: that Birendra was planning a 'coup,' while Dipendra had attempted another 'coup' by killing him, an attempt which somehow ended in his own death. Part of our conversation, held on 18 December 2007, went like this:

People look at the palace massacre, which occurred during your term as the chief of palace security from various perspectives. How do you see it yourself?

It should be looked at from two angles. One, Crown Prince Dipendra was in an extreme mental state at the time due to a family dispute. This was the point when the murders took place. Two, there is an element of political conspiracy and the involvement of foreign agencies. But this matter of political conspiracy remains draped in secrecy even now. Who were the foreign agents who provoked Dipendra into doing something like that? No investigation has been undertaken on this aspect. The way suspicions are cast on the role of some foreign intelligence services, that aspect too remains uninvestigated.

You are saying that the motive for the massacre was not probed?

Yes. Nobody looked into 'motive'. Investigations by experts were also not carried out. Everybody thought it was enough to form such a high-level investigation committee (with the then chief justice and speaker in it).

If you believe it was a conspiracy, then do you think that the conspirators targeted the frustration building up within Dipendra?

One hundred per cent, they seem to have targeted him. He might have been lured by the prospect of gaining the throne. That is because the family dispute was building to such a climax that Queen Aishwarya could sometimes be heard warning that if Dipendra chose to marry Devyani, she would have him stripped of the title of crown prince and give the same to Prince Nirajan. That really infuriated Dipendra. Someone closely monitoring his psyche could have provoked him.

So Dipendra thought of becoming king himself by killing his father and his mother?

In my analysis, he simply wanted to kill the king (Birendra) and replace him on the throne. He might have thought that, once he became king, he would be immune to any legal action. Someone who suggested this might have incited him. And King Birendra had already suffered a heart attack and had a pacemaker installed. The plan might have been to present his death as having been caused by a heart attack.

If he had only wanted to kill Birendra, then why were others shot?

He fired the first shot into the ceiling, probably to draw attention. Then the second shot was fired at King Birendra.

When the king fell down, Dhirendra was shot as he tried to jump at him. This was followed by another shot at the king. These things happened within seconds. It was an automatic weapon, capable of firing thousands of bullets in a minute. Thereafter, there was total chaos in the hall. And whoever tried to raise their head was shot one by one.

He was said to be totally intoxicated at the time. How was it possible for him to carry out such a massacre?

The reports of his drunkenness are not totally true. He had only been acting as if he was drunk. He took the lives of his relatives, then, I think, his sixth sense told him that everything was gone! In the ensuing state of extreme shock, he committed suicide. He seems to have fired a shot at the left side of his head from the weapon in his left hand. That pistol was later found to have dropped from his left hand into the pond beside him. He was a good marksman, equally adept at firing shots from both hands.

In your opinion, do you think the conspirators indeed wanted to make him king, or simply wanted to use him?

It looks like they simply wanted to use him.

So who were those conspirators?

They could be anyone, within or outside the country. The truth might emerge gradually.

Why do you think the palace massacre was staged?

It could be due to somebody's personal motive. But, more importantly, King Birendra was planning to take a decisive step very soon. The country was in bad shape. Was the massacre staged to stop him from taking that step? He had just returned from China after taking part in a conference in Boao. There was speculation about the imminent move. Those who did not want him to take such a step might have become apprehensive about whether he was doing so at the behest of the Chinese.

What sort of step was he planning to take?

A political step.

Something akin to what King Gyanendra did later, on 1 February 2005?

I would not know what the blueprint would have been, but he was definitely thinking about ways to resolve the Maoist problem, because it was taking a huge toll on the country. I understood that he was exploring ways to bring the Maoists on board the government, to hold some sort of a wider political dialogue.

Distancing Delhi

Shah claims that King Birendra was unable to implement his plan because he could not get diplomatic support from a close neighbour. It was a time when relations between Delhi and the Durbar were not warm. Birendra saw Delhi's hand behind the curtailment of his governing powers, and in the persistent instability of the country. Delhi, on the other hand, saw the palace as the power centre where anti-India sentiments were manufactured. Particularly due to his tussle with Rajiv Gandhi, King Birendra was unable to mend ties with the Indian establishment.

In fact, his relations with Rajiv's mother, Indira Gandhi, were very cordial, even though they did not see eye to eye on many matters. Following the failure of the Emergency in 1976, and the decimation of her party at the hands of the Janata Party in the parliamentary election, Indira had felt quite insecure. King Birendra had invited her to come to Kathmandu. She herself did not want to leave her country, but wanted to send her son and daughter-in-law (Rajiv and Sonia) to a political refuge to Kathmandu. It was after the intervention of the then RAW chief, R.N. Kao, who advised her against it, saying it could spell trouble for her politically, that Indira backed out. At least two senior RAW officials with knowledge of the events have confirmed the episode.[10]

After Indira was killed by her own bodyguards in 1984, Rajiv rose to power as the scion of the Nehru–Gandhi dynasty, but Birendra never had good relations with him. King Birendra's 'refusal' to attend a breakfast meeting hosted by Rajiv on the sidelines of the fourth SAARC Summit in Islamabad in 1988 became an issue of prestige for the Indian leader. Even as bilateral ties were becoming frosty, Nepal's decision to import sixty-five trucks full of weapons, including sixteen anti-aircraft guns from China irked Delhi so much that it refused to renew the bilateral trade and transit treaty and imposed economic sanctions. At the same time, in 1990, there was a people's movement within Nepal. India backed the democratic forces and helped to end the Panchayati party-less system under the king's direct rule. The mutual suspicion between the Kathmandu Durbar and Delhi could never be cleared after that episode.[11]

After Rajiv Gandhi was assassinated in 1991, P.V. Narasimha Rao, who was not a member of the Nehru–Gandhi family, became the Indian prime minister. King Birendra had good relations with Rao. He told Rao that under his leadership, 'a new era of friendship and cooperation' would begin. Rao replied that he expected the constructive contribution of the king in conducting mature relations with India, just like the Bhutanese king. It was, in fact, Rao's policy to cement multiparty democracy through the consolidation of ties with the constitutional monarchy, which later became the much-touted 'twin pillars' theory of India's relations with Nepal.[12]

And it was this policy of Rao's that the new ambassador, K.V. Rajan, came to represent in Kathmandu in 1995. King Birendra, too, wanted to indicate the normalization of ties during Rajan's term. In 1996, in a departure from tradition, King Birendra visited the Indian embassy to watch a performance by the Indian musical maestro Ustad Amjad Ali Khan. In 1998, accompanied by his family and a council of ministers and former prime ministers, he took part in the Independence Day celebrations organized by the Indian embassy. It provided a unique photo-op. When the photo was splashed across the front pages of newspapers the following day, the message was clear: Delhi–Durbar relations were warming again. In yet another clear signal of warming ties, King Birendra was invited to attend India's Republic Day functions in 1999 as the chief guest. Both the Indian president and prime minister heaped praise on him during their Republic Day addresses. Their theme was how the constitutional monarchy was playing a constructive role in cementing democracy amid the unsatisfactory performance of the political parties.

King Birendra was quite keen on improving ties with Delhi. He was planning to take an important political step, and he wanted to take Delhi into confidence. But India did not encourage him. He had sent his emissaries to the US, the UK, China and India with a message that he was planning to take steps to address the Maoist problem. According to Indian Ambassador Rajan, none of the world capitals except China backed him. He then hesitated to move ahead. It was amid this 'stress' that the king suffered a heart attack, according to Rajan.[13] In October of 1998, the King underwent a coronary angioplasty at the Cromwell Hospital in London.

The king was conflicted. He could neither give up his plans for a coup, nor could he remain stress-free. The Maoists were becoming increasingly bold in their attacks. He felt that the political parties were unable to play their role, despite having enough chances. He was also under family pressure for not taking a 'courageous step'. According to the former military secretary, Shah, Birendra was under tremendous pressure from the palace's 'illiberal' camp. 'Queen Aishwarya, Crown Prince Dipendra and Prince Gyanendra represented this camp. This camp looked up to the late King Mahendra as their ideal. They felt that the king should be firm, and should press ahead in sidelining the parties.'[14]

This camp did not conceal its unhappiness over how King Birendra had, in 1990, declared multiparty democracy and backed the liberals. They often remarked on his weak leadership. 'Impressed with this perspective, the crown prince used to regard his father as a feeble leader, and said he would become a strong leader when his time came,' Shah writes. 'The fact that some quarters praised Dipendra, calling him a good and strong leader, was no secret. So, it is my conclusion that by playing up the inherent family conflicts and weaknesses, a well-planned plot was hatched by domestic and foreign power-centres to incite Dipendra's ambition to carry out the massacre.'[15]

This was also the time when Dipendra was becoming increasingly frustrated over his mother's refusal to let him marry his sweetheart Devyani Rana. He was disappointed by his father's failure to intervene in the matter. There has been a traditional rivalry among Nepal's Rana families between descendants of Chandra Shumsher and Juddha Shumsher. Being among Juddha's descendants, Queen Aishwarya did not want her son to marry Devyani, who comes from Chandra's line. Devyani is the youngest daughter of Pashupati Shumsher Rana, himself a well-known politician and the grandson of Nepal's last Rana prime minister, Mohan Shumsher. The Maharaja of Gwalior Madhav Rao Scindia, an Indian minister belonging to the Indian National Congress, was Pashupati's brother-in-law, or Devyani's maternal uncle. And her grandmother was Vijaya Raje Scindia, a respected leader of the Bharatiya Janata Party. So it was not surprising that Queen Aishwarya would reject her marriage into the Nepali royal family. She was known to harbour anti-India sentiments, and she would not allow a daughter-in-law with such powerful Delhi connections to become Nepal's queen one day. The extreme family pressure on his private affairs rattled Dipendra, and it was this frustration that was played upon, according to Bibek Shah. As palace military secretary, he had wide access to security and intelligence information related to the Durbar, but he could not present any hard facts beyond his own conjectures to prove any 'design' behind the massacre.

Message from Tehran

Although he backed down from his first attempt to effect a coup, King Birendra again started exploring the option in 2000. Again, Delhi cold-shouldered him. One reason was a renewed coldness in ties between Delhi and the Durbar following the departure of the Rao government. Particularly, the security agencies and bureaucracy of Delhi treated the Nepali Durbar with some animosity. They routinely accused the king of harbouring anti-India elements in Nepal. Delhi felt that the activities of Pakistan's ISI intelligence service, and its 'protégé', Indian mafia lord Dawood Ibrahim, were expanding in Nepal. Incidents such as the discovery of RDX explosives headed for Delhi were becoming frequent in Kathmandu.

In a report entitled 'Nepal Gameplan', leaked by the RAW to the Indian media, some royal family members were accused of having links with Dawood.[16] It was felt that pro-monarchy and Pakistani ISI elements were behind the anti-India riots of the Hrithik Roshan episode.[17] Before that, Pakistani militants had hijacked an Indian Airlines plane from Kathmandu, and taken it to Kandahar, Afghanistan, forcing Delhi to make a 'shameful' agreement. A section of Indian officials believed that all these things were possible because of the 'soft posture' of King Birendra towards such elements.

Right at that moment, Birendra initiated procedures to reduce Nepal's political and military dependence on India. With his eye on the military's imminent involvement in dealing with the Maoists, he started the process of modernizing the Royal Nepali Army. Preparations were underway to replace Indian SLRs with German-made HK G36 rifles as the personal weapon for RNA infantry soldiers. A line of credit had been opened to import 5000 G36 rifles, initially from the German Heckler and Koch.

A secret plan was also set in motion to allow HK to set up an assembly line in Kathmandu with the aim of exporting weapons to Bangladesh, Sri Lanka and other south Asian and south-east Asian countries. The factory was to be set up in partnership with the Nepali army at Sundarijal. The plan was also to manufacture 5.56 mm calibre ammunition for the G36 rifles there. Delhi had made attempts to stop this plan; it wanted to sell India-made INSAS rifles to the army.

Former Crown Prince Paras has claimed that the HK scheme was one of the reasons for the palace massacre. In an interview he gave to a tabloid in Singapore, Paras lists the growing row over buying weapons for the army as among the causes, along with the Dipendra-Devyani love affair and disenchantment with the 1990 change, behind the massacre.[18]

Even though he was distancing himself from Delhi, King Birendra was making rapid advancements in forging a political and strategic alliance with China. He had made ten official visits to China. His latest was a trip to China at the invitation of President Jiang Zemin in February–March 2001. He had addressed the Boao Asian Forum, an alliance of twenty-four countries, as an 'special guest' in Hainan on February 27 and then went to Beijing as part of the state visit. Subsequently, the Chinese premier Zhu Rongji visited Nepal. During that visit, China agreed to build a second highway linking the two countries—the Rasuwa–Kerung highway.

According to a Chinese academic, 'the Indians disliked King Birendra for his attempt to implement independent and self-reliant foreign policies.'[19] Following his failure to win Delhi's support for his plan, Birendra had gone all out to woo Beijing. 'Operation Hawk' was the result of such planning.

Indian Ambassador K.V. Rajan recalls in his memoir a startling incident from that time. According to Rajan, just prior to the massacre, he began receiving sensitive messages from the king. When he came to know that there was going to be a big incident in Kathmandu, and that the king wanted to deliver some emergency message to Delhi, he sprang to action. He was part of the entourage of Indian Prime Minister Atal Behari Vajpayee in Iran at the time. So, along with External Affairs Minister Jaswant Singh, he went to Vajpayee's hotel room at midnight.

Vajpayee patiently listened to the details and looked at his foreign minister inquiringly. Jaswant said, 'Atalji, I think we should ask Rajan to go immediately to Kathmandu, meet the king and come back with a detailed report.'

Vajpayee closed his eyes for a moment and thought. He said, 'It might be better for us to invite a special emissary of the king.'[20]

But before Vajpayee and his officials could take any action after returning to Delhi, Kathmandu was struck by the tragedy. As King Birendra himself was killed, it was not clear what emergency assistance he had been seeking from Delhi.

'New Kot Massacre'

The Maoists were unaware of the state of mind that King Birendra was in. Nor did they have a whiff of the hurricane that was about to lash Kathmandu. But when they heard about the palace massacre, they immediately smelt a conspiracy. At that time, Baburam Bhattarai was staying in Manglapuri in Delhi. Early on the morning of 2 June 2001, he had gone to a railway station to see somebody off at 5 a.m. There, he received a call from an Indian journalist, Ananda Swarup Verma, about the incident at the palace. Baburam wanted to learn about Dhirendra, because it was through him that they were holding talks with King Birendra.

Bhattarai called a senior advocate, Sindhunath Pyakurel, who was once a parliamentarian from his party. When Pyakurel said, 'The fate of Dhirendra is also similar,' Bhattarai dispatched his representative to the residence of former Prime Minister Kirti Nidhi Bista in Gyaneshwore. He thought that Bista might divulge something of importance, since he was close to King Birendra and took a liberal view of the Maoists; but nothing new came from Bista. That evening, having analysed the information they had gathered the whole day, Prachanda and Baburam Bhattarai reached a conclusion—this must be a political conspiracy.

The Maoists were caught totally off-guard by the palace massacre. Birendra was killed amid preparations for his meeting with Prachanda. Dhirendra, who was arranging the meeting, was also killed. The Maoists were aware that Birendra did not want to mobilize the army against them, despite being under tremendous pressure to do so. So they saw the massacre as a grand conspiracy, and they blamed the new king, Gyanendra, Prime Minister Girija Prasad Koirala, India and the United States. The primary proponent of this conspiracy theory was none other than Baburam Bhattarai.

Sitting in a park in west Delhi, he wrote a famous article. The article was published in the daily *Kantipur*. He called the massacre 'a coup'. He compared the incident with the Kot massacre 150 years earlier, in which Jung Bahadur had slaughtered dozens of courtiers near Hanumandhoka Durbar to lay the foundation of the Rana oligarchy in Nepal.[21]

'His unwillingness to mobilize the army—which has a tradition of loyalty towards the King—to curb the People's Revolution taking place under the leadership of Nepal Communist Party (Maoist) became his biggest crime in the eyes of the imperialist and expansionist powers,' Bhattarai claimed, arguing that King

Birendra was killed simply because of his liberal views towards the Maoists.

Bhattarai's claim was that India had staged the palace massacre in order to carry out its political design of first turning Nepal into Bhutan, then merging it like Sikkim. He likened the role of King Gyanendra to that of then Bhutanese King Jigme Singye Wangchuk and the role of Prime Minister Girija Prasad Koirala to Sikkim's last prime minister, Lhendup Dorjee.[22] The Maoist claim seemed to be based more on conspiracy theory than on facts. Their claims extended to the involvement of American and Indian intelligence agencies, the CIA and the RAW, whose covert actions are generally invisible.

The Maoists had become more suspicious because of what Dhirendra had told them at their last meeting. According to Bhattarai, 'In his last meeting with our representatives, just weeks before the royal massacre, Dhirendra Shah had revealed a threat to his and other royalties' lives. This is one of the concrete proofs we have about the larger conspiracy behind the royal massacre on 1 June 2001.'[23]

Five years after the palace massacre, I asked Prachanda at a meeting in Delhi, 'Did you have any factual evidence to support your allegations of a conspiracy behind that incident?'

Without mincing words, he said, 'Well, we don't have any facts. Not anything you are looking for.'

Bhattarai, standing close to Prachanda, added, 'Some American journalists have written with quotes! (They have written) how the Pacific Command (of the US military) had come and plotted.'

Wayne Madsen, a former member of the US navy and a journalist, has written a piece in which he claims that the CIA dispatched a squad of special forces, under the cover of US military training on earthquake risks, to the Royal Nepali Army, and how the squad was used in an operation code-named 'Bailey Nightingale One'[24] to carry out the royal massacre. He further wrote that India's RAW and the then Prince Gyanendra were accomplices in the operation. He wrote that the Devyani link was deliberately raised to put the blame squarely on Dipendra.[25] In fact, a squad of the American military team did come to Nepal around that time and held a joint exercise with the Royal Nepali Army in Bhaktapur, but there is no evidence to support the claim that it had any link to the massacre.

The Maoists had reached their conclusion of an external conspiracy by an analysis of the political situation. Even that analysis was not without contradictions. In the statement he had released after the incident on 2 June, Prachanda pointed fingers at the 'Girija government and Indian ruling class'. In a subsequent statement on 5 June, he claimed the killings were carried out in collusion with an 'Indian intelligence agency and the Girija government.' In Baburam's article, published on 6 June, and in the politburo statement of 11 June, they also accused Gyanendra and the CIA as conspirators.

Who was the real murderer? The Maoists were perplexed, but they did try to exploit the massacre as a big political opportunity.

Failed attempt at revolt

The Maoists were fresh from their second national convention, which had endorsed the line also known as 'Prachandapath', that of seizing power through an urban insurrection. Three months later, the palace massacre occurred. When groups of youths with shaved heads (they cut their hair as a mark of respect to the dead royals) started enraged agitations in the streets of Kathmandu, the Maoists wanted to take advantage. A politburo meeting of the Maoists identified 'the arrival of a republic with surprising speed'.

Putting aside even his own proposal for an all-party conference, Prachanda called on other parties to directly form a united republican government. He also appealed to the army: 'the Royal Army loyal to King Birendra, and patriotic Nepali, should no longer protect foreign stooges and murderers. It should fulfil its glorious duty to the nation by supporting and cooperating in the process of formation of an interim government of patriots'.[26]

But there was no possibility of the army supporting the Maoists, because the palace was still there. A new king had been crowned, and its loyalty was to him. So nobody seriously believed the Maoists' prediction of 'the arrival of a republic with surprising speed'. It ended up as a mere political slogan.

The general public refused to believe the story of the palace massacre as it was being presented, but opinion had not swung in favour of a republic either. The ruling Nepali Congress and opposition CPN–UML, who had a great hold on the urban populace, were in a similar mood. Prime Minister Girija Prasad Koirala harboured doubts about the incident. Opposition leader Madhav Kumar Nepal backed out from the palace-formed probe committee for the same reason. But they wanted to appoint a new king and fill the royal void as soon as possible, so that none of the other forces—including the Maoists—could take advantage of the anarchy.

A proposal by a pro-Maoist student front for a united movement was rejected by student unions affiliated to the other parties. Their plan to instigate a rebellion by seizing the dead body of the newly proclaimed King Dipendra from the funeral cortège was also thwarted by the government, which imposed a curfew during the procession on 4 June. Their planned revolt ended up as a few scattered rallies in the gullies of Kathmandu. The mainstream forces, including the Nepali Congress and the CPN–UML, recognized the new king.

In their very first statement after the incident, the Maoists had made accusations against Prime Minister Koirala. This deepened their rift with the ruling Nepali Congress party. Koirala might have thought that he could get support from the new king for his plans for military mobilization against the Maoists. More importantly, despite the suspicions and doubts in his mind, Koirala decided to accept Gyanendra in order to give continuity to monarchy. The

Maoists therefore had to back down. Less than two months later, they came to the table for a dialogue with the government under the new king. It was, in effect, an indirect recognition of King Gyanendra. However, they had to pass through intense internal discussions to reach that point.

One a patriot, the other a murderer!

After the death of King Birendra, his eldest son Dipendra, still in a coma, was proclaimed the new king, even though it was clear to all that he was not going to make it. On the third day and after he passed away, his uncle, and the only surviving brother of Birendra, Prince Gyanendra, was crowned king.

The Maoists used to praise the late King Birendra as a patriot, but they were in a huge predicament initially as to what they should call the 'new, living king' Gyanendra, and whether they could still have 'unity in action' with him. In the first two statements he released after the massacre, on 2 and 5 June, Prachanda had not accused Gyanendra. It was in the article published in *Kantipur* on 6 June that Baburam first added Gyanendra to the list of 'murderers'. The party's politburo meeting, which took place subsequently in India, formally endorsed Baburam's line. Thus, the previous king became a 'patriot' and the new king became a 'murderer' in their eyes.

Not everybody in the party agreed with that conclusion. Rabindra Shrestha was one of the dissenters. He was in charge of the Maoists' valley bureau, and stopped the politburo statement from being released. As a result, it was not published in the Maoist weekly mouthpiece *Janadesh*. But another weekly, *Jana Ahwan*, said to be close to Baburam, did not obey his diktat. Immediately afterwards, he stopped the printing of the paper, citing financial reasons, and its editor, Om Sharma, was suspended as a district committee member.

I later asked Rabindra Shrestha about the incident. His logic was that Gyanendra, too, could be used like Birendra had been, so it was not appropriate to immediately accuse him. 'What I said was that although we could suspect 95 per cent that Gyanendra committed the crime, let's give him 5 per cent (benefit of doubt),' said Rabindra, who left the Maoists in 2006. 'Because that incident could have been carried out by Dipendra or someone else. At the end, we did not have evidence. I just said that if evidence emerged clearing Gyanendra of any crime, what would become of the party's image?'

Baburam, on the other hand, felt that the right environment for the transformation to a republic could be created by hitting out at Gyanendra. Ignoring Baburam's remarks, Rabindra, who was living underground in the Kathmandu valley, went ahead and held talks with Gyanendra's emissaries. The old palace sources also approached the Maoists, claiming Gyanendra's innocence in the palace massacre. They said that the 'king had international influence and recognition, while the Maoists had the people's support. So if the king and the Maoists come together, they can overthrow the parliamentary parties'. According to Prachanda, Gyanendra at one time proposed that if the Maoists took part in an election, he would see to it that they got a two-thirds' majority.[27]

One-and-a-half months after the palace massacre, King Gyanendra foiled an attempt by Prime Minister Girija Prasad Koirala to mobilize the army against the Maoists in Holeri. This led to unexpected cooperation between the palace and the Maoists. In July 2001, talks began between the Maoists and the government. Simultaneously, the Maoists also advanced their negotiations with palace emissaries. It was ironic, since the party still called Gyanendra a murderer. A section of Maoist leaders, including Baburam, was unhappy at talks being held with Gyanendra's representatives.

There was an extensive discussion at the Maoist politburo meeting that took place in Faridabad, India, in October 2001 of the issue of giving recognition to King Gyanendra. Rabindra Shrestha moved a proposal calling for recognition, arguing, 'We should not close our doors to Gyanendra. He can be used like Birendra.' Senior leaders like Badal and Kiran were amenable to his proposal. Their idea was to displace the parliamentary parties by aligning with the king and then sharing power.

Baburam opposed it. After the palace massacre, he was beginning to stand solidly for a republic. It was only after Prachanda supported Baburam's position, and ruled out any immediate possibility of an alliance with Gyanendra, that Rabindra Shrestha's proposal was rejected. Nevertheless, the door to that possibility was still left ajar.

Part II

The Climax

5

Gyanendra on the Throne—War and Jaw

'Until yesterday, Nirmal Niwas (King Gyanendra's residence) was Mecca for the Maoists. And today, they see it as a seat of American imperialism and Indian expansionism.'

—Ram Chandra Poudel, then deputy
prime minister and leader of the Nepali Congress,
pointing to the 'double game' of the Maoists[1]

It was 12 July 2001. The Maoists had called a *Nepal bandh* (general strike). To make it successful, they were planning to attack a police training centre in Bhaluwang of Dang district. Around 1200 guerrillas from the western region had gathered for the purpose. But they had to return midway after they learnt that their plan had been leaked. They still needed to strike a blow somewhere to make their bandh successful, so they targeted a police camp at Holeri in Rolpa district.

As usual, the policemen had all gone 'out' at night in case there was a Maoist attack. They were just returning to their post early in the morning, at around 4 a.m., when they found themselves surrounded. Just as the Maoists started firing, the policemen surrendered. One sub-inspector, Raj Bahadur Giri, was killed as he tried to flee. Including an inspector, Madan Gurung, sixty-nine policemen were detained by the Maoists and led away.

Just forty-one days after the horrendous palace massacre, Kathmandu was distressed by the news of over five dozen policemen being abducted by the rebels. Surprisingly, abiding by the government's instructions for the first time, the army dispatched commandos to the Rapti hills. The goal was to free the police and confiscate looted weapons from the Maoists at minimal cost.

On the morning of 13 July, at around 6 a.m., an MI-17 helicopter took off from Dang with the first platoon. The weather was inclement. It took half an hour to complete what should have been a ten-minute flight. They landed at Nuwagaun village in Rolpa. Less than a minute after the helicopter took off to collect the second platoon, there was a sound: clack . . . clack. Pilot Binayak Singh thought the engine had failed. Inexperienced in war, they did not know it was the sound of shots being fired. Then he saw he was already hit, a bullet in his thigh. Lt Rudra Poudel had a bloodied hand. And Sepoy Nara Bahadur Khatri had been struck in the abdomen.[2]

The shots had been fired from a hilltop to their left, from a .303. There were twenty-one holes in the MI-17, including in its tail unit and fuel tank.

It was the first incident in which the Maoist insurgents had attacked and injured soldiers of the Royal Nepali Army. The incident was unanticipated, even for Maoist Commissar Barshaman Pun 'Ananta' and Commander Nanda Kishor Pun 'Pasang', who were deployed in the Holeri raid. Upon hearing the helicopter, they had quickly led the policemen in their detention away, but when the chopper kept hovering over them, they had no option but to fire at it. Initially, they thought the police had come with a military chopper. But as it wobbled downwards to an emergency landing, they saw—it was the army.

The army had just been able to land one out of four platoons. And that platoon was immediately surrounded by around

500 guerrillas. The Super Puma and Puma helicopters carrying commandos dispatched for their rescue were also fired upon. Those helicopters were fitted with GPMGs (general purpose machine guns). The commandos tried to retaliate by firing the GPMG, but the operational commander stopped them. It prevented the army–Maoist clash. The central policy of not fighting the Maoists was still in operation.

The forty-two specially trained commandos had to return without landing. The Super Puma that was carrying them was damaged, and they were only just able to return to Dang. The weather took a turn for the worse. At the top of the hill, shrouded in dense fog, the one platoon (around forty soldiers) that had landed lost any hope of rescue.

The army was now faced with the challenge of rescuing their soldiers—after getting their nose bloodied in their first encounter with the rebels. The Maoists, on the other hand, were frantically trying to stop the incident from spiralling out of control. These two different goals brought them together temporarily. Despite their upper hand in Holeri, the Maoists were not in the mood to fight the army yet. Besides, that would bring King Gyanendra and Prime Minister Girija Prasad Koirala closer politically, which they did not want. So they went overboard in making use of all their contacts.

Pro-Maoist journalist Krishna Sen 'Ichhuk' talked to former zonal commissioner Surya Bahadur Sen Oli, who had contacts in the royal palace. Someone went to the former army chief, Satchit Shumsher Rana. A group of activists, including Padma Ratna Tuladhar, Dr K.B. Rokaya and Madhav Marahatta went to the army headquarters. There, they made a clear proposal—let the army stop its operation and we will make sure the abducted policemen are freed. They talked to Lt Gen. Pyar Jung Thapa, and the chief of the war operations department, Kalyan Rayamajhi. A mutual 'retreat' deal was reached. The plan was to send human rights activists to Rolpa, for the Maoists to hand over the policemen to them, and both sides would withdraw their armies.

Immediately, the rights activists were sent to Rolpa. The team included Dr Mathura Prasad Shrestha, Mukti Pradhan, Sudip Pathak, Dr Bhogendra Sharma and Kalyan Dev Bhattarai. In fact, Pradhan was a regional bureau member of Maoists. Many other rights activists did not know that they were already a part of the Maoist–army deal. The Maoists started releasing the policemen immediately after they reached Rolpa.

In line with the deal reached at the centre, the Maoists and the army had reached an understanding on the ground as well. At Nuwagaun in Rolpa, the Maoists' military commissar in charge of the western region, Ananta, was already in talks with the soldiers they had surrounded, first through megaphone and then through an exchange of letters. Both sides mentioned the deal at the centre in the course of their conversation. The first letter was written by Ananta, to which the army officer in command replied.

Here is what Ananta wrote:

Dear commander, Greetings!

As we came upon you in the course of our programme here, 2000 members of the People's Liberation Army have surrounded you. We are ready for talks and a way out, and remain firm in the 'gentleman's agreement' made by the centre. We will be morally forced to retaliate if attacked. With expectations of cooperation and understanding.

Commander
People's Army, Nepal

To his letter, the army commander's reply was:

Respected brothers and sisters!

We received your letter. The talks mentioned in the letter are being carried out at the central level. We don't have any animosity

against you. If you guys go your way and do not 'charge' us, we will
also not 'charge' at you. Just let our helicopter land. We will let you
know once we get the gist of the agreement reached at the centre. You
kindly go your way.

Commander
Royal Nepali Army[3]

That was the first exchange of letters between the Maoists' PLA
and the Royal Nepali Army. Following the exchange of letters,
two representatives of the PLA (Santosh and Abiral) and two
representatives of the Royal Nepali Army held face-to-face talks
for half an hour. And, in the spirit of the deal reached at the centre,
they took one another's leave and waved at each other.

The prime minister steps down

The Holeri 'hungama' had settled in Rolpa, but it continued to send
political tremors through the capital. When the army commandos
were dispatched to Rolpa, the government had come out publicly
stating that an army operation was on against the Maoists. It was
reported that the rebels had been 'gheraoed'. If one listened to the
news reports coming out of Kathmandu, one would believe that
a fierce battle was going on in Rolpa. But the reality was starkly
different. The army had not fired even a single shot. Rather, it was
'retreating' following a deal with the Maoists.

Perhaps Prime Minister Koirala was the one most deceived
by this illusion. He had actually been told by intelligence officials
the day after the army left for Rolpa not to rely upon the army's
information. The reports he was receiving from the chief district
officer of Dang were also totally different from what he was being
fed by the army. But the prime minister did not trust these. The
generals had spread a map on the table and briefed him on their
plans with military precision. They pointed at the map and told

him how they were tightening the noose around the Maoists. 'The operation is being carried out from here and this area has already come under our control . . .' was what he heard from the generals.

A meeting of the National Defence Council that took place on the afternoon of the day of the Holeri attack had taken the decision to mobilize the army. At the meeting, Defence Minister Mahesh Acharya said the army would be mobilized with a mandate under the existing Integrated Internal Security and Development Plan (IISDP). Under the plan, the military could only retaliate if attacked. Army Chief Prajwalla Shumsher Rana said that these rules of engagement were not adequate for his soldiers to free the abducted policemen. He also demanded that the council take a firm decision to mobilize the army, and that the army be allowed to operate even outside Rolpa because, he said, the insurgents would flee to other districts once the operation began in Rolpa.

But the army chief had to back down after the prime minister intervened and ordered the army to go with the IISDP mandate alone. So the army went to the field but was not fully prepared, mentally or physically, for the fight. The soldiers were dispatched without a pep-talk. There was no briefing even of the 'operational plan'. Only one of the four platoons was able to land in the field. That platoon was immediately surrounded by the Maoists. So the full force of commandos could never be dispatched. Two army choppers were damaged by rebel fire. Worse, the inclement weather ensured that the army could launch neither a ground nor an air offensive.

In the end, the soldiers who were sent to fight returned by striking a deal instead. Who instructed the soldiers to do that? The government itself was unaware. Enraged, the prime minister sought the resignation of the army chief, but the king demanded his resignation instead. The king was already displeased by the PM's decision to send the army without consulting him. He ordered a halt to the army operation midway. When the two entered into a heated debate over this, the king made an irrelevant accusation against him: 'Prime minister, people are saying you are corrupt.'[4]

Taken aback and seething with anger, the PM shot back, 'Your Majesty, it's not me alone they are talking about. Shall I start narrating what people are talking about Your Majesty relating to the palace massacre? Many people have told me that there you had a hand in the massacre.'[5]

That was the last conversation they had as king and prime minister. On the afternoon of 19 July 2001, Koirala threw at the king the letter of resignation he was already carrying in his coat pocket. From there, he went directly to the residence of senior advocate Ganesh Raj Sharma at Dhobidhara. During that period, Koirala used to go there whenever he wanted serious advice on anything. After hearing about the episode, Sharma told him, 'The king has committed a blunder. A day will come when he will have to cry tears of blood.'

His remarks came true. In future, a movement led by Koirala would force not only Gyanendra from the throne but would end the monarchy in Nepal, but there were many years still before that would happen. Five years after the incident, Koirala admitted his mistake. 'I should have publicly stated from Tundikhel that the army refused to obey my order of mobilization. That was my big mistake, a blunder.'[6]

Prime Minister Koirala could also have exposed in Parliament, which was in session at the time, how the army had disobeyed his orders. He could have sought an explanation from the army chief, in his capacity as the chair of the National Defence Council. Instead, he meekly resigned and exited the picture. The Dunai debacle the previous year had claimed the home minister's head. The Holeri hungama forced the prime minister out. These things happened because of the 'undeclared unity in action' between the Durbar and the rebels.

However, people in some quarters opine that the reason behind the meek resignation of Prime Minister Koirala was none other than his own intention to do so. They say that Koirala had already made up his mind to step down. He was under tremendous opposition pressure at the time to resign over accusations of his involvement in the 'scam' of leasing Lauda aircraft to the RNAC. The opposition parties, including the main opposition, CPN–UML, had halted parliamentary proceedings for fifty-seven consecutive days over this issue. Within his own party, Sher Bahadur Deuba was itching to move a resolution of no confidence against him. His deputy in the cabinet, Home Minister Ram Chandra Poudel, had resigned on 13 July over the Holeri incident. Trapped from within and outside, Holeri provided him with an opportunity to step down honourably. He was replaced by Deuba, who was considered close to the army, the Durbar and the Maoists.

Butwal talks

India, for the first time, showed an interest in government operations against the Maoists during the Holeri episode. The Indians thought the king was wrong not to allow army mobilization. According to the then Nepali ambassador in Delhi, Bhesh Bahadur Thapa, they believed that had the king allowed an army operation, the beginning of the end of the Maoist movement would have been initiated right there, because key Maoist leaders were already gheraoed.

Ambassador Thapa was asked in Delhi, 'Why did the king stop the operation despite a clear chance of weakening the ultra-leftist forces that have waged war against the state and raised anti-India slogans?' External Affairs Minister Jaswant Singh asked him directly, 'Why did the Maharaja stop the army operation against the Maoists?'

Summoning the ambassador to ask such a question clearly meant that Delhi wanted to register its extreme displeasure. But Thapa himself was unaware who had stopped the operation. Giving a diplomatic answer to South Block, he headed towards

Kathmandu for consultations. It was no use asking the foreign ministry or others, so he posed his questions directly to King Gyanendra.

'What would come of Nepali killing Nepali? Would it bring a political solution?' Gyanendra's reply was vague. It wouldn't address Delhi's concerns. 'On one hand, we were seeking weapons, training and intelligence information from the Indians, and on the other hand, it showed there was a big review going on regarding how we deal with the same insurgents we were seeking support to fight. It definitely raised doubts (in Delhi),' Thapa said.

Actually, the king was still exploring the possibility of a political understanding with the Maoists. Immediately after the Holeri episode, in the third week of July, Col. Dilip Jung Rayamajhi met two Maoist leaders—Top Bahadur Rayamajhi and Chakrapani Khanal 'Baldev'—in Butwal in western Nepal. D.R. Lamichhane had arranged the meeting: the same person who had previously arranged a similar a meeting in Butwal. The palace had been using Col. Rayamajhi since 1997 to study the Maoists and contacting them. Right at the start of that meeting, he shouted at the Maoist leaders, 'Why did you guys attack us? We no longer have any other option. Either you come for talks or get ready to fight the army.'

During the meeting, he also urged the Maoists to drop suspicions against the new king, and told them it was Crown Prince Dipendra who had committed the massacre. The Maoists had other ideas. One of the leaders at the meeting told him, 'Let us come together (army and Maoists). Let us give the king some respectful space. We can take Nepal to new heights together.'

The Maoists' attention was focused on the army. According to Dilip Jung Rayamajhi, 'They were actually trying to find out how they can influence the army in the name of cooperating with the monarchy'. But their efforts went in vain. In fact, the Maoists were talking to an army officer who, despite coming from a family background of communism, was personally anti-Maoist. So, back from Butwal, Col. Rayamajhi, who later promoted to the rank of Brig. Gen. and appointed as the military intelligence chief, reached a conclusion: the Maoists are ultra-communist and there can be no 'deal' with them.

Following the meeting at Butwal, the Maoists wrote a letter to the palace. D.R. Lamichhane carried the letter and handed it to Col. Rayamajhi, who passed it on to the palace military secretary, Bibek Kumar Shah, unopened. The letter then went to King Gyanendra. After that, the Maoists agreed to the first peace talks. Upon learning in Butwal that they could have no immediate deal with the army, they were now eager for peace talks.

The first peace talks

At that time, for the last few months, the new prime minister, Sher Bahadur Deuba, who had replaced Koirala, had been in talks with the rebels. The 'High Level Committee for Recommendation for Resolution of Maoist Problem', which he headed, had recently submitted its report to the government. Even before he took the oath of office, he called for a ceasefire on 23 July 2001. Prachanda accepted it the same day. Having pushed back the police and outsmarted the army in Holeri, the Maoists came to Kathmandu for the first peace talks in a victorious mood.

The week-long Maoist central committee meeting that took place in Siliguri, India, decided to form a talks team under the leadership of Krishna Bahadur Mahara, which would include Agni Prasad Sapkota and Top Bahadur Rayamajhi. Another Maoist leader, Krishna Dhwaj Khadka, was already in direct contact with Prime Minister Deuba and Home Minister Khum Bahadur Khadka.

On 26 August, PM Deuba wrote a letter to Prachanda about the talks. Four days later, their first formal negotiations took place at Godavari Village Resort in Lalitpur, but it ended as a fruitless round of introductions. However, the two sides parted after expressing a shared commitment to 'finding a way out of all differences and problems through the means of peaceful talks'.

The first round of talks did not lead to a reduction in differences. On the contrary, they increased. On 28 August 2001, the army detained Maoist cadres in Sindhupalchok while they were heading towards a party programme. Prime Minister Deuba publicly questioned the Maoists' intentions on 4 September. Three days later, the ministry of defence issued a stern warning to the Maoists for their 'attempt to incite the families of soldiers'. The following day, in Gorkha, the army opened fire at the Maoists, for the first time, when they conducted protests in Aanp Peepal. Four were injured. With that and without any formal declaration, the army was mobilized across the country.

The crisis of confidence between the two sides was fast worsening. The army was seen to be preparing for a fight. New barracks were erected, and it stepped up field inspections. The Maoists, too, were gearing up for the inevitable. They held training camps in various places. In the first week of September, they formed the 'People's Liberation Army, Nepal' at a central gathering of selected guerrilla leaders in Kureli of Rolpa. They also held a political assembly there, declaring the formation of the 'United Revolutionary People's Council' under the leadership of Baburam Bhattarai, intended to form a 'central people's government'.

Therefore, the second round of talks was nothing but a farce. The Maoists wanted to hold it in their 'capital', Rolpa. The government refused. The venue was later shifted to Thakurdwara of Bardiya district. Having just trained his guerrillas for the imminent war, Krishna Bahadur Mahara came down to Thakurdwara to lead the second round of talks on 13 and 14 September. He presented a thirty-one-point list of demands at the meeting. They included the 'abrogation of the Constitution,' 'formation of an interim government by dissolving Parliament and the current government,' and 'institutional development of a republic'. These were not demands that Deuba could fulfil. Deuba later said, 'They wanted a Constituent Assembly. I was not in a position to give them that. My party, the Nepali Congress, had not demanded such an assembly. The king was also against it. How could I have agreed to it? That is why the talks failed during my term.'[7]

When the army came to surround them in Holeri—not long after the murder of King Birendra, whom they thought had wanted to talk to them—the Maoists had reached a conclusion, that the possibility of partnership with the palace had ended. Their slogan must be for a republic, and they would have to fight the army. So they wanted breathing space and time to arrange their guerrilla force, to train them to fight the army, and they also needed to demonstrate to the people that they were not against peace talks. The Maoists decided that if the government rejected their demand for a Constituent Assembly, then they would fight the army. Following this broad conclusion, they took advantage of the period of the peace talks and ceasefire to advance their organization, mobilize people, penetrate urban areas and prepare for war.

Siliguri summit

During their talks with the government, the Maoists carried out a different experiment across the eastern border. They invited eleven top leaders of six different communist parties in the country for a conference on 15 and 16 August 2001 in Siliguri, India. The leaders included the general secretary of the CPN–UML, Madhav Kumar Nepal, and its standing committee member Ishwor Pokharel; the general secretary of the CPN–ML, Bamdev Gautam; the general secretary of CPN–Masal, Ram Singh Shrish; the general secretary of CPN–Unity Centre, Narayan Kaji Shrestha 'Prakash' and its leader Lilamani Pokharel; and the president of the Nepal Workers and Peasants Party, Narayan Man Bijukchhe 'Rohit', along with another leader, Sunil Prajapati. For the first time, Prachanda, Baburam and Kiran held collective talks with these leaders.

The general secretary of Unity Centre, Prakash, coordinated the invitations and organization of the Siliguri meeting. According to him, the goal of the meeting was to arrive at a common position of all the leftist forces which would be put on the talks table with the government, so that all of them could support the position and hold a joint movement, if need be. Prachanda presented his proposal—if the CPN–UML, the Maoists and all leftist forces were to conduct a joint movement, then a republic could be peacefully achieved in Nepal. But apart from Unity Centre, none of the other parties present at the meeting agreed to his plan.

Prachanda's second proposal was the establishment of a Constituent Assembly. Under this plan, he laid down a roadmap of how to dissolve the Parliament, form an interim government, hold an election to the assembly with a republic as a pre-condition and, thus, proclaim a republic in Nepal.

According to Prakash, except for the CPN–UML, all the other parties agreed to the proposal of a Constituent Assembly. Madhav Kumar Nepal told the meeting that though he was personally positive about the idea, he would need to hold a discussion in his party. He called a meeting of the central committee of the CPN–UML after returning to Kathmandu. The decision reached was: 'The appeals for interim government, new Constitution, Constituent Assembly and republic proclamation would ultimately pose a danger against national independence, and would jeopardize the gains made by the (1990) people's movement.'[8]

This decision was totally unexpected for the Maoists. In those days, the CPN–UML used to believe that the king would hijack power if there was even an amendment to the 1990 Constitution. It was totally unprepared to go with a demand for a republic made by a competitor leftist force. 'We were not in the mood to make a republic an immediate goal. Rather, we wanted to find an understanding by taking the king on board,' Madhav Kumar Nepal said four years later.[9]

Following the decision of the CPN–UML not to support the republican agenda, the Maoist mouthpiece *Janadesh* ran a story accusing Nepal of being a monarchist, and also briefing the king about the 'secret' decisions taken at Siliguri.[10] It was a setback not only to relations between the two parties, but also caused uproar within the Maoists. Baburam was unhappy over the news report, which was written by Rabindra Shrestha himself. Baburam felt that 'it was inappropriate to accuse somebody whom they should be utilizing'. It was only after he phoned Nepal to tell him that the article did not represent the official party line that relations between the two improved a little.

Fighting the army

Having failed to achieve a working partnership among communist parties, the Maoists went ahead and organized campaigns of public mobilization. 'It is possible to mobilize hundreds of thousands of people in the streets even during the peace talks and totally segregate the reactionaries and revisionist political cliques already embroiled in immense contradictions and indecision. It is also possible in this process to rip apart the army of the indecisive enemy, and to expand the army of the people with incredible speed,' was their conclusion.[11]

The Maoists had already conducted public assemblies in major cities. The climax was to be the public assembly in Kathmandu on 21 September 2001. They planned to bring half a million people to the assembly. They goal was forcing the government to meet their demand of a Constituent Assembly by flexing their activist muscle and bringing Kathmandu to a halt for three or four days; or, if possible, channelling the assembled mass towards an urban insurrection and, thereby, grabbing power. With these goals in mind, they started bringing in people to the capital from the beginning of the month. Schools, colleges, public places and private residences were forcefully asked to provide shelter to these invitees. A sitting of a 'people's court' was conducted in Kathmandu itself. Incidents of arson and physical assaults also occurred in places where the Maoists faced resistance.

They covered the walls of Kathmandu with posters showing groups of people armed with weapons and red flags marching towards the palace and demolishing its tower. Some cadres coming to Kathmandu were armed with lathis and khukuris. There were rumours that the rebels had smuggled thousands of armed insurgents into the capital. The police as well as the army conducted several raids in the hostels of various colleges in order to search for such a smuggled cache of weapons. King Gyanendra summoned Prime Minister Deuba and asked him to stop the Maoists from holding the assembly. Otherwise, he told him, the Maoists would declare the seizure of Kathmandu and render even the army helpless. Two days later, the government declared a month-long prohibition on any gathering or assembly in Kathmandu.

Right at that juncture, an astounding international incident occurred which pushed the Maoists onto the defensive: al-Qaeda terrorists attacked America on 11 September 2001. It sent ripples of shock across the world. The Americans started a 'global war on terror'. This greatly helped King Gyanendra and Deuba, who considered himself close to the US.

As the domestic and international tide turned against them, the Maoists were pushed to the back foot. They were forced to cancel their much-touted public assembly of 21 September. They saw that if they went ahead with the assembly and invited a clash, the ensuing scenario would go against them. Furthermore, they were already facing the anger of Kathmandu residents. They had no base in the capital, and they were inviting resistance through their abuses. Far from fermenting an urban insurrection, they were not even able to conduct a public assembly in the capital. They also had to shift the venue of the fifth convention of their student wing from Kathmandu to Biratnagar. In addition to that, they had to 'put on hold' the demand for a republic in the third round of peace talks. But despite this flexibility, the government refused to accede to their demand for a Constituent Assembly.

As they saw a clear possibility of the resumption of armed hostilities, senior Maoist leaders, including Prachanda, Baburam, Kiran, Badal, Ananta and Baldev, met in Chitwan to forge a war strategy. After a marathon discussion, they concluded that they would have to attack a military barracks in the western region, where they were comparatively stronger. In the eastern and central region, they planned to launch attacks to capture district headquarters, leaving the barracks alone. As such, the third and final round of talks held again at the Godavari Resort on 13 November was nothing more than a pretence. The government said it could find a resolution through the 1990 Constitution, whereas the Maoists stuck to their guns on their Constituent Assembly demand.

Nobody was allowed to carry a mobile phone into the venue for the talks. At around 8 p.m., the mobile of the PM's private aide Ratan Aire buzzed. It was a call for Mahara. After receiving the call, Mahara and his team hurried to leave the venue, wrapping up the negotiations quickly. Perhaps he got instructions from the party high command to leave the meaningless charade. From Godavari, Mahara and his team simply vanished. The chief government negotiator, Minister Chiranjibi Wagle, was in an equal hurry, as he was planning to go on an official visit to South Korea. So, without arranging a date for the fourth round of talks, he simply concluded the meeting.

In the middle of the confusion, Prachanda, on 21 November, issued a statement sounding the death knell for negotiations. He stated that the utility of the talks had ended. Two days later, the insurgents launched a vicious attack against an army barracks in the western district of Dang. The same night, they attacked a military camp in the central district of Syangja and a barracks in the eastern district of Solukhumbu three days later. Of these, the attack on the Ghorahi barracks of Dang was the deadliest. Around 1100 guerrillas of the newly formed People's Liberation Army launched simultaneous attacks at the military barracks, police posts and civil offices. In the course of the battle, fourteen army soldiers, including Major Naresh Uprety, seven policemen and seven insurgents died. The insurgents made off with 225 modern weapons, tens of thousands of rounds of ammunitions and eighty quintals of gelignite: almost twelve truckloads of materials.

The causes of defeat

There were several reasons for the failure of talks in 2001. Both the Maoists and the government were not wholly committed to their success; rather, they were preparing for a future war. They did not prepare any code of conduct for the ceasefire. Rights activists Padma Ratna Tuladhar and Daman Nath Dhungana were nominated as facilitators. But they were neither given any role nor any written mandate. Problems had surfaced even at the first round of talks in Godavari, when the facilitators were not even allowed in the meeting room. In Tuladhar's words, 'We felt really insulted. For hours, we were left alone in a separate room. Damanji wanted to go away from the venue. I, somehow, convinced him to stay.'

There were technical lapses as well. Even the joint statement had to be handwritten. The same thing happened at the second round of talks in Bardiya. Before presenting it to the government, the Maoist team had shown Tuladhar a handwritten letter listing their demands. 'There were typos and corrections. I told them that they should print it on a clean page, because it was a historic document. But a computer was not available, and it was presented in the same state,' Tuladhar recalled. The government negotiators also presented their reply as a handwritten letter. The lack of seriousness shown towards the talks by both sides was responsible for such needless lapses.

There were some objective reasons for talks and a ceasefire at that time. Due to the spate of killings, people were yearning for the suspension of hostilities anyhow. This exerted pressure on all sides for peace talks. For Prime Minister Sher Bahadur Deuba, who had recently come to power with the slogan of peace, holding peace talks—irrespective of the result—had become mandatory. Gyanendra was new to the throne and was still learning his way around the state machinery, so he, too, wanted breathing space. The police was almost totally defeated, and the army was not yet ready for the fight. After the Holeri shock, the army wanted some time to prepare.

The Maoists, too, had found themselves in a difficult position at Holeri. They had not yet readied themselves to take on the army, so time was necessary. Besides, the recently held second national convention had endorsed peace talks and asking for a Constituent Assembly on one hand, and passed the Prachandapath, a plan to forge a strategic 'fusion' of the people's war and urban insurrection, on the other. They had to build strength in the capital for this purpose.[12]

The Maoist central committee meeting held in July 2001 in Siliguri had decided to go for peace talks while taking into consideration 'two specific possibilities': to turn the talks into a people's victory if successful; and to mobilize the people for insurrection if they failed. However, neither were the talks successful, nor were they able to ignite an insurrection. They lost twelve cadres in different incidents during the ceasefire, but were able to free over 200 cadres from different jails. They could repair their party structure. They could enter the cities. Most importantly, they won recognition as a political force through the dialogue.

In the Siliguri meeting, the top leadership had decided to advance the demand for an 'unconditional Constituent Assembly' in the talks until the last moment, and to switch it to 'conditional Constituent Assembly' with constitutional monarchy only if they had to. In accordance with that decision, the Maoists did withdraw their demand for a republic, 'for the time being', at the third round of talks. But the government was not ready for a Constituent Assembly, conditional or unconditional. So the Maoists chose to break the ceasefire.

When they saw that the talks were breaking down and the ceasefire ending, the Maoists decided to seize the initiative and draw first blood. They dragged the nation's last guard, the Royal Nepali Army, into the fight at a time when the whole state machinery had been upset due to the palace massacre. Following the Maoists' attack on the army, the government declared them terrorists, imposed a countrywide state of emergency and began military retaliation. Consequently, the Maoists' covert activities in urban areas came to a halt. Many were arrested. There were many incidents of treachery and escapes. But the state of emergency had no significant military effect in rural areas.

A phase of so-called 'undeclared unity in action' between the palace and the Maoists came to an end with their declaration of war against the military. But the Maoists had already identified a second power centre for a new phase of partnership. It was Delhi.

6

Indian Abode

'Merely because Mr Madhav Nepal was able to meet some Maoist leaders at an undisclosed location in Lucknow does not mean that India is providing sanctuary to Maoists.'

—Indian Ambassador Shyam Saran, talking to journalists in Nepalgunj on 5 February 2003[1]

Prachanda was in Kathmandu when he launched the 'people's war.' For the next twenty-two days, he stayed in the capital, changing 'shelter' every day. When the risks grew, he left the Kathmandu Valley. For some time, he stayed at a village in the western district of Syangja. But he did not feel secure. 'We had just two rifles. What were we to do? Should we use them to safeguard the leadership or to attack the enemy? Likewise, we had only a few pistols, and most of them were out of order. And we see enemies roaming around, here and there. So we were quite distressed. It was in that situation that we decided that it would be easier if certain members of the leadership shifted outside.'[2]

Three months after the start of the 'people's war,' in May or June of 1996, Prachanda went to India. For three years, the border town of Siliguri was his 'shelter'. Subsequently, he shifted to Delhi, Ghaziabad and Noida. For brief periods, he would move to Indian cities such as Mumbai, Bhopal, Chennai, Dehradun and cities in Punjab. He spent eight-and-a-half years in India. His two daughters were married there, one in Jalpaiguri and one in Jalandhar. His son Prakash grew up in India.

Many Maoist leaders surfaced in India soon after the 'people's war' began. When police in Kathmandu raided a residence in Koteshwor its occupant, Hisila Yami, was busy presenting paper at an international seminar held (16–19 February 1996) by the All India People's Resistance Forum in New Delhi. Her husband, the Maoist leader Baburam Bhattarai, was also an underground resident of India.

In the initial years of the conflict, another Maoist leader, Ram Bahadur Thapa 'Badal', used to be seen in Dehradun along with his wife Nain Kala. Their children, Prateek and Pratima, studied there under the tutelage of their uncle, Chop Bahadur Thapa, who was an officer in the Indian army.

Ram Karki was underground as far as Nepal's official records were concerned. He lived in Sikkim and was widely thought to be an informal advisor to the state's top political establishment. He had married a lady, who was a Sikkim state government official and also related to the family of the former Sikkimese king, the Chogyal. His real name was Surendra Karki, but he used many aliases such as Ram, Partha Chhetri, P. Kanchan and Hirakaji Maharjan. He coordinated the open activities of the Maoists from Sikkim to Siliguri and in Delhi.

After the police launched Operation Kilo Sierra-2 in 1998, a considerable chunk of the top Maoist leadership started living across the border. They entered Nepal only as and when necessary. The headquarters of the Maoist Eastern Command were in Patna and Siliguri, while those of the Western Command were in Gorakhpur and Lucknow. Based on instructions from India-based headquarters, the field commissars, commanders and guerrillas conducted the insurgency in Nepal.

The first central committee meeting of the party after the people's war began was organized in Siliguri in June 1996. The following January, a politburo meeting was held in Lucknow, followed by an assembly of party organizations in Kanpur (in February) and another politburo meeting in Faridabad (in April). A document presented by Baburam to the party has an interesting list of Indian cities where party meetings took place. According to this document, during the eight years between June 1996 and June 2004, at least twenty-six central-level meetings and assemblies were held in various Indian cities.[3]

Meetings of high historic importance, such as the fourth plenum of 1998 (Faridabad) and the second national convention of 2000 (Bhatinda), took place in India. In fact, the first considerable public rally in support of the Maoists took place not in Nepal but in the Indian capital on 13 February 1999, organized by the Solidarity Forum to Support the People's War in Nepal. It was addressed by Maoist leaders of both countries: Suresh Ale Magar, Bamdev Chhetri, Varvara Rao, Tara Singh, Darshan Pal and others.

Prachanda and Baburam met leaders of the Nepali Congress and the CPN–UML not in Nepal, but in Indian cities like Siliguri, Delhi, Lucknow and Patna. When these facts came to light, and when Maoist leaders discernibly reduced their anti-India slogans, people started talking, asking whether the Maoists were actually 'run' by the Indians. And whether they were getting material support from the Indians.[4]

Living in Hindustan

Yet, if one skims through the forty-point demand list they presented to the government just before they launched the insurgency, one finds nine of them directed against India. These include:

- Abrogate all unequal treaties such as the 1950 Nepal–India Friendship Treaty, Mahakali Treaty

- Control and regulate the open Indo-Nepal border
- Close Gorkha recruitment centres
- Implement work permits for Indian workers in Nepal
- Immediately stop vehicles with Indian number plates from plying in Nepal
- Prohibit the import of decadent Hindi cinema, videos and newspapers/magazines

Although their demands were directed against India, they wanted to utilize Indian territory in practical terms, so they did nothing to irk the Indians. To be fair, it was not only the Maoists who used Indian territory. All major political struggles in Nepal's history, whether that of the Nepali Congress in 1950 or its armed struggle in 1961, or the bomb explosions by Ram Raja Prasad Singh in 1985, all had links to India and the Indo-Nepal border. The 1751-km-long open and porous border between Nepal and India has been a boon for all sorts of rebel activities. Once a person crosses the border into the huge Indian nation, they can simply vanish.

The Maoists made full use of the situation. They used Indian territory for shelter as well as smuggling of arms. They had a readymade base of hundreds of thousands of immigrant Nepalis spread across India in which to expand their networks. The Maoist-affiliated All India Nepali Unity Society and student organizations had been active in India since 1979. There were separate webs of underground party committees.

Another important element was the active Maoist movement in India, as part of which the Naxalites had been waging a decades-long people's war. There was also a wide section of leftists and socialists in India who didn't take part in any revolution themselves, but did not shy away from getting excited about one. Leftist intellectuals and writers emerged as well-wishers.[5]

Despite all these bases, it would be possible to direct armed activities in Nepal from India only if the Indian government overlooked them. And that was what happened. For Prachanda, it was the land of Gandhi that became favourable, not the land of Mao.

The Nepali authorities were not totally unaware of this. When the deputy inspector general and chief of the midwest regional police office in Nepalgunj, Sahabir Thapa, learnt about a training programme of Maoists in Gomti Nagar, Lucknow, he dispatched a team led by Sub-inspector Kanhaiya Singh Sardar. Sardar mobilized his contacts in bordering Bahraich and went directly to Gomti Nagar. He caught four Maoist leaders, including Haribol Gajurel and Jag Prasad Sharma 'Apar', on 1 December 1998. But they were not allowed by the Lucknow Police to take those detained to Nepal. It was later revealed that pressure had been applied from the very top. Gajurel and the others were released after forty-eight hours. Sardar's team returned empty-handed and Sardar was later killed by the Maoists in Nepalgunj in 2003.

Kathmandu got the message—the link was very strong.

A few months later, the Indian external affairs minister, Jaswant Singh, came to Kathmandu for a four-day visit. At the end of his visit, on 11 September 1999, he attended a press conference. A Nepali journalist asked, 'There are reports that the Maoists are being trained in India. Isn't this against the very spirit of the 1950 treaty?'

Singh's reply was, 'I can assure you that India provides no shelter to any terrorist that is to cause disturbances to the friendly country of Nepal.'[6]

Nepal had, for the first time, formally asked India to control Maoist activities on their territory. Initially, Singh just denied that there were any such activities taking place. When he was presented with evidence, such as photographs of their programmes in India, he promised help, but it was not translated into practice, as a Nepali minister who had attended the bilateral meeting revealed later.[7]

Nepal demanded that India arrest the Maoist leaders roaming freely in their country, but India did nothing even when provided with details such as time and venue of a central committee meeting. In the end, Nepal decided to mobilize its own intelligence machinery.[8] In order to coordinate efforts, the SSPs of the Nepal Police and the National Investigation Department (NID), Gobardhan Shrestha and Dhan Singh Karki, were posted to the Nepali embassy in Delhi under diplomatic cover in 2000. Karki later went on to become the chief of the NID. After closely observing the Nepali-speaking community in places such as Dehradun, he concluded that nobody was attempting to control Maoist activities.[9]

The role of the military attaché at the embassy was, however, different. While Karki was stealthily approaching Nepali-speaking communities to observe the Maoists, the military attaché, Kalyan Rayamajhi, could meet them easily. Even the ambassador, Bhesh Bahadur Thapa, came to know about Rayamajhi's meeting with the Maoist leader Krishna Bahadur Mahara in Dehradun in 2002. The military attaché would provide a copy of his weekly briefing notes to the ambassador, but mainly, he would abide by the directives of army headquarters and the ambassador would not know about all of his activities. The Dehradun meeting was one such covert move.[10]

Having observed these activities, Karki asked Thapa, 'Ambassador Sahib, I see a predicament here. The Indians and the palace both seem to want contact with everyone. So the picture is not clear, (it's not clear) which direction we should move towards.'

In fact, Ambassador Thapa himself was at a complete loss. He was at the helm of Nepal's Delhi mission during the crucial years between 1997 and 2003. He was in close contact with the four pillars of the Indian establishment at that time: Brajesh Mishra, Jaswant Singh, Yashwant Sinha and George Fernandes. Such wide contact is rare for any Nepali envoy. 'Talking to them, it would be difficult to believe that the Maoists could have covert relations with the Indian government,' Thapa said to me. 'We used to hear that the Maoists were getting support from Mulayam Singh Yadav's Samajwadi Party in Uttar Pradesh. We couldn't see them getting any support from the centre. But after 2002, they did build formal relations with the Indian establishment.'[11]

Prime Minister Girija Prasad Koirala, too, was in a fix. He suspected that the Maoists were receiving support either from the Durbar or from Delhi. When he went to India on 1 August 2000, he posed a direct question to his Indian counterpart, Atal Behari Vajpayee. 'What is this Maoist affair? If it has been staged by the Durbar, then its aim would be to topple us. And if it has been staged by you (India), then its aim would be to topple the monarchy.'

Ambassador Thapa was present at that meeting. Vajpayee was taken aback by Koirala's question. To change the subject, he merely replied, '*Girijababu, aap bhi kya kehete hain* (Girijababu, you say just anything).'[12] Despite his answer, Koirala's mind was made up—the Maoists were piggybacking on either Delhi or the Durbar.

For the general Nepali public, the 2001 Siliguri meeting of communist leaders called by the Maoists appeared to expose their Indian links. Soon after he returned from Siliguri, CPN–UML General Secretary Madhav Kumar Nepal stated, on 2 September 2001, that 'the palace could be using the Maoists as a back-up to end the multiparty system' and that 'the Indians could be supporting the Maoists to bring Nepal under their security umbrella.'[13] Five days later, Girija Prasad Koirala, then the Nepali Congress president, made similar remarks. He accused the palace of 'nurturing' the Maoists, and India of 'sheltering' them.[14]

Following these accusations, India gave a significant reaction. Upon returning from his Nepal trip, Indian External Affairs Minister Jaswant Singh termed the Maoist activities as 'terrorism' for the first time.[15] Up until then, the Maoists had not been termed terrorists even by the Nepali government. In fact, the Maoists had agreed to peace talks at that time, announcing their first truce. A day before Jaswant Singh's reaction, the Indian embassy in Kathmandu had issued a statement on preparations to mobilize 10,000 members of the paramilitary Special Service Bureau (SSB) along the Indo-Nepal border to control cross-border Maoist activities.[16]

A few weeks later, when the Maoists ended their ceasefire and attacked the Nepali army, the spokesperson of the Indian external affairs ministry, Navtej Sarna, called it 'unfortunate'. And, in the first strong statement against the Maoists from India, he said, 'We support the actions taken by the Nepali government to maintain peace and security in the country'.

'Royal American Army'

The gap between Delhi's walk and talk had created confusion in Kathmandu. So when the Maoists launched their attack on the army barracks in Ghorahi in November 2001, it was the United States, not India, that Nepal approached for help. The global political situation also helped push Nepal towards the US. It was a coincidence that America's global war on terror following the 9/11 attacks and Nepal's army operation against the Maoists took place around the same time.[17]

America's campaign against terrorism was limited primarily to Muslim countries. By supporting Nepal's campaign against the Maoists, it could show that America's campaign was against all forms of terrorism in the world. Furthermore, Sher Bahadur Deuba, who was said to be close to the Americans, was both prime minister and defence minister of Nepal at the time. For these reasons, Nepal became a part of the American-led 'global war on terror', as announced by PM Deuba.

Fifty-two years since the establishment of bilateral diplomatic ties, in January 2002, an American secretary of state made a maiden visit to Nepal. Soon after Colin Powell returned, the Maoists launched a vicious attack on the army in the distant western district of Achham. American Ambassador Michael Malinowski himself visited the site of the attack. He then said, 'There is no difference between the al-Qaeda and the Maoists.'

There was an increase in the activities of American army and intelligence officers in Nepal. In April 2002, twelve American experts, led by a lieutenant colonel from the US Pacific Command, toured Rolpa, Achham and Gorkha. It was the first time foreign military experts had visited the Nepali hills to forge a strategy for fighting the Maoists. Based on the team's report on the needs and capabilities of the Nepali army, the Pentagon decided to provide weapons, including M-16 rifles, to Nepal.

The team also visited the Nepali army's barracks in Gam, Rolpa, which were overrun by the insurgents a few days later. The barracks were fortified, as per the Americans' advice, by bringing together members of the Armed Police Force and Nepal Police under the army's command. This incident spurred further US support. On the day of the Gam attack, 7 May 2002, PM Deuba was in Washington DC. At his meeting with US President George W. Bush in the Oval Office, he quickly appealed for US assistance.

In June 2002, the US army opened an 'Office of Defence Cooperation' in Kathmandu to coordinate American assistance to the Nepali army. In the first year (2002–2003) alone, they provided military assistance worth $12 million. During the subsequent four years, they provided assistance worth $22 million. They handed over 10,000 M-16 rifles in two phases. Nepal's quota under the International Military Education and Training (IMET) programme was increased. In March 2003, the Nepali army established a 'Ranger Battalion', formed following consultations and training by the American military. And on 25 April 2003, the two countries signed a five-year Counter-Terrorism Agreement to provide Nepali security personnel with 'counter-terrorism training' and 'technical advisory support'. American trainers could be seen roaming around the Nepali hills.[18]

The Nepali army even admitted that it was able to stop the Maoists' victorious march only because of American support and training. 'We couldn't have reached here without that support,' the army's director of military operations, Kul Bahadur Khadka, told US Assistant Secretary of State Christina Rocca. 'I, on behalf of the RNA, would like to express our heartiest gratitude to the government of the United States for providing us the political, moral and material support to counter the Maoist problem.'[19] However, at that time, even within the Nepali army, there were voices that called for caution regarding the geo-strategic interests behind American military assistance.[20]

The Maoists, on the other hand, rechristened the Nepali army—basking in the glow of rising American support—the Royal American Army. They not only levelled accusations but even murdered two security guards of the American embassy in Kathmandu and took responsibility for both the murders. They also warned the embassy 'not to hide informers under any cover'.[21]

The Americans hardened their position against the Maoists. The US state department listed them as a foreign terror organization.[22]

Following in America's footstep, Britain, too, provided military assistance against the Maoists. After a visit by the British chief of Defence Staff, Admiral Sir Michael Boyce, in May 2002, London provided two MI-17 helicopters and two Islander spy aircraft. It also dispatched MI-6 officers to conduct a joint intelligence operation, codenamed 'Mustang', with the sleuths of the National Investigation Department. The covert action, costing NRs. 320 million, was not effective. Instead, when details of financial irregularities emerged, it appeared to be another scam.[23]

Britain also took the initiative to coordinate foreign financial assistance from donors, aimed against the Maoist movement. A London conference was organized for the purpose on 19 and 20 June 2002. The conference, for the first time, brought India and China together in a single forum to discuss the Nepali Maoist issue.[24] In February 2003, British Prime Minister Tony Blair appointed Sir Jeffrey James as special representative to Nepal in order to coordinate British agencies as well as help forge a common Nepal policy, mainly among the US, the UK and India. But India was not pleased with the UK and the US overtures near its border, and it soon demonstrated its displeasure.

India in the lead again

The 9/11 attacks had brought India and the US closer in international affairs on the issue of fighting Islamist extremism. But they had a clear difference of opinion when it came to the Maoist situation in Nepal. Delhi was becoming fretful about the growing American military involvement, its rising clout in the Nepali army, the supply of military hardware: in short, deepening military relations between the two.[25] The age-old Indian mindset that Nepal's military capability should be dependent on Delhi, and its anxiety over a superpower advancing in its backyard, came to the fore again.

Instead of Indian SLRs, Nepali soldiers were seen carrying American M-16s. When PM Deuba signed a deal to import 5,500 Minimi machineguns from Belgium, Delhi could no longer keep silent. It did not allow the aircraft carrying those guns to cross its airspace. For three weeks towards the end of 2002, the aircraft remained stranded in Kazakhstan. It was finally allowed after several requests from the Nepali side. During this episode, the Indian foreign secretary, Kanwal Sibal, openly advised Western countries, saying they should be 'careful about extending excessive military assistance to Nepal in order to avoid an increase in the lethality of the internal conflict and the leakage of arms to the Maoists'.[26]

The Indian ambassador in Kathmandu, Shyam Saran, was even less discreet. 'If the US and UK supply something that we cannot, or provide training on some areas where we cannot, then it is always welcome.' He meant to say that India itself would supply all essential military assistance in a concessional manner to Nepal.[27] India tried everything to stop Western forces from becoming any more active in Nepal. He also expressed his displeasure to the American ambassador to Nepal, Michael Malinowski.[28] Malinowski's successor as American ambassador, James F. Moriarty, has noted that he was enraged to know that the Indian embassy had complained to the prime minister's office in Nepal against US training to the Nepali army.[29]

Even as US–India relations in Nepal were going through a bad phase, another shocking incident came to the fore. It was revealed that the CIA's Kathmandu station chief was 'handling' a joint secretary-level officer of RAW, Ravinder Singh. In June 2004, Singh reached Kathmandu via Nepalgunj after fleeing Delhi. He was kept in hiding for a week before he was flown out on an American passport, accompanied by an American spy.[30] It was not clear whether the dozens of documents he photocopied from the RAW headquarters were related to Nepal, or whether his escape was related to Nepali affairs, but the episode was a setback to their intelligence relations.

However, the wider international context was pushing India and America closer. Although Pakistan was a traditional US ally in South Asia, the 9/11 attacks caused Islamist extremists to become a common enemy of India and the US. India was of strategic importance to the US in its war on Islamist extremists. In such a situation, the US did not want to continue needling India vis-à-vis Nepal affairs: a comparatively minor issue. Besides, the Nepali army, despite having increased its resistance capacity, had not been able to take a decisive step against the Maoists. Delhi reiterated that it alone had the desired experience and capacity to solve the problem in Nepal, which, it said, fell under its sphere of influence. As a result, American activity started decreasing in Nepal. It didn't mean that the US had changed any bit of its hard-line policy against the Maoists—only its role had changed.

In the Maoist analysis, until they attacked Beni in March 2004, the US strategy had completely failed and the Indians had come forward.[31] Instead of M-16s, the Indian INSAS started coming in. The Nepali army was visibly dissatisfied with the quality of the rifle, said to be an Indian edition of the Russian AK-47, but it was forced to buy it. Around 23,000 INSAS rifles entered Nepal— they were bought in a concessionary deal—with Nepal having to pay just 30 per cent of the price.

India had also given two light helicopters to Nepal after the imposition of a state of emergency. It gave two additional Lancer helicopters in January 2004. Four months later, it provided two helicopter gunships (HL Dhruva). It also gave seventy mine-protected vehicles, other vehicles, weapons and materials: assistance worth NRs. 5 billion in total. This was the highest amount of military assistance Nepal obtained from any country from 2001 to 2004.

The primary motives behind Indian military assistance were preventing rise of US–UK influence in the Nepali army, maintaining Indian dominance, and weakening the Maoists. But India never saw the people's war as an ideological challenge. Rather, it was looking to take diplomatic advantage of the situation. Therefore, it could be seen hunting with the hounds and running with the hares—on one hand, it was providing abundant support to the Nepali army, while on the other, the Maoists were allowed to conduct their activities on Indian soil. Meanwhile, in a planned conspiracy, a new game was played to dissolve the elected Parliament and empower the king.

7

Midnight at Narayanhity

'The king promised the election symbol of tree to me. At least he should have frozen the symbol if that was not possible. I was betrayed by the king. I don't know how many more times he will let me down.'

—Sher Bahadur Deuba, after dissolving
Parliament on the king's advice[1]

After he stepped down as prime minister over growing differences with the new king, Gyanendra, in July 2001, Girija Prasad Koirala found himself in a tight spot politically. Sher Bahadur Deuba, who replaced him as prime minister, was rapidly advancing his influence within the party, whereas the new king was growing in confidence with the imposition of a state of emergency and the mobilization of the army. Koirala felt that his role in national politics was shrinking. A person with a penchant for power, he now started a different kind of activism. He realized he could satisfy his ambition through proximity to one of the two existing powers: the king and Prachanda.[2]

While he was the prime minister, Koirala was the number one enemy of the Maoists. Baburam even said, 'Girija is the worst murderer of people in the history of Nepal. In the viewpoint of international law, he is an evil war criminal like Hitler'.[3] Koirala, too, was known for harbouring extreme contempt for the communists. In 1990, Koirala made a famous statement lumping together all shades of communists: 'Whether *Male* (the CPN–UML), *Mashale* (the CPN–Mashal, mother party of the Maoists) *or Mandale* (pro-royalist vigilantes), they are all the same.'

For Koirala, the Maoists were nothing but communist terrorists! But the manner in which he was forced out of office by the king in the aftermath of the Holeri incident sowed the seeds of anger against the monarchy within him. So he started meeting the emissaries of Prachanda with the intention of holding peace talks. Up until that point, King Gyanendra was Prachanda's first choice of interlocutor. Prachanda still thought that any pact with the king would be the shortest route to the Singha Durbar. But the new king was so filled with hubris that he deliberately belittled the elderly Girija Koirala.

During the winter months of 2002, there were times when the politically isolated Koirala would wait the whole day for a phone call from the palace chief secretary, Pashupati Bhakta Maharjan. His political secretary, Puranjan Acharya, remembers how, bewildered at not getting a call from the palace, Koirala would yell at his daughter Sujata and others for not hearing the phone ring. Acharya was then assigned the duty of attending to phone calls. Maharjan would assure Koirala that he would make the call after talking to the king, but he never did. It was not hard for Koirala to understand that the whole charade was being played to snub him. The wound from Holeri was still fresh in Koirala's mind. One evening, at his nephew Shashank Koirala's residence, among his coterie, he felt enough was enough and announced: this king has crossed the limit; I will show him now, I will talk to Prachanda.

Koirala felt that it was essential for him to talk to Prachanda and seek a resolution to the conflict in the country as a means of getting back to power. He had already reached the conclusion that the Maoist conflict was not going to be resolved by military means, and that the state of emergency would ultimately be used to target the political parties, to further shore up the king's power. The Maoists would naturally be pleased to build contacts with a leader of international stature such as Koirala. Following the failure of their overture to communist parties (at the Siliguri and Lucknow meetings), the Maoists were already on the lookout for chances to build bridges with parties like the Nepali Congress, even though they represented a different ideology.

Contacts and sources

The initial contact between Prachanda and Koirala was through the leftist leader Gobinda Neupane. A founding central leader of the CPN–ML, Neupane had left the party in 1981 to work for Plan International, an international non-governmental organization. One of his colleagues in that organization was Puranjan Acharya of Biratnagar, who went on to become the political secretary to Koirala. Having left Plan, Neupane had moved closer to the Maoists, though he was not in any official position in the party. In 1999, he had written a book advocating federalism based on ethnic identity, and a Constituent Assembly in Nepal—both ideas that were later embraced as party policy by the Maoists.[4]

Though the two men had gone in different political directions after leaving the Plan office, Acharya and Neupane were in regular contact. Neupane had also been acquainted with Prof. Krishna Khanal, who was once Koirala's political advisor in 1999. The three used to have political discussions occasionally. Later, Congress leader Narahari Acharya also joined the group. Around January 2002, Neupane proposed talks on the Maoists' behalf: 'Tell Girija Prasad Koirala (about the Maoists' interest),' he said with Khanal.

As the state of emergency had recently been imposed, Khanal could not see any possibility of this happening. 'How can one accept the logic of a proposal for talks less than two months after they dropped the earlier dialogue and went to attack Dang? It is not possible. If the Maoists are really honest about talks, then we will cooperate,' Khanal told Neupane.[5] But Neupane continued trying. Finally, he reached Koirala, who himself was in a hurry to contact the Maoists. Koirala's circle started a series of long discussions on what their meeting point with the Maoists could be.

In fact, Koirala was in contact with several Maoist 'channels' at the same time. He had met people like Mumaram Khanal and Manoj Jung Thapa. One such channel went on to become the most important: that of the poet and pro-Maoist journalist Krishna Sen 'Ichhuk', who was one of the interlocutors during the Holeri crisis. Koirala and Sen held a series of meetings. Sen communicated Koirala's messages to Prachanda by telephone.

Sometime in March 2002, a meeting was held at the residence of a high-ranking government official, after which the Congress–Maoist contact rose to a different level. Soon, Prachanda and Koirala started having direct telephone conversations. Preparations were on for a direct meeting. Chakra Prasad Bastola was added to Koirala's team of Krishna Khanal, Narahari Acharya and Puranjan Acharya. Narahari had proposed that the team needed a leader like Bastola because Koirala had little knowledge of the principles or organizational structure of the Maoists, and he would not listen to most people. Bastola not only belonged to the Koirala family but was also knowledgeable about Marxism and communism. He also had wide diplomatic experience and contacts in Delhi, where the Maoist leaders stayed.

Bastola returned from Delhi after holding one round of talks with the Maoist leadership in March 2002. Meanwhile, Neupane presented to Koirala possible meeting points for a Congress–Maoist understanding. Not convinced about a Constituent Assembly, Koirala, instead, agreed to the Maoists' proposal to add a clause enabling referendums under Article 3 of the 1990 Constitution, along with some amendments in other clauses.

On 10 May 2002, all the seven political parties represented in the Parliament (Congress, CPN–UML, Rastriya Prajatantra Party, Sadbhavana, United People's Front, National People's Front and Nepal Workers and Peasants Party) held a joint public assembly in Khula Manch of Kathmandu. Koirala and Prachanda had reached an understanding whereby Koirala was to make an appeal for dialogue from Khula Manch, and the Maoists were to issue a statement supporting it. The Maoists were officially regarded as 'terrorists' and the country was in a state of emergency at the time, so they had applied extreme caution in these efforts. It was decided that they would proceed with talks through Parliament, involving all major parties. However, Prime Minister Deuba was in no mood for any dialogue unless the Maoists gave up arms. Koirala blasted this position from Khula Manch and said, 'If the government is not willing, then the parties should take the initiative together for a peaceful resolution of the problem.'

Koirala also asked the Maoists to reply within seven days if they were interested. Prachanda responded within four days by dispatching similar letters to all the parties on 14 May, stating that the Maoists had 'most positively taken the initiatives by the parties'. He further stated, 'It is a matter of pleasure and glory for us that the whole country is standing behind dialogue and political resolution. The time has come to take a concrete action based on this public mandate'.[6] The exchange of letters further improved the environment for a direct meeting between Prachanda and Koirala.

Delhi meeting

Amid the efforts for talks with the Maoists, Koirala suddenly left for China in early June. It was not clear whether it had anything to do with the talks process, but he certainly intended to deliver a message to both Delhi and the Durbar through his Beijing sojourn. Isolated in national politics, he probably wanted to build international linkages. Interestingly, when he was in Beijing, he received a call from Prachanda to fix a meeting in Delhi. Koirala, instead of returning to Kathmandu, headed for Delhi from Beijing via Shanghai and Hong Kong. He termed it 'a private visit'.

Chakra Prasad Bastola was with Koirala. He called the Nepali ambassador in Delhi, Bhesh Bahadur Thapa, from Beijing. 'We are reaching tomorrow. Could you please arrange for a vehicle to pick us up at the airport?' There was no reason why he could not send a vehicle to pick up the former prime minister. It was only later that Thapa heard rumours that Koirala was coming to Delhi to meet Prachanda.

Bastola had chosen the residence of his friend, then Delhi editor of the daily *Telegraph*, Bharat Bhushan, for the meeting. He later shifted the venue because, apparently, the residence of the economic counsellor at the Nepali embassy, Gobinda Regmi, was close to Bhushan's home. They thought of meeting at the India International Centre, but later decided on Moti Bagh in south Delhi.

The meeting took place the very night Koirala arrived from Hong Kong, on 6 June 2002. Bastola and Baburam were also present. Baburam introduced Koirala to Prachanda. There were many rumours regarding the identity of Prachanda at the time. He had been living underground for several years. In fact, on one occasion, the *Times of India* had published a picture of the rights activist Padma Ratna Tuladhar, identifying him as Prachanda. Koirala had to depend on Baburam, whom he knew from the past, and take his word that the person to whom he was introduced really was Prachanda.

There were also rumours circulating of Maoist leaders having met King Gyanendra in Kathmandu. Without any preamble, Koirala made a direct statement: 'Well, you guys have also met the king!'

Prachanda admitted that his emissary had met the king. 'So what did the king say?' Koirala asked.

'We received a proposal for the Maoists and the monarchy to come together, sharing power and sending the leaders of parliamentary parties behind bars.'

'And what did you say?'

'We didn't agree.'

Koirala mentioned in his autobiography that he doubted Prachanda's reply.[7] Though he was getting closer to the Maoists due to the adverse political situation, he suspected that the Maoists and the palace could still come together. A fan of detective novels during his younger days, Koirala was interested in stories of political conspiracy.

Prachanda, on the other hand, immediately told Koirala in Delhi, 'If you guys accept a republic, we will accept the multiparty system.' But Koirala did not support a republic. Instead, he proposed amending the 1990 Constitution. 'Let's amend all things except its preamble. Come to the mainstream,' he told them.

I interviewed Koirala immediately upon his return from Delhi. According to him, after long discussions, Prachanda and Baburam seemed ready to drop their demand for a Constituent Assembly and join the mainstream by accepting the amendment of the 1990 Constitution.

There was a fundamental difference in those two options. Joining mainstream politics after simply amending the Constitution meant being part of the 1990 political framework, which included the monarchy and the parliamentary system. A new Constitution through an elected Constituent Assembly, on the other hand, could be a fresh start with the aim of establishing a republican set-up, and also held the possibility of a new kind of governance system.

'They too are in a tight spot,' Koirala said, adding, 'They asked for fifteen days to discuss which amendments they wanted, and to get the party's endorsement. They have said they will get back to me after that. I have returned to Kathmandu with that understanding.'

Although the Maoists talked of dropping their main demand for a Constituent Assembly, accepting mere amendments and the monarchy, this appears to have been a part of their cunning diplomacy. A Constituent Assembly remained their 'bottom line', which they raised immediately afterwards in another meeting.

Many understood that there was an Indian backing to the dialogue between Koirala and Prachanda. Koirala himself told Narahari and Puranjan that the Indian agencies learnt of his meeting with Prachanda, but did not obstruct it. According to one report, the first meeting between Koirala and Prachanda was arranged by the then Indian defence minister, George Fernandes.[8] Bastola had long-standing relations with Fernandes. A socialist leader, he had allowed the Burmese rebels to open office in his ministerial quarters. His residence was a nest for all sorts of radical outfits.[9]

Durga Subedi, who had played the role of negotiator in the government–Maoist talks in the past, was one of the few Nepali friends of Fernandes. I asked him about Fernandes' role in that first meeting between Koirala and Prachanda. Subedi said, 'Fernandes did give a green signal to the meeting with the Maoists. But he was not directly involved. He just said that they would not obstruct it. He used to say that there should be dialogue with the Maoists because India could not send a force like they did in Sri Lanka to control the communist rebellion in Nepal.'

Such an Indian position was adequate to create a positive atmosphere for Maoist–Congress talks, but King Gyanendra did not want that. He was not pleased with Girija Prasad Koirala's efforts for talks.

Midnight dissolution

When the monarchy was in power, there was one attitude prevalent among political parties in Nepal—get to power by winning the monarchy's confidence. Koirala was no exception.

In 1999, it was he who had hobnobbed with King Birendra to force his party colleague Krishna Prasad Bhattarai out of power. He wanted to use the same weapon to oust Prime Minister Sher Bahadur Deuba. For that purpose, he wanted to build bridges with King Gyanendra even though he personally did not like the new king. Koirala made the wrong calculation. He could not foresee that the king was harbouring the ambition of becoming the executive chief himself. Koirala admitted this in an interview with me later.[10]

Upon his return from Delhi, he shared the substance of his talks with Prachanda with the king. The king asked him, 'What will my role be?' His second question was, 'What is the bottom line of the Maoists? Find out and we will meet again.'

As he came out of the palace, Koirala says he was overwhelmed by a sense of apprehension. 'I had talked to the king, but I suspected that the Maoists might betray me. However, it would be the king, and not the Maoists, who would do the betraying,' Koirala told me later in an interview.[11]

Even though he had asked Koirala to discern the Maoists' bottom line, the king already knew what it was. The perceived Maoist bottom line was that they would drop their Constituent Assembly demand and accept constitutional monarchy, though that was only a part of their tactical manoeuvre. However, the king was not willing to give any space to Koirala. He was looking to create his own. He felt that bringing the Maoists into the mainstream would serve his desire to be more assertive. The king had ambitions of sidelining the parliamentary parties and grabbing power. The Maoists' entry into the mainstream under his efforts could open the door to this outcome. But the elected Parliament had become an 'eyesore' to him. Its dissolution would undercut the influence of parliamentary forces and put a brake on Koirala's campaign to woo the Maoists with constitutional amendments. It would also concentrate power in the palace. So he started weaving an intricate scheme designed to dissolve the Parliament, and Prime Minister Deuba was chosen as his instrument to carry out this design.

The day Koirala told the king about his conversation with Prachanda was the day his peaceful overtures started unravelling. The king played a double game.[12] He urged Koirala to go ahead even as he filled the ears of Prime Minister Deuba with Koirala's 'plans to replace him'. Deuba was already very suspicious about the manner in which his party president had dashed to Delhi—without informing him—to talk to the Maoists. It was interesting to see how Koirala and Deuba lacked mutual trust, but were opening up to the king. Getting 'free' information from both leaders, the king was plotting to 'ambush' the elected Parliament and the Congress party, both.

Sensing a risk from Koirala, Deuba drew closer to the palace. When Koirala raised the slogan of 'wider democratic unity' by recruiting even the CPN–UML, and talked of amending the Constitution to bring the Maoists on board, Deuba raised obstructions in his path by saying that 'they would need the consent of the king in order to change the Constitution promulgated as part of a tripartite agreement'. He added, 'There is no possibility of talks with the Maoists unless they abandon arms.' On 23 April 2002, hours after Party President Koirala directed Deuba's Congress party government 'to keep the doors of dialogue with the Maoists open', Deuba announced, at a parliamentary party meeting, a prize money of NRs. 1 to 5 million on the heads of Maoist leaders.[13]

The Royal Nepali Army was also used to obstruct Koirala's campaign. When Koirala went to Delhi to meet Prachanda on 24 April, the army issued a statement warning anyone against 'contacting the terrorists'. In another incident, when Koirala said, 'The state of emergency was imposed by the army and not the government,' Army Chief Prajwalla Shumsher Rana retorted, 'Was the state of emergency declared at the request of the army or was it declared because of the emergence of a serious threat to national security? Is the army or the bad governance responsible for this situation in the country?'[14]

The same state of emergency was used as the ostensible reason for dissolving the Parliament. The six-month period of the state of emergency, imposed after the Maoists attacked the army, would expire on 25 May 2002.[15] The Maoists wanted to avoid its extension at any cost. Koirala, too, did not want its extension, because of the growing clout of the army and the king.

When he returned from a visit to the United States, Prime Minister Deuba indicated to journalists that he, too, was not in favour of an extension. But he changed his mind after getting different suggestions from the army and the palace. He moved a proposal in the House of Representatives to extend the emergency. Party President Koirala instructed him to withdraw the proposal. He declined. The parliamentary session had been scheduled for 22 May. Deuba feared that Parliament would reject his proposal and, instead, he would have to face a no-trust motion. So, the night before the session, Parliament was dissolved in a dramatic manner. The date for elections to constitute a new Parliament was set for 13 November 2002.

The prime minister had signed the Parliament's death warrant by agreeing to the king's idea. The palace military secretary, Bibek Kumar Shah, was one of the witnesses to what transpired at the palace at midnight on 21 May 2002. He writes:

> At the palace that night, Prime Minister Deuba sent for the letter pad and stamp from his office. Once they were brought in, the chief secretary of the king, Pashupati Bhakta Maharjan, typed, on behalf of the PM, a letter about the dissolution of the House of Representatives and a new election date. The letter was written as a recommendation to His Majesty. The PM signed it in the presence of the king. Immediately afterwards, the king dissolved the Parliament and announced a mid-term election as per the recommendation of the prime minister.[16]

Since the end of the reign of King Birendra, the palace coterie had wanted to grab power by dissolving Parliament and fomenting a political crisis to prevent an election from taking place. That 'readymade roadmap' was followed during Deuba's term. Deuba saw it as a chance to teach Koirala a lesson and acquiesced. He thought that he would dominate in both the party and the government if there were mid-term polls at a time when he was being backed by everyone from the king and the army to the United States.[17]

In fact, even his ministers were unaware of the midnight dissolution. Party President Koirala was seething with anger. He expelled Deuba from the party on 26 May. Deuba registered a new party at the Election Commission: the Nepali Congress (Democratic).

The state of emergency was merely used to veil the real cause. Actually, the king wanted to stall Koirala's peace talks efforts by any means. Such efforts would have undermined the role of the king. Besides, the palace's wings could have been clipped further were there to be an amendment to the Constitution. According to Koirala, 'I was trying to resolve the problem through Parliament. The king had understood the bottom line of the Maoists (constitutional amendment). So he dissolved the Parliament to take the initiative himself and earn the credit.'

The efforts for peace talks with the Maoists were stopped. Koirala's Maoist contact in Kathmandu, Krishna Sen, was arrested from Kathmandu a day before the dissolution. Sen was later mercilessly killed in army custody on 27 May 2002.[18]

King Gyanendra now had his new destination in mind, which the Maoists had already identified before him—Delhi.

8

Dual Diplomacy

'India's ultimate aim in its security concept vis-à-vis Nepal appears mysterious given its substantial support to the government army including military materials, training and funds, and allowing the rebel leaders to take shelter in their country at the same time.'

—Col. Bijaya Thapa, a Nepali army official,
expressing doubt about India's Nepal policy[1]

For a whole year after he was crowned king, Gyanendra did not go on any foreign tours. A year after the palace massacre he went to India, where there was much excitement about the visit by the new king. He had an official meeting with the Indian prime minister, Atal Behari Vajpayee, on 24 June 2002. Right after the meeting, Vajpayee's principal secretary, Brajesh Mishra, took Ambassador Bhesh Bahadur Thapa aside and asked, 'Ambassador, what's your king up to? He was asking for three years.'

It was because of their close personal rapport that Mishra had questioned Ambassador Thapa in such a manner. Thapa asked him, 'What did he say?'

Mishra was forthright. 'He was asking Vajpayee*ji* to endorse his dictatorship.'

Thapa was unaware of this but replied, 'Oh, did he ask?'

According to Thapa, King Gyanendra had outlined the need for his intervention for a maximum of three years, due to the growing armed challenge of the Maoists, the parties' inability to address it, and the lack of effective political leadership in the country. In the context of the feeble leadership demonstrated by Prime Minister Sher Bahadur Deuba during his India visit three months earlier (20–25 March 2002), and his tendency to look up to the palace as the ultimate source of guidance, India was starting to believe that power in Nepal was gradually being concentrated in the palace. It could not, therefore, brush aside Gyanendra's application altogether. Vajpayee merely told him that India was willing to provide all kinds of support to Nepal's efforts to overcome armed conflict while there was constitutional monarchy and multiparty democracy. Upon his return to Kathmandu, Gyanendra told his close aide and business partner, Prabhakar Shumsher Rana, that the visit 'had gone better than he expected'.[2]

Former Ambassador Thapa believes that this was the point from which a decisive turn in India's Nepal policy began. India had learnt of the king's intention of grabbing power and initiated its own plan accordingly. It performed a series of contradictory moves, encouraging both the king and the Maoists, which greatly reduced the role of parliamentary parties like the Nepali Congress and the CPN–UML.

It was around January 2002 that the Maoists, too, posted a letter addressed to Indian PM Vajpayee, appealing for political support. They had not received a reply. When India learnt of the king's intention in June, it wrote a reply to the insurgents the same month. And a few weeks after the king's coup, India established formal contact with them, in November 2002, details of which are discussed in the later part of this chapter.

The Maoists and the monarchy were fighting each other, but both were seeking support from Delhi. Delhi maintained parallel relations with the conflicting parties of its neighbouring country. India's support to the palace, which led the Nepali establishment, was understandable. But why did democratic India engage in the contradictory exercise of also bolstering the guerrillas? It probably had no 'democratic' answer. That is why this duty was entrusted to the RAW, which had expertise in political intelligence. One goal of the Nepal mission shouldered by RAW in 2002 was to topple the monarchy and establish a republic in Nepal. It took them only six years to achieve this goal. High-ranking Indian and Nepali sources have confirmed this special mission of RAW, but whether the agency was given any further goal is still a mystery.

The year 2002 was a watershed year in recent history in terms of Nepal–India relations. It represented the point from which the role of the Indian external affairs ministry and political leadership started shrinking, as far as the duty of formulating and enforcing Nepal policy was concerned. The Indian PM's national security advisor, who is regularly briefed by intelligence agencies such as RAW and IB, became increasingly influential. The responsibility of the Nepal policy, entrusted to Brajesh Mishra during Vajpayee's term, was later transferred to his successors: J.N. Dixit, M.K. Narayanan, Shivshankar Menon and Ajit Doval. The first significant Nepal incident after Indian policy took this turn was the royal coup of 4 October 2002.[3]

First coup

King Gyanendra had exhibited his 'itch' for power ever since he'd been crowned. He was building the image of an 'active', not a 'constitutional', monarch. He gave interviews to many newspapers and magazines. Perhaps he was the only Nepali king to give so many interviews to the media. He used to say, 'I cannot sit silent like my brother (the late King Birendra),' 'I want to be constructive, not active,' and so on.[4]

He was giving enough indications that he was not averse to taking a suitable step as and when the opportunity presented itself. After the dissolution of Parliament and the announcement of a mid-term election, there was no legal body left to constrain him. Prime Minister Deuba had been reduced to a rubber-stamp of the palace. The loyalty of all state agencies, including the army, the police and other security agencies, was towards him and not the government.

On 8 September 2002, the insurgents attacked the Sandhikharka barracks and killed seventy-four soldiers. The assistant chief district officer was abducted. Four days later, at a meeting called by the Election Commission, Inspector General of Police Pradeep Shumsher Rana, proposed the postponement of the 13 November election by at least three months. The home ministry expressed its displeasure by seeking a clarification from him, but it was in vain because he had spoken the king's mind. King Gyanendra summoned the prime minister and said, 'PM, it is not possible to hold the elections. So you please resign. I will help form another government by including all under your leadership, again. You run the government and also strengthen your new party. Then hold the elections at a more appropriate time.'[5]

Deuba asked for some time to study the king's proposal. He then left for South Africa to take part in a world environment conference, but under heavy pressure, he returned from Brussels. A birthday celebration was held for Crown Princess Himani at the palace, where the king again asked Deuba the same question. Deuba didn't say anything. The king then told Deuba's wife, Arzoo Rana, 'Please, convince the PM.'

A few days later, at a meeting of the National Defence Council, Army Chief Pyar Jung Thapa called for a decision at the political level, since the elections could not be held on the specified date due to the unimproved security situation. Deuba saw no alternative to postponing the polls, so he called a cabinet meeting on 2 October.

The cabinet had appealed to the king to 'remove constitutional obstacles' by invoking Article 127 of the Constitution to postpone the 13 November 2002 election.[6] But the king did not postpone the poll. Instead, he invoked the same article to dismiss the prime minister on the charge of 'inability to hold the election' at 10.45 p.m. on 4 October 2002.

The 1990 Constitution had no provision whereby a prime minister could be sacked by any person or authority other than Parliament. Therefore, the king's step was clearly a 'coup'. It sent the 1990 Constitution into a 'coma'. The king proclaimed that he removed Prime Minister Deuba by exercising 'the state power inherent in us' according to the Constitution. He took over executive powers himself. A few days later, he appointed an old palace loyalist, Lokendra Bahadur Chand, as the new prime minister. This was his fourth time in this position. Last time, he was prime minister in 1997 when the Maoist insurgency had just begun.

Rajan–Rasgotra's rush

Just before the king sacked Deuba on 4 October, former Indian Ambassadors Maharajkrishna Rasgotra and K.V. Rajan arrived in Kathmandu. Rajan had been Delhi's ambassador to Nepal from 1994 to 2000, while Rasgotra had been there from 1954 to 1956 as the second secretary, and from 1973 to 1976 as the ambassador.[7] Later, he had gone on to become foreign secretary (1982–84). Both had cordial relations with the royal family of Nepal.

They were welcomed as Indian emissaries in Kathmandu. According to the then minister Jaya Prakash Anand, they met NC leaders Sher Bahadur Deuba and Girija Prasad Koirala separately and told them that the Congress, which was freshly divided, would lose to the UML if the elections took place then. They advised them both to recommend to the king that polls should be put off, since it was better than having a communist government in Nepal.[8]

Nepali Congress President Koirala, and president of the newly formed NC (Democratic) Deuba, both found the suggestion to their liking. So Koirala agreed with his arch-rival Deuba in making the recommendation. The UML was unaware of it all; it became a part of the conspiracy hatched against it. Prime Minister Deuba, in accordance with the suggestion of all parties, made the recommendation to postpone the election to the king on 2 October. The same day, Rajan and Rasgotra met the king. Two days later, King Gyanendra sacked Prime Minister Deuba.[9]

Delhi was keeping a close watch on Kathmandu. On 4 October, a palace secretary informed Indian National Security Advisor Brajesh Mishra about the impending royal announcement. Deuba's dismissal was no surprise for Delhi, so it did not give any strong reaction. Rather, it portrayed the king's actions as borne out of compulsion, due to the failure of the political parties to hold the elections on the specified date.[10]

India described the '4 October' step as 'a minor violation of the Constitution'. It saw that the king in a role as 'referee', with the power to dismiss the prime minister, but not bent on sidelining the political parties altogether, was in its interest. There were people in and around the Indian establishment who supported King Gyanendra, owing to his long association with Indian joint ventures like Surya Tobacco, Himalayan Goodricke and a Tata Motors distributorship for Nepal.[11] His son had married into the former Indian princely family of Sikar, Rajasthan.

In the immediate aftermath of 4 October, there was a problem in Durbar–Delhi relations. The king picked Lokendra Bahadur Chand as the new prime minister, who was seen as 'anti-India' previously. The king 'corrected' this a few months later when he replaced Chand with Surya Bahadur Thapa, who had very good relations with the Indian establishment.

Contact with the Maoists

Around the same time, Delhi made it possible for the Maoists to get close to them. After the failure of the first peace talks in 2001 and the initiation of a war with the army, the Maoists were increasingly concentrating on their goal of a republic. They would need international, particularly Indian, support for the purpose.

Prachanda and Baburam had a long discussion on how to go about building relations with the Indians. According to Prachanda, they identified a professor at Delhi's Jawaharlal Nehru University (JNU), S.D. Muni, whom Baburam had known from the 1970s.[12] A professor in the International Relations department of JNU, Muni was among the few academics who took an interest in Nepali affairs. Having written books on Nepal–India relations, he was considered an authority on Nepal affairs. A staunch republican, Muni believed that democracy would not be consolidated, nor would India's interest be safeguarded, while there was a monarchy in Nepal. His argument was that 'India cannot meaningfully get engaged with the peace process (in Nepal) unless it gets constructively engaged with the Maoists'.[13]

Prof. Muni had good contacts with PM Vajpayee's principal secretary and NSA Brajesh Mishra. The Maoist leaders decided to write a letter to Vajpayee via Prof. Muni. Baburam drafted the letter, and they sent it bearing the signatures of Baburam (as the coordinator of the United Revolutionary People's Council) and Prachanda (as party chairman). They wrote the letter on 3 December 2001, but were able to hand it to Prof. Muni only two months later. For a long time, they were unsure if the letter had reached the addressee.[14] According to Muni, Vajpayee told him that he had received the letter when they met at a programme four or five months later.[15]

The Maoist leadership had dispatched similar letters addressed to the presidents of China and the United States, the chairman of the European Commission and general secretary of the United

Nations. In the letter, they argued that they were fighting against autocratic monarchy and appealed for the international community to recognize the 'people's regime' they were establishing. At the end of the letter, it was written: 'We would, hence, expect all the countries, international bodies and particularly the two immediate neighbours, India and China, not to interfere in the internal affairs of Nepal and let the Nepali people decide their own political future themselves. Looking forward to cordial and mutually beneficial relations in the days to come.'[16]

Other letters were handed over to the missions of foreign countries in Kathmandu, but the letter to India was handed over directly in Delhi. The Maoist leadership came to know in June 2002 that their letter had reached the Indian PMO. Delhi subsequently asked them to write another letter with concrete issues. After they sent the second letter to Vajpayee through Prof. Muni in November 2002, institutional contact between the Maoists and Delhi was established.[17] Previously, though they were given a free run to stay and organize activities on Indian territory, they had not been able to build formal relations with the Indian establishment.

What was in the second letter? Prof. Muni himself has described its contents thus:

Packaged in radical rhetoric, the letter written by the Maoist duo, Prachanda and Baburam Bhattarai, assured the Indian leaders that they wanted the best of relations with India and would not do anything to harm its critical interests. The response to this letter came after a couple of months; the intelligence and surveillance and restrictions on the Maoists' movements in India were relaxed, and an IB team held discussions with the Maoists' representatives. The Maoists reiterated their position again in writing to the IB sleuths. This was followed by more contacts and meetings between the Maoists and the RAW. Maoists could now move with greater ease and could also contact other Nepali political leaders in India.[18]

The Indian political leadership did not want to publicly establish formal relations with a group conducting an insurgency in a neighbouring country. That is why they instructed their intelligence machinery to 'covertly' engage them.[19] India has been mobilizing its intelligence agencies in Nepal's internal affairs since 1950s. When they heard that the Ranas, freshly ousted by the 1951 revolution, were plotting against King Tribhuwan, an IB officer, K. Sankaran Nair, was dispatched to Kathmandu. Nair, who later became chief of RAW, smelt a conspiracy against 'India's friend' King Tribhuwan. He later described how Delhi had acted on his suggestion in foiling the Ranas' conspiracies and bolstering Tribhuwan.[20]

So the involvement of Indian intelligence in Nepal's affairs was not new. But as being the political force, the Maoist party failed to realize the consequence of building relations with India through an intelligence agency. According to Muni, they went to the extent of writing letters not only to the Indian PMO but also to the IB, and promised the bureau that they 'wanted the best of relations with India' and 'would not do anything to harm its critical interests'.[21]

Such a show of approval was totally against the Maoists' professed policy of terming India an 'expansionist' power. Once they entered into institutional relations with India, their customary anti-India voices vanished from both slogans and practice. They even stopped calling India 'expansionist'. Some—such as the former palace military secretary, Bibek Kumar Shah, in his autobiography—even claimed that they started receiving training and material support from the Indians.

The source of Shah's information was an inspector of the Armed Police Force (APF), who had returned from a Chakrata military facility near Dehradun in Uttarakhand, India. A company level unit of the APF had gone there in June 2003 for commando training. An inspector in the team came to know that a month earlier, a team of Maoist guerrillas had received similar training at the facility. He shared the information with APF Chief Sahabir

Thapa upon his return. Thapa told the same to Shah and Shah shared it with King Gyanendra. Subsequently, a former deputy chief of the intelligence department was dispatched to the cantonment town of Chakrata to investigate the matter. However, the officer later went incommunicado and Shah claims that he lost his job after trying to investigate this matter further.[22]

It is a fact, published in several books, that in the past, the secret military installation called 'Establishment 22' in Chakrata had been used for training Khampa rebels, the Mukti Bahini of Bangladesh, and Tamil rebels.[23] However, over the years, both the Maoists and the Indian external affairs ministry have rejected allegations that the Nepali rebels received any training there.

On 4 December 2003, US Ambassador Michael Malinowski asked Indian Ambassador Shyam Saran about the alleged training given to the Maoists. When he raised the matter of some Nepali women Maoists obtaining training at a Chakrata military facility, Saran termed the information as 'unfortunate'. In a report he sent to his government after the meeting, Malinowski wrote that Ambassador Saran may have been unaware of all the activities of RAW in Nepal.[24]

It is true that intelligence agencies do many things covertly in the name of 'national interest', like Malinowski pointed out. According to Girija Prasad Koirala, during their struggle against the Panchayat regime, then RAW Chief R.N. Kao not only advised them to hijack an airplane and loot NRs. 3 million belonging to the Nepal Rastra Bank, but also turned a blind eye to the smuggling of Indian currency and even uranium.[25]

Though it is still a matter of speculation whether the Indian government lent material support to the Maoists, I am certain that it allowed Maoists to stay and carry out their activities on Indian soil. India was apparently eyeing the chance to become a decisive force and sort out its outstanding strategic and economic interests in Nepal. But India never wanted the instability to go out of its control in Nepal. It was thinking on the same lines as the royal palace and the Royal Nepali Army before 2001. Simply put: Let the Maoist activities grow to a certain level but let us be able to come forth and control them as and when required.

There may be several reasons for Delhi's decision to provide concessions to the Maoists. The main reason was the monarchy, which was emerging as the ultimate power centre and was clearly an obstacle to Delhi's desire of becoming a decisive force in Kathmandu. There were also strong voices in Delhi that felt Nepal's monarchy was becoming a centre for anti-India sentiment; though King Gyanendra was perceived as a friendly force in his initial days, he also followed the same path as his predecessors. The second reason was the growing advances of the United States in Nepal, something Delhi detested. For instance, American Ambassador Malinowski once had to complain to Indian Ambassador Saran that certain agents of RAW in Kathmandu were portraying 'America's policy and intention in Nepal as being tantamount to overlooking Nepal's sovereignty'.[26]

India did not want to see an expansion of the role of any other country, be it the US or China, in Nepal. Had the America-army alliance been able to thwart the insurgency, there would have been a possibility of a transformation in the traditional power structure in Nepal, which would have greatly reduced India's dominance. Delhi could not allow that to happen. So it chose to lend various sorts of support to the Maoists.

The Maoists, on the other hand, wanted to make Delhi their shield as they saw America helping the army–palace combine, against which they were fighting. They wanted to concentrate their attack on the monarchy by joining hands with the parliamentary parties at the behest of the Indians. The Indians, too, worked to bring the Maoists and the parties together against the palace. All these activities were taking place clandestinely. On the surface, Delhi had a different position, which was seen during the visit of the Indian prime minister, Atal Behari Vajpayee, to Kathmandu to take part in the SAARC Summit in January 2002.

Vajpayee was prime minister from March 1998 to May 2004, during the height of the Maoist insurgency in Nepal. He held a long interaction with Nepali journalists in Kathmandu. The main theme of the interaction was the Maoist affair. The editor of the fortnightly *Himal*, Rajendra Dahal, asked, 'Your Excellency, what does India think of the Maoist problem? Is it seen as part of global terrorism?'

Vajpayee's reply was, 'What is important is how Nepal looks at it . . . We don't want to interfere in this. We are only helping Nepal out. We are helping so that there is peace in Nepal, there is stability in Nepal, and Nepal continues to develop.'

Another journalist, Ram Chandra Neupane, interjected, 'But India has declared the Nepali Maoists terrorists.'

'Yes, that is correct.'

Then the editor of the daily *The Kathmandu Post*, Shyam K.C., asked, 'Sir, there is a feeling that a lot of the arms for the Maoists are coming from India and also some of the top Maoists seek shelter there. Is India going to do anything about it?'

Expressing surprise, Vajpayee answered, 'Arms coming from India?'

The editor of the daily *Gorkhapatra*, Kishor Nepal, added, 'Not only arms, but there are training centres also in India.'

Vajpayee said, 'No!'

Ram Chandra Neupane wanted to prove his claim and said, 'I will give you one example. When Girija Prasad Koirala was prime minister, he give an interview to M.J. Akbar. He said in that interview that there is a training centre of the Nepali Maoists in Hisar in Haryana.'

'In Hisar? He did not find any other place for this?' It did not look like the Indian PM was serious about the matter. 'Lots of things are published in the newspapers. We should not believe them all. We would not like our territory being used against our neighbour Nepal, and I am confident that this is not happening.'[27]

9

No Meeting with the King

'I think India always had demonstrated two contradictory positions: one professed building relations with the king and the other encouraged clashing with him.'

—B.P. Koirala, indicating Delhi's
point of view towards the Durbar[1]

In the second year of his rule, King Gyanendra was in a very favourable position. He had usurped power after dissolving the Parliament. He had won support from India, the most influential external player in the internal politics of Nepal. He also took the third step: initiating dialogue with the Maoists.

The Maoists, too, wanted to hold talks with the king. They had concluded that the earlier talks in 2001 had failed because the real state power was in his hands. Following the king's 4 October 2002 coup, they saw that the political condition evolved to their liking. Less than three weeks later, Prachanda issued a surprising statement, on 24 October, in which he, for the first time, cordially addressed the monarch as 'King Gyanendra'. The statement urged the king to 'make necessary sacrifice for the benefit of nation and the people'. What the 'sacrifice' meant wasn't clear, but what was clear was that the Maoists became unnaturally soft towards the king.

There were lots of preparations going on behind the scenes. Maoist leader Haribol Gajurel had secretly come to Kathmandu for informal talks with Prime Minister Lokendra Bahadur Chand. In November, a Maoist politburo meeting formed a team of negotiators, including Krishna Bahadur Mahara and Dev Gurung. King Gyanendra depended on two reliable channels for talks: the Geneva-based Centre for Humanitarian Dialogue, called the HD Centre, and his minister Narayan Singh Pun.

The HD Centre, which had played the role of mediator in resolving conflicts in other countries, had been active in Nepal since 2000. The director of the centre, Martin Griffiths, and his deputy Andrew Marshall had visited Kathmandu and held meetings with several leaders, journalists, rights activists and facilitators. They had built contacts with several key figures, from ministers to Sher Bahadur Deuba, then the coordinator of a team formed to study the Maoist problem, and to the Durbar and Maoist leaders. Marshall had contacted Maoist leaders through rights activist Padma Ratna Tuladhar. Initially, Griffiths met Maoist leader Rabindra Shrestha in Kathmandu. Two other meetings were held in foreign countries. One was held in Bangalore, India, and another in Geneva, Switzerland. Those meetings were attended by the Maoist leader Mumaram Khanal and Tuladhar, as Khanal revealed during an interview with me.[2]

In November 2002, the HD Centre submitted a proposal for mediation to the prime minister, Lokendra Bahadur Chand, through Tuladhar. The plan in the proposal was to fly government and Maoist negotiators, along with facilitators, including Tuladhar, secretly to Geneva for talks. The process was to be formalized if the talks succeeded, but if it failed, then the Maoists would be flown back to where they came from. Accordingly, Sharad Chandra Shah and Kamal Thapa were nominated as government negotiators while Krishna Bahadur Mahara and Suresh Ale

Magar were named as the Maoist negotiators. The HD Centre flew in a six-seater aircraft to Nepal for the purpose. It was kept waiting in a hangar of the Tribhuwan International Airport in Kathmandu for three days, but King Gyanendra concluded it was more appropriate to mobilize one of his ministers, the helicopter pilot Narayan Singh Pun, for the negotiations instead. The HD Centre's proposal was thus discarded.

A retired lieutenant colonel of the Royal Nepali Army, Pun was involved in the helicopter business. He was also affiliated to the Nepali Congress and had become an MP and minister. In 2002, he left Congress and floated a separate party, the Nepal Samata Party, under his own leadership. He became the minister for works and physical planning in the Chand cabinet formed after 4 October. He wanted to use negotiations with the Maoists as a bridge to further personal success. He nursed the ambition of becoming prime minister soon, as he told close associates.

Birendra Jhapali, a key member of Pun's party, was friends with the old communist leader D.R. Lamichhane, who, in turn, was in contact with the Maoists' regional bureau member Sagar Chhetri. In this manner, Pun met Chhetri and subsequently established contact with the senior Maoist leader Badal. Palace Military Secretary Bibek Kumar Shah played a role in convincing King Gyanendra about Pun's proposal. Pun would report to the king via Shah. The chain of contact went something like this: King Gyanendra—Bibek Kumar Shah—Narayan Singh Pun—Birendra Jhapali—D.R. Lamichhane—Sagar—Badal—Prachanda.

There was no direct contact between Gyanendra and Prachanda, but the Maoists felt they were dealing directly with the king. They formally agreed to talks after the palace accepted Pun as its emissary. The Maoists were informed in writing about Pun's nomination as the coordinator of a 'high-level commission for resolution of Maoist and other national problems.' On 17 January 2003, Pun wrote a letter on the commission's letterhead—registration number 1-2059-60—inviting the Maoists to join a ceasefire. The letter stated that if the Maoists were willing to resolve the problem peacefully through dialogue, the state was willing to withdraw accusations of terrorism, red corner notices and the prize money on Maoist leaders' heads, and also call a 'roundtable conference' to discuss their demands for an interim government and a Constituent Assembly. A ceasefire was the precondition for all of this.[3]

Two days later, Prachanda replied that he was willing to agree to a ceasefire, but the palace did not respond for a week. In fact, the royal family was busy with the wedding of Princess Prerana. Meanwhile, there was a sensational incident: the assassination of the chief of the Armed Police Force, Krishna Mohan Shrestha. After he was shot to death by the Maoists in Lalitpur on 26 January, the Maoists spread the rumour that they had a hit-list of high-ranking officials. The king condemned the assassination as 'the height of terrorism'. But even before the blood spilt on the site had dried, he ordered a ceasefire. On the third day after Shrestha's assassination, at midnight on 28 January, a cabinet meeting decided, under instructions from the palace, to withdraw terrorism charges and red corner notices against the Maoists and the prize money on their heads. A copy of the government decision was sent to Maoist Chairman Prachanda overnight. The following day, both sides announced a ceasefire.

Dispute over 5 kilometres

For two-and-a-half months, Pun alone had coordinated the government's initiative for negotiations.[4] But when, on 16 April 2003, the government formed its negotiating team, Deputy Prime Minister Badri Prasad Mandal was put in charge, while Pun was relegated to being a mere member. Even so, Pun's role was much more significant. Other members of the team included ministers Ramesh Nath Pandey, Upendra Devkota, Kamal Chaulagain and Anuradha Koirala.

The Maoist team was headed by Baburam Bhattarai and included Ram Bahadur Thapa 'Badal', Krishna Bahadur Mahara, Dev Gurung and Matrika Yadav. The first round of talks was held at the Hotel Shankar in Kathmandu on 27 April 2003, where the Maoists presented their 'Agenda for Forward-Looking Political Resolution.' Their demands were the same as in 2001: roundtable conference, interim government and Constituent Assembly. They also demanded that the army be recalled to the barracks within a week. On 9 May, when they met for preparatory talks a day before the second round of dialogue, the two sides discussed the matter of restricting the army. After the government refused to meet their demand for a 'full withdrawal of the army to the barracks', they discussed the possibility of restricting army movement to the periphery of its camps.

The second formal round of dialogue was to take place at Hotel Shankar the following day. Baburam messaged the prime minister, suggesting that the army's movements be restricted to within 5 kilometres of its barracks. Prime Minister Chand shared the message with Pun, who took it to his 'boss', Palace Military Secretary Bibek Kumar Shah. Shah advised the prime minister to 'consult with the army chief'.

PM Chand then spoke to Chief of Army Staff Pyar Jung Thapa. General Thapa (a person who normally speaks his mind) replied, 'Well, we would be okay (with this) if the limit were set for 20–25 km rather than 5 km.' Perhaps he thought that patrolling over this distance would be enough to ensure that barracks could not be targeted by the 'long-range' weapons of the insurgents. Shah briefed the king. The king also said that '20–25 km would be ok.' But the king, the army chief and Shah were all surprised when they heard on the news later in the evening that it had been agreed that the army would be restricted within 5 km of its camps.

This happened because the government negotiators were unable to resist the Maoists' persuasion. Maoist leader Mahara made the announcement at a press meet following the talks. Sitting by his side, Pun just kept mum.

This deal—that the army would be restricted while no such restrictions were laid down for the insurgents—was played up as a victory for the rebels and it demoralized the government side. Congress Party President Girija Prasad Koirala, who had been critical of the king and the army, seized the opportunity and stated that the deal 'devalued the national army'. It created a ruckus within the military leadership. The top generals said that it was not a matter of 5 or 25 km: it was a matter of principle. How could a national army be geographically restricted within the country? The army's response came in the form of a statement by its spokesperson, Deepak Gurung: 'The army will continue its operations unless the looted weapons are returned.'

Dark clouds had gathered over the future of talks.

Hapure and violence

In the end, Prime Minister Chand was made a 'sacrificial lamb'. Though he was not directly involved in the 5 km dispute, it was felt that his ouster would pave the way for scrapping that deal. The king made him resign and replaced him with Surya Bahadur Thapa on 4 June 2003. A new team of government negotiators was formed, led by minister Prakash Chandra Lohani and including Kamal Thapa as member secretary. The new team stated that the issue of 5 km was only under discussion and no decision had been made about it. The foundation of trust was breached by the formation of a new government and a new talks team.

Actually, the Maoist negotiators said they suspected a plot to kill them. They started vanishing from Kathmandu one by one. Lohani's team rarely got to meet them in person, depending instead on exchanges of letters. On 27 July 2003, the Maoists laid down five pre-conditions and warned that they would consider it a 'unilateral breach of ceasefire by the government' if the conditions were not met within four days.[5] The government tried to reduce the tension by releasing three Maoist leaders—Rabindra Shrestha, Mumaram Khanal and Bamdev Chhetri—from detention, but in vain.

Fearing arrests, the Maoist negotiators declined to travel to Kathmandu. The third round of talks began in Nepalgunj, where Baburam held a two-hour-long chat with his former college classmate and then minister, Kamal Thapa, at the residence of Dhawal Shumsher Rana. The talks centred on ways to resolve issues by giving some recognition to the monarchy. They did not result in anything concrete, however. Having opened the third round of talks in Nepalgunj, at the Maoists' suggestion, the teams travelled to Hapure village in nearby Dang district for further talks.

When the government team reached Hapure on 17 August, they were welcomed with garlands and treated to local delicacies. Both sides knew that nothing was going to come of the talks, though. The government side presented its 'Resolution for Forward-Looking Reforms in State System' at the meeting. It amounted to a proposal for rewriting the 1990 Constitution. The Maoists did not accept it, sticking to their demand for a Constituent Assembly.

Meanwhile, an army operation totally derailed the dialogue process. On the day of the Hapure talks, the military killed two civilians and seventeen unarmed Maoists cadres, including their local people's government chief, Baburam Yonjan, in the village of Doramba in the central district of Ramechhap. The government claimed this happened in an 'encounter'. In reality, they were killed execution-style after being arrested—a fact later corroborated by the National Human Rights Commission.[6]

The incident indicated that the government thought the ceasefire was over. And the Doramba massacre enraged the insurgents. Their talks coordinator, Baburam Bhattarai, left for Delhi in the third week of August. His new address was a pink, four-storeyed house in Rohini's Sector 15. Prachanda, too, was staying in Delhi. In that house, the two leaders held a long discussion on 27 August and prepared a statement about the end of the ceasefire. It was released the same day. It said that the talks were derailed by the government: politically through its resolution (presented at Hapure) and, militarily, through the Doramba killings.

The following day, on 28 August, the Maoists shot two army colonels in Kathmandu: one was killed while the other was seriously wounded. The 'terrorist' tag, which had been removed seven months earlier, was reinstated.[7] The cycle of violence and counter-violence was resumed with greater ferocity.

There were numerous reasons for the failure of the talks. It had taken three months after the ceasefire to even hold the first round. The gap between the first and the second rounds of talks was also around three months. The government changed its team of negotiators three times. The government itself was changed in the middle of talks. The dispute over the restriction of the Royal Nepali Army to within 5 km of barracks became a major issue. Those who opposed the talks became active in the government side. Actually, a serious trust deficit developed a few weeks after the ceasefire and ultimately led to the failure of peace talks. And the new government led by Surya Bahadur Thapa was in no mood to find a peaceful solution.

Couldn't meet the king

When serious differences arose during the course of talks, the Maoists had wanted to hold direct talks with the king. In Prachanda's words, 'He was, after all, the supreme commander of the Royal Nepali Army. So we thought about talking to the person who held the reins of power.'

Baburam was the person who had written the 'acidic' article in the aftermath of the palace massacre, calling Gyanendra a 'murderer'.[8] He was the one pushing the 'no truck with monarchy' line within the party, and Prachanda had sent the same fierce republican leader as the coordinator of the team that would talk to the king. The king paid no heed. Describing Baburam as an 'Indian agent,' he sent the message that he was ready, instead, to talk to the 'nationalist' Ram Bahadur Thapa 'Badal'. There was a perception that Badal was comparatively soft towards the monarchy and the palace tried to implement a divide-and-rule policy. But Prachanda did not permit Badal to meet him. So Badal ended up meeting the king's son-in-law, Raj Bahadur Singh. One of their meetings took place at the office of Karnali Airlines, Narayan Singh Pun's helicopter company, at Sinamangal, Kathmandu. Another meeting was held at the residence of Khadga Bahadur Gharti Magar, the son-in-law of the old Rolpa communist leader Burman Budha, at Kusunti in Lalitpur district.

The Maoists were also under tremendous pressure from the military onslaught, and from the growing cooperation between Delhi and the durbar. They were in desperate need of breathing space, to prepare and organize themselves, if nothing else. But the insurgents who came to Kathmandu to talk to the king were not able to meet him, despite several attempts. The king had changed his mind. Initially, the king was willing to permit a Constituent Assembly if the existence of the monarchy was guaranteed. But subsequently, he hardened his position because he felt he had Delhi's support. When the rebels were in the capital looking to meet him, he took off to spend six weeks to Britain on the pretext of 'health treatment'. His attitude was enough to send the Maoists into tizzy. They smelt a rat.

Thapa's rise to power

In the first week of December 2002, Delhi began to closely watch the efforts towards a Maoist–government dialogue. The RAW special secretary, J.K. Sinha, visited Kathmandu and met several leaders and officials. He urged the leaders to work with the Maoists to thwart what he called 'conspiracies' by the king. On the other hand, in his meetings with security officials, he urged them not to get distracted by talk of dialogue, and promised all kinds of support from India.[9]

The aim of this dual game was to prevent dialogue between the government and the Maoists, but the ceasefire was announced anyway. Just before its announcement, the foreign minister had gathered the heads of diplomatic missions in Kathmandu at the Mirabel Resort in Dhulikhel to brief them about the government's position. At that gathering, Indian Ambassador Shyam Saran kept asking one question: How did they contact the Maoists?

In other words, India was not pleased that the government and the Maoists were preparing for talks without its knowledge. If the rebels and the Durbar made a deal to end the conflict, Delhi would be denied any diplomatic benefit. Conditions, therefore, favoured the removal of Prime Minister Lokendra Bahadur Chand's government. Chand was never considered close to India. Delhi saw Surya Bahadur Thapa as a better alternative.

In the past, too, Thapa had replaced Chand in Baluwatar. The cycle was repeated. Thapa suddenly 'took ill' and rushed to Delhi, where he had long discussions with the Indian leadership. Before he left for Delhi, he visited the palace. He again went to meet the king upon his return. A few days later, the king replaced Chand with Thapa.

'I have not become prime minister under Indian influence,' Thapa felt it necessary to claim right after he was appointed. The Indian ambassador, Shyam Saran, also insisted that only negative perceptions made people see an 'invisible hand' behind the change in government. Rarely had such a clarification been made in respect to a change in government.[10]

There was an attempt to change the strategic balance within the Nepali regime during Prime Minister Thapa's term. He made several concessions with long-term significance to India, including allowing the Indian embassy to directly approach the local bodies for funding under the 'Small Development Project Schemes'; allowing it to station additional armed commandos on its premises; and permitting the opening of an Indian consular office in the key border town of Birgunj. In the past, Nepal had refused several of these provisions.

Prime Minister Thapa was also rather cool about the ongoing peace talks. His government's activities were directed not at convincing the Maoists, but at discouraging them. In this, Thapa was encouraged by discontent among army generals. The generals believed that the Maoists had chosen to hold talks because of the success of military operations.

The Maoists also used the seven-month-long truce to repair their organization, hold meetings and training exercises, and gain strength. Because King Gyanendra was scared by their tactics, his military officers convinced him that he could achieve victory through military means. The palace chose this option. It was in this context that the massacre in Doramba occurred. This was not the handiwork of a rogue military officer, but the consequence of a well-thought-out military policy. It was believed that the incident would push the Maoists away from the path of dialogue, and that is what happened. In any case, the Maoists were also becoming dishonest in their own negotiating proposition. They had just one concern: that they did not want talks to break down because of them. Doramba provided them with a sound excuse.

The level of rage that the military was harbouring against the Maoists was exposed in the manner in which they dealt with Khadga Bahadur Gharti Magar. Magar's only 'crime' was to allow the Maoist leaders to hold talks with the king's son-in-law and the palace military secretary at his residence. Immediately after the breakdown of the ceasefire, he was arrested and detained by the Bhairabnath battalion, on 22 September 2003. He was mercilessly tortured and died in custody on 24 February 2004.[11]

Government negotiator Narayan Singh Pun had fled to Britain by then because he was 'feeling insecure'. Palace Military Secretary Bibek Kumar Shah was also dismissed from service on 7 November 2003.

A new phase of war had begun in which Delhi and the Durbar were on one side, and the Maoists on the other.

10

Startling Raids

'There were other leaders, too, in Siliguri during that period. But it was only Comrade Kiran who was arrested. Kiran was aggressive towards India and was the main aide to the revolutionary headquarters.'

—Anil Sharma, a Maoist leader who
was arrested in Patna, India, claiming
that Kiran was singled out for arrest[1]

On 18 July 2002, senior Indian journalist and member of the Upper House, Kuldip Nayar, expressed anger as he sought an answer from the Indian authorities about the deportation of some Nepali Maoists from India. Speaking in the Rajya Sabha, he asked, 'I would like to know whether it is a part of the new policy of the government of India after the visit of the king . . . that the police would just pick up and deport anybody who is attending some open meeting or watching something. Is there no law, no authority or no court in the country?'

Responding to his query, Minister of State for External Affairs Digvijaya Singh said that four Maoist cadres, including

Ram Karki, had been arrested for taking part in a programme of the banned All India Nepali Unity Society. He added that they had been extradited under the Foreigners Act.[2] The Society, which was actively working to spread the Maoist network in India, had been banned under the Prevention of Terrorism Act 2002 on 1 July 2002, three days after King Gyanendra returned from a visit to India. The king had made a special request to Home Minister Lal Krishna Advani and other Indian leaders to control Maoist activities on Indian soil.

Following the order to ban the organization, on 11 July, the Indian authorities arrested Ram Karki, Maheshwar Dahal, Aditi and Moti Prasad Rijal as they came out of the Triveni Kala Sangam in Delhi. They were handed over to Nepal. Another Maoist leader, Bamdev Chhetri, was arrested on 5 September in Delhi and was also handed over. Three months later, in November, six Maoist leaders, including the Jhapa district in-charge Chatur Man Rajbanshi and the district secretary, Govinda Pokharel, were arrested from Siliguri. Sources claim that they were later shot dead after they were delivered to the authorities in Jhapa.[3]

India didn't take these steps only to keep the king in good humour. Its own dialogue with the Maoists had not proceeded well. Before his arrest, Bamdev Chhetri had himself talked to representatives of the Indian government in two to three phases. 'Our contact with the Indians at the diplomatic level had been established and ongoing since 2001,' said Chhetri, adding, 'They arrested and handed us over to Nepal after seeing that there was (going to be) no meeting point.'

Chhetri, the general secretary of the banned Unity Society, was a member of the library staff of the Indian government-funded Jawaharlal Nehru University. Two months after the ban, he was detained at the university premises at 10 p.m. As he was a Maoist leader openly active in Delhi, Kathmandu had been clamouring for his arrest for a long time.

Gaurav's arrest

Politburo member Chandra Prakash Gajurel, aka Gaurav, was the first leading figure to be caught. He was arrested from Chennai airport on 20 August 2003, just before the second peace talks were derailed in Nepal. He was attempting to fly to London via Frankfurt by using a passport in the name of a British well-wisher, Mark Avilon Digby (number 700882754).

Digby had exchanged his photo with that of Gaurav, and had sent the passport to him with an Indian visa—stamped by the Indian embassy in Paris. But the immigration officer at the airport was not convinced. Coincidentally, a staff member of the British Consular Office in Chennai happened to be in the airport at the time. When Gaurav could not answer ordinary questions related to London, his cover was blown. Then he no longer tried to hide his identity.

Gaurav had thought that Chennai airport would be safer than Delhi or Mumbai, but he hadn't realized that due to its use by Tamil rebels fighting in Sri Lanka, the monitoring there was quite strict. Instead of going to London, Gaurav ended up in a jail in Tamil Nadu. He had planned to lead a month-long organizational campaign in European cities such as Frankfurt, London and Brussels before meeting a representative of the Revolutionary International Movement (RIM) to exchange experiences of a people's war.

Though India had already handed over mid-level Maoist cadres, it showed no sign of doing so in Gaurav's case. India did not even allow a Nepali security team to interrogate him in Chennai. The Maoist leadership immediately inquired about Gaurav's arrest with a RAW official they were in contact with, and were told that the intelligence agency had no hand in his arrest. Gaurav fell into the net on technical grounds, because of his false passport. Judging by the way events unfolded in Chennai, it is likely that the RAW official was speaking the truth.

IB stepped in with support

The royal government in Kathmandu wanted India to arrest other Maoist leaders as well. After his 4 October 2002 dismissal of the government, King Gyanendra was at the centre of the Nepali power set-up. First Lokendra Bahadur Chand and then 'pro-India' Surya Bahadur Thapa were made prime ministers in quick succession. The king and Thapa both had close coordination with Delhi. Despite this coordination getting warmer at the political level, the security agencies were not whole-heartedly supportive.

The Nepali intelligence agency, the NID, has institutional relations with RAW. There used to be many bilateral visits. In 2003, NID Chief Haribabu Chaudhary and his deputy, Devi Ram Sharma, visited the RAW headquarters in Lodhi Road, New Delhi. They held a long discussion with RAW Chief Vikram Sood and his deputy, J.K. Sinha, who looked after the Nepal desk. After his retirement, Sharma recounted to me what happened in that meeting. According to him, they complained to their Indian counterparts: you guys detect even an ant walking in Nepal, but you say you have no knowledge of Maoist leaders staying in your country? How can we trust that assertion?

Albeit in a light-hearted manner, they went to the extent of saying, 'The weapons you provide our government at the central level, we hear that you provide similar weapons covertly to the Maoists.'

Though expressed informally, the charge was serious. The RAW officers rejected it firmly. But they were compelled to reply, 'Give us information if you have it and we will help'.

Yet, the Nepali side did not get any help, even after providing information. For instance, in November 2003, CPN–UML General Secretary Madhav Kumar Nepal was leaving for Lucknow for 'health treatment'. It was not hard to surmise that Nepal was in fact heading to Lucknow to meet the Maoist leaders. The NID knew that the western regional headquarters of the Maoists was based in Lucknow, under the command of Post Bahadur Bogati 'Diwakar'. Before Madhav Nepal reached Lucknow, the NID had alerted the Kathmandu station and Delhi headquarters of RAW, but they were not forthcoming. They tried to downplay the incident, saying, 'We don't think there will be a meeting with the Maoists.' Meanwhile, Madhav Nepal was already back after holding two rounds of talks, on 19 and 20 November, with Prachanda, Baburam Bhattarai and Krishna Bahadur Mahara.

Two months later, there were home secretary-level talks between the two countries, on 2 and 3 February 2004, in the Hyatt Regency hotel in Kathmandu. Such meetings are also attended by officers of RAW and IB. DIG Bhagwat Chaudhary attended on behalf of the NID. When the matter of the Maoists came up for discussion, the Indian side reiterated its old stance: We will certainly help if you give us information.

DIG Chaudhary was not amused. He said, 'Well, you guys did nothing when our chief informed you about the meeting that was taking place in Lucknow between CPN–UML General Secretary Madhav Kumar Nepal and Maoist leaders.'

That was an odd situation for RAW and IB officials when Chaudhary made this complaint in the presence of senior officials, including the Indian Home Secretary N. Gopalaswamy. They later complained to the newly appointed NID Chief Devi Ram Sharma. After the bilateral meeting, a joint secretary at the IB, Nehchal Sandhu, who later became the IB chief in 2010–12, went to the NID headquarters in Baraf Bagh, Singha Durbar. Sharma had known him for many years Sandhu gave assurances of 'real' help and collected mobile numbers and other information about Maoist leaders living in India from the NID.

Sandhu also held a separate meeting with the chief of the Directorate of Military Intelligence (DMI), Brig. Gen. Dilip Jung Rayamajhi, at Dwarika's Hotel in Battisputali, Kathmandu. Rayamajhi made requests similar to those made by NID's Sharma. The Nepali side wanted India to at least hand over politburo-level leaders. 'We are not assisting Maoists. We will soon prove it,' Sandhu said before returning to Delhi.

Following the decision of the bilateral security meeting of 22 and 23 September 2003, the IB and DMI had freshly established institutional relations. The Siliguri, Patna and Lucknow offices of IB had 'hotline' contact with the Royal Nepali Army. The IB was fighting Naxalites within India. Though they had built good relations with Nepali Maoists at one point of time, they were no longer in the mood to continue turning a blind eye. And, based on information from Nepal, it identified a few Maoist shelters in Delhi.

The NID and Nepal Police had each installed SSP-level officers at the Nepali embassy in New Delhi under diplomatic cover. The military attaché would also gather some information. But a large part of the intelligence gathering was done from Kathmandu itself. The army had created its small network in Delhi for this purpose. As assigning a senior official was not prudent, it had dispatched a *jamadar*-level junior officer and established him in an apartment in Delhi. He had been able to recruit various agents within the Maoist network. The most reliable among them was a person who presented himself as being close to the Nepali Congress party, but secretly helped Maoist leaders find shelter.

'In fact, that person even provided us with a list of army barracks in Nepal that would be targeted by the insurgents. Initially, we did not trust him. But later, his information proved to be accurate,' former DMI Chief Rayamajhi revealed to me. 'He gave us regular information for two years. He was the most useful of our agents in Delhi.'

The IB was preparing for a large operation based on information from the Nepali side.

'Attack on headquarters'

According to then NID Chief Sharma, three days after Sandhu returned to Delhi, he sent a message back: 'Some leaders have been identified'. The hiding places of Ram Singh (Matrika Yadav) and Minham (Suresh Ale Magar) had been detected.

'Didn't you find the big fish?' the Nepali official asked Sandhu, referring to the top leaders.

'The mobile numbers you gave did not work,' Sandhu replied.

'They are still there, according to our information,' the Nepali official said.

Sandhu did not show much interest in his remarks, but said, 'We will send you Matrika and Suresh, if you want.' He had a condition: 'They must not be harmed!'

In other words, the IB was looking for assurance that they wouldn't be killed. NID Chief Sharma immediately called the palace military secretary, Gajendra Limbu, but he was already aware. Prime Minister Surya Bahadur Thapa had also been informed by Delhi. And Sandhu had informed DMI Chief Rayamajhi. It showed how many channels Delhi had when it wanted to contact Kathmandu.

Actually, even the biggest fish, Prachanda, was about to be netted, but he got lucky. On the evening of 7 February 2004, Prachanda was about to leave for the apartment of Suresh Ale Magar in Delhi, according to prior arrangement, but his wife Sita asked him to stay back, saying it was already dark. Prachanda took off his shoes and stayed. That night, IB officers 'raided' the apartment and arrested Suresh Ale Magar, Matrika Yadav and Upendra Yadav.

Matrika had recently been elected president of Madhesi Rastriya Mukti Morcha at its second convention, but he had immediately resigned because the party had refused his proposal for 'one Madhes, one province'. Prachanda had summoned him from Patna to talk about the dispute. Matrika had come with a Madhesi intellectual he trusted, Upendra Yadav. On 6 February, Prachanda had held talks with Matrika and Upendra from 12 noon till 6 p.m. They had dispersed, promising to meet the following day. Prachanda escaped arrest only because he did not keep that promise. It is not clear whether the Indians would have handed him over to Nepal or would have clandestinely released him, had they been able to nab him. But Prachanda concluded that the raid was targeted at him. Overnight, he left for Mumbai.

Of those arrested, Upendra said he was taken to Narela near the Delhi–Haryana border and detained for one-and-a-half months at the Restricted Foreigners' Detention Camp. Republican leader Ram Raja Prasad Singh later said that he approached officials in South Block and used his contacts to free Upendra.[4] Matrika and Suresh, on the other hand, were put in a jeep and swiftly rushed to Gaddachowki near the Nepal border. DMI Chief Rayamajhi himself was there to receive them. They were then flown by helicopter to Nepalgunj, and from there to Kathmandu by a military skyvan.

A central member of the Maoist politburo, Suresh Ale Magar was one of the organizers of the World People's Resistance Forum in Mumbai, held not too long before his arrest. The IB considered it a Maoist front. Politburo member Matrika Yadav was a rising Maoist star in Madhes, but was 'unreliable' in the eyes of Indian officials. Not long before, he had rejected the offer of cash from Indian intelligence officials in Patna.

The Delhi 'raid' was the first result of a partnership between the NID, the Nepali Army and the IB, and the RAW was not in the picture in this episode.

Detention of Kiran

Two months after the Delhi raid, the number two leader of the Maoists, Mohan Baidya aka 'Kiran', was arrested from Siliguri. On 28 March 2004, Kiran had just been discharged from a local hospital in Sewak Road, after a cataract surgery in his right eye, when he was nabbed from the hospital gate. Along with him, Narayan Bikram Pradhan, a local Maoist cadre from Jalpaiguri and the son-in-law of Prachanda, was also arrested.

As the eastern command in-charge, Kiran was found to be operating from an office at Haidarpada in Siliguri. A team led by intelligence officer S.K. Mitra seized a radio transmitter, two computers, a photocopy machine and party documents from there. According to Kiran, he was interrogated by an IB official in custody.

The IB officials had many questions. What is the relationship of your party with Nepali speakers in West Bengal? Are you here to smuggle weapons to Nepal? Kiran claims that when they were dissatisfied with his replies, they even tried to use some force.[5] He was handed over to the local police three days later. He was charged with trying to revolt against the Indian government by working with Indian Maoists, and sent to Jalpaiguri prison.

Kiran was surprised that the IB knew his whereabouts. 'I had told the party about my trip to the hospital that same day. It must have been leaked from there,' he said. 'From my conversation with the IB officer, I came to know that a section of our leaders were somehow in contact with them.' Kiran did not want to divulge the names of those leaders.

When Kiran was arrested in Siliguri, Baburam was in Allahabad and Prachanda in Mumbai. Baburam was going to meet Prachanda. At the railway station, Prachanda's son Prakash came to receive him. He told him, 'Uncle, they have arrested Kiran uncle in Siliguri!'

The Maoists had already established institutional relations with the RAW. So, after consulting Prachanda, Baburam made calls to RAW officials. Madan Pyasi was one of the officials he talked to. Baburam had met Pyasi (then the Kathmandu station chief) when he was in Kathmandu for peace talks in 2002–03, with the full knowledge of the party. Baburam asked him, 'Why was Kiranji arrested?' But the RAW official denied any role, and said that the West Bengal government might be responsible.[6]

This reply did not convince Prachanda. He later obtained information that a top intelligence officer of Nepal had worked with the same Pyasi to arrest Kiran, and later taken him to Kathmandu. However, due to unknown reasons, the Indian side did not hand Kiran over.

Predicament in Patna

Soon after the RAW had washed their hands of the arrest of Kiran, the agency asked the Maoist headquarters, 'Are you guys holding any programme in Patna?' In those days, Patna and Siliguri each had a liaison office of the Maoist Eastern Regional Command. Following Kiran's arrest, Ram Bahadur Thapa 'Badal' had been appointed to head the regional command. Several leaders, including Badal and the military chief of the eastern command, Barsha Man Pun 'Ananta', were congregating in Patna en route to a training programme in the Nepali eastern bordering district of Panchthar.

According to a top Maoist leader, the RAW contact even cautioned them, 'Guys, be alert if you have any programme in Patna!' The headquarters then informed Badal and Ananta to be 'watchful' in their moves. They were heading to Patna from a politburo meeting in Mysore. After the RAW's warning, the leaders, including Badal, Ananta, Hitman Shakya and Agni Prasad Sapkota, took extra caution. They limited their contacts with cadres to phone calls, and moved only at night. Thus, they escaped arrest. But the mid-level leaders from the Valley bureau, who had also gathered in Patna, were not so lucky. They were a bit carefree in their movements—walking in groups, going to the cinema, and staying openly in a hotel—which made it easier for the intelligence officers trailing them to arrest them.

Kul Prasad KC 'Sonam', of the Valley bureau, his wife Tara Gharti 'Anjali', and Anil Sharma 'Birahi', were arrested from Arpit Hotel on Station Road. Kumar Dahal 'Bijaya', in charge of the Valley bureau, and Chitra Bahadur Shrestha, general secretary of the All Nepal Peasants Association, were picked up from a nearby cyber café. Hit Bahadur Tamang 'Shumsher', and his 'staff' Suman Tamang, were arrested from New Asian Hotel on Exhibition Road. Dilip Maharjan, chief of the Newa National Liberation front, and other cadres Shyam Kishor Prasad Yadav and Min Prasad Apagai, were also arrested from the city.

These eleven Maoist leaders and cadres were arrested from five different parts of Patna on 2 June 2004, all within half an hour. Those arrested included two politburo members, Sonam and Abhyas, and three central members, Shumsher, Bijaya and Birahi. Which agency made these arrests? Why did the RAW leak the operation? Was RAW itself involved in the arrests? Some people believed that there were no answers to these questions.

Anil Sharma 'Birahi', who was among those arrested, believes that the targets included leaders such as Badal and Prachanda. According to him, 'The intelligence wallahs had information that both those leaders were coming to Patna. Immediately after arresting us, they asked us for the whereabouts of those two leaders. The Indian expansionist power had attacked us with the aim of seizing our headquarters.'[7] In fact, the information that Prachanda was in Patna was incorrect, but Badal was indeed in the city.

The Patna arrests took place on the same day that, in Kathmandu, King Gyanendra re-installed Sher Bahadur Deuba as prime minister. Two days later, the Indian minister for external affairs, K. Natwar Singh, visited Kathmandu. He did not have to listen to complaints of India's non-cooperation in Maoist affairs this time.

There were several reasons why the Indian action, which started with the arrests of Ram Karki and Bamdev Chhetri, was beginning to get closer to Prachanda. These reasons included the cross-border spread of Maoism, the growth in Tarai violence, Maoist organization among Nepali-speaking communities in India, their hobnobbing with separatists groups, etc.

The spread of Maoism

Prachanda was playing with two different forces in India. Diplomatically, he was in contact with the Indian establishment. But he also had ideological, and to a certain extent even a material, partnership with the Naxalite rebels who were fighting that very Indian establishment. Like the PLA of Nepal, the Naxalites had their PGA or People's Guerrilla Army. The Indian Maoists also started calling 'bandhs' and holding 'peace talks' with the government. The level of these attacks increased. On 6 February 2004, the Indian rebels launched a coordinated attack against thirteen government offices in Koraput, a district headquarters in Orissa state (now Odisha), in a tactic that was quite similar to how the Nepali Maoists operated. It was a new kind of incident in India. A series of such incidents then followed, forcing Prime Minister Manmohan Singh to finally announce that Naxalism had become the greatest internal security threat to India.[8]

India had confronted Maoist rebellion since the 1960s. Because it started from Naxalbari in West Bengal, the movement was known as 'Naxalism' and the rebels called 'Naxalites'. The government partly suppressed the rebellion, but around the time that Maoism grew in Nepal, the wave of Naxalism re-intensified in India. In states such as Andhra Pradesh, Chhattisgarh, Jharkhand, Bihar, Maharashtra and Orissa, the movement emerged as a big challenge.[9]

There were several factions of ultra-communists in India that went by names such as the CPI–ML (People's War), and Maoist Communist Centre (MCC). They were not even on speaking terms, and fought each other often.[10] It was the Nepali Maoists who helped in the reduction of animosity between them. The Nepali Maoist leader Dinanath Sharma, who had worked closely with his Indian comrades, said, 'The situation was so bad that if we attended any programme of one group, the other group would get angry and refuse to speak to us. Gradually, we brought them closer and an environment was created wherein they could, at least, take part in a discussion together.'

The second task was party unity. In 1998, a smaller faction, CPI–ML (Party Unity) of Bihar, was merged into the People's War, based in Andhra Pradesh. In 2002, four smaller factions were merged into MCC of Bihar. The influence of Nepali Maoists was significant when two of the largest Naxalites groups, the People's War and the MCC, unified and formed the Communist Party of India (Maoist) on 21 September 2004. Their new name resembled that of their Nepali counterparts.

The ambitions of the Nepali Maoists grew from party unification to the creation of a regional front. During the period that it was in talks with the Nepali government, on 1 July 2001, a new regional umbrella organization of far-left rebels was formed, the Coordination Committee of Maoist Parties and Organizations of South Asia (CCOMPOSA), which brought together most of the Maoist groups active in Nepal, India, Sri Lanka and Bangladesh.[11]

The IB and the Indian home ministry sat up and took serious note of the spread of Maoist propaganda and insurgency across South Asia. They claimed in their annual reports that there were plans to form a 'Compact Revolutionary Zone' from Nepal to Andhra Pradesh.[12] The scattered Maoist movements in India were getting integrated, as evidenced by the mergers of Party Unity, MCC and People's War. Delhi thought that this could spell great trouble if the Nepali Maoists, too, joined the bandwagon. Consequently, Indian officials tightened their leash on the Nepali rebels.

The Tarai shock

Another reason for Indian apprehension was the growth of rebel activities in Nepal's southern plains, which bordered India. India was somewhat indifferent to the spread of Maoist activities in the high hills of Nepal. But when the insurgency rolled down the hills to the plains, it became alert. As the Tarai had an open border with India, and people on both sides had deep contacts and even family relations with each other, Delhi feared that the insurgency could easily spread to its villages in Uttar Pradesh and Bihar. The PWG from southern India had come right to the doors of Bihar by merging with the MCC. If Nepali Maoists, too, came down from Rolpa–Rukum, the combined force could be deadly. Prachanda wanted to make the Madhes (or Tarai) a centre of his political strategy. That was the reason he himself attended the first convention of the Madhesi National Liberation Front, held in Barhathwa of Sarlahi district, from 21 to 24 August 2001. It was his first attendance at a semi-public programme.

It is necessary here to recall how India treated the east–west highway in southern Nepal as its strategic border, not the Himalayas, as in the past. Delhi's concept that any breach of peace below the highway would hurt its national security came under challenge when the Maoists spread their activities to the region. Most Indian industrial investments in Nepal were located in this region. India had also demonstrated its interest in the region by opening a consulate office in Birgunj in 2003. This is the background to the arrest of the Maoists' Madhesi (Tarai) leader Matrika Yadav, and his extradition to Nepal.

Organizing the Nepali-speaking community

Another warning bell for Delhi was Maoist activity among the Nepali-speaking community in Siliguri and the nearby Dooars–Darjeeling–Sikkim region. For a long time, the Maoist headquarters were based in this region. It was chosen for its proximity to Nepal and the presence of a Nepali-speaking community (95 per cent in Darjeeling and 35 per cent in the Dooars) in large numbers, whose members the Maoists had started recruiting.

An Indian of Nepali origin, Narayan Bikram Pradhan, married (and later divorced) Prachanda's youngest daughter, Ganga. The son of a former Indian MP of the CPM, the old communist leader Badri Narayan Pradhan, Narayan was a teacher at a school in the Luksan tea estate in the Dooars. He was a former president of the All India Nepali Students Association, who later joined the Maoist movement, and was arrested along with Kiran.

Kiran's eldest daughter Lata, too, married a local, Rupesh Sharma, who used to work on a Nepali language weekly, *Sagarmatha*, published from Siliguri with government funding. Besides journalism, he was also engaged in Maoist politics as Narayan.

Top Maoist leaders Prachanda and Kiran were active in this region, India's so-called 'chicken's neck', where, in the 1980s, the Nepali-speaking community had organized a bloody struggle, demanding a separate 'Gorkhaland' state. The struggle had led to a deal to set up a 'Gorkha Hill Council' with a limited mandate. The anti-Gorkhaland policy of the CPM, which formed the West Bengal government, had piqued even the leaders and cadres of the party in this region. They floated a separate CPRM (Communist Party of Revolutionary Marxists) in 1997. Expressing solidarity with their position on Gorkhaland, the Maoists advanced their relations with the CPRM.[13]

The Maoists mobilized members of the Nepali-speaking community under the All India Nepali Unity Society. The Unity Society was winning support mainly through social work. For instance, they lent support to demands such as the recruitment of Nepali-speaking teachers in the Dooars, education in the Nepali language, etc. In September 2001, the society passed a resolution in support of a separate Gorkhaland at its programme organized at Rishi Bhawan, Siliguri, which was attended by some Nepali Maoist leaders. The programme was part of a campaign called 'From Mechi to Sunkosh' (a river separating Assam and West Bengal). The Indian establishment did not wish to see the

Nepali-speaking community become organized and powerful, and was startled by the Maoist activities.[14] Result: The Unity Society was banned and leaders in the region, including Kiran, were arrested.

Delhi's headache grew with the rapid advances made by the Nepali Maoists into Nepali-majority areas like Siliguri, Darjeeling, the Dooars and Sikkim, and its role in bringing about 'emergence' in 'Nepali nationalism'. The 'chicken's neck' is an area of great strategic importance for India, not more than 22 km wide and located between Nepal and Bangladesh, joining the rest of India with Darjeeling, Sikkim and the seven north-eastern states. It is also very close to the international borders with China and Bhutan.

In the eyes of Kathmandu, Siliguri was emerging as an even worse hotbed of insurgents than Rolpa. Therefore, King Gyanendra, in June 2002, and Prime Minister Sher Bahadur Deuba in March 2002, went to Kolkata to talk to the chief minister of West Bengal, Buddhadeb Bhattacharjee. Their request was the same: please arrest the Maoists who are active in Siliguri. CPM leader Bhattacharjee himself was not fond of the Maoists because, he felt, they were eating into the CPM's support base among the Nepali-speaking community. He saw the CPRM becoming stronger and the Gorkhaland demand re-emerging. The interests of both the centre and the state government converged. As a result, not only were activists Kiran and Ram Karki arrested, their Indian supporters, too, were jailed.

Cosying up to the separatists

The Maoists getting cosier with the separatist elements became another point that needled Delhi. The Maoists had maintained years-old relations with separatist organizations such as the National Socialist Council of Nagalim (NSCN), United Liberation Front of Asom (ULFA) and National Democratic Front of Bodoland (NDFB). Some leaders of these north-eastern Indian separatist groups occasionally visit Kathmandu to hide and meet others. Some Nepali-origin Indians from Assam and Nagaland also became the bridge between the separatist leaders and Nepali Maoist leaders.

According to Prachanda, even before he declared the people's war, people associated with ULFA and Naga rebels used to come to meet and 'hold good discussions' with him in Lalitpur.[15] They had also helped in the preparation for the people's war. Maoist Commander Chakrapani Khanal 'Baldev' had once gone to stay at ULFA camps. But the Maoists wanted to keep these relations hidden as far as possible in order not to irk the Indians. When the Maoists formed the 'South Asian Peoples' Journalists Association', they also included the editor of the Assamese daily *Aaji*, Ajit Kumar Bhuyan, who had been arrested numerous times and was accused of links with the ULFA.[16]

Several arms smuggling syndicates were active in north-eastern India, which smuggled arms from Cambodia and Myanmar through Cox's Bazaar and the Chittagong Hill Tracts. The ULFA and NSCN were involved. The Maoists, too, brought in consignments of ammunition through that channel. A few AK-47 rifles, smuggled by this route, were found in the hands of some Maoist insurgents. It was enough to scare the Indians.[17]

Were these the only reasons?

Not at all.

When India initiated the arrest of Maoist leaders, the Maoists had already established institutional relations with the Indian establishment, particularly its intelligence agency RAW. The underground relations with RAW grew at an amazing speed. In little time, the RAW knew the Nepali Maoists inside out. So it selectively targeted those Maoist leaders whom it saw would be 'unfriendly'. Mostly, they let leaders close to Baburam Bhattarai (who favoured peace talks) alone, arresting those close to Kiran and selectively targeting those close to Prachanda. Ram Karki and

Bamdev Chhetri were the only pro-Baburam leaders who were arrested in the initial phase. Later, most of those arrested (Kiran, Gaurav, Matrika Yadav, Suresh Ale Magar, Sonam, Lokendra Bista, etc.) belonged to the Kiran–Prachanda camp, who adopted a harder line and did not favour peace talks.

There was no single opinion within the Maoist party regarding the endgame of the people's war. Baburam and Kiran adopted different lines. Since 1999–2000, Baburam had advocated the establishment of a republic and a peaceful transformation of the people's war through a Constituent Assembly. However, in Kiran's eyes (he had been party general secretary even before Prachanda), this proposal was 'rightist'. He believed that the new people's regime could only be established through a communist revolution, as envisaged when the people's war was launched.

Prachanda, on the other hand, had concluded that he would not reach his destination on the basis of the people's war alone. He kept open the possibilities of completing the revolution through a Constituent Assembly, or through tactical flexibility, or by getting closer to the Indians. Tactically, therefore, he was closer to Baburam, but his strategic objective was closer to Kiran. Besides, he had not forgotten Kiran's past role in establishing his leadership. Kiran also had the respect of the party rank and file. Therefore, due to all these personal, organizational and strategic reasons, Kiran–Prachanda were on one side and Baburam was on another. It was not hard for Indian intelligence to discover these differences. They saw Baburam as a long-term strategic partner who wanted to return to the mainstream through a Constituent Assembly, and who harboured no ill feeling toward India.

It was only after Kiran's side was weakened that the Maoists could shift towards Baburam's line. All India's actions were geared towards sidelining the 'revolutionaries' and bolstering those who favoured compromise. But their tactic was counterproductive. Prachanda felt that he himself had narrowly escaped arrest. His close comrade Kiran was detained, as were youth leaders close to him. He reached a conclusion: instead of compromising with the Indians, he would return home and explore an alliance with the king instead.

It was the start of a new war within the Maoists, over the issue of Delhi versus the Durbar.

11

Struggle between the Comrades

'Their people's war is going nowhere. They will finish us off.
Please help.'

—Hisila Yami, wife of Baburam Bhattarai, appealing
to CPN–UML leader Madhav Kumar Nepal[1]

One in November 2003, the top Maoist leaders, known as 'the
headquarters', were in Delhi. The head of the overseas bureau, Top
Bahadur Rayamajhi, hosted a party on the occasion of Prachanda's
birthday at his hideaway in Gurgaon. Baburam Bhattarai and
Hisila Yami soon took their leave. Others were beginning to
depart too. But Prachanda and Badal were busy dining. Chums
since their college days, both leaders loved to drink. In informal
settings like this, they enjoyed their drink a good deal.

After a couple of pegs of whisky, Badal started getting angry.
In front of his friend Prachanda, Badal started yelling, 'How
dare you insult my family? How dare you say just anything to my
family? I cannot take it anymore; I will join hands with Baburam!'

Prachanda was taken aback. Whether intoxicated or not,
Prachanda's ears were always alert. He would not have minded

165

if Badal had only made some loud comments. But declaring his willingness to change 'camps' and side with Baburam was entirely unpalatable to Prachanda. Kiran had already been jailed. If the two remaining senior-most leaders, Baburam and Badal, came together, then his position could be challenged. The party lost its lustre after Badal's outburst.

Prachanda started investigating the reasons for Badal's 'revolt'. The reason, as he found out, was lingering petty disputes among the families of Maoist leaders and supporters, a large crowd of whom had gathered in Delhi. Leaders such as Prachanda, Baburam, Badal and Top Bahadur Rayamajhi used to stay in Delhi along with their families. Even as the families were mixing together well, there were also disputes brewing among them.

Badal's wife, Nainkala Thapa aka Barsha, was not amused with the manner in which Prachanda's wife Sita always talked about how she had 'saved' her marriage. Back in 1996, when an affair between Badal and another Maoist leader came to light, Sita had worked hard to bring about a reunion between him and his wife Nainkala. Thus, she had 'saved' the family. But Nainkala became furious when she kept mentioning the topic.

Badal, too, fumed when his wife complained to him. The reason was that the party had, in the past, not only accused him of 'sexual indiscretion' but also of 'demonstrating the Lin Biao tendency'. Lin Biao was once the closest comrade-in-arms of Mao Tse Tung in China. He was later accused of plotting against Mao and fell from grace. The accusation was therefore quite serious. Badal admitted only moral indiscretion, but never the charge of following Lin Biao. Yet, the party found him guilty of both and suspended him for two years from 1997 onwards. He was reinstalled in the party's central committee only after 1999. The charge that he followed in the footsteps of Lin Biao was only withdrawn in 2005, after the Chunbang conclave. Badal had always seen the hand of his close comrade Prachanda in these incidents. So the domestic issue in Delhi had reignited old wounds.

Return home

That domestic disputes had taken a political shape was obvious during the politburo meeting in Mysore in April 2004. Initially, Prachanda criticized Badal for demonstrating 'personalized problems' and 'narrow-minded communism'. Baburam said the problem was between Prachanda and Badal. Then Badal himself admitted his differences with Prachanda. Subsequently, leaders such as Top Bahadur Rayamajhi, Hisila Yami, Chakrapani Khanal 'Baldev' and Mani Thapa lent their support to Badal, and pointed fingers at Prachanda.

For the first time, they also raised questions about his role in connection with the series of arrests of senior leaders, including Kiran and Gaurav, and the failure to push the people's war in Nepal according to their expectations. Prachanda seemed to be in a minority in the politburo. In the fourteen years since he had taken up the party leadership, he had not faced such serious dissension.

Another leader, Narayan Sharma, came to his rescue. He said, 'Blood is being shed in the revolution. How can you question the leadership? The movement will not move ahead if somebody replaces the leadership by raising politico-organizational issues to corner Prachanda.' He asked Baburam, 'Can you become the alternative (party chairman)?' Baburam replied that he could not, adding that he had no interest in becoming party chairman.[2]

Middle-rung leaders such as Barshaman Pun 'Ananta', Netra Bikram Chand 'Biplav', Agni Sapkota, Hitman Shakya and Shakti Basnet were startled by the fast-evolving partnership between Baburam and Badal. They wanted a Badal–Prachanda alliance, and accused Baburam of being a 'rightist'. A recent article by Baburam published in *Nepal* magazine, in which he championed the cause of a 'democratic republic' and advocated partnership with parliamentary parties, was nothing but another example of his 'rightist credentials', according to them. Mostly active within Nepal, these young leaders had made up their minds to criticize Baburam in the politburo. But they came to know of the growing differences between Prachanda and Badal only upon reaching Mysore. So they decided among themselves that they must concentrate their attack on Baburam, if only to break the Badal–Baburam alliance. They, therefore, argued that there was no ideological contradiction between the chairman and Badal, and that they had just had family related emotional problems. The actual political contradiction, they added, was between Baburam and the chairman. Prachanda was quick to get their point, agreeing that 'it is just as the comrades have said'. With the environment in the meeting taking a new turn, Badal, too, quickly evaded further criticism by agreeing he had no ideological differences with the chairman.

Baburam was furious at the sudden unravelling of his new equation with the chairman. He then declared, 'Yes, I have an ideological difference with the chairman.' In an insurgent communist party, it is unimaginable to harbour differences with the main leadership. This was a 'crime' by Baburam. Besides, Baburam again stressed that he was correct in calling for an alliance with the parliamentary parties. Other, more hard-line Maoist leaders termed it nothing but a 'rightist' concept. In the end, the majority in the politburo was back on Prachanda's side.

The politburo meeting was taking place inside a decrepit factory. Three days after the meeting began, somebody started yelling that the factory owner was arriving, and they all dispersed without reaching any conclusion. The first thing Prachanda did after the meeting was to win Badal's confidence and attack Baburam. Prachanda resolved the personality tussle with Badal easily as they had had a close friendship for decades.

In the course of two years, one dozen central leaders, including five politburo members, had been arrested in India. Additionally, around 137 cadres of different levels had been similarly nabbed. In Prachanda's words, 'We all feared arrest.' He thought it would be suicidal to continue living in India. 'I thought that if I did not return in time, we would have met the same fate as Peru's Shining Path after the arrest of Gonzalo, or India's Naxalite movement after Charu Mazumdar was killed.' Prachanda, sensing conspiracies to control or terminate the party leadership and bring about dissolution of the movement, made up his mind to return home.

He faced a situation akin to that faced by the Nepali Congress's exiled leader B.P. Koirala, who returned home in 1977 calling for a reconciliation. India had allowed the Congress party to launch an armed struggle with the Nepali state from its territory three times in the past: in 1950, 1961 and 1973–74. But when their interests clashed, Indira Gandhi compelled B.P. to leave India. B.P. returned with the slogan of reconciliation, aimed mainly at a partnership with the king.

After eight-and-a-half years of enjoying the opportunity to launch war in Nepal from Indian soil, Prachanda also had to return. In June 2004, he reached Rolpa, tracing the long underground route to the district. Upon his return to the base area, Prachanda embarked upon a policy to mend ties with the palace.

Tantrum of tunnel war

Prachanda's first task upon reaching Rolpa was to organize a central committee meeting, the first one to be held inside Nepal since the launch of the war. The central members began to assemble in the northern Village Development Committee of Thabang, in some cases, after trekking for a month. The ten-day-long meeting, which started on 29 July 2004 in Phuntibang village, decided to make 'nationalism' the main agenda while pushing janabad as a supporting agenda. It announced a phase of 'strategic counter-attack' and made a 180-degree turn in the party's stance vis-à-vis India, concluding that 'Indian expansionism is the main obstacle to a progressive resolution' in Nepal. It decided that the silence adopted by the party on issues such as the 1950 bilateral treaty, Gorkha recruitment, Kalapani and other border incursions was a grave mistake.

The Phuntibang meeting concluded, 'The Indian expansionist power is plotting to cunningly proceed with its strategy of Bhutanizing or Sikkimizing Nepal, in a clear adherence to the expansionist Nehruvian doctrine of considering the Himalayan mountain range as their northern border.' It also concluded that India was planning a military offensive for the purpose and, therefore, decided to call for resistance by 'turning the whole country into a war zone and militarizing the ordinary people and, thereby, carrying the people's war to a new height.'[3]

After the Phuntibang meeting, Prachanda declared at a public assembly in Thabang, the historic centre of their 'people's war', 'In order to resist attacks by the Indian air force, we will dig tunnels and caves across the country. We will carry out a military campaign for the security of the people and their families.'[4]

After this announcement, Maoist cadres started to dig tunnels and bunkers across the country. Their so-called 'tunnel war' got a lot of attention. 'India was planning military intervention owing to its foolhardy hooliganism,' Prachanda thundered, adding, 'The intervention will lead to the spread of the people's revolution in India itself. They will be digging a grave for themselves. It will negatively assist in spreading revolutions across South Asia. And it will achieve the historic glory of modern Vietnam.'[5]

The Maoists planned to ally not only with the Naxalites, but also non-communist separatist groups. The Maoist mouthpiece envisaged it thus: 'It is certain that revolutionary parties like the People's War Group and Maoist Communist Centre, as well as organizations advancing national liberation movements such as ULFA, Bodo, KLO, will come to the field for such resistance. Likewise, it will ignite a fierce storm of people's revolutions in Bhutan, Bangladesh and Sri Lanka. The CCOMPOSA under the coordination of the CPN–Maoists will give leadership for a volcanic eruption of the revolutionary lava in the whole of South Asia.'[6]

The CCOMPOSA was formed as an umbrella organization of all Maoist parties and organizations in Nepal, India, Bangladesh and Sri Lanka. Not long before, a Communist Party of Bhutan (Maoists) had also been formed with the help of the Nepali Maoists. They wanted to cause a setback to Indian dominance in Bhutan through the spread of the people's war in Bhutan. The Nepali Maoists were even training a few Bhutanese refugees languishing in Nepali camps.

The Maoists determined that if India undertook military intervention in Nepal, it would rankle China due to its sensitive Tibetan affairs. It would increase tension between India and China, and, ultimately, undermine peace and order in all of South Asia. They also plan a campaign to evict Indian-origin traders from Nepal, to trigger a corresponding eviction of Nepali migrant workers from India, forcing those workers into the welcoming arms of the Maoists. In fact, their imagination was way out of proportion.

However, scattered violent incidents targeting India did take place. In March 2004, the insurgents torched eighteen Indian tankers in Kailali and one truck in Bhairahawa. They set off an explosion at the Modern Indian School in Chobhar, Kathmandu. They also bombed a Hetauda-based factory of Nepal Lever, then a subsidiary of Hindustan Lever. They also held fourteen unarmed soldiers of the Indian Gorkhas for three days in Kailali.

Talking to Indian Prime Minister Manmohan Singh on the sidelines of a BIMSTEC meeting in Bangkok, Prime Minister Sher Bahadur Deuba proposed jointly facing the Maoist challenge. Talking to journalists upon his return home, on 3 August 2004 at Tribhuwan Airport, Deuba declared that 'the Indian prime minister has told me that India is ready to support us in resolving the Maoist problem'.

Soon afterwards, Deuba went to Delhi, where he received a commitment from his Indian counterpart on joint action against the Maoists. The joint communiqué issued at the end of his visit described the Maoists as a 'common security challenge'. India increased the volume of its military aid to Nepal. Around that time, the Maoists obstructed the trunk road linking Kathmandu. Amid rumours of dwindling supplies of essential goods in the capital emerged reports of the Indians making 'contingency plans' to 'bread-bomb' by mobilizing their air force.[7] The strength of the Sashastra Seema Bal (SSB) posted along the Nepal border was further increased.

The quickly unfurling events pointed to one thing—that plans were afoot for war. Maoists cadres were given a different brief by their leadership. They were told about a partnership with the king to confront 'Indian expansionism', sowing confusion among the rank and file of the Royal Nepali Army, sidelining the parliamentary parties with the support of the king, and, finally, overthrowing the monarchy to complete the 'people's revolution'.

Following the Phuntibang meeting, the Maoists had come back to their pre-palace massacre analysis of the king and the army. They adopted a line to work together with Gyanendra, whom they had till recently accused of the murder of King Birendra. They concluded that once war against India began, they would have to 'cease the war with the Royal Nepali Army and declare a national war in order to safeguard the survival of the nation'.[8]

The Maoist assumption was that, 'The Indian military offensive will divide the Royal Nepali Army clearly into two sections. One section will favour national capitulationism and the other will be composed of patriots.'[9] Claiming that a few army generals had reacted positively to their assertions, the Maoist mouthpiece wrote after the Phuntibang meeting, 'Patriots will stand against the intervention and join the national revolutionaries after effecting organized revolt. Or they would aid and abet the people's revolution by various means.'[10] The insurgents calculated that the dissolution of the Royal Nepali Army would begin from that point onwards.

But these claims and assertions were mere fantasies or figments of fertile imaginations. The Indians were neither in any mood for armed intervention, nor were the objective conditions ripe for such action. Actually, Prachanda had radically raised the issue of nationalism when compelled to change tack and had joined hands with King Gyanendra. Thus, he spread the propaganda of a 'tunnel war'. The main aim of these statements was to get closer to the monarchy. Prachanda coined a phrase: 'We will hold talks with the master, not his servants'—a clear reference to his willingness to talk to Gyanendra and a snub to the political parties.

Holding hands with the master

The Maoists had not been able to forge any understanding, despite holding talks with the party leaders in Siliguri, Delhi, Patna and Lucknow, and despite two rounds of peace talks with the government in Kathmandu. Therefore, they were gradually concluding that they would need to talk directly to the king to have any fruitful dialogue. It also became a matter of compulsion once they returned home vowing war with India.

The Phuntibang meeting dropped previous slogans such as 'Down with monarchy', and also passed a resolution advocating 'dialogue with the master', i.e., the king. That resolution was enough to get the palace excited. The king was again itching to sack Deuba, like he did on 4 October 2002. In the meantime, Kathmandu witnessed unanticipated rioting. After news reports of the brutal murder of twelve Nepali workers in Iraq, an enraged mob took to the streets on 1 September 2004, setting fire to and ransacking dozens of offices of manpower companies (agents responsible for sending Nepalis overseas), and offices of media houses including *Kantipur* and *Space Time* as well as a few foreign airlines. Subsequently, the honorary ADC of King Gyanendra, Maj. Gen. (Retd) Bharat Keshar Simha, advised Deuba to step down. Caught in a tight spot, Deuba asked the king what he should do. Although the king answered, 'Bharat Keshar does not represent me,' Deuba was bewildered upon receiving information that the king was indeed using Bharat Keshar to pressure him.

The Royal Council was organizing countrywide programmes to boost the monarchy. At its central convention, also attended by the king, in Kathmandu in November 2004, it formally advocated active kingship. The streets were filled with painted slogans such as 'Come King, Save the Country'.

Having already suffered a summary dismissal back in 2002, Prime Minister Deuba was quick to smell conspiracy this time, so he was planning to announce a date for parliamentary elections. He had been handed the premiership with a specific mandate to hold elections. But the king was not amused. Instead, the king dismissed Deuba, for the second time, on 1 February 2005, accusing him of being incompetent. Like Prachanda had said, 'the master' had now seized power.

Baburam's revolt

If there was anybody dead set against Prachanda's policy of 'approaching the monarchy and maintaining distance from Delhi', it was his own comrade Baburam Bhattarai. During their return to Rolpa, Prachanda came together with Baburam through the Rapti hills, while Badal traced a different route; he first went to Darjeeling and then crossed the border into Panchthar, where he conducted training for cadres. He finally reached Rolpa after a month of trekking through the hilly villages. Throughout all this, close aides of Prachanda such as Ananta, Hitman Shakya and Agni Sapkota were with Badal. And they helped convince him to favour Prachanda's approach.

Prachanda himself held long talks with Badal at Rangkot in Rolpa. Other leaders also 'convinced' him. In the end, Badal even refused to meet Baburam ahead of the Phuntibang meeting.

At the meeting, Badal declared, 'The chairman is our leader. I will follow him.'

Baburam found himself isolated. After the central committee adopted nationalism as its main agenda, Baburam was painted as 'India-leaning', and was even accused of trying to hijack the leadership. In Baburam's words, he was 'gravely accused of forging a grand design by inciting Badal and other comrades against the headquarters (Prachanda) and, in the long run, seize the headquarters itself'.[11]

Even while in India, Prachanda had expressed suspicion that an internal leak was responsible for the arrest of his staunchest ideological ally, Kiran, and his own near-arrest in Delhi. His suspicion grew with the arrest of the group of Maoist leaders in Patna. In Patna, those considered close to Prachanda had been selectively targeted while those considered close to Baburam, such as Devendra Poudel 'Sunil', Devendra Parajuli and Kalpana Dhamala, had been left alone.

'Did you suspect Baburam's involvement in those arrests in India?' When I put this question to Prachanda in the presence of Baburam, while they were still underground in Delhi, Prachanda said, 'No, no,' four times. I could see that Baburam wanted to say something at that point, but he held back.

'So what is the reality?' I asked.

'It is not that I suspected him directly,' Prachanda said, pointing to Baburam. 'But I got a written report from comrades that in Patna, they were asked questions like "which faction do you belong to, Prachanda's or Baburam's?" And, in custody, the police official would thrash them, saying that I had not made a certain comrade a politburo member because he sided with Baburam. It did raise suspicions regarding the fact of the matter.'

Misgivings within the Maoists grew to such an extent that a large section started to believe that Baburam was planning a 'coup' against the headquarters with Indian support. That he was finishing off Prachanda to grab the leadership. This was why leaders and cadres close to Prachanda and Kiran were arrested in India.

Nobody could actually prove these accusations. So far as ideological norms are concerned, Baburam ought to have been the number one enemy in the eyes of India, because he was the architect of the concept paper that provided the ideological basis for the people's war. The paper terms 'Indian expansionism' the 'principle external enemy'. He had not only 'factually analysed' that 'subjugation and tyranny of Indian expansionism is the biggest example of imperial oppression', but also concluded the need to 'redefine relations with India in order to make Nepal independent in the truest sense'.[12]

Even after the launch of the people's war, Baburam's articles and writings were offensive towards India. He regularly raised the bogey of Sikkimization. In 1999, analysing the composition of the newly elected Parliament, he wrote, 'Actually, except for one Rohit, it can be said that all the members in the Parliament are, directly or indirectly, loyal to Indian expansionism. One cannot easily discount the possibility of this Parliament filled 99.9 per cent with Lhendup Dorjees, Sikkimizing the country at any time.'[13]

Baburam had also openly advocated a partnership between the monarchists and the Maoists on the agenda of nationalism. He had claimed to see the hand of RAW behind the palace massacre. However, after that period, he changed his mind. In his later opinion, 'The Narayanhity massacre was such a historic watershed or landmark, it represented a qualitative leap by the Nepali monarchy in its character, from feudalism to mainly comprador and bureaucratic capitalism.'[14] And then he fully committed to a republic instead of exploring any kind of alliance with the monarchy.

In fact, after the royal massacre in 2001 pushed the Maoists to stand against the Durbar–army combine with the objective of establishing a democratic republic, it fell on Baburam's shoulders to build the party's relations with the Indian establishment. As he had spent more than fifteen years living and studying in India, he was automatically considered a potential ally by the Indians. He was acquainted with leaders such as Sharad Yadav, D.P. Tripathi and Dr Karan Singh. Many of his college mates went on to become key officials in the Indian government. He now utilized those contacts and channels to establish a republic in Nepal. But, at the same time, Prachanda returned home and started advocating the issue of nationalism.

Baburam considered his party's changed policy of pointing guns at India without first taking its fight against the monarchy to a conclusion as 'wrong-headed'. 'As the foreign enemy forces, particularly Indian expansionism, have not as yet made a direct military intervention, the principle contradiction of the revolutionaries would be with the monarchy. This is a straightforward and crystal-clear question. It is quite worrisome when there is occasional lack of clarity and vacillation on this issue.'[15] He hit out at Prachanda, saying, 'It cannot be proper and correct to be seen as confused on the question of sub-stage of the democratic revolution born in our own specific revolutionary context and the tactics of the democratic republic, and to be seen looking toward the monarchy with hopeful eyes.'[16]

Should they fight the king with Indian support, or fight India with the king's support? This question led to a 'warlike' situation between him and Prachanda. Baburam thought that they should join hands with parliamentary parties and India, and all other amenable powers, to topple the monarchy. Prachanda, on the other hand, wanted to drop the issue of a republic for the time being, as he saw the 'nation under threat'.

Consequently, the Phuntibang meeting relieved Baburam of his responsibility as coordinator of the so-called central parallel government, the 'United National Revolutionary People's Council', and also of his leadership of the party's schooling and propaganda and publications department. Fuming at the decision, Baburam resigned from the standing committee. After an informal meeting with Prachanda, he withdrew his resignation—but the discord continued to fester.

Action, finally

On 11 November 2004, Baburam wrote a letter addressed to Prachanda, expressing his dissent on all of the decisions made at the Phuntibang meeting. And three weeks later, on 30 November, he listed his dissent in thirteen points, criticizing everything from the party's action plan to Prachanda's style of functioning.

Baburam's greatest objection was to the party's decision to join hands with the 'feudal' monarchy against 'republican' India. He also expressed dissatisfaction over what he called the centralization of leadership, in making a single person head of all three organs: the party, the People's Liberation Army and the political front (United Revolutionary People's Council). Baburam noted, 'The establishment of single leadership on the party, military and the political front is in violation of the letter and spirit of the thoughts crystallized by the second national convention and the resolution on development of people's democracy in the 21st century.'[17]

The second national convention of 2000 was an important turning point in the transformation of the Maoists. It had concluded that it was no longer possible to attain the party's goals through the path of a people's war alone, and adopted the path of the Constituent Assembly as a way out. Subsequently, the central committee meeting in May 2003 passed a liberal resolution entitled 'Development of People's Democracy in the 21st Century', thus leading a party that had espoused unitary politics to accept multiparty competition.

Baburam, therefore, felt that the Phuntibang meeting had embraced a regressive line by abandoning this long-held view of progressive reforms, which had corrected the weaknesses seen in the communist movement elsewhere in the world. Prachanda, however, only saw personal ambition behind Baburam's assertions.

A personality clash was a major factor behind the tussle between the two leaders, which both of them tried to disguise in ideological garb. For example, Baburam raised this question after Phuntibang: 'If responsible persons keep on presenting "Prachandapath" as synonymous with the person of Com. Prachanda, what would be its essence and relevance? Is it correct and prudent to put the photograph of Chairman Com. Prachanda alongside those of Marx, Engels, Lenin, Stalin and Mao?'[18]

Prachanda saw red when 'pro-Indian' Baburam turned against him. So he made up his mind to take a decisive step. On 25 January 2005, a politburo meeting was called in Labang, Rukum. Calling for action against Baburam, Prachanda presented a resolution at the meeting titled 'Comrade Laldhwaj's letter and other activities'. The fifteen-member politburo discussed it for six days and, at the end, passed the chairman's proposal by a majority of ten votes on 31 January.[19]

Charging him with 'violating the party procedures', the proposal relieved Baburam of all party duties and reduced him to an ordinary party member. Baburam's wife and alternative politburo member Hisila Yami (code name 'Rahul') also faced similar action for inciting her husband. Dinanath Sharma (code name 'Ashok'), who was close to Baburam, was forced to resign from the politburo on the charge of leaking secrets to the *Jana Dharana* weekly paper, which was run by his son-in-law. The paper had been accused by Krishna Bahadur Mahara of having secret links with royal elements.[20]

Baburam was served a three-point charge sheet: first, he was accused of attempting to run a parallel party headquarters; second, he was accused of advancing divisive policies; and third, he was accused of breaching party policy and discipline through his articles published in *Kantipur* daily and *Samaya* magazine. During the height of internal bickering, he had written an article in *Samaya* calling for permission to make public the internal dissension within the party. In *Kantipur*, he had made a veiled attack on Prachanda by stating that the 'tendency of princely fiefdoms exists in the party'.[21]

Although informally, Baburam was also accused of plotting against the party leadership and hobnobbing with the Indians, the charge sheet did not mention these accusations. Rejecting the charges levelled at him, Baburam spoke at the meeting, 'I did not register my thirteen-point note of dissent with such an intention. If you do not trust me, then, Pasang (commander of the PLA) is right here. Let him shoot me.'

Pasang quickly retorted, 'These are bullets exchanged for the blood of martyrs. They will not be spent on rightists.'[22]

12

The Royalist Turn

'During the course of peace talks, our leaders wanted to meet with the king but in vain. There was a strong chance of resolving the problem, had such a meeting taken place. Why shouldn't the king, who frequently meets with the people who have destroyed the country, meet with our leaders to resolve the main problem facing the country?'

—Matrika Yadav, in a letter addressed to the
king after he was handed over to Nepal by the
Indian authorities, who had arrested him in Delhi[1]

Baburam was in the custody of his own party. Dinanath Sharma and Hisila Yami shared the same fate. With nothing but a box full of books and a chair to his name, Baburam was escorted through snow-covered hills to Mirul village of Rolpa on 7 February 2005. They were lodged in a two-storeyed wooden house. Baburam Bhattarai and Hisila were given a room facing north on the upper floor. Dinanath had a room facing south. In a room between those two was posted a squad of guerrillas to keep round-the-clock vigil on them.

There was pain in his voice when Dinanath recalled those harrowing moments:

> Sleep left me completely at around half past two in the morning. I slowly opened the door and came out onto the veranda. Taking great care not to make any noise, walking carefully over those wooden planks, I tried to go outside to attend nature's call. But the comrade at the entry is quick. He is alerted by the smallest of the noises I make. They have been told to be extremely alert in guarding us . . . I used to find that comrade Laldhwaj (Baburam) also went through the same painful ritual. We feigned ignorance but we both knew it—we were suffering the same pain, the same fate. How could sleep come to us in such times?[2]

Ten days after they were taken to Mirul, on 16 February, when they were preparing to celebrate the anniversary of the people's war, suddenly, they saw an army chopper in the sky. 'When the chopper whirred over the house, I thought it was the end of us. We were peeping through the gaps in the wooden window. Then we heard the loud explosion of a bomb. Only after the helicopter flew over the hill did we heave a sigh of relief,' Sharma remembers.[3]

They were cut off from all contact with the outside world. Their communication equipment had been confiscated. Their meetings were controlled. They had no idea when they would be released. They felt they were in danger: there were leaders around calling for their 'head'. Politburo member Rabindra Shrestha made provocative remarks, saying, 'Baburam and Hisila should be jailed and hanged.'[4]

Ram Karki, a close aide of Baburam, was in Delhi. 'We used to hear about demands to bury Baburam alive,' he recalls. 'My eyes would well up while reading the letters he sent to me and (his daughter) Manushi from the war zone.'

Unable to bear it any longer, Karki contacted Prachanda in Rolpa via satellite phone and asked him the reasons for detaining

Baburam. Prachanda replied that it was untrue: 'Where have we detained him?'

Karki continued, 'We have heard he doesn't have good security. He has no phone.'

'Okay, he will contact you.' The following day, Karki received a call. Baburam was speaking in English. 'He never spoke to us in English. Perhaps there were people close to him and so he had chosen to speak in English to prevent them from understanding what he said.'[5]

The Maoists were suffering a serious upheaval. But the outside world didn't have any inkling. When we got a whiff of it, and when we got our hands on the four and thirteen-point letters presented to the party by Baburam, I wrote a cover story in *Nepal* magazine about their crisis.[6] When the news of the three leaders' confinement became public, after fifty-two days of detention, Baburam and Hisila were allowed to speak, albeit in a controlled environment. They revealed that they were in detention through this statement: 'We feel no resentment but extreme glory and joy to stay within the security perimeter provided by the People's Liberation Army.'[7]

Love–hate relations

The same age, from the same groups in school and college, from the same rural Brahmin family background—Prachanda and Baburam were contemporaries who had nevertheless entered politics through different routes. Even before the launch of the people's war, they'd had a love–hate relationship. The party rank and file was familiar with their ups and downs as well. Initially, the root of the dispute seemed to lie in ideology. Their debates used to focus on the direction of the people's war: whether they should follow Mao and establish a single base area (like Chinkangshan in China), or several such areas. Should they limit themselves to launching the people's war in rural areas, or expand to organize urban insurrection? They had heated debates over those questions.

Gradually, personal issues also crept into their debates. Baburam was better known to the public thanks to his stellar performance at school (he had topped the countrywide annual school board exams in his batch), and because he was a PhD holder. We in the media also used to carry Baburam's photograph whenever posting news related to the Maoists because most journalists did not know Prachanda, nor was his photo available. The fourth plenum of the party, in August 1998, decided to 'establish leadership in a planned manner'. Under this plan of 'centralizing leadership', they released a photo of Prachanda and made it mandatory for leaders to quote him in any political writings. Baburam criticized the decision as 'feudalistic' and indicative of a 'petty capitalist tendency of deifying'.[8]

The disputes arising from this were resolved somewhat after the central committee meeting of 1999. A middle point was reached whereby the pair would help each other in 'establishing Baburam within the party and establishing Prachanda outside the party'. A politburo member, Yan Prasad Gautam 'Alok', was detained on charges of 'inciting' the two leaders against each other. Alok was rising within the party, and he went to the extent of presenting himself as second only to Prachanda in the hierarchy. His ambition crumbled in an instant after the disciplinary axe fell on him. He was killed in an army attack while in party custody in Rolpa in April 2002.[9]

The process of establishing Prachanda's leadership, which started from the fourth plenum, reached its climax at the second national convention held in 2000, which elevated him from the post of general secretary to party chairman. It also declared 'Prachandapath' a guiding principle of the party. Both Baburam and Kiran supported it. A former general secretary, Kiran considered Prachanda to be one of his 'disciples'. Baburam, too, thought he had no need to worry so long as the party remained on the path he had shown. He once wrote, 'I never considered leading the party as number one.'[10]

But Baburam never gave up the position of number two, from which he sometimes challenged the number one, Prachanda.

Preparations to meet the king

Preparations to meet the king were proceeding when the party took action against Baburam. News reports emerged that the king's former secretary, Chet Bahadur Kunwar, had been abducted by insurgents from Rupandehi in November 2004. He had a long talk with Maoist leader Dev Gurung during his ten days of detention. It is not clear whether the Maoists had abducted him to hold talks. But immediately after he was released, Kunwar came to Kathmandu and gave the rebels' message to the king.

'We were in talks with some generals of the royal army,' Prachanda revealed. 'We talked about a one-to-one meeting between us (the king and Prachanda) and discussion over the way out. The talks were taking place via one particular general.'

In Prachanda's words, 'One of our politburo members was to first talk to him, and then arrange for the meeting between the heads. He (the general) assured us about arranging the meeting, but he kept on pushing the date. Besides, we were also facing serious dissension in the party.'

Finally the date and venue were determined: 4 February 2005 at the army-controlled Dhorpatan Wildlife Reserve in the upper side of Rolpa. The king was to arrive in a helicopter. The king's son-in-law, Raj Bahadur Singh, was the main medium of communication, and he was in contact with the Maoist leader Krishna Bahadur Mahara. Singh had frequented Delhi when Prachanda was based in the Indian capital, carrying royal messages. He had even stayed in Maoist safe houses at times. Apart from Mahara, Rabindra Shrestha was also active in arranging such talks (he had advocated dialogue with the new King Gyanendra even in the immediate aftermath of the royal massacre).

The general whom Prachanda had mentioned, who was opening the door of dialogue from the king's side, was none other than Rookmangud Katawal. He was considered loyal, having been brought up in the palace by King Mahendra, who brought him to the capital from Okhaldhunga in his childhood. Working in various capacities, such as the chief of the Department of Military Intelligence (DMI), midwest division commander and co-convener at the National Defence Council, Katawal was intimately involved in the Maoist conflict.

There were many channels for palace–Maoist negotiations. One was the chief of the NID, Devi Ram Sharma. Born in the western district of Pyuthan, Sharma had grown up in the company of local communist leaders. He was related to the Maoist leader Kiran. Their houses were close. In fact, Kiran and his father had tutored him in his early days. Sharma had contact with several Maoist leaders, from Krishna Bahadur Mahara to Krishna Dhwaj Khadka. And he was also trusted by King Gyanendra as his chief intelligence officer.

Via Sharma, the Maoists sent a message to the king: 'We will establish the king with the same speed that we are currently discrediting him. But he will also have to agree to empower the people. We will guarantee his respectful position.' Their conditions were: the king should keep his distance from parliamentary forces, such as the Congress and UML, and also from India.

The royal emissaries, on the other hand, imposed the following condition for 'nationalist partnership': take action against Baburam. There could be a pact between 'patriots' only after 'pro-Indians' were sidelined. Just as the palace wanted, the Maoists took action against Baburam on 31 January 2005. The following day, the king effected his coup. There was a planned king–Prachanda meeting set for 4 February. Was it only a coincidence that the party took action against Baburam just before the royal coup? Wasn't the scheduled meeting between the king and Prachanda related to the incident?

A few months later, I got to meet both Prachanda and Baburam together. I asked, 'You took action against Baburam at the same time as the king's coup and your planned meeting with the king. How did that happen?'

A candid person, Prachanda shrugged and laughed loudly in his characteristic way. 'That is where the timing was wrong! We later evaluated that the timing of our internal contradiction was wrong. We resolved it (the crisis), but at a high price.'

Due to a continued threat from the army, the party's internal rift, Baburam's revolt and pressure from India, Prachanda had thought that the 'partnership' with the king might be a favourable option. But he calculated wrong. On one side, there was the possibility of a party split after the action against Baburam, and on the other, the coup was going to empower the king.

Royal coup

The very evening of the day when the Maoists took action against Baburam, on 31 January 2004, King Gyanendra summoned four of his top security officers to the palace: army chief, Pyar Jung Thapa, police chief, Shyam Bhakta Thapa, chief of the Armed Police, Sahabir Thapa, and chief of NID, Devi Ram Sharma. They were briefed about the secret plan for a power grab by the king the following day. At the meeting, held in Mángal Sadan of the Narayanhity palace, the security chiefs were read the one-and-a-half page royal declaration that would be aired the next day. Sharma was surprised because the declaration did not mention anything about the Maoists. He shared his concern when he was asked his opinion. The others did too. Sharma was asked to add a phrase and Bangalore amend the draft. He added a sentence stating that the royal step was aimed at establishing peace and appealing to the Maoists to initiate dialogue.

Prachanda was informed, through Krishna Bahadur Mahara, that a royal address was on the anvil, with an appeal for dialogue. Prachanda also received similar reports from others. The politburo meeting that day had taken action against Baburam, and the members decided that they would declare the meeting closed only after listening to the royal address the following morning. Many of them had thought, 'The King will come out with a positive message on a Constituent Assembly or something similar.' Their expectations turned out to be totally misplaced. The king had carried out a blatant coup.

Actually, the draft of the royal declaration had been further edited after the security chiefs left the palace. It no longer made an appeal for dialogue with the Maoists. Rather, it warned the insurgents. 'We urge those who have lost their direction and have raised arms against the state and the people, committing crimes against peace and democracy, to return peacefully to the mainstream of national politics by giving up their arms,' the king intoned. 'If terrorist activities against the country and countrymen continue, the people will not tolerate it and the law will prevail.'

Prachanda fumed with anger at the royal statement. 'As we were in the middle of an internal contradiction, Gyane (a derogatory term for Gyanendra) came out with that statement, calling us terrorists who'd lost direction. Besides, he had seized all powers from the political parties and that closed the door for dialogue.' Immediately, he went inside a room to draft a response, which was issued within hours. It not only rejected the royal statement, but also included threats of retaliation and the announcement of three days' of Nepal bandh (general strike), starting the next day.

The establishment faction of the Maoists may have taken part in the meeting had the king given them some space by calling an all-party conference. Prachanda saw no meeting point. When he made his statement on 1 February, Gyanendra thought that the Maoists had already taken action against Baburam and had, thus, split. He foresaw a faction coming to the mainstream.

His calculation was to split the Maoist party, compel one side to come closer to the palace, sideline the parliamentary parties and, ultimately, take care of the Maoists too, ensuring a system of governance of its preference. But the wind of politics did not move in line with the palace's calculations. Nor did it move as per Prachanda's dream of an 'all-out victory'.

Dashed dream of 'all-out victory'

Following his 'betrayal' by the king, Prachanda planned to gain the upper hand by dealing a military blow. The Maoists planned a fierce attack on Gulariya, the district headquarters of Bardiya, in February 2005. It had to be cancelled at the last moment, however. The insurgents in that squad were instead mobilized to lay an ambush against government forces at Ganeshpur on the Nepalgunj–Gulariya road on 28 February 2005.

Perhaps the army was pre-informed. Anyway, it surrounded the insurgents. Thirty-seven of the 'best' Maoist fighters, including Brigade Commander Jeet (Prem Bahadur Roka from Jajarkot district), were killed in the ensuing action. They also lost sixteen additional guerrillas and two dozen modern weapons, including M-16 rifles. Prachanda called it the 'worst loss in the history of PLA'.[11]

The Ganeshpur rout put psychological pressure on Prachanda and created a 'political need for carrying out a big centralized military attack to deal a setback to the king'.[12] The target were the Khara barracks in Rukum. The central and western divisions, headed by Commanders Pasang and Prabhakar, were summoned and a joint attack was launched on 7 April 2005.

The Maoists were facing defeat on every front. Desperate for a victory, they had built up a force of 6000, including 2000 guerrillas, 2000 militias and 2000 party cadres. Two of their three divisions were thus brought in to attack Khara. Possibly, the Maoists had never before made such big preparations for an attack—what may have been their biggest attack till then. Yet, it was not successful. In the fight at Khara, they lost seventy-two guerrillas and over thirty weapons.

This was actually their second defeat at Khara. They had attacked the barracks on 27 May 2002 also. Nearly 150 guerrillas had died in that attack. Subsequently, the Royal Nepali Army had strongly fortified the hilltop location. The Maoists launched their second attack without a proper study of the barracks. Their two commanders did not coordinate successfully, mobilizing their divisions on their own. Their loss was inevitable.

The Maoists' internal politics might have taken a different turn had the attack been successful. Their plan was to capture Khara, then force the army out of Rolpa, Rukum and Salyan districts, assemble domestic and international journalists and declare a 'permanent base area' amid a huge public presence. Then they planned to install Prachanda as the chief of the central people's government (Revolutionary People's Council)—in other words, start a parallel government. That might have pressured King Gyanendra and opened avenues for a political give-and-take. They would also have implemented the Phuntibang decision to launch a 'strategic offence'. Inside the party, Baburam would be further weakened. Perhaps Baburam would not have been released so soon then.

Prachanda had painted the Khara attack as the one 'to open the door of all-out victory'. Its failure exerted pressure not on King Gyanendra or Baburam, but on Prachanda.

Prachanda under attack

Meanwhile, attempts were made not only to pressure Prachanda, but to kill him. After Khara, a unit of the Royal Nepali Army was in hot pursuit of fleeing rebels. They entered the Maoists' base area and launched a fierce aerial assault on the Rangsi region, where Prachanda was taking shelter. For the first time since he launched it nine years earlier, Prachanda came face to face with the war on the ground.

Prachanda's son Prakash Dahal, aka Sakar, was one of his staff at that point. He recalls, 'We felt a bit unsafe during the Khara assault. There were enemies everywhere. When we went to a village, we would hear of enemy patrols nearby and had to flee. The same thing would be repeated when we went to the next village. Helicopters hovered above us constantly. We were hiding and running helter-skelter.'[13]

It was difficult for them to save their skin. Prachanda felt additional psychological pressure due to the intense military attack on them. He concluded that it would only invite further risk to prolong the war. He had narrowly escaped an attack just before the Khara assault too.

That was a few months earlier, on 16 February 2005. The Maoists were celebrating the ninth anniversary of their people's war. That day, a military chopper dropped bombs targeting a house in Rangsi—the same one in which Prachanda had been living for three months. He escaped with his life only because he had changed shelter three days earlier. The house was destroyed. How did the army know about Prachanda's shelter, which was kept secret even from the Maoist rank and file? Because this happened at a time of internal conflict, suspicions of a leak floated around. Later, they came to know that the informant was one of the milkmen who supplied milk daily to that house.

Having returned to Nepal after feeling unsafe in India, Prachanda was now confronted with the same feeling at home. Not only did he have to save his own skin, he also had to protect one Andrei, a representative of RIM (Revolutionary Internationalist Movement), an international Maoist network, who had come to visit the war zone. The Maoists had already lost a few of their best fighters at Ganeshpur and Khara, and in the offensive the army launched after the coup. Among them were Brigade Commander Jeet, Brigade Vice Commander Basant (Prakash Rijal of Lamjung) at Rangkot, the Rolpa clash in April, and another brigade vice commander, Jwar (Dil Kumar Pun of Rolpa) in a clash in Arghakhanchi in June.

A month after the defeat in Khara, the insurgents launched a coordinated attack on four army facilities in Siraha, but only the unified command at Mirchaiya came under their control. The main target, the Bandipur barracks, held out. Three dozen insurgents were killed, including a battalion commander–commissar. The Maoists were getting pushed back to a 'state of defence'.

A message from across the border

Prachanda encountered challenges from every side. The king had betrayed him. The party was almost vertically divided into two camps following the action against Baburam. None of his armed attacks were successful. The Royal Nepali Army was turning more aggressive by the day. Rumours flew thick and fast. Prachanda heard a rumour that India was mulling a military operation to rescue Baburam. All these events had shaken him. So he had no option but to grasp with both hands Delhi's proposal of partnership.

Though he had come to Rolpa from Delhi, Prachanda had maintained his contacts in the Indian capital. Now the Indians invited him to side with Delhi rather than with the Durbar. The royal coup of 1 February 2005 drove a deep wedge between the Durbar and Delhi. Around that time, RAW got a new chief in P.K. Hormis Tharakan. He immediately contacted Prachanda via sat phone. Prachanda told me that after his conversation with Hormis, he also let Baburam talk to him, perhaps to indicate that he was not being detained. From a hilltop in Rolpa, Prachanda asked Tharakan to release Kiran from Siliguri jail. Tharakan inquired about the action against Baburam and indicated that he ought to be released too.[14]

The RAW chief invited Prachanda to Delhi for further talks. Prachanda invited him instead to Rolpa. Following the Khara defeat, Prachanda sensed a turning of the tide, and decided to send Baburam and the party's international bureau chief, Krishna Bahadur Mahara, to Delhi. He made this public through a statement, saying they had gone to 'understand the position of various political parties in India and the Indian government and to apprise them about the party's position'.[15]

It was a test that Baburam passed with flying colours. Even in the capacity of an ordinary member of the party, Baburam was able to hold fruitful talks not only with leaders of the Nepali Congress and the CPN–UML, but also with Indian emissaries. Meanwhile, the Royal Nepali Army attempted to foil the growing camaraderie between Prachanda and Baburam. At a press meet at the army headquarters on 19 May 2005, it released a covert audio recording in which one could hear Prachanda speaking:

> They (Indians) have got a report that Baburam is pro-India and, therefore, the party took action against him. We have got a message from "government level" that they will not release Kiranji and Gauravji before this matter is cleared. They are trying to give a message that (Kiran and Gaurav) will be set free only after (Baburam) is reinstalled in the party. Please understand that this has come from the Indian government itself.

In this secret briefing of his commanders and commissars, Prachanda further said:

> They are saying that the party headquarter (Prachanda) should go to India for talks . . . they want us to go there and want party headquarter there. What we have told them is . . . we have asked them to come here in our base area and we will provide a security guarantee. We have told them that Baburam and CM (Chairman Prachanda) will talk to them together.

The revelation of this conversation also put India in a diplomatic tight spot. Hours after the army released the tape, the Indian embassy in Kathmandu issued a press note stating it was unaware of its authenticity.

Two days later, Prachanda responded by saying it was indeed his voice. But he added, 'It is an old tape belonging to a totally different time, context and circumstances.' He said, 'The subsequent development of events has already proved many things related to Baburam wrong.'

Although Prachanda said the tape belonged to an 'old context', he could be clearly heard terming Baburam 'pro-Indian' and claiming that he had received Indian pressure to withdraw action against him. Baburam, who was in Delhi at that time, angrily responded with a statement on 24 May, stating, 'It is self-evident that anybody terming me pro-Indian will automatically be a pro-monarchist.'

The chief editor of the Maoist mouthpiece, the weekly *Janadesh*, Maheshwar Dahal, asked Prachanda, 'Comrade chairman, how do you feel being charged with being pro-monarchist when you are engaged in a life-or-death fight against the royal regime?'

Prachanda gave a sharp reply: 'Look, if anyone calls a black person black, it will invite rage. But if anyone calls a white person black, it will invite laughter. Terming us pro-monarchist is nothing but a joke.'[16]

The pro-Prachanda leader Ananta went a step further and suggested, 'Perhaps terming Prachanda pro-monarchist in his statement was a cover to hide his other leanings.'[17]

The relationship between Baburam and Prachanda, which was gradually warming, was damaged by the accusations and counter-accusations of being 'pro-Indian' and 'pro-monarchy'. It was suspected that the tape had been leaked to the army by someone in the party, but it later turned out that the army had found the tape in a bag of one of the insurgents killed at Khara. Amid this unexpected turn of events, Prachanda decided to 'take a big risk' and go to Delhi. In his own words, 'There were suspicions that the party's responsible leader himself (read Baburam) would orchestrate Prachanda's arrest there.'[18]

Nothing of that sort happened! Prachanda and Baburam engaged in a long conversation. They reached a pact. Prachanda made a 'self-criticism' about the content of the audiotape, while Baburam withdrew the notes of dissent he had submitted to the party. Right there in Delhi, the action taken against Baburam in Rolpa was rolled back. On 18 July, the party publicly announced that Baburam was reinstalled in the standing committee, while Dinanath Sharma and Hisila Yami were reinstalled in the politburo.

Intellectuals and rights activists from Devendra Raj Pandey to Mahesh Maskey played a role as catalysts in the truce between Baburam and Prachanda. Politics and geo-political compulsions also worked in their favour. A Nepali Congress leader, Pradeep Giri, was lobbying in Delhi for the release of Baburam in Rolpa. Once, he took his friend Durga Subedi to a meeting with the former Indian Prime Minister Chandra Shekhar. At the meeting, Chandra Shekhar wondered, 'Are these Maoists being used for pressure tactics by the Indian government?' Subedi later said to me, 'I was surprised by such a remark from India's former prime minister. But I did not give it much thought at that time. Later, when I recalled his words, I found they were quite meaningful.'

With the reinstatement of Baburam, the Maoists declared the Durbar, instead of Delhi, to be their principle enemy and made the establishment of a democratic republic their main goal. The new path now compelled them to get closer to the parliamentary parties and the international community, including India, and they were also compelled to adopt a political rather than a military path.

No success in solitude

When they launched the people's war, the Maoists had set an ambitious target—of fighting alone and completing their revolution by defeating the whole world. Over time, they concluded this was practically impossible. Then they tried to partner with the palace. That, too, was in vain. Their attempt to work with Delhi had also not been fruitful. Although they did utilize their relations with Delhi and the Durbar from time to time, in pursuit of tactical objectives, they could not gain strategic success. Neither could they capture Kathmandu by a military offensive, nor could they unleash a people's revolt. So they reached a conclusion: they could establish a republic and come to power only by working with the parliamentary parties. The parties enjoyed international legitimacy, which they themselves lacked. This conclusion forced them towards a political rather than a military line. Several circumstances compelled them to this conclusion.

Failure of the military line: When the Maoists fought the army, they were initially successful in attacks at Dang, Lisne, Gam and Achham, but after that their gains diminished. The army restricted itself to heavily fortified camps. American military experts had stressed the heavy fortification of army barracks in 2001–2. The insurgents incurred major losses trying to breach such fortifications. For instance, the Maoists lost sixty-four insurgents in the Sandhikharka attack, fifty in Jumla and ninety-two in Beni. Hundreds of others were injured.

The Maoists made numerous attacks on army barracks and district headquarters. But they could never hold them permanently. They had easily outdone the police, but failed to deal a decisive blow to the army. Their plan to instigate revolt within the army also failed. Only a few soldiers joined their force.

Inability to form a base area: The reason for the failure in their strategy of people's war was that they could not form a permanent base area, like in China, where they imposed their own regime and the enemy could not enter. In the Maoists' definition, 'Establishing a base area would mean sanitizing it totally of the presence of the reactionary regime and begin practicing the new people's democratic regime.'

The Maoists had passed the slogan of 'Let's move towards the great direction of establishing a base area' through the fourth plenum held in August 1998. They later declared the Rapti region a 'permanent base area', but it was merely propaganda. The Maoists did practise their 'people's regime' and 'people's courts', but these were of a temporary nature and partly symbolic. They did claim to have 80 per cent of the country under their control, but those territories were not permanent base areas like those created by Mao in China. The Maoists dominated those regions, having displaced the government machinery, but if the government's security forces reached those regions, the insurgents fled. Indeed, it was because of their failure to establish permanent base areas that the main leadership of the party had to stay in India for almost the entire period of the insurgency. In the one year they stayed in Rolpa–Rukum, the leaders, including Prachanda, faced tremendous pressure, as mentioned earlier.

Lack of international support: One of the major problems of the Maoists was their inability to win international support. They had good contacts with Indian Naxalites and armchair revolutionaries in Europe and America. The Revolutionary Internationalist Movement (RIM) did organize a few limited campaigns in a couple of European cities, but this was meaningless in terms of domestic political change.

In order to successfully complete their revolution, they would have needed the support from neighbours, either India or China, or a superpower such as America. Following the 11 September 2001 attacks by the al-Qaeda on America, the world situation changed drastically against them. They concluded that even if they somehow managed to seize power, they would be unable to hold on to it due to external intervention.

America was critical of the people's war from the very start. After 9/11, they hardened their position. China termed the Maoists 'anti-government elements' and adopted a hands-off policy. So far as relations with India were concerned, the Maoists did not encounter any tension with Delhi for the first eight years of their insurgency. For a year after 2004, the two sides were bitterly opposed. Finally, the Maoists decided to attempt political dominance in Kathmandu with Delhi's support. Delhi, on the other hand, never allowed them to capture power alone, only encouraging them to participate in the multiparty system.

The threat of destruction: With time, the Maoist leaders began to see the real threat of people turning against them on account of their growing internal problems, lack of discipline and anarchic behaviour. In November 2004, the people of Dullu in Dailekh district organized a campaign of resistance against them. In Naumule, they manhandled Maoist leader Khadga Bahadur B.K., handing over four of his aides and over 200 Maoist cadres to the local administration. Some of them were beaten black and blue by the mob.

The Maoists were taken aback. How could their war succeed if the people stood against them? In the central district of Chitwan, on 5 June 2005, thirty-nine innocent civilians were killed when the insurgents ambushed a passenger bus in Madi. The incident pushed the Maoist leadership further onto the defensive.

Although the Maoist organization and guerrilla strength had grown numerically, they had not all been well-trained. The organization was sliding towards anarchy and crime. These challenges exerted great pressure on the leadership, especially when they suffered other setbacks. As the road ahead seemed confusing, the clash among leaders was inevitable. This was one of the reasons for the collision between Baburam and Prachanda.

The only way out of all these problems was to find a soft landing for the people's war as soon as possible, ensuring maximum political gains. Therefore, they made a Constituent Assembly their bottom line, and decided to work with the political parties and India.

13

Decisive Drift

'I have told every leader of yours: there is no use of monarchy now in Nepal. The monarchy never gave anything to Nepal. But I would tell them, you should bring the change. I am very happy to be a part of that historic change in Nepal.'

—Shiv Shankar Mukherjee,
recalling his role as the Indian ambassador[1]

On the evening of 31 January 2005, Minendra Rijal, a Congress leader close to Prime Minister Sher Bahadur Deuba, was at a cocktail party. The deputy chief of mission at the Indian embassy, V.P. Haran, approached him and asked, 'Is the king up to something?' Rijal had no knowledge of anything, so he quickly contacted Home Minister Purna Bahadur Khadka.

The minister contacted the police chief, Shyam Bhakta Thapa. IGP Thapa took the call as he was returning from the palace with the chief of the Armed Police Force, Sahabir Thapa, and chief of the NID, Devi Ram Sharma. They had just been briefed about the royal step planned for the next day. But since they were told to keep it top secret, IGP Thapa was unable to reveal details, even to the home minister. He just hinted that 'something was cooking'. Minister Khadka then told Rijal that 'security was on red alert'. Perhaps the minister himself did not know anything more than that.

Early on the morning of 1 February, a well-known Indian national working at the Everest Hotel was told by a person who delivered flowers to the palace that 'something is about to happen'. The Indian shared the information with the Indian embassy. Quickly, the information was relayed to Delhi.

According to Devi Ram Sharma, the RAW chief called him and said in a warning tone, 'We are following the policy of supporting the twin pillars of constitutional monarchy and multiparty democracy. But if the king breaches it, we will no longer be compelled (to continue doing so).' Sharma informed the palace about the conversation, but King Gyanendra had already made up his mind. At 10 a.m., he addressed his subjects through radio and television and declared the royal takeover by invoking Article 127 of the 1990 Constitution.

Actually, the king had wanted to take this step after taking the Indian political leadership into confidence. He had therefore been trying to visit Delhi for a long time—but Delhi kept postponing his visit. He was finally scheduled to go to Delhi on a ten-day visit beginning 23 December 2004. The royal couple was about to get in the car for the airport. The prime minister had already reached the airport to see them off. Right at that moment, Indian Prime Minister Manmohan Singh himself called King Gyanendra, to inform him about the demise of former Indian Prime Minister P.V. Narsimha Rao. He regretted that the visit had to be postponed.

Three days later, India faced a natural calamity in its coastal areas caused by the tsunami. The king's visit was as good as cancelled. The king had wanted to make his move only after visiting Delhi, so that he could garner support there. When it became impossible, he went ahead anyway on 1 February 2005, planning to gain Indian support later.

Strong reaction

Immediately after the royal coup in Kathmandu, Indian PM Manmohan Singh called an emergency meeting of his cabinet security committee to review the latest Nepal situation. After the meeting, India took a strong position against King Gyanendra, which was evident in the statement issued by the external affairs ministry.[2] Shyam Saran, who had maintained a hawkish attitude against the palace during his stint as ambassador in Kathmandu, was now the head of South Block.

Saran issued a strong statement deploring the royal step: 'India has consistently supported multiparty democracy and constitutional monarchy enshrined in Nepal's Constitution as the two pillars of political stability in Nepal. This principle has now been violated with the king forming a government under his chairmanship. The latest developments in Nepal bring the monarchy and the mainstream political parties in direct confrontation with each other.' The statement added that such a step would only benefit the Maoists as a force that stood against both the democracy and the monarchy.[3]

India had not objected earlier when King Gyanendra had appropriated some executive power. But on 1 February, India concluded that the king had gone too far. Neither democracy nor constitutional monarchy was being maintained. Besides, the king had kept Delhi in the dark.

Five days after he took power, the thirteenth SAARC Summit began in Dhaka, on 6 February. The king's plan was to attend the summit himself, brief the regional leaders about the 'compulsion' that forced him to take the step, and win their support. He was preparing to extend a hand of friendship to Indian PM Manmohan Singh at the summit. But when the Indian prime minister declared his inability to attend, on security grounds, Bangladesh was compelled to suspend the summit. Earlier, on the third day after the royal step, the Indian army chief, J.J. Singh, had cancelled his scheduled visit to Nepal.

These were all attempts to pressure King Gyanendra. But he did not appear to be under pressure. Rather, he kept on trying to contact the Indians for support. He instructed his Foreign Minister Ramesh Nath Pandey to talk to Indian Ambassador Shiv Shankar Mukherjee two days after the coup. On 8 February, he sent the army chief, Pyar Jung Thapa, to meet Mukherjee. The following day, he himself spoke to Mukherjee. None of the three meetings were fruitful. Talking to journalists in Bangalore, Indian PM Singh said, 'What has happened (in Nepal) is a setback for democracy. India hopes that there will be a change for the better and democracy will be restored at the earliest.'[4]

The palace had expected political opposition to its step from India, but what really startled it was when Delhi stopped the supply of military material. India made a formal announcement on 22 February that it was stopping military assistance and supplies to Nepal, to apply pressure on the king. After its Foreign Secretary Jack Straw visited India and consulted with Delhi on Nepal, in the third week of February, the UK also announced the suspension of military assistance. And on 16 March, US Secretary of State Condoleezza Rice, during a visit to Delhi and after talks with Indian External Affairs Minister Natwar Singh, stated that India and the US were in full agreement that Nepal should return to the path of democracy at the soonest.[5]

The Royal Nepali Army was piqued at the decision of India and other countries to stop military aid. The army spokesperson said, 'It is an unfortunate decision. It will ultimately assist terrorism and the so-called people's regime of the Maoists.'[6] The palace was under pressure to ensure the resumption of military aid in order to prevent soldiers from becoming demoralized. Foreign Minister Ramesh Nath Pandey had a 'working lunch' with his Indian counterpart Natwar Singh in Delhi on 7 March. He tried to convince Singh about the necessity of the royal step. He was actually carrying with him a list of military wares they needed.[7]

Jakarta encounter

The Indonesian capital Jakarta was hosting a conference of Afro-Asian nations a few days later. King Gyanendra wanted to meet Manmohan Singh in Jakarta. So, on the eve of his departure to Jakarta, he released a few political detainees, including former Prime Ministers Girija Prasad Koirala and Sher Bahadur Deuba, and declared municipal elections. Still, Singh was not willing to meet him. It was only after he sought help from Singh's National Security Advisor M.K. Narayanan that the meeting could be confirmed.

When he spoke to Singh for forty-five minutes on 23 April, King Gyanendra basically made two points. One, if the Indians did not resume military supplies, the Maoists could take over. Two, Nepal would be compelled to seek help from China and Pakistan if India remained adamant. Meanwhile, the king had held a telephone conversation with the Pakistani prime minister, Shaukat Aziz, to seek assistance. Pakistan extended full support to the royal regime.[8]

India was in a fix. It neither wanted to see a Maoist takeover, nor wanted China or Pakistan to step into its zone of influence. Therefore, it exhibited flexibility by setting some conditions. NSA M.K. Narayanan was trying hard to repair Delhi–Durbar relations, while External Affairs Minister Natwar Singh also lent a hand in this direction. Natwar Singh, in fact, hailed from the same Jat princely family of Rajasthan whose daughter had married Gyanendra's only son, Paras.

The Indian Army, which considers the Nepali Army its 'brother army', was also pressuring the Indian government for a resumption of supplies. Their logic was that the army was the strongest institution in Nepal, and India should not reduce its influence over the army. The Indian army leadership reiterated that if they did not help, China or Pakistan would come forward. It was also said that continued pressure on Nepal would negatively affect the morale of over 50,000 Gorkha soldiers in the Indian army.[9]

Due to these reasons, India was ready to resume military supplies. The condition was that the king should be clearly seen to be restarting the political process. The king had also committed, in Jakarta, to release all political leaders, talk to them, call an election, and form an elected government. Yet, on 28 April, former Prime Minister Deuba was rearrested on charges of corruption in the Melamchi water project.

However, possibly having understood Delhi's predicament, the king lifted the state of emergency on 30 April and released a few more detainees. On 8 May, on her way to Nepal, the US Assistant Secretary of State Christina Rocca visited New Delhi, and was able to convince the Indians to give the king the benefit of doubt. The next day, Indian Ambassador Mukherjee informed the king of Delhi's decision to resume military supplies.

Military supplies, including few a Mahindra jeeps, bulletproof jackets, bunker protection devices and mine-proof vehicles entered Nepal by the Raxaul border. But Indian PM Manmohan Singh had to face a storm of protests after dispatching the first lot of military supplies. He could do no more. He had basically heeded the advice of Natwar Singh, but Natwar Singh had been unable to even take his bureaucracy in South Block along with him in this matter. The announcement of partial resumption of supplies had 'surprised' the Foreign Secretary Shyam Saran, and Nepal desk chief, Ranjit Rae (who incidentally became ambassador to Nepal from 2013 to 2017). They were unhappy. The major supporter of the coalition government in Delhi, the leftists, also created an uproar over the resumption, and so did the intellectual community in the capital. King Gyanendra also did nothing except to lift the state of emergency to help his cause in Delhi. Amid these adversities, military supplies were stalled again from 22 May onwards, never to be resumed during the royal regime.

Worsening relations

Though the king sent a few emissaries to Delhi, none were effective. Prabhakar Shumsher Rana, the king's business partner, was sent often. But after an incident involving a supposedly drunken brawl in Kathmandu, in which his son Siddharth was beaten by the Crown Prince Paras, he also drifted away from the palace. He later publicly stated that 'the 1 February royal step has helped neither the king nor the country'.[10]

Ostensibly to take part in the *India Today* conclave in the third week of February, the king dispatched his trusted aide Sharad Chandra Shah to Delhi. He mainly met with leaders of the opposition Bharatiya Janata Party (BJP). Since the Vishwa Hindu Parishad's Ashok Singhal had backed the royal step, the king expected the BJP to do the same. But that was not to be. BJP leaders Lal Krishna Advani, Jaswant Singh, Yashwant Sinha and Brajesh Mishra all toed the 'official line', that they could not support an active monarchy. Shah had a close friendship with Foreign Secretary Saran. Private friendships do play a part in diplomacy, but not always. Shah returned empty-handed from Delhi.

The Nepali mission in Delhi was headed by former Chief Secretary Karna Dhwaj Adhikari, who had an 'anti-India' image. He could not forge close relations with leaders of the ruling coalition United Progressive Alliance (UPA), which included the Indian National Congress, which had been at the helm of the Indian government since May 2004. The party did not have the best relations with the Nepali monarchy. Other coalition partners were also mostly supportive of a republic.

The king had enjoyed broadly two kinds of traditional backing in India: from the group of Hindu leaders and former princes active in politics (such as Natwar Singh, Jaswant Singh and Dr Karan Singh), and the indirect support of the Indian army establishment (who had traditional relations with the Royal Nepali Army), the

North Block (home ministry) and the IB, which were confronting the Naxalite challenge in India. Crucially, though, the king failed to win the confidence of powerful and decisive forces in India, including the ruling political parties, the bureaucracy of its external intelligence agency, RAW and South Block (the external affairs Ministry). Furthermore, there occurred some incidents which worsened his relations with India:

- The Nepali foreign ministry summoned Indian Ambassador Shiv Shankar Mukherjee and sought his explanation for some remarks he had made.
- The Royal Nepali Army blamed its defeat in the Pili clash in July 2005 on 'substandard' Indian INSAS rifles, which riled even the Indian army generals who were backing them.
- The army released an audiotape of Prachanda, which proved India's contact with him. In both the tape and the INSAS episodes, the Indian embassy had to issue a statement to refute the army's stance. Referring to the Prachanda tape, Nepal, on 20 May, issued an 'aide-memoire' warning India to stop interfering in its internal affairs.
- As per the three-year 'umbrella agreement' reached during the term of Prime Minister Surya Bahadur Thapa, the Indian embassy could undertake direct investment of up to NRs. 30 million in any part of Nepal, just by informing the foreign ministry in Kathmandu. This was stopped after the 1 February takeover.
- Delhi was enraged with the decision of the royal government to block the services of United Telecom Limited, which had investment from Indian government bodies.

Indian diplomats often remarked that they could not trust King Gyanendra because he did not 'walk the talk'. India's bitterness towards Gyanendra grew when he failed to keep his word given to Indian PM Singh in Jakarta. Then, at the Dhaka SAARC

Summit (October 2005), he proposed to make China a member despite India's opposition, while opposing the membership of Afghanistan, proposed by India.

Delhi started openly backing the mainstream political parties. The external affairs ministry even issued a statement on 16 May welcoming the common programme of protest against the royal regime announced by the seven parliamentary parties. Subsequently, the ministry spokesperson indicated a softening Indian approach towards the Maoists, saying there was no purely military way of resolving the problem.

Following his release, former Prime Minister Girija Prasad Koirala went to Delhi for 'medical treatment', where he had a long conversation with Manmohan Singh. He also met Sonia Gandhi, other leaders and former prime ministers there. Defence Minister Pranab Mukherjee praised him for his leadership in bringing the seven parties together.

Actually, the palace never imagined that the seven parties and the Maoists could reach an alliance, so it did not take things very seriously when the royal step pushed them closer together. The king had taken over by pointing a finger at the armed challenge of the Maoists. The Durbar was making every effort to convince Delhi that the first impact of any escalation in the civil war in Nepal would be felt by India, with which it had an open border. The king was under the illusion that Delhi would choose him over the parties. He failed to see the changed equation in Delhi.

Eyes on China and the US

With Delhi unamused, King Gyanendra started hinting that China was on his side. 'We should not be surprised by the displeasure of some of our friends towards our step. There are other friends who have supported it,' he said, adding, 'We have to do what we have to do. They have to say what they have to say.'[11] It was an open challenge to India—if not you, there are others to help the palace.

The king also looked to the US for support. During the twelve-point pact between the political parties and the Maoists, the American ambassador in Kathmandu, James F. Moriarty, travelled to Delhi to lobby against it. He later told a television programme that the twelve-point understanding was not aimed at ending violence, but rather at getting the support of the parties for the violence. After the 1 February royal step, Moriarty had said that the king should be given a period of one hundred days.

This was not Moriarty's personal opinion. Due to the Maoist threat, the US did look at the king differently from India. At the centre of the US and India's bilateral strategic partnership was the endorsement of India's civil nuclear programme by the US President George W. Bush in 2005. In most other world affairs, the two countries saw eye to eye, but in Nepal, they exhibited clearly different points of view. India was bent on bringing the Maoists and the parties together, whereas the US was against the idea. The US could not continue to support an autocratic king in Nepal and damage its wider relations with India. When the king attempted to build relations with China, and sought Chinese military assistance, the US rebuked him publicly.[12] In the end, it endorsed Indian policy on Nepal.

China, thus, was the final hope of King Gyanendra. The northern neighbour had not opposed the 1 February royal step. It kept mum on Nepal's 'internal affair'. A few days before he carried out the 'coup', King Gyanendra had shut down a liaison office of the Dalai Lama in Kathmandu. China was grateful to the king. Tibet being the main concern of its Nepal policy, China saw that it could gain much from the king's rule. Besides, the Chinese establishment has considered the Nepali monarchy to be a reliable institution since the time of Mao. In this context, Chinese Ambassador Sun Heping even lobbied a bit in the king's favour. Implying a reference to India, he said, 'Nepal itself is capable of resolving all its problems including that of terrorism (Maoists).'[13]

Actually, India had only one concern at that time: What if, indeed, the king aligns himself with China? On 21 March 2005, the vice-chairman of the royal government, Kirti Nidhi Bista, an ex-prime minister known to be 'pro-Chinese', announced that the two countries would sign a military deal during the upcoming visit of the Chinese Foreign Minister. Indian Foreign Secretary Shyam Saran immediately headed to Beijing. Fluent in Mandarin, Saran spoke to Chinese foreign minister Li Zhaoxing. He not only apprised him of the role being played by India in Nepal, but also requested China not to assist the Royal Nepali Army.

China did not seem to heed the Indian request. Foreign Minister Li arrived in Kathmandu on 21 March. His Nepali counterpart, Ramesh Nath Pandey, visited Beijing in July. Later, the Nepali Army Chief Pyar Jung Thapa visited China from 18 to 25 October. He signed a bilateral pact on military assistance, and even made a political statement praising China. Subsequently, there were news reports that eighteen trucks of weapons, including 12,000 rifles, 80,000 grenades, and 4.2 million rounds of 7.62 mm ammunition, had entered Nepal from China.[14] These events infuriated India. India's defence minister, Pranab Mukherjee, indicated he had taken a 'diplomatic step' regarding it.[15]

Another incident further enraged Delhi: Nepal's proposal to make China a member of the SAARC. This was the point of no return for the worsening Delhi–Durbar relations. The disagreement in Dhaka paved the way for the twelve-point understanding.

Despite having traditionally warm ties with the Nepali monarchy, China could not play a political role in Nepal. The Chinese had neither a wide political network in Kathmandu nor, really, the desire to play such role. Besides, it was not possible for China to continue supporting the king when it clearly saw that public opinion was quickly turning against him. In the end, the king was totally isolated—within and outside the country.

In this situation, the second Delhi agreement was signed in November 2005. In a striking historic coincidence, both the

Delhi agreements, I and II, kicked out the same king from Nepal. Gyanendra was enthroned (and removed) twice in his life. In 1951, a minor Gyanendra had been made king for a short period after his grandfather, King Tribhuwan, sought political exile in India along with the rest of his family, while the Nepali Congress militarily attacked the regime from Indian territory, leading Delhi to broker an agreement in Nepal, ending a century of the Rana family's dictatorship. Now, once again, Delhi was involved in brokering an alliance of opposition forces against the aristocratic regime in Kathmandu.

14

Delhi Agreement–II

'The decisive battles in this struggle (in 1950), however, had not been fought in the hills of Nepal but in the halls of New Delhi.'

—Leo E. Rose, an American scholar,
writing about the first Delhi Agreement[1]

After the seizure of power by King Gyanendra, all the seven parliamentary parties (NC, CPN–UML, NC–Democratic, People's Front, Nepal Workers and Peasants Party, United Leftist Front, and the Nepal Sadbhavana Party-NSP) had come together for the first time—and their consensus leader was NC President Girija Prasad Koirala. He had actually hit the streets after the king's first coup (on 4 October 2002), but his 'agitation' had not flourished. When parliamentary parties NC–Democratic and UML joined the government after 4 October, the unity among the parties had evaporated.

Having closely monitored the unfolding situation, Koirala decided to side with the Maoists after the 1 February royal coup. To do that he would have to, at the very least, accept the Maoist demand for a Constituent Assembly. The meeting of the seven

211

parties on 8 May 2005 came up with a joint commitment that
they could go up to the point of a Constituent Assembly for the
sake of 'total democracy and establishment of peace', through the
'restoration of Parliament, all party government and peace talks
with the Maoists'. Thus it was actually King Gyanendra who drove
the parties to it. Craving executive power, the king had trampled
over the 1990 Constitution and sidelined the mainstream parties.
Despite being republican by belief, the general secretary of the
UML, Madhav Kumar Nepal, had expressed his loyalty to King
Gyanendra after the palace massacre. Despite his misgivings,
Koirala had also played a major role in establishing Gyanendra on
the throne. Even when he was forced to resign the premiership
after the army, loyal to the palace, refused to carry out his orders,
Koirala did not make the incident public in order to prevent
further damage to his relations with the monarchy. After he first
met Prachanda, Koirala hastened to brief the king. The king later
misused the information he got from Koirala to provoke Deuba to
dissolve the Parliament and started the journey towards his ruin.

Prime Minister Sher Bahadur Deuba had always abided by
the king and the army's orders. He even split his party at the king's
instigation, but he was, in the end, sacked by the king. However,
for a week after the king sacked Deuba, Koirala and Nepal did not
react in the hope that the monarch would call them to form the
government. Only after the king installed his loyalist Lokendra
Bahadur Chand as prime minister did the leaders formally start
opposing him.

The parties again looked to the palace when the king made
Chand resign. Madhav Kumar Nepal went to the length of
registering a petition at the palace to become prime minister.
Again, the king chose another loyalist, Surya Bahadur Thapa,
over him. Even then the leaders continued to run from Nagarjuna
bungalow, located north of Kathmandu, to Narayanhity palace
to meet the king. Amid increasing national and international
pressure, the king reinstalled Deuba as prime minister. Deuba

was happy to get 'justice'. The UML, too, joined the Deuba government, touting it as a 'partial correction of regression'. But, as the palace insiders later disclosed to me, the king had other plans. He was still plotting his strategy to grab power.[2] Then came 1 February 2005. The leaders came to their senses only when the king grabbed power and sent them to prison.

The king's steps led the political parties to embrace the agendas of a Constituent Assembly and a republic. Due to its growing distance from the Durbar, Delhi, too, encouraged them to move closer to the Maoists.

The first round of talks

Girija Prasad Koirala went to Delhi on 4 June 2005. During his ten-day stay in Delhi, he met senior leaders including PM Manmohan Singh, chairperson of the ruling Congress party Sonia Gandhi, Defence Minister Pranab Mukherjee, and External Affairs Minister Natwar Singh. These meetings were brought to formal notice. But his meeting with Prachanda was kept under wraps.[3]

Koirala, who had flown to Delhi after his release from house arrest in Kathmandu, was hosted at the five-star Taj Ambassador hotel. From there, he travelled to Gurgaon, just outside Delhi, to meet Prachanda. It was their first meeting in three years. Many tumultuous events had occurred in the meantime—the dissolution of Parliament, the first royal digression of 4 October 2004, Maoist dialogue with the royal government, the breakdown of the ceasefire, and resumption of hostilities and so on. The three years had also been wasted in the Maoists' attempt to talk to the king instead of Koirala. So they tried to repair their ties. They reviewed the past and tried to find a common roadmap for the future.[4]

Baburam Bhattarai and Krishna Bahadur Mahara had reached Delhi in April, ahead of Prachanda's arrival. Their mandate was to talk to leaders of the seven parties and representatives of the Indian government. Many leaders of the seven parties had gathered in Delhi around that time. These included Krishna Prasad Sitaula, Mahantha Thakur and Shekhar Koirala of Nepali Congress; Pradeep Giri of NC–Democratic; Jhala Nath and Bamdev Gautam of UML; Hridayesh Tripathy and Rajendra Mahato of NSP; and Chandra Dev Joshi of United Leftist Front.

Most of them had individual and collective meetings with the Baburam–Mahara team. In the second week of June, a joint meeting was called at the residence of a Maoist sympathizer in Gurgaon, at which Sitaula, Shekhar and Girija Prasad Koirala from NC; Khanal from UML and Prachanda, Baburam and Mahara from the Maoists were present.[5]

The Maoists were eager to join hands with the seven parties, having concluded that they would not be able to hold a decisive agitation in Kathmandu single-handedly. Besides, they could also count on international support if they piggybacked on the seven parties, otherwise they were still 'terrorists' in the eyes of the international community. The seven parties also sought partnership with the insurgents in order to fight the royal regime and restore peace. They were trying to find a meeting point.

Prachanda made a proposal—to give a written form to the discussion. But Koirala was not yet ready to enter into a written pact with an armed group. Perhaps he was still exploring the possibility of a pact with the king. So when he returned to Kathmandu in the third week of June, Koirala did not seem in the mood for immediate agitation.[6] Instead, he started sending up trial balloons by saying that the Maoists were extremely flexible, and would accept 'ceremonial monarchy'. He added that he could not do anything more because he was out of power. As I heard from Koirala, he wanted to take a peace initiative with the Maoists after reaching some sort of an understanding with the palace.[7] He was getting positive feedback from the palace. In fact, this was aimed at keeping him under an illusion. The palace wanted to prevent the coming Eleventh Convention of the NC, set for August 2005, from discarding its long-held policy of supporting constitutional monarchy in favour of an outright republic. The palace, however, was in no mood to hand over power to Koirala. It saw no need to do so.

Fed up with the palace policy of 'divide and rule', the parties became increasingly aggressive and revolutionary upon their return from Delhi. A meeting of the NC Central Working Committee, in July, decided to keep all options, including amendment of the 1990 Constitution, a referendum and a Constituent Assembly, open. In August, the party convention formally decided to discard the policy of 'constitutional monarchy' from its statute. A continuous campaign for a republic, carried out by leaders like Narahari Acharya, greatly helped the party reach this point.[8] The UML held its central committee meeting in July–August. The two-week-long meeting decided to make a Constituent Assembly its immediate demand and determined to give 'complete shape to multiparty democracy through democratic republic'.

Attack in Pili, ceasefire in Delhi

Despite their continued negotiations in Delhi with the parties, the Maoists had not ceased their attacks inside Nepal. The biggest attack of this period was the attack on an army camp at Pili in Kalikot district on 7 August 2005. Fifty-eight soldiers were killed, and sixty abducted. The Maoists captured 200 weapons, losing thirty insurgents in the skirmish.

The army had set up their camp there just twelve days earlier. They had gone there to assist in road construction. The camp had not yet been fortified. For the first time since their success at Arghakhanchi, the rebels took full control over an army camp. It created a sense of enthusiasm among the increasingly demoralized guerrillas.

Prachanda wanted to extract political mileage from his military victory. He announced a unilateral ceasefire for three months on

3 September. This played a decisive role in isolating the king and bringing the parties closer. Apart from encouragement from the Indians, the Maoist leadership had taken this decision following their meeting, towards the end of August, with the special envoy of the UN general secretary, Lakhdar Brahimi, and another official, Ian Martin. The seven parties, India, the European Union and the United Nations welcomed the ceasefire.

The king found himself cornered by the Maoist ceasefire. However, he did not reciprocate. He was forced to cancel his plan to visit the UN general assembly at the last minute. His intention to garner international support against 'Maoist terrorists' was pre-empted. Besides, he also learnt that he would not be invited to a reception hosted by the American president. His decision to cancel the visit revealed the impossibility of defending his coup in the international arena.

The people were excited by the prospect of peace raised by the Maoists' unilateral ceasefire, but the king's government termed it a conspiracy. Perhaps the situation might have changed if the government had reciprocated. Instead, the king announced elections for local bodies. The people took it as the king's attempt to invite further discord with the parties. He'd blundered, again.

After announcing the ceasefire in Delhi, Prachanda headed to Chunbang for a crucial party meeting.

New course from Chunbang

The Maoists were going through two significant processes around that time. The first was the reunion of Prachanda and Baburam Bhattarai; and the second was building trust with the seven parties. Both these events needed to be discussed and endorsed by the party. So Prachanda called a central committee meeting in September in Chunbang, Rukum district, in midwestern Nepal. The meeting endorsed the demand for a Constituent Assembly and a democratic republic.

The previous year, the Phuntibang meeting had termed India the 'principal enemy'. The Chunbang meeting mellowed this stance, instead targeting 'American imperialism'. And, unusually, it criticized China for trying to expand its role in the traditional Indian zone of influence in South Asia. 'Having made economic progress by handing over the keys of the market to American imperialism, the revisionist rulers of China have engaged in a cunning process of expanding their influence in South Asia.'[9]

The Chunbang meeting also resolved internal dissension. Baburam found it comfortable to accept Prachanda's leadership once the party took up his political line. He withdrew his notes of dissent and Prachanda withdrew allegations of 'rightist capitulation' levelled at Baburam, ending the party's action against him.

Baburam's address at the meeting was filled with praise for Chairman Prachanda. 'What I have seen in our comrade chairman, and what I have found myself attracted to are his qualities of Lenin. I find him almost equal to Lenin.' He added, 'I will play my role as a noble aide to the strong headquarter that we have established in the leadership of comrade Prachanda. My role will not be anything more than that. I feel as if I have merged with him.'[10]

The Chunbang meeting also settled the years-long festering tension between Prachanda and Badal. 'Am I Lin Biao? Did I conspire to overturn comrade Prachanda's leadership?' Badal asked in an emotional appeal, once again refuting the charges once levelled at him of undermining the leadership of Prachanda. He eloquently admitted having made mistakes. 'I may have tried to overtake the commander, whether unknowingly or deliberately. It created problems. It compelled tears to flow. I should have lost before my commander. I should have obeyed my commander's order without question. Perhaps I did not do that, sometimes. I lost when I tried to overtake the commander. I accept my loss from this platform of history.'[11]

It was in 1997 that Badal had faced the party's disciplinary action on charges of conspiring to seize party leadership and demonstrating 'Lin Biao-oriented tendencies'. After he, like Baburam, declared that he, too, had 'merged' into Prachanda at the Chunbang meeting, all the previous party actions against him were withdrawn. Both the two leaders, who had only the year before challenged him at Mysore, were now submitting to his unchallenged leadership, which made Prachanda more powerful. The party that had drifted to the brink of division had united.

Following the Chunbang pact, Baburam started working to 'establish' Prachanda. He kept a low profile in the subsequent series of interviews, press meets and assemblies, and let the chairman hog all the limelight. Thus started the exercise for a gradual and planned push to make Prachanda public. Baburam was pleased at the fact that the whole party now espoused his demand for a Constituent Assembly and a democratic republic—a position for which he had to face the party's wrath only a year before.[12] But there were leaders on both sides who were not happy with Chunbang's conclusion. Rabindra Shrestha, close to Prachanda, and Mani Thapa, close to Baburam, walked away from the party in February 2006 to form a 'new cultural revolution group'. The party expelled them as 'deserters of revolution'.

The party projected the decision of the Chunbang meeting as an extension to the preamble passed by its second national convention. That convention had, in 2000, proposed a Constituent Assembly. In 2004, the party had made 'nationalism' its main agenda, and the agenda of Constituent Assembly was effectively set aside. The Chunbang meeting reverted the party to its old position. There was a possibility of other forces interpreting their 'republic' as a 'communist/people's republic'. Therefore, the Maoists added the qualitative epithet 'democratic' before republic. They planned to use 'democratic republic' as a vehicle to reach their strategic goal of 'people's republic'. The document passed by the Chunbang meeting reads:

> The party takes the democratic republic neither as a form of bourgeois parliamentary republic, nor directly the new people's republic. This method of republic alongside extensive restructuring of the state aimed at resolving the existing class, ethnic, regional and gender problems, will the play the role of a transitional multiparty republic. It is certain that the reactionary class and their parties will make every effort to turn it into a bourgeois parliamentary republic but our party of the proletariat will try to turn it into new people's republic.[13]

Although the Maoists had adopted the policy of working together with parliamentary forces against the monarchy, they had not abandoned their ultimate goal of 'new democracy': something which many mainstream parliamentary parties took to mean establishing a 'communist republic'. In other words, the Maoists wanted to take advantage of the parliamentary parties in their forward march. Therefore, the Chunbang meeting also decided to establish seven divisions of the People's Liberation Army and expand their military strength.

Unable to capture urban areas and unable to exert decisive pressure on Kathmandu, they were restricted to the rural regions. If this stalemate continued, they saw the risk of the local population turning against them. So the Chunbang meeting also changed their slogans and made urban areas the focus.

They planned to orchestrate a united movement with the seven parties in Kathmandu. They also planned to turn the movement into a 'people's revolt'. Even if that did not happen, they thought at least the royal regime would collapse under the pressure of a joint movement. So Prachanda declared at the Chunbang meeting, 'A big storm is coming to Nepal very soon. It will be a big storm, and it won't be too long before it comes.'[14]

Rolpa deal

Coinciding with the Chunbang meeting in Rukum, the central committee of the UML decided to take an initiative to bring the Maoists to a more peaceful path through dialogue. UML leader Bamdev Gautam left for Rolpa in October. Gautam had been in contact with Maoist leaders for a long time. When he reached Rolpa, the Maoist leaders had just concluded their Chunbang meeting. As per its 'mandate' to reach an understanding with the parliamentary parties, the Maoists struck a first agreement with the UML.

After long discussions, the leaders of the Maoists and the UML signed a six-point deal in October 2005. The deal was signed by Prachanda, Baburam and Krishna Bahadur Mahara on behalf of the Maoists, and by Gautam and Yubaraj Gyawali on behalf of UML. It was essentially aimed at targeting the monarchy, adopting a Constituent Assembly and a democratic republic as key positions, and reducing distrust between the two parties through enforcement of a code of conduct. According to the six-point code of conduct, a mechanism would be formed to investigate past incidents aimed at each other, district secretaries of both parties would be in regular contact, the parties would inform each other about their programmes, and so on.

In the course of agreeing to the six points of the deal, Gautam had talked to Madhav Kumar Nepal, who was in Delhi at that time, via Prachanda's satellite phone. The Royal Nepali Army intercepted the conversation and subsequently dispatched Ranger commandos to the Nuwagaun area on 24 October. They searched the whole area, inquiring after the 'whereabouts of Bamdev Gautam'. In fact, their target was Prachanda. But when they reached there, Gautam was already back in Dang, whereas Prachanda had reached a safe area.

The Maoist–UML deal would not have been possible if Gautam had not travelled to Rolpa. Without it, the door for the Maoists and the seven parties' twelve-point understanding a month later would not have been opened.

Twelve-point understanding

It was difficult to reach Delhi from Rolpa at that time. The Maoist leaders could face serious trouble from Nepali security personnel posted at the border. They were therefore late. Eleven days after they left Rolpa, Prachanda, Baburam and Mahara reached New Delhi on 7 November 2005.

Most of the bilateral and multilateral talks in Delhi were arranged by the Maoists. Interestingly, the Indian authorities did not obstruct them, but rather were found to be supportive in some instances. Special care was taken to avoid their programmes being leaked to Nepali spooks.

Nepali Army Colonel Padma Bilas Karki, Nepal police SSP Deepak Shrestha, and NID SSP Bishan Shahi—all posted at the Nepali embassy in Delhi—had enlisted some local Nepali youths to keep an eye on the visiting leaders. The main target of Nepali intelligence was Koirala, for obvious reasons.[15] But Koirala easily duped them. He was provided with three cars by the Indian government. Under the pretext that they were small and uncomfortable, he asked for a vehicle from the Nepali embassy. Ambassador Karna Dhwaj Adhikari provided his own Prado SUV (registration 51 CD 1) to the former prime minister. The intelligence guys thought that their driver alone would be enough to report on his whereabouts. But Koirala cleverly used the car only for official visits. Information related to such visits was quickly transmitted to the palace secretary, Pashupati Bhakta Maharjan, and from there to King Gyanendra. But this information was useless.

Prachanda would secretly enter the hotel when Koirala was away, and they held talks when he came back. However, most of their bilateral and multilateral talks were held at the Tel Bhawan in Noida. Whenever Koirala had to go there, he would inform the driver that he was resting in his room and would ask him to go out for lunch. Leaving the embassy-provided car at the hotel, he would sneak out and travel in a Maoist-provided car or, at times, take an auto.

The meetings between the Maoists and the seven parties separately had been taking place in Delhi since the second week of November. The decisive meeting was held on 17 November. The top flat of a four-storey house belonging to a Nepali-speaking Maoist sympathizer at Deoli Gaon of Khanpur, Delhi, was chosen as the venue. Maoist leaders Prachanda, Baburam and Mahara reached there in the morning. UML General Secretary Madhav Kumar Nepal, his comrade K.P. Oli, NC leaders Krishna Sitaula and Shekhar Koirala, and Unity Centre leaders Amik Sherchan and Narayan Kaji Shrestha 'Prakash' also arrived. Koirala was the last, as he took time to shrug off the spooks on his trail, but he was unable to walk up to the top floor due to his health. A nearby one-storey building was immediately selected. The leaders conducted their dialogue sitting on the eight available plastic chairs and a bed.

According to the leaders, the bilateral and trilateral meetings of the Maoists, NC and UML had begun from early morning. They formed a team to draft the agreement. The team included Baburam, Oli, Sitaula and Prakash. Giving the team necessary instructions and authority, UML General Secretary Nepal left for Kathmandu the next day. NC President Koirala followed him the day after.[16]

The team continued meeting for five days. The first draft was made by Prakash. UML leader K.P. Oli went through it, adding some points to make it eighteen points altogether. Then came the turn of Baburam, who reduced it to twelve points. Krishna Prasad Sitaula made a few changes. After five versions, the draft was finalized. Baburam's aide Bishwodeep Pandey typed it on his laptop. The twelve-point understanding declared: 'We are committed to ending autocratic monarchy and the existing armed conflict, and establishing permanent peace in the country through Constituent Assembly elections and a forward-looking political outlet.'

Both the Maoists and the seven parties agreed to elections to the Constituent Assembly, but they differed over how. The seven parties first wanted the reinstatement of the Parliament dissolved in 2002. The Maoists wanted to form the assembly through a round-table meeting. Koirala pressed for the Parliament's reinstatement. He seemed to care for nothing else. He was constantly asking, 'Have you written (about) the restoration of Parliament?', returning to Kathmandu only once he was assured of its inclusion in the draft. Finally, the parties agreed to meet midway by 'continuing talks and finding common understanding', and expressed both their positions in the twelve-point document.

Another technical argument was over the joint signature. Koirala proposed releasing the same agreement but with separate signatures. He wanted to avoid any national or international complexities arising out of joint signature in an agreement with the Maoists, who were still 'terrorists'. In the end, he won. The Maoists and the seven parties released the twelve-point understanding separately, from Delhi and Kathmandu, respectively, on the same date.[17]

In the course of drafting the twelve-point understanding, the Maoists and the UML had already agreed on a republic. But when Congress said it could not immediately accept a republic, the language of the twelve-point understanding was adjusted, and its aim was stated as 'to end the autocratic monarchy' and 'to establish total democracy'. The Maoists interpreted this as a republic, whereas the leader of the seven parties, Girija Prasad Koirala, interpreted it as being in favour of a 'ceremonial monarchy and establishment of democracy'. Anyway, the agreement had brought both the forces together against the monarchy. The existing three poles of Nepali politics—the parliamentarians, the monarchists and the Maoists—were now reduced to two.

By entering into a partnership with the Maoists, the leader of the seven parties, Girija Prasad Koirala, had totally changed his party's traditional political direction. Even after he was dismissed by the king in 1961, the then Congress leader and prime minister, B.P. Koirala (Girija's elder brother), had never abandoned his belief in constitutional monarchy. Instead, the elder Koirala had returned to his country from exile in India in 1977, calling for 'national reconciliation' to explore ways for a compromise with the monarchy. He always rejected a partnership with the communists. His younger brother Girija Prasad, on the other hand, had sided with revolutionary communists and sought Indian blessings for that partnership. The strategy brought about a major shift in the ideological principles of the NC.

In the past, the parties had been the main targets of the Maoist insurgency. They had lost hundreds of their cadres. The party governments of recent years had also carried out campaigns of repression against the insurgency. A high number of insurgents, too, had lost their lives in this process. With such opposing forces coming together, Nepali politics had reached a significant landmark. The international community, including India, the United Nations and the UK, welcomed the twelve-point deal.

Entering into an agreement with the warring Maoists meant endorsing the violent aspects of their people's war. In other words, the parties were prepared to execute a fusion between their peaceful movement and the rebels' violent insurgency. As such, one could see simultaneous organization of rallies by the seven parties in urban areas against the local elections (called by King Gyanendra), and the attacks on government installations by the Maoists. Meanwhile, the twelve-point understanding also included a point that read, 'With the end of autocratic monarchy and in the course of holding elections to a Constituent Assembly, the armed force of the Maoists and the Royal Nepali Army will be kept under the UN or other reliable international supervision.'

Common course of Constituent Assembly

The Maoists presented the Constituent Assembly as a vehicle by which they could return to mainstream politics. For the Nepali Congress, the demand was something it had made way back in the 1950s, but had subsequently dropped. On 18 February 1951, when then King Tribhuwan returned to Kathmandu from Delhi, he announced at Kathmandu airport, 'Let the system of governance of our people, from now onwards, be in accordance with the *ganatantratmak* (republican) Constitution formed by an elected legitimate assembly.'[18]

The king had just returned after the first Delhi Agreement, which dismissed the 104-year-old Rana oligarchy from Nepal and paved the way for cooperation between the palace and the then revolutionary Nepali Congress party.

The legitimate assembly the king talked about was a Constituent Assembly. The NC made this its main agenda. But once Tribhuwan was back on the throne, he broke his promise. His successor, King Mahendra, went a step further and arranged for the drafting of a Constitution through a commission and, in 1959, held elections to a Parliament instead of a Constituent Assembly. Eventually, the Nepali Congress dropped the agenda. It continued, however, to remain an agenda among a section of communist parties. In 1962, at the Darbhanga plenum of the Communist Party, its leader Mohan Bikram Singh proposed backing a Constituent Assembly. Later (after the restoration of democracy in 1990), his party, the CPN–Masal, boycotted the general election in 1991, calling for the election of a Constituent Assembly instead.

When they launched their people's war, the Maoists had not advocated for a Constituent Assembly. They wanted to establish a 'new people's democracy'.[19] Had they been able to conquer the state of Nepal through military means, they would probably have termed the demand for a Constituent Assembly as 'rightist'. But when they concluded that on their own they would not even be able to establish a 'bourgeois republic', let alone a 'new people's democracy', they chose to embrace a Constituent Assembly. They also saw the possibility of winning the support of various leaders and workers of the Nepali Congress, intellectuals, common people and the international community by giving a 'rebirth' to this agenda.

Less than four years after they launched the people's war, the Maoists' central committee meeting, in 1999, advanced the slogan of 'abrogation of reactionary Constitution and the right of the people to make their own Constitution'. It was from that point that writing a Constitution by the people or, in other words, through a Constituent Assembly, was envisaged as a point of landing for their people's war. The issue started being discussed when they presented this demand during their attempts at a dialogue with the government of Krishna Prasad Bhattarai. As they began the first peace talks in 2001, the Maoists crystallized their demands as 'round-table conference, interim government and new Constitution through a Constituent Assembly'.

In the eyes of the Maoists, accepting the 1990 Constitution and becoming a part of the old regime would be tantamount to abandoning the justification of their people's war. However, the Maoist leaders concluded that they could, at least, achieve a republic through a Constituent Assembly, and create a launch pad to establish a 'new people's democracy'.

The first Delhi Agreement in 1951 had toppled the Rana oligarchy and restored the Shah dynasty's rule in Nepal. The second Delhi Agreement, in 2005, paved the way for toppling that Shah dynasty.

15

Seen and Unseen Actors

'Since RAW was not answerable to any outside agency—and the control of the PMO was perfunctory, at best—many officers thought that they were not only above the law but a law unto themselves.'

—Maj. Gen. (Retd) V.K. Singh, a military officer who worked as a joint secretary at RAW, describing the mindset in the organization[1]

The day was 17 August 2009. I had never before witnessed such a fierce windstorm in my life. The traffic in the Indian capital was blocked by fallen trees and branches strewn everywhere. We reached the Taj Mahal Hotel on Mansingh Road an hour later than scheduled. Thankfully, the person we had gone to meet was still waiting for us. He was the former chief of RAW, P.K. Hormis Tharakan. This man had played a decisive role from behind the scenes to forge the twelve-point understanding.

Akhilesh Upadhyay, the editor of the *Kathmandu Post*, and I were there to attend a meeting arranged by one of our Indian journalist friends. Tharakan had come from Bangalore that day. We made our way into the Machan restaurant on the ground floor.

Tharakan began the conversation, saying, 'I have read your articles. Tommy also used to talk about you.' Tommy, or Thomas Matthew, had worked as an associate editor at the *Himal South Asian* for a long time when I was working at its sister fortnightly magazine, *Himal*. He was a relative of Tharakan. In the course of our conversation, it became clear that he knew a lot about us. It may have been natural, for he had worked as RAW's Kathmandu station chief for two years (1999–2001), and had gone on to become the chief of RAW.

Tall and soft-spoken, with a thick white moustache, he appeared to be a quintessential south Indian. Tharakan did not look like a spymaster from any angle. But his professional record had established him as a successful intelligence operator. He also had a significant hand in shaping Indian policy firmly in favour of a republic in Nepal.

An IPS (Indian Police Service) officer of the Kerala cadre, 1967 batch, he had, coincidentally, taken over as chief of RAW on the very day King Gyanendra executed his 'coup' in Nepal. On that morning of 1 February 2005, the first 'briefing' he made as the director of RAW, to his boss PM Manmohan Singh, was about Gyanendra's coup. For the next two years of his term, the situation in Nepal was never off his desk. The period witnessed tumultuous events: the twelve-point understanding, the second people's movement, the peace process, Constituent Assembly election and the declaration of a republic. In all these events, Tharakan played an invisible role.

When we met him, Tharakan had already retired from RAW. He was working as a member of the National Security Advisory Board. In the course of two hours of conversation on his Nepali experiences, he was quite open. 'The main credit for whatever we did should go to Prime Minister Manmohan Singh. He always encouraged us to think and work differently, not in a mere traditional manner,' Tharakan said, adding, 'The twelve-point understanding took place in special circumstances. It was possible only because of many factors. Such opportunities do not come always in history—that is simply not possible.'

Tharakan did not try to seek the credit of bringing the Maoists to the mainstream, and sidelining the monarchy, for himself alone. 'Many played important roles to make it possible,' he said, recalling the roles played by the CPM General Secretary Prakash Karat, its leader Sitaram Yechury, and D.P. Tripathi of the Nationalist Congress party, among others. He seemed to have a lot of hope and trust in the Maoist leadership. 'I have interacted with almost all the main leaders of Nepal. Among them, I have seen the firmest political will in Maoist leaders. I have many expectations, particularly of Baburam Bhattarai.'

According to the Indian professor S.D. Muni, the association between Baburam and Tharakan goes back a long way. 'A good personal connection between the new RAW Chief Hormis Tharakan and Baburam Bhattarai facilitated better understanding between the Maoists and the RAW, which kept in regular contact with the Maoist leadership.'[2] Muni, who knew both closely, wrote, 'Tharakan was politically progressive and viewed Nepal's Maoists as leading a genuine struggle for Nepal's socio-economic transformation.'[3]

When he worked in the position of 'minister consular' at the Indian embassy in Kathmandu, Tharakan was known for his disdain of the parliamentary parties such as the Nepali Congress and the CPN–UML. Naturally, he may have been attracted to the Maoists as a new force. Professor Muni mentions Baburam having spent some time in Hormis's home state of Kerala in the course of his education. Baburam has had an association with Kerala since his school days. Verghese Thomas, from Kerala, was the principal at Baburam's Luitel School in Gorkha. Baburam had a great respect for the principal. Tharakan had contact with Verghese when he came to Kathmandu.

During his term as RAW station chief in Kathmandu, political leaders, security officers and businessmen gathered regularly at Tharakan's residence at Bishalnagar. Baburam instructed his confidante Mumaram Khanal to pay a visit to Tharakan. Khanal has said that while he did not meet Tharakan, he instructed Om Sharma, a Maoist worker under him, to make contact.

A few weeks after the palace massacre, Tharakan returned to India, handing over his role to Madan Pyasi. Around that time, the Maoists established institutional relations with RAW and the exchange of letters began, which has been discussed in the chapter 'Dual Diplomacy'.

Upon his return from Kathmandu, Tharakan first became the Director General of Kerala Police, and then chief of RAW. He then renewed his Nepal contacts. Before he sent Baburam (facing party action at the time) to Delhi, Prachanda had a chat with Tharakan via satellite phone. Later, Tharakan held long conversations, first with Baburam, then with Prachanda, in Delhi. He not only reduced tensions between Baburam and Prachanda, but also created an environment conducive for the Maoist–seven party alliance against the king.

When, on 4 June 2005, Congress President Girija Prasad Koirala reached Delhi after his release from house arrest, the first person who met him at his room number 105 at the Hotel Taj Ambassador was none other than the RAW Chief Tharakan. He also met other leaders of Congress and the UML. All these efforts led to the signing of the twelve-point understanding.

The twelve-point deal brought the Maoists to the mainstream. But, as Tharakan wrote in an article, the entry point for their transformation was the political document entitled 'Development of People's Democracy in the 21st Century', passed by the Maoist central committee in May 2003. The document includes their first-ever commitment to returning to political competition. At the time of that decision, the RAW was building its relations with the Nepali Maoists. The document, probably, was the reason they trusted the Maoists thereafter. In one of his *Indian Express* articles, Tharakan states that this document, not the king's coup, played the decisive role in the Maoists accepting multiparty competition and entering into a partnership with the parliamentary parties.[4]

Tharakan was closely associated with the twelve-point understanding, the toppling of monarchy, and the Maoist transformation. But he wanted to give much of the credit to the then foreign secretary, Shyam Saran. He said to us, 'He had much influence over the PMO and the political leadership. He played the most important role at that time.'

Saran, like Tharakan, had spent an important stint in Kathmandu, as Indian ambassador in Nepal, before he became foreign secretary. A 1970 batch Indian Foreign Service officer, Saran superseded over half a dozen senior officers to reach the top. In Nepal, he had overseen the establishment of an Indian consulate office in the key border town of Birgunj; expanded India's relations in the southern Tarai plains; and built close relations with political parties. When he became foreign secretary, it was in Nepal that he could really show some achievements. So he pushed Nepal to the top of the list of priorities in South Block.

Like Tharakan, he also wanted to clip the wings of the Nepali monarchy and bring the Maoists to the mainstream. In the last press meet he hosted as ambassador in Kathmandu, on 9 July 2004, he had said, 'India has stated quite clearly that this is a problem which cannot be eliminated by military means alone. It is a problem which also has economic and social roots.'[5]

While Saran was in favour of curtailing the rights of the king, the then minister for external affairs, Natwar Singh, was more favourably disposed to the palace. Natwar Singh was forced to step down amid an oil-for-food scandal in November 2005. The minister of state for external affairs, Anand Sharma, was closer to the foreign secretary's position as he was also associated with the 'Nepal democracy solidarity committee, India', formed under the chairmanship of Marxist leader Harkishan Singh Surjeet, to support democracy movement in Nepal after King Gyanendra's coup.[6]

Moreover, Saran's views were shared by the ambassador to Kathmandu, Shiv Shankar Mukherjee. The new ambassador had given an interview after the twelve-point understanding, and said that they (India) did not want to obstruct any talks between the parties and the Maoists.[7] The Indian ambassador stated publicly that India was not going to do anything to rein in the activities of the group that had raised arms against a neighbouring state.

The Maoist leaders had earlier failed to meet any senior official of the Indian external affairs ministry despite repeated attempts. This changed. In June 2005, Saran met Baburam and Prachanda. The meeting was organized with the help of Professor Muni. Saran used his diplomatic skills to the fullest to bring the twelve-point understanding to fruition. Three weeks after the signing of that understanding, Saran landed in Kathmandu, in December 2005, and met the king and the army chief. To the press, he only had this to say: 'It is necessary for constitutional forces to work together.'[8]

Saran was pressing the parties and the then unconstitutional force, the Maoists, to reach an agreement, while at the same time coming to Kathmandu and highlighting the need for constitutional forces to come together. After his retirement, Saran said the twelve-point understanding was not 'imposed' by India. 'We only played the role of facilitator. The deal was reached among the Nepali sides,' he told an interviewer.[9]

Muni takes the initiative

Without the initial steps taken by Professor S.D. Muni, even Foreign Secretary Saran and RAW Chief Tharakan may not have been able to push Nepal policy in the direction that they did. He was the person through whom the Nepali Maoists had first contacted Indian PM Atal Behari Vajpayee back in 2001.

South Block used to listen to Prof. Muni on Nepal matters, even though his views did not always shape policy. The author of four books on Nepal, Muni used to openly advocate the establishment of a republic in Nepal, for which reason the royal government even demanded that Delhi rein him in.[10] Ever since the first royal regression of 4 October 2002, Muni had called for an alliance between the political parties, especially the NC and the Maoist rebels, against the royal regime. He argued that such an alliance would gradually push the Maoists to leave their path of violence and would have a salutary effect on Indian Naxalites. In 2002, he wrote a long paper, also available in book form, arguing that India needed to build relations with the Maoists and play a role in forging their relations with the parliamentary parties in order to present the image of a people-friendly neighbour.[11]

After the second coup by King Gyanendra on 1 February 2005, Muni's proposal for a Maoist–party alliance became officially palatable. He said, 'India was not happy with Gyanendra's takeover. The king did nothing to please India (even after the coup). Otherwise, India's line was that the parties and the king should work together. But my line was that India should help bring the Maoists and the parties closer. In the end, things turned out like I wanted.'

The politics of the CPM

The lobbying by Tharakan from RAW, Saran from MEA, and Prof. Muni as an influential intellectual, was given the necessary political thrust by the Communist Party of India (Marxist) (CPI(M)). The liberal communist parties of India, the CPI(M) and the CPI, backed the campaign to mainstream the Nepali Maoists. These parties were influential in the government led by the Indian National Congress as key constituents of the United Progressive Alliance (UPA). They supported the government from outside, but the withdrawal of support by the CPI(M) alone could have toppled Manmohan Singh's government.[12]

The problem the Indian government faced was that it could not engage directly in any political or diplomatic relations with the Maoists, who were categorized as 'terrorists'. This job was conveniently handed over to the CPI(M). The Maoists welcomed the prospect of building bridges with the ruling Indian parties. Earlier, the Maoists did not have any bilateral relations with the CPI(M). In fact, in the eyes of the Maoists, the CPI(M) was a 'revisionist party immersed in the marsh of parliamentary politics'. The CPI(M) itself had a much closer relationship with the CPN–UML in Nepal. And it had demonstrated a hawkish tendency towards the Maoists in the state of West Bengal, where they led the state government. Several leaders, including Kiran, had been arrested in that state. However, the royal regression and subsequent changes in the CPI(M) leadership altered the equation. In early 2005, Prakash Karat took over the reins of the CPI(M) as its general secretary, from Harkishan Singh Surjeet. He had once publicly declared that Gyanendra would be the last king of Nepal.[13]

The most important role of the CPI(M) was in the formation of the 'Nepal Democracy Solidarity Committee'. Surjeet was its convener, and it counted former Indian prime ministers such as V.P. Singh, Chandra Shekhar and Inder Kumar Gujral, apart from Congress General Secretary Digvijay Singh, General Secretary of the Nationalist Congress party D.P. Tripathi, and politburo member of the CPI(M) Sitaram Yechury, as its members. The solidarity committee included representatives of over one dozen Indian parties. It was in contact with the Indian government, the Maoists, and the seven parties. It created a political environment and public opinion in favour of the anti-monarchy movement in Nepal.

Following the king's coup, Baburam met CPI(M) General Secretary Karat in Delhi in April 2005. Karat instructed his comrade Sitaram Yechury, a well-known Nepal-watcher, to coordinate with the Nepali Maoists. Tripathi was also active alongside Yechury. Both had easy access to PM Manmohan Singh.

Tripathi has said that they were in contact with the Maoists and the seven parties on PM Singh's instructions.[14] Tripathi, who was once an aide of former Prime Minister Rajiv Gandhi, had close contacts with the Indian political leadership, security agencies and business houses.

JNU was the thread that connected Tripathi, Yechury and Karat—each of them had headed the student union during their student days. Baburam Bhattarai had also done his PhD there. So this connection helped them to gel. And another bond that brought all four together was a professor of that university, S.D. Muni.

RAW's road map

The Dubai-based *Gulf News*, on 17 May 2005, published a report saying that Nepali Maoist leaders Baburam Bhattarai, Krishna Bahadur Mahara and Kishan Pyakurel (an alias of Top Bahadur Rayamajhi) had met Indian leftist leaders Prakash Karat and A.B. Bardhan, who were with the governing alliance, with the help of Indian spooks. The report, published from the Gulf, did not get much attention. But a similar one published eight days later, on the front page of the *Times of India*, generated a lot of comments.[15]

Karat and Baburam both accepted the meeting had occurred, but denied the involvement of any spy agency. Certainly, these two leaders, who shared an alma mater, did not require any intermediary to meet each other. But India's leading daily linked them with RAW, and questions flew thick and fast on the relations between RAW and the Nepali Maoists.

The BBC Nepali Service asked a former major general of the Indian army, Ashok Mehta, who takes a keen interest in Nepali matters, 'How long has it been that Indian intelligence agents have been in contact with the Nepali Maoists?' Mehta, who had access to the establishment, replied, 'At least two to three years.'[16]

The Maoists had tried to use the intelligence agencies as a means to get access to the Indian establishment. There had been a debate within the party as to how appropriate it was to build contact with a spy agency. At the Phuntibang meeting of September 2004, Chairman Prachanda himself admitted his weakness in not being able to raise the party's diplomatic contacts beyond RAW. 'Although it was correct to advance clandestine diplomatic relations (with India), we failed in raising our open political relations to the same level,' he said.[17]

At this meeting, the party even decided to stop meeting spy agencies in its pursuit of diplomatic relations with the Indian government. 'Yet, the Indians did not want to meet them at the political level. They dispatched RAW agents. Prachandaji met with them,' said former Maoist leader Rabindra Shrestha.[18] Part of the issue was that the Indian government did not wish to demonstrate its direct contact with the Maoists. It was in this context that the *Times of India* published its report, stating how spooks had hosted the Karat–Baburam meeting.

Apart from Tharakan, two of his senior officials, Amitabh Mathur 'Tony' and Shashi Bhushan Singh Tomar, also held periodic talks with the leaders of the Maoists and other parties. Tomar had extensive knowledge of Nepal, having already served at the Indian embassy in Kathmandu under cover as its first secretary (political). He was one of the passengers on IC 814 when it was hijacked from Kathmandu on Christmas eve in 1999 and taken to Kandahar, Afghanistan. The hijackers had no idea about his official identity and he was, thus, spared any complications.

The RAW team prepared a two-page 'future roadmap' to resolve the Nepal crisis. It was handed over to Girija Prasad Koirala when he landed in Delhi. It was also made available to some Maoist and UML leaders. A high-level source privy to the note says it basically included the following points:

- To make a Constituent Assembly the 'bottom line' for understanding between the parties and the Maoists.

- Kingship to be reduced to 'ceremonial monarchy'. The army to be brought under the control of Parliament.
- To integrate Maoist guerrillas in various security agencies (the army and two police forces), based on their 'capability' and 'training'.

The leaders involved in forging the twelve-point understanding admit Indian assistance in the process, but reject their direct involvement. Prachanda said, 'It did not happen without their knowledge. It would not have been possible had they not closed their eyes. But the meetings did not take place with their direct involvement.' Many years later, the Indian ambassador to Nepal, Jayanta Prasad, also claimed in an interview that India had not arranged the twelve-point understanding. India had only used its goodwill to enable the leaders to reach an understanding among themselves, he said.[19]

But Prof. Muni has clearly mentioned that a draft of the agreement was shown to Indian officials and mediators. According to him, he had the opportunity to examine the draft a number of times.[20] He says India was able to use its role to emphasize three elements of the twelve-point understanding:

> First, the document was officially called an 'understanding' and not an 'agreement', so that it was not binding on any side.
>
> Second, it did not have joint signatures, nor was it issued by the Maoists and the seven party leaders from one place. This was done to treat the Maoists as outsiders and not immediately provide them with political legitimacy.
>
> Third, the understanding did not refer to a 'republic' anywhere. The Maoists were compelled to accept the phrase 'total democracy'. In other words, the idea was to corner the monarchy, not completely kick it out.[21]

After the twelve-point deal, the Maoists were able to carry on their activities more openly in India. On 13 February 2006, they held a public assembly at Ramlila Maidan, where the police installed a 'walk-through' metal detector to provide security. The CPI(M)'s Sitaram Yechury addressed the assembly. In the eyes of Delhi, the Maoists were no longer 'communist terrorists', but adherents of democracy and a republic.

A large section among intellectuals, the bureaucracy and politicians in India were traditionally opposed to monarchy. In the eyes of RAW officials, the Nepali monarchy was a nest for inciting anti-India sentiments in Nepal. They argued that Indian interests could be safeguarded only after removing the monarchy. This can also be inferred from the article that was written by the newly retired special secretary of RAW, J.K. Sinha. Published around the time when intensive talks were going on among the Nepali leaders in Delhi, it began by claiming that a prediction by Swami Gorakhnath on the demise of the Nepali monarchy was coming true. Legend had it that Gorakhnath had predicted that only ten of Prithvi Narayan Shah's descendants would sit on the Nepali throne. Sinha observed that King Gyanendra was the tenth, and by his actions, was likely to fulfil the prophecy.[22]

Anti-monarchy sentiment among the Indian political leadership and bureaucracy gained traction after Gyanendra seized power in Kathmandu without seeking their support or consent. It also coincided with the rapidly increasing anti-monarchy feeling among the Nepali masses following the royal coup. From the seven parties to the Maoists and the general public, all were coming together on an anti-monarchy plank. The Indian establishment, including RAW, was quick to understand the changing equation and forge a corresponding policy. And they had some specific goals.

The first was to tame King Gyanendra. There were two streams of opinion on this. One felt the wayward king should be taught a lesson, but the two-pillar policy of 'multiparty democracy and constitutional monarchy' should not be abandoned. Another felt India should no longer back the source of India-baiting in

Nepal, the palace, and should support its removal in favour of a republic. Both agreed on the need to tame the king.

Second, the alliance with the seven parties was necessary to bring the insurgent Maoists into the mainstream. It was thought that it would peacefully resolve Nepal's instability, and would set an example for the Indian Naxalites to follow.

Third, India could get credit from the international community if it could establish peace in a neighbouring country. A candidate for permanent membership of the UN Security Council, India wanted to demonstrate its key role in establishing peace in the region so that it could present the successful example of Nepal to strengthen its bid in New York.

Fourth, to be able to fulfil its own economic and social interests after effecting political transformation in Nepal.

The external affairs minister, Pranab Mukherjee, who went on to become president of India, once revealed the role played by India in bringing the Maoists to the mainstream. On 28 January 2009, he was asked by Riz Khan, during an interview with Al Jazeera television, 'Minister, how do you see India's rising status on the world stage?'

In his reply, Mukherjee talked about the role played by India in establishing peace in the neighbourhood. He emphasized Nepal. 'I am just giving you an example when there was trouble in one of our Himalayan countries, our neighbour Nepal, we persuaded the political parties which resorted to guns and violence, the Maoists in Nepal, that they give up violence (and) participate in the mainstream national political activities. They agreed, listened to our advice and in collaboration with other democratic parties, they formed the government, they are leading the government.'[23]

Was the 'roadmap' of RAW limited to this?

It is hard to be definite because the strategies of intelligence agencies are mostly kept under wraps. In many cases, they even carry out clandestine operations without the knowledge of their political masters. For example, in the 1970s, when the Indian

Prime Minister Indira Gandhi asked how long it would take to start operations to merge Sikkim with India, a RAW official replied that it could start within twenty-four hours. Indira was surprised by the answer. In fact, when she asked the question, the RAW was already in the final stages of its operation.[24]

16

Spring Revolt

'There were two main bases for the movement: popular discontent prompted by the repeated failures of the king's direct rule, and hope that the twelve-point agreement between the mainstream parties and the Maoists would bring peace.'

—An International Crisis Group report[1]

The internal dissension within the Maoists had been resolved after the meeting of Chunbang. They had also struck the twelve-point understanding with the seven parties. After a long gap, they had finally dealt a military blow to the Royal Nepali Army at Pili in Kalikot. It was around December 2005 that a team of Kathmandu-based journalists left for a trip to Rapti hills.

First, we reached Bhabang in Rolpa where we met one of the four deputy commanders of the PLA, Janardan Sharma 'Prabhakar'.[2] He spoke in a tone that seemed to be threatening us. 'We will now focus all our attacks on Kathmandu. It is the head of the central regime. To hit at it, we will first stamp on its spine.'

The Maoists were, indeed, directing all their strategies at the capital. They understood that they could topple the royal regime only by hitting there. The Chunbang meeting, therefore, had formulated a strategic plan—crush the spine and strike at the head (of the enemy).

'What do you mean by spine?' I asked.

'We have termed as the 'spine' all those places where the enemy has raised obstructions to protect its centre, the head,' the man in charge of the Rapti region—the so-called capital of the Maoists— Netra Bikram Chand 'Biplav' said. He added, 'If you look at the geography, you will find that one side of the spine of the enemy lies prostrate in the Gandak region while the other side is in the Janakpur region. And it has a head like Ravana, in Kathmandu. We want to cross it from both sides. So we will stamp on its spine and strike at its head.'

This meant undertaking military action against the main lifelines and strategic points of the state. Instead of rural regions, they now adopted the strategy of striking at government offices near the capital. 'Let's now march to the capital and hit at the enemy's nerve-centre,' Hemanta Prakash Oli 'Sudarshan', commissar of the fifth division, told a public assembly in Rukumkot. Carrying a pistol in his belt, he asked the participants, 'Are you guys ready to head to the city?'

By attacking police posts at two entry points to the capital, at Thankot and Dadhikot, the insurgents sent a message of their impending arrival. But the centre of their attack was the Lumbini– Gandaki region to the west of Kathmandu. In December 2005, the Maoists initiated their 'Gandak campaign', the commander of which was the same Prabhakar under whose command the insurgents had recently made a devastating assault on the Royal Nepali Army at Pili.

All the divisions (fourth, fifth, sixth and seventh) of the western region were gathered to one area for the Gandak campaign, aimed at breaking the back of Kathmandu. Somewhat akin to the 'long march' of China, around 10,000 fighters, militias and cadres were mustered by the end of December. A big battle ensued at Chitre in Syangja district, when the Royal Nepali Army tried to stop them.

Maoist leaders Prachanda and Baburam Bhattarai during a central committee meeting held in 1994 before the start of the people's war

A Maoist street protest before the people's war in Kathmandu in 1995

Prachanda during his underground days near New Delhi in 2006

Maoist leader Netra Bikram Chand 'Biplov' at a mass meeting in Rukum in 2005. He formed a new party—NCP—and is still in the armed movement.

Photo courtesy of Nepal magazine

The Maoist PLA at a cantonment in Shaktikhor, Chitwan, in 2007

Photo courtesy of Kantipur Publications archive

Prachanda and Baburam Bhattarai with local villagers in midwestern Nepal

Photo courtesy of Nepal magazine

Indian Maoist leader Balaji at a training camp in Rolpa in 1999

Photo by Sudheer Sharma

A wall painting of international communist leaders in a remote village of Rolpa district in 2005

King Birendra and Queen Aishwarya in Tanzania in 1986. They were killed during the 2005 palace massacre.

During the announcement of the first district-level people's government by Maoists in Rukum in 2000

PLA cadres at a Maoist mass meeting in Rukum district in 2004

During the people's movement in Kathmandu in 2006

The then prime minister, Girija Prasad Koirala, and the Maoist chairman, Prachanda, after signing the Comprehensive Peace Agreement on 21 November 2006

The former king, Gyanendra, speaking at a press conference before leaving the royal palace in 2008

The then Nepali prime minister, Prachanda, along with the deputy prime minister, Upendra Yadav, during a meeting with the then Indian prime minister, Manmohan Singh, in 2008

Indian Prime Minister Narendra Modi during a visit to Nepal in 2014

A few days later, the insurgents launched another successful assault on Palpa, but they failed to destroy army camps in Taulihawa and Butwal.

Pokhara was the target of the Gandak campaign. This city was where King Gyanendra had based himself at that point. Under all-round pressure, the king took the advice of an astrologer and went to stay at the Ratna Mandir palace on the banks of the scenic Phewa Lake. He reached there on 17 February and spent two months on its serene shore. The fighters were advancing quickly towards the tourist attraction.

The Maoists hatched the ambitious plan of organizing several armed assaults in the region and taking Pokhara under control, before advancing towards Kathmandu. It would not be possible, however, due to two main reasons. One, they faced stiff resistance from the Royal Nepali Army at several places. Two, the Maoist leaders had reached an understanding for a joint peaceful movement with the seven parties. Prachanda therefore announced a ceasefire. Prabhakar's team had to return midway. After that episode, all the energy of the Maoists was spent making the people's movement in Kathmandu successful.

The people's movement

Despite the preparations for the people's movement, the problem was that the people had very little faith in the political parties and their leaders. In the initial days, the movement, therefore, was led by civil society leaders such as Devendra Raj Pandey and Krishna Pahadi. The political leaders were in the background. Amid the growing disenchantment with the royal regime, people were looking hopefully at the prospect of peace offered by the deal between the Maoists and the political parties. Although they had signed their understanding in November 2005, the two sides were unable to come up with a joint agitation programme for some time. Meanwhile, the Maoists unilaterally announced a *chakka jam* (transport strike) from the third week of March 2006, and *aam hartal* (general strike) from April. This compelled the leaders of the seven parties to rush to Delhi in the first week of March to talk to the Maoist leaders.

Prachanda and Baburam held a series of talks with Krishna Prasad Sitaula and Mahantha Thakur of the NC, Jhalnath Khanal and Bamdev Gautam of the UML, and Narayan Kaji Shrestha and Amik Sherchan of CPN–Unity Centre. On 11 March, they reached a three-point deal: the Maoists and the seven parties would issue a joint appeal to make the movement successful; the seven parties would ask the Maoists to withdraw its blockade; and the Maoists would then withdraw them and lend support to the programme of the seven parties.

Although it was agreed that the joint appeal would be issued from Delhi, Girija Prasad Koirala refused. Earlier, he had also refused to put a joint signature to the twelve-point understanding. The leaders were scared that the king could lump them together with the Maoists, declare them 'terrorists', and ban the parties if they formally launched a joint agitation. Finally, they reached a compromise whereby they issued a similarly worded statement separately on 19 March, in which they expressed their commitment to 'firmly implement the twelve-point understanding'.

The announcement of a joint movement against the king by the parliamentary forces and the Maoists sent a positive message, coming as it did amid rising dissatisfaction with towards the regime and the intensifying conflict. People hoped that they could win both peace and democracy. Following three days of a joint general strike, beginning on 6 April, the movement intensified. On the very first day, an army chopper was destroyed, for the first time, by the insurgents during a clash in Sarlahi. This encouraged the protestors. Since the Royal Nepali Army was seen as the supporting force of the king, it was losing popularity day by day.

A worker of the UML, Darshan Lal Yadav, died in a police baton charge at Rajbiraj on the first day of the movement. When the government resorted to indiscriminate repression, it had the effect of bringing more people out on to the streets to protest. The seven parties decided to extend the three-day general strike indefinitely from 9 April onwards. The Maoists supported them. There was countrywide defiance of government-imposed restrictions and curfew. There was, in fact, no meaning to the curfew when the sea of people spilled into the streets in open defiance. A campaign to declare 'republic regions' started from 10 April. People started replacing boards of 'His Majesty's Government' with 'Nepal Government'. Government employees took part in the agitation within the central secretariat of the Singha Durbar. A slogan was raised everywhere: *Gyane chor, desh chhod* (thief Gyanendra, leave the country).

The first people's movement of 1990 was mainly urban-centric, involving primarily the Kathmandu middle class. But the second people's movement of 2006 was not focused in Kathmandu. People rose up in the villages. There was agitation even in the rural Karnali region. The involvement of the lower class was notable. However, the most impressive agitation took place in Kathmandu. The parties claimed that they mobilized one million people during the nineteen days of the movement in the capital. And despite the involvement of hundreds of thousands of people, it was mainly peaceful.

The agitation attracted people from all walks of life, including professionals such as journalists, lawyers, teachers and doctors. The mass media, such as television, FM radio and newspapers, openly sided with the movement. The government did not have the strength to face such a juggernaut. One reason the protests swelled was the involvement of the Maoists.

Street full of sticks

During the people's movement, the Maoists participated in the urban agitation as well. They played a key role in sending people to the city from surrounding areas. One could see that a section of people participating in the agitation carried sticks. Initially, this was done by Maoist workers in order to identify each other and coordinate. Later, it became a sort of symbol of mass demonstration.

The Maoist in charge of the Valley 'special command', Barshaman Pun 'Ananta', was responsible for mobilizing Maoist cadres in Kathmandu. The Maoists mobilized a large number of people from what they called 'ring areas' around the capital. He himself was based in Kamidanda of Kavre district to the east of Kathmandu. He instructed his field commanders from mobile and satellite phone. He had no party permission to enter the city, but, unable to suppress the excitement, he sometimes came up to the nearby town of Panauti to witness the mood of the movement.

The Maoists deployed their workers and general public from the surrounding districts of Kavre, Sindhupalchok, Nuwakot, Dhading, Rasuwa, Dolakha and Makwanpur. If caught, they were taught to tell the authorities that they belonged to the Nepali Congress. They were the ones who marched with the sticks. Upon learning this, Home Minister Kamal Thapa repeatedly claimed Maoist infiltration in the agitation, but could do no more than that. According to Ananta, the Maoists mobilized around 91,000 people in total from the surrounding districts. Since they gathered at different points on the ring road, those places became the flashpoints of demonstration.

Around ninety Maoist fighters led by the brigade commander of the Special Task Force, Chandra Bahadur Thapa 'Sagar', participated in the mass movement. The police rounded up around a dozen of them, including the battalion commander. Some, like Lalitpur district committee member Dinesh Chapagain, received bullet wounds. Subsequently, the guerrillas started demanding that they be allowed to shoot back.

On 21 April, the army raised barricades and positioned Ferret armoured cars, which look like small tanks, on the road leading from Narayan Gopal Chowk to Nirmal Niwas (the residence of King Gyanendra). Sagar phoned Ananta and asked, 'The army has come out with tanks. We also have weapons. Should we charge?'

According to Ananta, he replied, 'We are currently in a peaceful agitation, Comrade. Do not use weapons.'

Army Chief Pyar Jung Thapa had received information that tens of thousands of Maoist cadres and a few thousand armed guerrillas had entered into the capital. He said in an interview later, 'They could have unleashed any kind of mayhem. We feared that they would organize a massacre by infiltrating the mass demonstration. It could have provoked the protestors. The army wanted to carry out some sort of defensive operation.' He reported this to his commander-in-chief, King Gyanendra. According to Thapa, the king's reply was, 'This army is public property handed down from the time of King Prithvi Narayan Shah (the founding king of unified Nepal). No operation, only defence.'[3]

Nevertheless, there were scattered incidents of shots being fired, which resulted in the deaths of twenty-one protestors.

Rejection of the royal decree

After two months' stay in Pokhara, the king returned to Kathmandu to find that the movement had grown more intense. On 16 April, he called the ambassadors of the US, India and China and held consultations with them separately. Then he met former Prime Ministers Surya Bahadur Thapa, Lokendra Bahadur Chand, Marichman Singh Shrestha and Krishna Prasad Bhattarai.

The first effort of the palace was to appoint Krishna Prasad Bhattarai as prime minister. The king's chief secretary, Pashupati Bhakta Maharjan, and a minister in his cabinet, Prakash Koirala (the eldest son of B.P. Koirala), went to Bhattarai's residence separately, carrying the royal message. Seeing no possibility of getting support from the agitating parties, Bhattarai declined the offer. Then, two more names were floated for the position of prime minister. 'We discussed making Madhav Kumar Nepal the prime minister,' said Army Chief Thapa. 'But India wanted the king to hand over power to Girija Prasad Koirala.'[4]

Indian PM Manmohan Singh called an emergency meeting of ministers and security chiefs to discuss the situation in Nepal on 17 April. Defence Minister Pranab Mukherjee, Home Minister Shivraj Patil, National Security Advisor M.K. Narayanan and the chiefs of the army and air force were present at the meeting. After the meeting, on 19 April, the Indian PM dispatched Dr Karan Singh, the chief of the foreign cell of the Congress party and the son of the last king of Kashmir, as his special envoy to Kathmandu.

On the very day of his arrival in Kathmandu, Singh, who also happened to be a distant relative of King Gyanendra, met several political leaders. He met the king the following day, and handed over a sealed letter sent by the Indian PM. Foreign Secretary Shyam Saran had accompanied Singh. According to him, Singh apprised the king of the Indian evaluation of the rapidly developing environment in Nepal and 'warned' him that in the absence of quick steps, the situation could further deteriorate. Speaking at a press conference, Saran added that Singh advised the Nepali king to respect democratic principles and the clamour for democracy among the Nepali people.[5]

India had a clear message: talk to the seven parties. Saran and Singh both returned to Delhi on 20 April, shortening their visit by a day. Singh told journalists that the king would soon make an announcement. The rest of the job was left for Ambassador Shiv Shankar Mukherjee. On 21 April, Mukherjee held two-hour-long talks with the king. In the end, the king agreed to the Indian proposal of handing power to the seven parties and allowing the restoration of Parliament through them.

The Indian ambassador himself carried the king's message to Girija Prasad Koirala. Koirala agreed. In the evening, Gyanendra made a seven-minute-long public address. In the address, he invoked Article 35 of the 1990 Constitution to appeal to the parties to form a new government. 'We urge the seven-party alliance to submit the name of a new prime minister to constitute the Council of Ministers as soon as possible,' the king said. He did not make any reference to the restoration of Parliament. The parties did not find it acceptable. The protesting mass was further enraged to hear the king speaking in a condescending tone of 'granting the prime minister's position' even as they were demanding a republic.

At that point, foreign powers, including the US, the UK, China and India also failed to read the writing on the wall. Their diplomats put pressure on the leaders of the seven parties to accept the royal decree and continue dialogue with the king. At 9 a.m. on the morning of 22 April, a team of ambassadors from eight European countries went to Koirala's residence, where the seven parties were holding a meeting. They tried to persuade the parties to accept the royal declaration by 'impressing' two points upon them. First, the king could resort to fierce repression in case they did not agree, which would lead to bloodshed. Second, the Maoists could seize power amid the ensuing anarchy.

Indian special envoy Karan Singh termed the royal declaration 'a courageous step'. Manmohan Singh, who was en route to Germany, told a PTI reporter on his aircraft that it was 'a step in the right direction'.[6]

But the people of Nepal refused to budge. In the streets, one could hear the slogan 'The royal declaration is a betrayal'. Most Nepali leaders rarely resist diplomatic pressure. But this time they did. The leaders, instead, sided with the people and continued the agitation against the king.

Closely watching the events in Kathmandu, Delhi was quick to see the changing mood. It corrected its position. Foreign Secretary Saran hurriedly called a press meet in Delhi on 22 April. He urged the journalists not to take India's position as either an endorsement or a rejection of the king's announcement. He said that India had stressed the need for the king to hand power over to the people of Nepal. He added that the king had agreed to this in his latest announcement. But Saran also added that India would always stand by the democratic forces of Nepal.[7]

Saran's remark was clearly against the king, and in favour of the agitating parties. It was the clearest indication yet that Delhi was about to abandon its two-pillar policy of supporting constitutional monarchy and multiparty democracy.

Abandoned by the army

Saran had supported India's two-pillar policy just two days earlier, when he arrived in Kathmandu. He had told the army chief, Pyar Jung Thapa, that 'India still stands by the two-pillar policy of constitutional monarchy and parliamentary democracy'.[8] Delhi's rider was that King Gyanendra should hand over power to the leader of the agitation, Girija Prasad Koirala. The special envoy, Dr Karan Singh, had said the same thing to King Gyanendra. Saran's mission was to bring the army leadership on board for that proposal. So he spent one-and-a-half hours at the army headquarters with the chief, whom he knew from the past.

According to Saran, he told Army Chief Thapa that the army should not be seen killing its own people. 'I said, somewhat provocatively, that he had a choice—to be the chief of the Royal Army or the chief of Nepal's Army,' Saran has written in a memoir of that meeting. 'I said it was his duty to convey to the king that the situation was becoming dangerous and untenable, that the army could not risk a violent confrontation with massive crowds and that defusing the situation politically was the only way out.'[9]

After the agitation did not subside, even after the royal declaration of 22 April, the senior generals held a heated meeting at the army headquarters the following day. One of those generals later told me, pointing to the red sofa at the western corner of the chief's boardroom, 'The chief was sitting on that sofa. He appeared to be in a state of confusion. We were all around him. We pressed him to go and talk to the king.'

Under pressure from outside and within his own organization, the chief went to the palace on 22 April. He said the king's declaration had failed to arrest the swell of the agitation and advised the monarch to take a political step, warning that the institution of monarchy itself could be under threat if he did not do that. He advised the king, 'When Your Majesty is already in the mood to hand over power, wouldn't it be better if Your Majesty just restored the Parliament as they have demanded?'[10]

This was a clear indication of the army standing against the royal position. The army chief gave a rare interview to CNN a few days later, which conveyed the same message. He said in the interview, 'The Royal Nepali Army doesn't believe in flexing muscle against its own people.'[11] Later, when he was summoned by the Rayamajhi Commission, formed to investigate charges of repression against the people's movement, Thapa told the commissioners, 'More people died in the first people's movement of 1990.[12] This time, fewer died despite the larger protests. It happened not due to our repression, but due to our caution.'

The main reason why the army abandoned the king was that it had been forced into the worst crisis of its history due to the monarch. Engaged in a bloody battle with the insurgents, the army was faced with international sanctions after the king's coup on 1 February 2005. Not only was military assistance suspended, it could not even purchase ammunition and guns from its traditional sellers. The king was unable to do anything to help them. The army concluded that if it continued to back the king, despite the protests, it could compromise its institutional interests. It refused to 'commit suicide'. Instead it heeded the advice of the Indian army, its 'brother army'. Things might have changed had Gyanendra dared to sack the army chief who did not obey him, and who undermined the army's loyalty to the palace. But the king himself was thoroughly beleaguered.

The king yields

The parties were planning the climax of the agitation for 25 April 2006. When the king heard of their intention to bring hundreds of thousands of people to the streets, announce a parallel government and get Indian recognition, he found himself under unnatural pressure. There were even rumours that India was deploying its air force.

Rumours flew thick and fast. Information that the Maoists planned to push the people in the street towards the royal palace was also bandied around. If the agitation took such a turn, it could only mean the direct establishment of a republic. The king would have only one option, of using the army, but the chief had already given up.

In Delhi, Defence Minister Pranab Mukherjee called a meeting of the cabinet committee on political affairs on 24 April. In the absence of Manmohan Singh, who was on a tour to Europe, Mukherjee was in charge of handling Nepal. Besides ministers Shivraj Patil, Lalu Yadav, Arjun Singh and Sharad Pawar, the meeting was joined by the leftist leader Sitaram Yechury, Foreign Secretary Shyam Saran, and the chiefs of the army, the air force and the navy, as well as the heads of RAW and IB. The two-hour session discussed what India should do in the event of things going bad the following day in Kathmandu.[13]

With no other alternative in sight, the king was now ready to restore the House of Representatives dissolved in 2002. He made a second royal announcement through state television on the night of 24 April, and stated, 'In order to resolve all problems of the country, including the violent conflict, as per the roadmap of the seven-party alliance and the opinion expressed by the people through the people's movement, we have, hereby, restored the House of Representatives, which was dissolved on 22 May 2002, at the recommendation of the then prime minister and, in accordance with the Constitution of Kingdom of Nepal 1990.'

The royal statement had been finalized with the consent of the leaders of the NC and the UML. The king's secretary, Pashupati Bhakta Maharjan, had rushed from Koirala's residence to Balkhu (the UML headquarters) in order to complete the draft.[14] Indian Ambassador Mukherjee also rushed between the palace and the parties at least three times that day.[15]

For the first time, the king admitted that 'The people of Nepal are the source of state power and that sovereignty and state power are vested in the people of Nepal.' He was forced to hand over power, but he did not budge from his stand against holding direct talks with the party leaders. In 1990, his brother King Birendra had called the agitating party leaders to the palace to hand over power; but Gyanendra refused to meet them till the very end. Instead, he dispatched his secretary to meet them before making his announcement.

India, the US and other members of the international community had urged the king to restore the Parliament 'in view of the threat of capture of power by the Maoists'. According to the American Ambassador James F. Moriarty, 'a lot of blood could have been spilt in the streets'.[16] Later, Prachanda confirmed it by saying, 'If the agitation had been allowed to proceed for a few more days, it was certain that the fate of the Nepali king and his family would not have been different from that of the Romanian leader Ceausescu. It would have triggered division in the royal army and made the country's entry into a new era of democratic republic possible.'[17]

Events might not have developed in the manner Prachanda and Moriarty suggested, but the king surrendered because the situation was rapidly spinning out of his control. The Maoists wanted to continue the agitation, calling the parties' decision to withdraw the movement following the second royal announcement 'a betrayal'. But they were not successful.

The rebels issued three rapidly shifting statements in the aftermath of the second royal announcement. In the first, issued on 25 April, they announced they would 'continue imposing blockades on the capital and district headquarters until the unconditional announcement of the election of a Constituent Assembly'. In the second statement, on 26 April, they called off their blockades and other programmes 'as per the request of NC President Girija Prasad Koirala'. The third, issued the same day, announced a unilateral ceasefire for 'three months'.

It was natural for the Maoist leaders to be suspicious as they were neither involved nor informed when the parties called off the people's movement. But the success of the movement not only restored Parliament and democracy, but also opened the door to let the Maoists into the mainstream politics and peace process.

If there was anybody who was most pleased with the restoration of Parliament, it was the commander of the second people's movement, Girija Prasad Koirala. He had constantly raised the demand for its restoration since it was dissolved on 22 May 2002. Many had termed his demand impractical and impossible. In his words, 'There was no international support for the demand. America used to say: you are asking for the impossible, the restoration of Parliament is not legitimate. The European Union, China and India were also against it. Even our own friends who spoke English used to say: the old man has gone senile. In the end, my determination and conviction prevailed.'[18]

17

Treacherous Transition

'Till the last moment I tried to push for the curtailment of
the king's authorities through the amendment of the (1990)
Constitution and giving it the role of interim Constitution . . .
It was a political blunder to replace the 1990 Constitution with
an interim Constitution.'

—Prime Minister Girija Prasad Koirala[1]

Despite the success of the people's movement, Prachanda had not
come to Kathmandu. On 8 June 2006, he was addressing party
cadres of the Rapti–Gandaki region at Sikles in Kaski in western
Nepal. One party cadre asked him, 'Comrade Chairman, shall
we now return to our villages to raise our cattle? Have our tasks
finished?'

Prachanda replied, 'No, Comrade. Your tasks will never be
finished. You have fought for so many years. Now let me fight.'

A few days later, he appeared in the capital. Thus began his
political fight, which appeared, at times, totally incomprehensible.
On one hand, he had taken up the policy of a Constituent
Assembly and establishment of peace. On the other, he was still

secretly telling his party cadres of his plans for revolt and power capture. A republic was his declared agenda, but he did not forget to appeal for partnership with the royalists.

It was difficult to determine who the real Prachanda was, which his serious agendas were and which make-believe. His attempts during those initial years of transition indicated that Prachanda actually wanted to carry out revolt and capture power, but could not do it because of national and international complexities. His goal of a republic was fulfilled. However, in the course of achieving that goal, the country was subjected to a series of schemes by Prachanda, which we will discuss in this chapter.

April thesis

In April 1917, following the 'February revolution', Lenin was returning to St Petersburg from Switzerland, and during the journey he prepared a brief proposal, which subsequently led to the October Revolution. Those point-wise directives for power capture, provided to his Bolshevik cadres, were known as the 'April Thesis'.

The Nepali promoter of Maoism, Chairman Prachanda, personally admired Lenin more than Mao. In the course of returning from India to Nepal, following the successful April movement, he, too, had drafted a point-wise programme for the future course. The Nepali Maoists called it 'April Thesis in the Nepali Context'. It was endorsed by the central committee meeting held from 7 to 10 May at Talwara, Punjab. It concluded that the seven parties had conspired to reach a deal with the king. It vowed to take the movement to its logical end by establishing a republic in Nepal under the leadership of their party. Two working policies were endorsed for the purpose: 'the peaceful entry into the regime' and 'the creation of powerful revolt'.

The strategy was, first, attempting to establish a democratic republic peacefully through dialogue and the election of a

Constituent Assembly. Otherwise, to unleash a movement in urban areas under the party's leadership and turn it into a people's revolt to establish a republic. Carrying the 'April Thesis', Prachanda entered Nepal with the goal of executing an 'October Revolution' like the one carried out by his idol, Lenin.

When the Maoists entered Kathmandu, they could not conceal their desire for revolt. During a public assembly at Khula Manch on 1 June 2006, the fifth anniversary of the royal massacre, many of the participants broke the gate and entered the nearby Army Pavilion. They sat on the seat reserved for the king. They covered the army statues with red flags everywhere. Soldiers stood nearby watching helplessly. Prachanda praised his cadres, 'The public assembly held peacefully under the leadership of CPN–Maoists challenged the 237-year-old feudal monarchy and captured the army pavilion. It has written a new chapter in history.'[2]

But it was mere illusion. Real power was quite far away from the Maoists.

'Nepali Magna Carta'

The parliamentary forces had been restored to government. With the success of the people's movement, Congress President Girija Prasad Koirala took oath as the new prime minister on 25 April. King Gyanendra administered it. But in a break with tradition, Koirala did not take his ministers to the palace to take their oaths. Subsequently, he started clipping the wings of the king. The same Parliament, which was dissolved by the king in 2002 and was restored through royal proclamation, was used for this purpose.

The restored Parliament declared itself 'sovereign' and the 'supreme authority of the country' on 18 May. Its main goal was to curtail royal power and assert control over the army. It took numerous far-reaching decisions: declaring a change in the name of the army from 'Royal Nepali Army' to 'Nepali Army'; authorizing the council of ministers to appoint the army chief and mobilize the army; and removing the king as supreme commander-in-chief. It also decided that Parliament would have the authority to frame, amend or rescind laws on royal succession. It declared a change in the official title of the government from 'His Majesty's Government' to 'Nepal government'; changed the national anthem; and declared Nepal a secular state. Many analysts termed these unprecedented measures a 'Nepali Magna Carta'.[3]

The army did try to intervene when Parliament began to curtail the authority of the king. Chief of Army Staff Thapa, accompanied by seven senior generals, including the future chief, Rookmangud Katawal, went to the prime minister's official residence at Baluwatar on the morning of 13 May. During the forty-five-minute meeting, they 'advised' the eighty-four-year-old prime minister to talk to the king before curtailing his rights.[4] In 1990, too, the prime minister, Krishna Prasad Bhattarai, was pressed by the generals, led by Chief Satchit Shumsher Rana, against curtailing the rights of the king. But in 2006, five days after the meeting, through a parliamentary declaration, the palace's control over the army was formally severed.

Delhi was in total agreement with whatever PM Koirala was doing. He received an unprecedented welcome reception in Delhi when he visited on 6 June. Manmohan Singh broke protocol and personally went to the Indira Gandhi International Airport to receive him. Singh praised Koirala, saying there was no other leader in South Asia like him.

During the visit, India announced huge bilateral aid and a concessional loan totalling NRs. 10 billion to Nepal—the largest till then. It was too much for the Maoists. Yearning to go to Kathmandu, the Maoists were equally suspicious of the unfurling events.

Actually, after sidelining the king, the seven parties were taking decisions unilaterally, with no involvement of the other party in the movement, the Maoists. Following the Punjab meeting, the Maoists dispatched a talks team comprising Krishna Bahadur

Mahara, Dev Gurung and Dinanath Sharma. The government gave similar a responsibility to ministers Krishna Prasad Sitaula, Pradeep Gyawali and Ramesh Lekhak. Yet, the peace talks could not proceed as expected, apart from issuing a twenty-five-point ceasefire code of conduct.

Prachanda and Baburam entered Nepal from the Raxaul border point on 23 May. But they still did not feel safe enough to travel to Kathmandu and appear overground. Exasperated at seeing a series of important decisions taken by the restored Parliament, and the isolation of his party, Prachanda expressed his outrage from a village in eastern Nepal, saying, 'The seven parties are demonstrating their cowardice by acting as if they have done the killing.'[5]

Baluwatar pact and the after-effects

With the Maoists becoming increasingly vocal against the government, Prime Minister Koirala dispatched his Home Minister Krishna Prasad Sitaula to Sikles, in Kaski district, on 16 June 2006. Prachanda was training his party cadres there. After a chat with Sitaula, Prachanda, his wife Sita and Baburam Bhattarai boarded a helicopter and came to Kathmandu, accompanied by the home minister. They rode in the minister's vehicle to enter the nerve centre of Kathmandu's political power. Prime Minister Koirala was waiting for them at his official residence at Baluwatar. It was their first direct meeting after Delhi. After half an hour of catching up, they attended a joint meeting with the seven parties, but it was not easy to find common ground. The meeting went on for ten hours. Towards the evening, they signed an eight-point pact. The points included an understanding to promulgate an interim Constitution and form an interim Parliament, to 'restructure the state', and request the United Nations to assist in the management and supervision of arms and armies of both the sides in the conduct of the Constituent Assembly election.

PM Koirala did not come out of the residence after signing the pact, but Prachanda did. It was for the first time in twenty-five years that the underground leader was showing himself in public before a horde of waiting cameramen and journalists yearning to get a glimpse of the master rebel. In the darkened (due to a power outage) makeshift tent erected outside the main building of the PM's residence, Prachanda declared, 'This is an important break in the history of Nepal.'

Sitting side by side, both Prachanda and Baburam were wearing similar grey safari suits. At his first public appearance, Prachanda presented himself as a practical orator rather than as a dogmatic communist leader. He avoided using communist jargon and instead chose to speak in simple language, in an attempt to communicate with the urban middle class. Despite their love for football, many Nepalis—otherwise watching the World Cup tournament—tuned in to hear what he had to say. In that hurriedly called press conference, Prachanda managed, succinctly, to outline his policies and programmes. He talked about his plans for the restructuring of the state, mobilizing Nepalis in a ten-year development campaign, bringing down the strength of the armed forces to 20,000, providing military training to all able Nepalis and so on.

That was the day when Prachanda was at the pinnacle of the public imagination. He could not maintain that hold in subsequent years. Gradually, people started to oppose the eight-point pact. It was thought that the Maoists were dominant in the pact. Members of the restored Parliament were not pleased, because it talked about dissolving their house and replacing it with the new interim Parliament. Relations between the Maoists and the seven parties slowly started growing frosty. Meanwhile, the Maoists were furious when Prime Minister Koirala unilaterally wrote a letter, on 2 July, to the UN secretary general asking for his assistance in the peace process. They wrote a separate letter to the UN on 24 July. In the end, like they did during the twelve-point understanding, the Maoists and the government separately wrote similarly worded letters to the United Nations. This created the right environment for the arrival of a UN mission to monitor the Constituent Assembly election, but it did not assuage the distrust between the Maoists and the government.

The 27–31 August central committee meeting of the Maoists, held in Kamidanda of Kavre district, clearly showed the seemingly unbridgeable differences between the two sides. It concluded that the seven-party alliance had betrayed them after gaining power. It decided to carry out 'revolution' in a new manner. 'One should never forget that the party has reached today's stage by adopting the belief that revolutions cannot be repeated, but their development is possible,' read the political document passed by the meeting. 'For the success of the Nepali people's revolution, it is necessary to strike a balance among the armed people's war, armed people's movement, peace talks and diplomacy.'[6]

The Maoists thus advanced four tools to complete their proposed revolution: people's war, people's movement, peace talks and diplomacy. They believed that having come to open politics from the path of 'people's war' and 'people's movement', they could create an environment for revolt through the initiatives of 'peace talks' with the domestic parties and 'diplomacy' with the international community. With this strategy in mind, they intensified urban-centric activities through the meetings of their sister affiliate organizations. They hosted the fourth convention of CCOMPOSA, the umbrella body of the Maoist parties of South Asia, in Kathmandu. They also took part in the meeting of the global body RIM. With the renewal of their ties with rebels elsewhere, the Nepali Maoists demonstrated that they were headed further towards extremism.

Guerrillas in the cantonments

Delhi was closely monitoring the Maoists' extremism-oriented activities. Indian Ambassador Shiv Shankar Mukherjee was in close contact with Prachanda and Baburam. He used to visit Prachanda's residence at Naya Bazaar or the Maoists' contact office at Shankhamul for formal conversations. But for informal chats, he used to call the two leaders to the Indian embassy. When the media got wind of one such clandestine visit to India House, in breach of protocol, on 21 October, it was publicly exposed in the media.[7]

According to Prachanda, during that visit, the Indian ambassador had encouraged him to participate in the soon-to-be-held Constituent Assembly election. Prachanda accused Prime Minister Koirala of attempting to hold the election unilaterally. The Indian ambassador then worked informally to mediate between the two sides. Finally, on the night of 8 November, at around 1.15 a.m., the Maoists and the seven parties announced another deal incorporating six different issues. They committed to form an interim Parliament and interim Constitution and hold elections to a Constituent Assembly by mid-June 2007. They prepared points of bases for the interim Constitution. They agreed not to provide any authority to the king and agreed that the decision of keeping or dismissing the monarchy would be taken by simple majority at the first meeting of the elected Constituent Assembly.[8]

The deal also decided to keep the Maoist fighters in the seven main cantonments at Kailali, Surkhet, Rolpa, Palpa, Kavre, Sindhuli and Ilam, besides twenty-one other satellite camps nearby. The government was made responsible for the maintenance of the camps and its inhabitants. It was also agreed that the weapons of the guerrillas would be stored in containers inside the camps. The containers were to be fitted with sirens and kept under UN supervision. They agreed to store the same number of weapons belonging to the Nepali Army under similar conditions. The government army was to be restricted to its barracks.

Initially, India had shown interest in being involved in the supervision, but both Prachanda and Koirala believed that it would be better to involve the UN instead. When the US, too, stressed the involvement of a UN mission in post-conflict management, India backed down.[9] In the end, the UN Mission in Nepal (UNMIN) came with a 'limited mandate' as per India's conditions. The first job for UNMIN was to register and monitor the guerrillas gathering at the cantonments. It was also entrusted with the monitoring of the forthcoming Constituent Assembly election.[10]

If one didn't count the militia, the Maoists had less than 10,000 guerrilla fighters at the height of the insurgency. As preparations were being made to keep the fighters in the cantonments, the Maoists quickly took out a few thousand and organized them under the newly formed Young Communist League (YCL). The YCL was formed as a youth wing to be used in open politics. And in order to increase the number of their guerrillas in the cantonments, they recruited militias, party cadres and ordinary youths. A large number of youths rushed to be recruited when they were promised salaries the same as soldiers of the Nepali Army. The number of guerrillas who came for UNMIN registration rose to 32,250, but 8640 of them did not attend when UNMIN started the verification process. After being identified as minors or as joining the guerrillas after the enforcement of the ceasefire code of conduct, 4008 more were subsequently dismissed. As such, only 19,602 were officially registered as former combatants. The Maoists listed 3428 items of weaponry.[11]

According to information provided by the Nepali Army to the UNMIN, the insurgents had looted a total of 3430 weapons from various security agencies. The Maoists' list was thus just two short. Obviously, given the number of weapons they had bought from Indian and Chinese markets, and the weapons they confiscated from people in villages, the number of weapons in their possession ought to have been much higher. It was suspected that the Maoists had concealed a large number of weapons. But the government chose to ignore this discrepancy to let the peace process move forward.

Finally, on 21 November 2006, the government and the Maoists signed a Comprehensive Peace Agreement (CPA). The agreement signed by Prime Minister Girija Prasad Koirala and the chairman of the Communist Party of Nepal–Maoist, Pushpa Kamal Dahal aka Prachanda, formally declared 'the end of the armed insurgency that started in 1996'. It not only addressed the technical aspects related to the management of arms and armies, it also laid down as its major agenda the establishment of a durable peace and removal of socio-economic disparities through the election of a Constituent Assembly.

Based on the CPA, the two sides also signed a deal on the monitoring and management of arms and armies of the government and the Maoists on 8 December. But the promulgation of the interim Constitution was delayed due to differences among the parties on several issues. Originally planned to be completed by 26 November, the interim statute was finalized on 15 January 2007. The parties had reviewed and amended the draft submitted by the Interim Constitution Drafting Committee. The interim Constitution gave unlimited authority to the prime minister. The prime minister was also given the powers hitherto reserved for the king as the head of state. There was no provision for relieving the prime minister from his position—this was later added.

As per the interim Constitution, a 330-member interim Parliament was formed. It had eighty-five members of NC and eighty-three each of the UML and the Maoists. The NC and UML members continued from the reinstated Parliament as it was converted into the interim Parliament. The Maoists had got the same number of seats as the UML on the basis of a political agreement. This formalized the entry of the Maoists into mainstream politics. The new interim legislature-Parliament had many young faces and those from usually under-represented communities, mostly belonging to the Maoists.

Red carpet in Delhi

India was pleased that, through its facilitation, it could bring the Maoists back to the peace process. Prachanda received an invitation to his first official foreign visit from Delhi, to be a guest speaker at a 'leadership summit' hosted by *Hindustan Times*—an indication of his growing legitimacy.

Prachanda received a good welcome when he addressed the session titled 'India: The Next Global Superpower', which was inaugurated by Sonia Gandhi, chief of the Indian coalition. Janata Dal (United) President Sharad Yadav hosted a lunch on 19 November at his residence, where Prachanda was seen sitting between former Indian Prime Ministers Inder Kumar Gujral and V.P. Singh. 'I had read the history of revolution. But you guys showed that to us in reality,' Gujral said, praising Prachanda as a revolutionary leader. 'I thank you for that opportunity.' Prachanda also met another former prime minister, Chandra Shekhar. The Maoist chairman was pleased at the roaring reception he received in the Indian capital. 'I am unable to distinguish if this is reality or a dream—getting such a warm welcome from you,' he said, revealing he had spent his underground life on Indian soil. 'In the course of the ten years of our movement, I have ended up developing a deep emotional attachment with the people of India. I want to meet those Indian people . . . where I had stayed and where I took shelter.'[12]

He also did not forget to speak of two things that are always music to Indian ears. First was related to the Indian Maoists. Prachanda said, 'There are ideological differences between the Nepali and Indian Maoist movements. We never had a working relationship with them.' The second was related to Pakistan. Upon his return, he spoke to journalists at Tribhuwan International Airport, revealing that after the start of the people's war, he had refused an offer from the Pakistani intelligence agency ISI 'to provide us with truckloads of weapons'.

However, the honeymoon between Prachanda and India was short-lived. The Maoists saw Indian activities in the Tarai region as being aimed against them. Then, there was a bloody incident in which twenty-eight of their YCL workers were massacred in Gaur, behind which the Maoists also saw the hand of Indian criminal elements. The Maoists termed these incidents 'expansionist conspiracies'.

During the period of frosty relations following the Gaur incident, a Gandhian leader named Nirmala Deshpande came to Nepal carrying a message from Sonia Gandhi. Deshpande, a member of Acharya Binoba Bhave's Bhudaan movement of the 1950s, had known Prachanda from his underground days in Delhi. She used to call the Nepali Maoists her *saathi* (companion), and used to say that her advice was also behind their decision to join peaceful politics. She held a secret meeting with Prachanda at a hotel in the western town of Butwal.[13] But it did not bridge the growing gap between the Maoists and India.

Peeved at Delhi

The central committee meeting of the Maoists that ended on 17 April 2007 made the conscious decision to accord top priority to the agenda of nationalism, besides that of the republic. A leader from Rolpa, Netra Bikram Chand 'Biplav', who enjoyed the blessings of hard-line leaders such Kiran, Gaurav and Badal, emerged as the champion of this cause, aimed at altering the party line. Kiran and Gaurav had just returned after being released from Indian jails and wanted to 'free the party from Indian influence'. At the meeting, Biplav made a scathing attack at what he called the 'compromise-prone tendency' of the party leadership. Claiming that the party had failed to make any achievement despite holding several talks in Delhi and Kathmandu in the past year, he said, 'This style of rushing to Baluwatar (the Nepali PM's residence) and holding on to the thread of assurances is not going to solve our contradictions. A new method and struggle is necessary for this purpose.'[14]

The Maoists looked upon the announcement of the Election Commission, of its inability to hold the Constituent Assembly elections in May that year for technical reasons, as a conspiracy by the seven-party government. 'The basis of unity among eight parties has been finished by this inability to hold the election in May,' Prachanda said. In fact, it was implicitly an announcement by the Maoists that the basis of unity with India, too, had collapsed.

Having cunningly manipulated various power centres, from the parties to the palace, ever since the start of the people's war, the Maoist leadership was confident: Girija Prasad Koirala and India could also be trapped by their scheming. They had therefore merged their 'new regime' into what they called the 'old regime'. They even declared the end of the people's war. They agreed to store weapons they had so assiduously collected in the ten years of war in Indian containers under UN supervision. They forced their guerrillas to live in tents sent by India, in camps that were ringed by Indian barbed wires and supervised by ex-soldiers of the Indian Gorkha regiments. They even rushed at times to India House in breach of diplomatic protocol whenever they were called by the Indian ambassador. They had joined the interim government even though they were not given the position of deputy prime minister, as had been earlier promised. After all these developments, when they looked back, they were scared to find that their status was rapidly getting reduced to a mere 'eighth party'.

When they weighed the benefits and losses that had accrued since the twelve-point understanding signed at India's behest, the Maoist leaders were dumbfounded. They were not using India— instead, it was the other way around. They were being used by India. As a consequence, the party's central committee meeting of April 2007 decided to take up the agenda of 'nationalism' (read India-bashing).

The Maoist leaders concluded that the Indians gave one kind of 'assurances' to them, but in practice, they had plotted to blunt them. They also concluded that India was orchestrating a proxy war against them in the Madhes (Tarai). Around that time, Indian Ambassador Shiv Shankar Mukherjee informed US Ambassador James Moriarty that the Maoists were divorced from their earlier relations with the Indian spy agencies.[15]

Just as India–Maoist relations were dipping, the Maoists held their fifth plenum at Balaju, Kathmandu, from 3 to 8 August 2007. Around 2200 cadres participated in the party's largest gathering since it had joined the peace process. Prachanda was under tremendous pressure to abandon the line of the Constituent Assembly in favour of renewed revolt. His political document was not passed without amendments. It was the first time in twenty years, since he assumed party leadership, that Prachanda had to adjust his document to get it endorsed. He had to add an 'action plan' for 'revolt' and incorporate the 'spirit of the plenum' before the document was duly endorsed.

Pointing at Indian activities, the document stated, 'Today, the increasing hold of foreign power centres over the country's armed forces, bureaucracy, information machinery, economy and politics has raised grave questions over the nation's future.'[16] After the plenum, the Maoists presented twenty-two demands to the government, demanding the immediate declaration of a republic and a proportional representation system of election—even though they themselves were a part of the government. They posed those demands as pre-conditions for the Constituent Assembly elections. In case those demands were not met, the Maoists announced their boycott of the elections scheduled for November that year.

On 18 September, four Maoist ministers walked out of the government they had joined five-and-a-half months earlier. One of those ministers, Krishna Bahadur Mahara, told party cadres, 'We have closely watched the government structure and carried out a recce of their activities from inside. Now we will capture it with your help.'[17] Remarks like these clearly pointed to their drift towards the agenda of revolt. As a result, the second scheduled date for the Constituent Assembly election (November 2007) also passed without voting.

Slogan of nationalism

Following the Balaju plenum, the Maoists appeared to be rapidly drifting away from the path of understanding. Prachanda urged pro-monarchists to join his anti-India campaign of nationalism. He said, 'There are people and forces in this country who honestly supported the king in their belief that he would save the nation . . . All forces should unite to safeguard national unity, independence and territorial integrity.'[18]

According to a top Maoist leader, they were planning to advance their dominance over the Nepali Army by getting close to the monarchists. They concluded that they could, sooner or later, seize power if they could take this armed force, which remained intact despite a decade-long conflict, into confidence. They thought that at least isolating the army would pave the way for the smooth declaration of a republic.

With these ideas in mind, Prachanda expanded his contacts with senior army officials. In informal conversations, he even told them that he would accept a 'ceremonial monarchy'. Prachanda said: the Maoists do not want a republic at this time, because if it comes it will come under the NC's leadership and would merely be a 'Bihari republic', it wouldn't make any objective difference other than the dismissal of the king and the increase of Indian influence. So he indicated his willingness to accept Gyanendra's grandson Hridayendra as a 'symbolic king' for a certain period. The then Army Chief Rookmangud Katawal was also advocating a similar position for a 'baby king'.[19]

It was the internal calculation of the Maoists that their proposal of a 'nationalist partnership' could either work in their favour, or it would scare Delhi and expedite the implementation of the agenda of a republic in the country. Prachanda had hit the bull's eye in this calculation. On 15–16 September, Delhi dispatched its foreign secretary, Shivshankar Menon, to Kathmandu. The Maoists had just decided to walk out of the government and foil the Constituent Assembly election. Menon met leaders of all the major parties, including the Maoists, and told them that the election was Delhi's top priority.

Close on the heels of Menon's visit, Delhi sent former Foreign Secretary Shyam Saran as its special envoy. Saran had worked closely with the Maoists since the twelve-point understanding. He arrived in Kathmandu on 10 October and met Prachanda at his Naya Bazaar residence the same evening. They met again the following morning at Dwarika's Hotel, where Saran was staying. Saran pointed out that the Maoists had no option but to take part in the Constituent Assembly election. But Indian efforts could not ensure the polls in November, and the Maoists were not interested in elections without the assurance of a republic.

After Saran's visit, the Maoists opened up another front— that of leftist polarization. On 4 November, a stricture motion in favour of a republic was passed by the Parliament at the joint initiative of the Maoists and the UML. The Parliament directed the government to implement the motion. The Maoists planned to replace PM Girija Prasad Koirala with UML General Secretary Madhav Kumar Nepal, if need be. They could not dislodge the powerful interim prime minister, but the UML–Maoist alliance in the Parliament, which threatened to push the government into a minority, forced the Congress to take steps towards the establishment of a republic.

The Maoists were playing two games at the same time. While they were creating the right environment for the declaration of a republic, they were also intensifying their clandestine talks with the king in order to find a point of partnership. Until then, their ultimate goal was to capture power, not the Constituent

Assembly.[20] And they were prepared to ally with any individual or force to reach that goal. The third date of the Constituent Assembly election had just been fixed for 10 April 2008. They made former Home Minister Kamal Thapa a medium to talk to the king. 'I talked to Prachanda and Baburam numerous times in Kathmandu on behalf of the king,' Thapa said. 'They told me that it was possible to cross the NC and UML if we joined hands with them.'

During their second such meeting, Baburam reportedly said, 'If the king gives us the go-ahead, we will come down to the street on various pretexts such as inclusion and derail the election.' According to Thapa, Baburam's proposal was this: The Maoists would take to the streets and unleash anarchy, inviting the king to intervene with the help of the army. The plan was hatched in the belief that the army was still loyal to the palace. Three weeks before the April election, Thapa carried their message to the king. But the plan was derailed after the king backed down fearing 'great bloodshed'.[21]

Perhaps the king saw that the Maoists were only trying to use him. He probably saw that once they captured power in an alliance with the palace, they would advance their influence in the army and would, at some point, sideline him. So he tried to look at other options to save the monarchy.

First step towards republic

The country was headed, sooner or later, towards a republic. The Maoists' posture only hastened its arrival. But the apprehension in Delhi was whether the Maoists would turn out to be dominant in the army once the king was dismissed. Besides, taking advantage of the transitional confusion, China was strengthening its contacts with both Maoists and the army. India was not pleased.

In fact, after the second people's movement, India was keen to distance itself from the army. They did not like the new chief, Rookmangud Katawal, who grew up under the care of King

Mahendra. Therefore, they had not yet invited the chief to a customary visit to India, even though a year had passed since his appointment to the post. Delhi saw that the Maoists and China would gain by its continued indifference. In this context, it finally invited Army Chief Katawal.

Incidentally, just a month earlier, Katawal's training mate at Dehradun's Indian Military Academy, General Deepak Kapoor, had been appointed as chief of the Indian army. He played a role in bridging the gap between Katawal and the Indian establishment. On 9 December 2007, Katawal flew directly to Dehradun on an Avro army aircraft. He was invited as a special guest to the silver anniversary ceremony of the Academy, which Indian Prime Minister Manmohan Singh attended as the chief guest. Apart from the Indian PM, Katawal also met External Affairs Minister Pranab Mukherjee, Foreign Secretary Shivshankar Menon, and National Security Advisor M.K. Narayanan. In Delhi, President Pratibha Patil decorated him with the honorary title of General of the Indian Army (the custom of the two armies decorating each other's chiefs as honorary generals had been suspended after the 1 February 2005 coup of King Gyanendra).

Despite being a military officer, Katawal took a keen interest in politics. He was seeking a way to save the monarchy in some form. After the Maoists–UML passed a motion in favour of a republic in Parliament, Katawal concluded that the former rebels' hobnobbing with the monarchists was a mere ploy and that they were bent on carrying out a strategy to capture power. So he understood that only Delhi now had the capacity to save the monarchy.

Delhi concurred with him on the dangers of integrating Maoist combatants into the army, believing that this would lead to an increase in Maoist influence on the army. The former fighters should be integrated into other security agencies or into society, was the common opinion. Katawal thought that if there was a breakdown over the issue of integration or in the peace process, it would derail the Constituent Assembly election, save the monarchy and spoil the Maoist plan of capturing power. Back from India, Katawal issued a statement opposing integration. But his attempts to seek Delhi's assistance in saving the monarchy did not work. The major parties of Nepal were already in favour of a republic. India, too, thought that its interest would be best served by supporting this republican wave in Nepal.

The then chief of RAW, Ashok Chaturvedi, landed in Kathmandu on 18 December 2007. He had taken over the reins of RAW a year earlier, following the retirement of P.K. Hormis Tharakan. At around 1 p.m. on 20 December, he went from the Hyatt Hotel in Boudha, where he was staying, to Baluwatar, in an Indian embassy car, to meet Prime Minister Girija Prasad Koirala. He was accompanied by RAW's Kathmandu station chief, Suresh Dhundiya. He had a half-hour conversation with Koirala, centred around the alliance with the Maoists, the restoration of the Maoists in the interim government, holding the Constituent Assembly election, and the growing Chinese influence in Nepal.[22]

Apart from Koirala, Chaturvedi met a number of leaders including Prachanda, Baburam Bhattarai, Madhav Kumar Nepal, and Army Chief Katawal. He returned on 22 December. Subsequently, the Nepali Congress and the Maoists started growing closer. Parties that had been unable to reach an understanding for the past three months, signed a pact a day after Chaturvedi left. On the night of 23 December, the top leaders of the main parties signed a twenty-three-point deal. It formally laid the foundation of a republic.[23]

According to the deal, the interim Constitution was to be amended to declare Nepal a federal democratic republic; the declaration of a republic was to be formally enforced by the first meeting of the elected Constituent Assembly (with a rider that the interim Parliament itself could implement a republic by a two-thirds majority before the Constituent Assembly, if the king resorted to any mischief), dissociating the monarchy from any aspect of governance, and letting the prime minister take up the role of head of state in the interim period. These were far-reaching decisions. With this, the Maoists re-joined the interim government; they toned down their anti-India and pro-nationalism rhetoric, which they had taken up since the Balaju plenum; and the country headed towards the 10 April 2008 election to a Constituent Assembly. But at around the same time, the southern plains of Nepal threw up an unexpected challenge, which pushed national politics in a different direction altogether.

18

Madhes Explodes

'When one looks at the Madhes and Maoists' people's war, one could see them as contradictory. But this perspective or understanding is not true. In fact, the Maoists' people's war and Madhesi revolt are two sides of the same coin.'

—NC leader Pradeep Giri, analysing the
relative aspects of the Madhesis and the Maoists[1]

The American professor Leo E. Rose was a prominent and oft-quoted foreign scholar who studied the geopolitics of Nepal. It was his student, Frederick H. Gaige, who carried out an extensive study of Nepal's southern plains, known as the Tarai or Madhes, bordering India. His book *Regionalism and National Unity in Nepal,* published in 1975, is considered a seminal work on the people of Madhes. He writes, 'Despite resentment against the Nepali government's economic policies in the rural areas of the Tarai and resentment against the government's efforts at Nepalization in the urban centres, the Tarai is not a sea of discontent, ready to drown the government in a high tide of revolution.'[2]

Gaige's conclusion that communities living in the Tarai region were unhappy over the government's economic policies and attempts at 'Nepalization' was correct. But his second conclusion, that this sentiment was not ready to boil over, no longer applied. Thirty-two years after his book was published, two successive political storms hit this region, just a year before the Constituent Assembly election.

These movements were not aimed against any political system. They were identity-based campaigns that raised socio-political issues. People expressed fury over discrimination and marginalization of the Madhesi community. The first movement established terms such as 'Madhes' and 'Madhesis' in the political lexicon and sought to gain recognition for their rights. The second movement propelled the country towards the path of federalism.

Issues of Madhes

According to the 2011 census, 50.27 per cent of the total population (or around 13.3 million people) lived in the Tarai region of Nepal.[3] These included natives, migrants from the hills, and Indians who have come across the open border. For years, the region had been seething with concealed anger over the tendency of Kathmandu to lump together the natives and Indian migrants and treat them with disrespect and discrimination.[4] Besides, the locals were also furious over the growing migration of people from the hills, and their dominance of the prime real estate of the region. From the time of the Rana regime (before 1951), it was customary to grant estates in the Tarai to people close to the regime. When the wave of migration to the Tarai swelled following the eradication of malaria from the dense forests there, suspicion and resentment among Madhesis and other communities increased.[5]

In recent years, the Madhesi community had been unhappy over difficulties in getting Nepali citizenship, prohibitions on the official use of local languages, minimal representation in major organs of the state and so on. They were equally angry over some of the decisions made by the Supreme Court on these issues. For instance, the decision by the apex court in May 1999 of stopping Rajbiraj municipality and the Dhanusha District Development Committee from using the Maithili language in official communication hurt their sentiments. They were also livid over the court's decision regarding citizenship. A committee on citizenship monitoring and evaluation, led by UML leader Jitendra Dev, had recommended the bestowing of citizenship on 3.4 million people of the Tarai. The government had formed teams to award citizenship in twenty districts. But the apex court intervened and rescinded the legitimacy of even the 30,000 citizenship cards that had been awarded by the teams.

The government in Kathmandu had a mistaken view, always looking at the problems of the Tarai through the prism of India. It held that the problems of the region were related only to illegal migrants. But if it felt the open border was problematic, it should have taken steps to regularize it. It shouldn't have refused to give justified recognition to this section of Nepal's diverse society. Yet, the government continued to follow the tradition established by King Mahendra, of imposing and promoting unitary nationalism based on the Nepali language and traditional dress of the hills. A few hand-picked Madhesi leaders enjoyed their position at the top levels of the mainstream regime, but the majority of Madhesis, who had no such access, were always fuming with discontent.

An attempt at invoking a regional political awareness in the Tarai was first made by the Nepal Tarai Congress, formed by Bedananda Jha in 1951. When the government promoted the use of the Nepali language, the party launched a campaign in favour of using Hindi in the region. But after all of its twenty-one candidates lost badly in the general election of 1959, Jha's political line gradually changed. Subsequently, he became a great supporter of King Mahendra and was appointed Nepal's ambassador to India.

Towards the end of the Panchayat regime, Gajendra Narayan Singh restarted Tarai-based politics by launching the Nepal Sadbhavana Parishad. After the restoration of democracy in 1990, he turned it into the Nepal Sadbhavana Party (NSP). Although the party did not win many seats, it persistently raised issues of citizenship and advocated the need for federal structures in the country.[6]

The Maoists advanced the slogan of federalism raised by the NSP. The CPN–Maoist leaders had envisaged way back in 1995 that they could exploit the discontent brewing below the surface in the Tarai and make it one of the bases for their people's war. The 'Proposal on Ethnic Policies in Nepal', passed by their first national convention stated, 'Regional discrimination against Tarai people must be ended to ensure their smooth access to government service, administration, etc.' They said that all the people of the Tarai should get citizenship without any obstruction, but added that in the course of citizenship distribution, no Indians should receive it.[7]

For a couple of years after the beginning of the people's war, the effect of the insurgency could not be felt below the Mahabharat hills. In order to expand their activities in the Tarai, the Maoists formed the Madhesi National Liberation Front in 2000 under the leadership of Mahendra Paswan. During the period of the first peace talks in July 2001, the first convention of the front was held in Barhathwa, Sarlahi, and chose a new central committee headed by Jai Krishna Goit. In August 2001, the Maoists formed a United Revolutionary People's Council under the leadership of Baburam Bhattarai. The council was intended to function as 'central people's government'. They envisaged nine autonomous provinces within that government, including 'Madhes', which was to incorporate Abadh in the mid-western Tarai, Bhojpura in the eastern Tarai, and Mithila, around Janakpur.[8]

The Maoists deliberately chose to use the term 'Madhes' instead of the Tarai to describe the plains bordering India. The Tarai is just a geographical term while Madhes has a political connotation. Those who lived in the Tarai, except hill-origin people, were called Madhesis. Maoist leader Bhattarai tried to explain it thus: 'Madhesi problems have emerged mainly due to the internal colonialist policies adopted by the feudal ruling regime of the Khas hill-origin community,' he wrote, adding, 'There can be no worse form of dishonesty if one tries to cover up one's cunning by claiming it was a creation of a neighbour.' Baburam's argument was that Madhesi problems did not emerge due to provocation by Indian expansionists, but that internal exploitation was primarily responsible.[9]

In the western districts of Rolpa and Rukum, the Maoists had established their organization on an ideological basis, whereas in Madhes, they tried to do so at gunpoint. As they rushed to expand, lumpen elements also joined their party. When such people received political backing and a gun, they went on a spree of terrorizing and extorting the public. The higher-class community of the region was already unhappy with the manner in which the Maoists were empowering Dalits and the lower classes. Along with middle-class people from various parts of the region, they stood against the Maoists.

The unruly Maoist cadres gradually came to the notice of security authorities on both sides of the border, who attempted to use these cadres to control the party. They were successful in exploiting Maoist cadres with financial or other incentives, luring them with motorbikes and turning them into informers. The Royal Nepali Army on this side of the border, and Indian intelligence agencies on the other side, did this in a planned manner. The army was able to infiltrate the insurgents better in the eastern and central Tarai than they had been able to do in the hills. Consequently, many Maoist leaders and cadres were killed in the region.[10]

Interest across the border

Indian security officials were not very concerned with the rise of violence in the hills of Nepal. They allowed the orchestrators of the violence to operate from their territory. But they became alarmed when it spilled over to the plains. The Madhesi Front of the Maoists had, in their first appeal, portrayed India as the enemy: 'Our struggle is against the Hindu high-class community, feudalism, imperialism and Indian expansionism.'[11]

Indians felt that the India policy of the Maoists was neither reliable nor trustworthy. Therefore, Indian officials saw a real threat in the merger of Nepali Maoism with Bihari Naxalism, especially among the Madhesis, who had the same features and sociocultural outlook as people in the bordering Indian states, besides relations with the latter. They concluded that the advancement of Maoism below the belt of the East–West Highway of Nepal was a security threat to India. Therefore, they quickly shifted tens of thousands of SSB border security personnel from the Chinese border, and posted them along the Nepali border.

The highway had replaced the Himalayas as India's strategic frontier. It deployed several tools to prevent the people's war from expanding below the highway. 'Indian expansionists came with full force. They tried to get cosy with the Madhesis by raising slogans of "*bhai-bhai*", and tried to divide the community,' Prachanda remarked during a phase of the people's war when his relations with Delhi were cold. 'India has invested millions of rupees in Madhes, in schools, parties and even in individuals. It has invested untold amounts to create informers. It is plotting to break the Madhes away by doing all this.'[12]

India's interest in the Madhes grew exponentially following the appointment of Shyam Saran as Delhi's ambassador in October 2002.[13] He mainly undertook two efforts.

First, until 2003, India had concentrated its development assistance to Nepal primarily in large projects in the hills. Under Saran, these were brought down to the Tarai, because of the large population in the region. The actual reason was strategic. During his term as prime minister in 2003–04, Surya Bahadur Thapa gave an unusual permission to the Indian ambassador, to spend up to

NRs. 30 million (which was later increased to NRs. 50 million) of monthly development assistance anywhere in the country, directly. Saran concentrated this assistance in the Madhes.

After he wrapped up his ambassadorial term in Kathmandu in July 2004, Saran returned to Delhi to take up the reins at South Block as foreign secretary. Later still, he was appointed as Officer on Special Duty at the Prime Minister's Office. Working in these capacities, Saran was instrumental in promoting large central highway road projects in his home state of Bihar, and played a role in linking those highways with the Nepal border through subsidiary roads. Saran was in favour of expanding not only social, but also political and economic relations between India and the Madhes.

The second important task Saran performed during his stint in Kathmandu was the opening of an Indian Consulate Office in the heart of the Madhes, at Birgunj. India had first proposed to open a consulate in Birgunj way back, during the visit of Prime Minister Inder Kumar Gujral in 1998. The agenda was broached by the Indians during several bilateral talks in subsequent years. Nepal kept declining the proposal on the grounds that there was no need for a consulate in a town that was only a few hours away from Kathmandu. In the end, the prime minister of the royalist government, Surya Bahadur Thapa, acquiesced in 2003. Allowing India to open a consulate in Birgunj meant allowing the Indian embassy to spread its network across Madhes. Coinciding with the opening of the Indian consulate, the Madhes witnessed unanticipated turmoil.

India's Madhes interest was closely linked to its security interest. According to an analysis by the International Crisis Group, a think-tank on global conflicts, India's 'key security concerns (in Nepal's Madhes) include what policy-makers see as the rising influence of Pakistani intelligence agencies, the increase in madrasas in the Tarai, links between Maoists and Indian Naxalites, large-scale cross-border crime and possible Chinese intervention'.[14]

Certainly, the Indians were guided by their security interest in Madhes, where they could not tolerate the influence of any other power. Therefore, they continued to raise different bogeys at different times. Such security concerns may have been understandable, but the problem was, as the Crisis Group noted, 'Many Indians do not see the Tarai as "foreign". Many politicians talked about Madhesis as "our own people who settled in Nepal".'[15]

Amid the tendency of many in Nepal to see them as 'Indians', and a similar condescending attitude from Indians themselves, the identity of the Madhesi community was assailed by prejudice from both sides. The Indian government was guided by strategic interest and had therefore shown sympathy to Madhesi concerns. Kathmandu, for a long time, neglected Madhesi concerns by mixing them up with the Indian interests.

By-product of the Maoists

During the period of the second peace talks in 2003, Maoist politburo member Matrika Yadav was approached by a RAW officer in Kathmandu, who promised him all kinds of help. After the breakdown of talks, Matrika returned to his old shelter in Patna, but he could not get away from the prying eyes of Indian spooks. Once, when his wife was ill, a RAW operative approached him with a 'bundle of notes'. 'They tried to force them on me on the pretext of helping my ill wife,' Yadav recalled, 'I declined. Then the Indians knew that I was not for sale. Consequently, they arrested and handed me over to Nepal.'[16]

Their other attempt was based on the policy of divide and rule. Shortly before he was arrested, the second convention of the Madhesi Front, in June 2003, had replaced Jai Krishna Goit with Matrika Yadav as its chief. The Maoist leadership calculated it was better to entrust this key responsibility to a trusted member of the party old guard, rather than Goit, who had joined the party only in 1998 and came from a CPN–UML background. After being reduced to an advisor of the front, Goit revolted along with his supporters. On 26 July 2004, he formed the even more radical Janatantrik Tarai Mukti Morcha (JTMM). He became further radicalized after walking out of the Maoists, calling for an independent 'Madhes state'.

Those who later became disenchanted with the Maoists either joined Goit's group or surrendered to the Nepali or Indian security agencies. Goit himself did not want to be surrounded by anarchists. When he tried to control the widespread extortion practised by his followers, his organization split. In July 2006, his eastern regional commander, Nagendra Paswan aka Jwala Singh, challenged his mentor and formed a separate group. Once a journalist based in Siraha, Jwala Singh had first joined the Maoist movement in 1996. He also raised separatist slogans.

Less than a year later, Jwala Singh's group also split. Another group was formed by Bisphot Singh. There were also numerous others. In this way, several small outfits emerged in the Madhes within a short span. Though most of them raised political demands, they were engaged in all sorts of criminal activities including killings, extortion, kidnapping and so on.[17] They took advantage of the transitional politics that had thrown the police and administration out of gear. Many of them received political protection from non-Maoist party leaders and enjoyed the Indian concession of shelter across the border.

Most of the violent and armed outfits that emerged in the Tarai were thus by-products of the Maoist insurgency. Yet all of them targeted the Maoists, and the security agencies were seen encouraging them in this course. It was clearly seen during the Constituent Assembly election that India could easily control them if it so desired. When the holding of the election became certain, Indian security agencies marshalled the leaders of around one dozen such outfits and forced them to stay in one place for a week. They were warned of 'encounters' if there was any explosion or violence in the Madhes. Those leaders immediately made frantic phone calls to their followers and asked them to refrain from any violence. The Constituent Assembly election, thus, passed off largely peacefully in the Madhes.

The rise of the Forum

The Maoists did not envisage a single province in the Tarai–Madhes at the time of their organizational expansion in the region. Besides the Tharu-majority area in the western Tarai, they had thought of at least three autonomous units in the east. In its first appeal, the Madhesi Front had declared, 'Based on the right of ethnic self-determination, we will separately operate autonomy in Maithili, Bhojpuri and Abadhi region.'[18]

Their initial plan for Maithili, Bhojpuri and Abadhi autonomous units based on local language groups could not be sustained for long. Then they talked of 'Tharuwan' in the west and 'Madhes' province in the remaining region. The idea of 'one Madhes, one *pradesh*' or a single Madhes province had already penetrated the Maoist mindset around that time. It later went on to become the central slogan of Madhesi politics. The Maoist leadership claimed to see an Indian interest behind the call. 'It is an Indian strategy to join Tharuwan and eastern Tarai. Its ultimate strategy is to amalgamate all of Tarai into India. Some of our comrades flowed along with the conspiracy of expansionists without comprehending it,' Prachanda told his cadres. 'They even spread rumours that Comrade Matrika Yadav was an agent of RAW!'[19]

Around that time, Matrika was advocating a single Madhes province including the Tharuwan region. Prachanda said that he did so without understanding the 'expansionist plot'. Expressing his discord over party policy, Matrika resigned as chief of the Madhes People's Government on 25 January 2004, immediately after he was elected to the position. His main supporter in the demand of 'one Madhes, one province' was one Upendra Yadav.

Upendra had become disenchanted with the politics of the CPN–UML, joined the teaching profession in Biratnagar, and become closer to the Maoists. At their suggestion, Yadav formed a non-governmental organization called Madhesi Janadhikar Forum (MJF) in March 1998, and engaged in intellectual discussions on Madhes issues.[20]

When the debate on including 'Tharuwan' into a 'Madhes province' intensified within the Maoist party, Matrika travelled, in January 2004, from Patna to Delhi to talk to Prachanda. He was accompanied by Upendra. Both Matrika and Upendra were arrested at the Delhi shelter of Suresh Ale Magar. As described earlier, Prachanda had a close shave when he cancelled his plan to go there for the meeting at the last minute. Prachanda suspected Upendra Yadav of conspiring with the police. He remembered how, in an earlier meeting, he had refused when Upendra told him, 'There is no option besides cooperating with the Indians.'[21] Besides, the Indian authorities subsequently released Upendra while they handed Suresh Ale Magar and Matrika over to Nepal. The Maoists accused Upendra of 'treachery' and decided to 'eliminate' him, though much later, Prachanda came to the conclusion that Upendra had no hand in the incident.

Madhes movement I

Since the Maoists had not withdrawn their decision to eliminate him, Upendra used to move with extreme caution when he came to Kathmandu after the success of the second people's movement. However, by that time, he had already turned the MJF from an NGO into a proper political party. He was supported in his campaign by a former leader of the Nepali Congress, Jaya Prakash Gupta, who joined him as general secretary of MJF.

When the interim Constitution was promulgated on 15 January 2007 without any mention of federalism, Upendra decided to emerge in open politics by raising this issue. The following day, under his leadership, the MJF burnt a few copies of the interim Constitution at Maitighar Mandala, close to Singha Durbar in Kathmandu. Home Minister Krishna Prasad Sitaula immediately ordered the arrest of twenty-eight leaders and cadres of the MJF, including Upendra, and slapped them with charges of treason.

This spark in Kathmandu ignited a big flame in the Tarai. Protesting Upendra's arrest, the MJF called a bandh. A team of Maoist cadres led by Ram Karki were on their way to a party meeting in Chitwan when they were blocked by bandh organizers in Lahan, Siraha district, on 19 January. Their confrontation blew up into a bigger incident after a local lad, Ramesh Mahato, was shot dead by one of the Maoist cadres. Demonstrators kept the dead body in the street. The following day, Matrika Yadav reached the spot with a large gang of his supporters. They snatched the dead body from the agitators and forced Mahato's family to perform his last rites. The Maoists had already committed one mistake by killing Mahato. They committed a second one by snatching the dead body. Snatching of a dead body is no small matter in Hindu society. Besides, when 'atheist' communists did so, it triggered an extreme response.

Maoist politburo member Matrika Yadav, who had been instrumental in promoting the Madhesi cause, had become the main provocateur. The Maoist leadership had groomed Matrika as their main Madhes leader and the successor of their central leader Ram Brikchhya Yadav after his assassination on 18 August 1994 at the hands of a criminal gang at Barmajhiya, Dhanusha. After the second people's movement, Matrika had painted the public walls of Kathmandu with slogans that urged Madhesis to protest discrimination and take pride in their ethnicity.

He played a key role in establishing words like 'Madhes' and 'Madhesis' in the social lexicon at a time when Kathmandu was accustomed to denigrating the Tarai community with derogatory terms like 'Marsya'. He was also behind the mass circulation of a video depicting an incident in Nepalgunj of hurtful disrespect by hill people towards Madhesis during a Nepal bandh called on 26 December 2006 by the NSP. Emotions were becoming charged. A foundation for future agitation had been laid. But when the same Matrika resorted to snatching the body in Lahan, the whole of the Tarai revolted against the Maoists. Their party cadres and offices were targeted by protesters. Gradually, the targets expanded to include government offices, police posts, banks and media offices. The agitation sparked in Lahan spread to almost all cities of the Tarai. Although the immediate causes behind the agitation were the Maoists and Upendra's arrest for burning the interim Constitution, the objective conditions for such an uprising had been festering for a long time.[22]

Party workers of the Nepali Congress, UML and even the underground JTMM took part in the Madhes agitation. They were backed by local leaders from across the border.[23] The leaders of the Nepali Congress and the UML were initially pleased with the agitation because it targeted the Maoists. According to then minister Hridayesh Tripathy, during his meeting with UML leader Madhav Kumar Nepal on 23 January 2007, Prime Minister Girija Prasad Koirala had said, 'The Madhes agitation is against the Maoists. Let's allow it to continue for a few more days.'[24] Only after they saw that the situation was rapidly going out of their control did they call an all-party meeting on 30 January. The Maoists proposed to deploy the Nepali Army and their own combatants to repress the Madhes agitation. This further fanned the fire of anti-Maoist feeling in the region.

Initially, the Madhes agitation seemed to be anti-Maoist. Soon, it began to target members of the hill community living in the region. Demands to harshly suppress the Madhesi movement were matched by provocative and communal Madhesi slogans against the hill community.[25] As a result, families who had been settled in the Tarai for generations were displaced. The most negative aspect of the Tarai agitation from the perspective of national unity was its communal tone and psychological demarcation of the communities into *pahadis* (i.e., people of hill origin) and Madhesis.

The Madhes agitation was not a planned campaign by the MJF. But when it intensified, the MJF leaders based in Kathmandu came down to the Tarai to lead the movement. The forum declared it would continue the agitation indefinitely till there was an amendment in the interim Constitution. About thirty-nine Madhesi protestors were killed by security forces in the course of repressing the agitation. Prime Minister Girija Prasad Koirala addressed the people on 31 January. For the first time, the government recognized the Madhesi community and, after attempting to suppress the movement by force, it called for ending the agitation through talks.

The agitators discarded his address, since it made no mention of their main demand for federalism. A week later, PM Koirala made a second address, on 9 February, in which he expressed his commitment to 'making necessary provision on federal state structure and demarcation of electoral constituencies through amendment of the interim Constitution'. The three-week-long Madhes agitation (19 January–9 February) finally drew to a close, forcing the parties and the government to amend the interim Constitution. The MJF welcomed the second address by PM Koirala and took part in dialogue. The agitation gradually cooled off, but some of its jolts were still to come.

Indications from Gaur and Patna

The next major incident was again aimed at the Maoists. On 21 March 2007, both the Maoists and the MJF had announced public assemblies at the same venue in Gaur municipality of Rautahat district. When the two sworn rivals gathered at the same place, a clash naturally ensued. The MJF workers dismantled the podium erected by the Maoists. The enraged Maoist cadres attacked the podium erected by the MJF. Right at that moment, shots were fired, mysteriously, from houses surrounding the ground. Five Maoist cadres died on the spot. Twenty-two more were hunted down and butchered mercilessly. In total, twenty-nine Maoist cadres were killed and over thirty-five injured.

According to the Maoists, somebody other than the MJF workers had opened fire at their cadres. A few weeks later, the fifth plenum of the Maoists passed a separate resolution on Madhes, claiming that there were 'deliberate and planned attacks and terrorism against the party in Madhes as per the plots by feudal and imperialist elements'.[26] The Maoists suspected an Indian hand in the incidents but it did not directly mention India in the document, as it was participating in the forthcoming Constituent Assembly elections in cooperation with India.[27]

The Gaur massacre lent strength to the objective of stopping the Maoist advance in Madhes on the eve of the Constituent Assembly election. The Maoists' strength in the eastern Tarai had weakened their due to their mistake at Lahan. The Gaur incident reduced their activities in the central Tarai, too. In the western Tarai regions, including Rupandehi and Kapilvastu districts, the Maoists were already under pressure due to 'resistance committees' of local 'goons' (or criminal elements) formed to fight them. Although the Gaur incident was deplorable, it propelled the MJF forward as a political force.

Less than two months after the Gaur massacre, on 27 May, there was an attempt to assemble all the armed and unarmed forces of Madhes together at a meeting in Patna, Bihar. Madhesi leaders of all hues, from the MJF Chairman Upendra Yadav to Jwala Singh, the leader of an armed outfit that raised separatist slogans and engaged in violence, were present. The unseen organizer of the meeting was the newly opened Patna RAW station. The aim was to form a common front of all Tarai forces, selecting a consensus leader of the front, and start a campaign for an 'independent Madhes' by seeking international support.

'By establishing cordial relations and, in coordination with the Indian embassy in Kathmandu, the Tarai struggle should be carried forth in line with the aspirations of the people of the Tarai, and to provide a desirable resolution as per the time and context and by instituting solidarity for such a resolution,' read the two-page concept note circulated among the participants of the Patna meeting. It also stated that they should proceed in establishing a separate country by recognizing the Tarai as the motherland of Madhesis, and by formulating a ten-year policy to enable Madhesis residing in the Tarai to become citizens of the Tarai able to compete in all spheres of public life.[28]

Ram Raja Prasad Singh, then a prominent republican leader from Saptari, was projected as the leader of the campaign. He was invited as the chief guest of the meeting. But when he himself remarked at the meeting that he 'could not even imagine becoming the president of the Tarai by disintegrating the nation', the Patna mission collapsed.[29] No other personality could come forth to bring both the armed and unarmed Tarai groups together. The groups with a political base had no option but to join the mainstream. The forum chief, Upendra Yadav and the coordinator of the government talks team, Ram Chandra Poudel, signed a twenty-two-point agreement on 30 August 2007. The deal recognized the Madhes agitation as a continuity of the people's movement of 2006. It also agreed to establish a 'federal system of governance along with autonomous provinces'. It was the largest and most explicit step in Nepal's path towards federalism.

Madhes movement II

The MJF won recognition as a political power through this deal with the government, but its internal conflict was worsening. Its general secretary, J.P. Gupta, who used to be a Nepali Congress MP in the old Parliament, had been restored as an MP by the restoration of Parliament. Differences between him and Upendra Yadav grew. Gupta started initiatives to form a separate new force in the Madhes. He held discussions with Congress leaders

Mahantha Thakur and Bijaya Kumar Gachhadar, NSP leader Hridayesh Tripathy and Rastriya Prajatantra Party (RPP) leader Sarbendra Nath Shukla. But the issue of who would be the leader prevented agreement. Gupta and Gachhadar walked away from the process, while the rest of the Madhesi leaders announced the formation of a new Tarai Madhes Loktantrik Party (TMLP), under the leadership of Mahantha Thakur on 12 December 2007.

This also served Indian interests. India had wanted to see the rise of a new force in the Tarai that would loosen the traditional Congress stranglehold in the region and also prevent the Maoists from gaining ground. So the TMLP was born by attracting Madhesi leaders and workers from all sorts of parties such as Congress, UML, RPP, NSP, etc. Congress had to face a bitter loss in the Tarai in the subsequent election. However, many believe that had the TMLP not been formed, the Maoists would have gained seats in the Tarai as a new and alternative force.

Given the rise of the forum, why was there any need of a new party like the TMLP? The main reason was that Delhi could not fully trust Upendra Yadav, even though it had assisted his rise. Yadav, with his communist background, was less reliable than the former minister Mahantha Thakur, who had severed his thirty-seven-year-old association with the Nepali Congress to form the new party. He also had almost 'universal' respect in the Madhes due to his long political career. So the Indian establishment pressed for his leadership. Shyam Saran worked the Delhi end while the deputy chief of mission at the embassy in Kathmandu coordinated at the local level.[30]

Interest of both Delhi and the Durbar: The MJF chief, Upendra Yadav, had joined hands with NSP leader Rajendra Mahato to form the United Democratic Madhesi Front (UDMF). Subsequently, the TMLP also joined the UDMF. Posing various demands before the government, the UDMF called for a fresh agitation in the Madhes from the third week of February 2008.

The first Madhes movement of the previous year was a sort of automatic revolt, from which various power centres tried to extract benefits. The second movement attracted the interest of Delhi and the Durbar for different reasons. The palace wanted to stop the forthcoming Constituent Assembly election by capitalizing on any disorder. Delhi, on the other hand, wanted to establish the newly formed TMLP, extract additional political rights for the Madhes and strengthen the agenda of federalism.

The name of a RAW operative, Jaya Gopal, appears prominently as someone who worked closely with the Madhesi leaders in the initial phase. When Delhi set up a RAW station in Patna with the intention of monitoring the Madhes, it dispatched Jaya Gopal to take up command, equipped with blanket authority to mobilize financial and other assistance. The son of a Nepali-speaking mother and a native of Dehradun, Gopal had been posted at the embassy in Kathmandu in 2002–03, when he had developed close contacts with Nepali leaders and officials. The role he played during the second Madhes movement, when he even crossed the Nepal border at times to assist, was considered 'unprecedented' by those in the know, as some highly placed sources shared with me.

According to journalist Prashant Jha, India's Intelligence Bureau had several offices in Bihar, which closely monitored Madhesi politics and briefed Delhi. But with the onset of the Madhes movement, RAW, which had access to greater resources not subject to direct accountability, also became active. Gradually, the RAW officers forged direct contacts with Madhesi groups.[31]

Around same time, the Durbar tried to develop relations with Upendra Yadav of the MJF. After the Gaur massacre, Upendra was again scared of the Maoists and sought assistance from various power centres in Kathmandu. At this time, he first met army brigadier Dilip Jung Rayamajhi at the residence of a former judge, Parmananda Jha, in Gaurighat (Jha later became vice-president of Nepal). Rayamajhi proposed, 'Would you like to join hands?'

Close to the palace, Rayamajhi believed the monarchy should be preserved. As he was politically isolated at the time, Yadav replied in the affirmative. Rayamajhi then arranged for a meeting with King Gyanendra. The king's ADC, Binoj Basnyat, picked him up from Lazimpat near the Hotel Ambassador and took him, clandestinely, inside Narayanhity palace. There, he held talks with Gyanendra for forty minutes. Subsequently, he had another important meeting with the Army Chief Rookmangud Katawal. Rayamajhi himself escorted Yadav to the army chief's residence at Shashi Bhawan.

The second Madhes movement intensified from 13 February 2008 onwards. Yadav was encouraged by gaining access to two major power centres of the country. Yadav did not want to take part in the Constituent Assembly election before gaining political strength for his party. The Durbar wanted to foil the election altogether. It naturally brought them closer. Besides, the relationships that Indian Hindu nationalist outfits such as the Rastriya Swayamsewak Sangh (RSS) and Bharatiya Janata Party (BJP) had with the palace also worked in their favour, since Upendra, too, had contacts with them.

The main player here was Mahant Yogi Adityanath of the Gorakhnath Math in Gorakhpur, who was later to become the Uttar Pradesh chief minister. Kings of the Shah dynasty considered Gorakhnath their family deity (*kul devata*). As such, Adityanath had a close relationship with the king's honorary ADC, Bharat Keshar Simha. Upendra used to participate in several programmes organized by Adityanath.[32]

An attempt to mobilize the army: The Indian Hindu nationalist group, the Seema Jagran Manch, backed the second Madhes movement from across the border by stopping petrol tankers headed for Nepal.[33] Normal life was thrown completely out of gear in the Tarai due to continuous bandhs. Kathmandu, too, felt as if it was under siege. The date of the thrice-scheduled CA election (10 April) was fast approaching. Prime Minister Girija Prasad

Koirala was under tremendous pressure. He wanted to hold the elections at any cost.

Army Chief Katawal proposed mobilizing army to ensure the election could take place. He proposed to deploy the army from Birgunj to Amlekhgunj, in order to clear the route for essential supplies, and also in other key towns. He said that the Nepal Police and Armed Police Force were demoralized and were not up to the task. The recently held assembly of army corps chiefs (10 and 11 February) had advised that the army should be brought out of the barracks 'to control the anarchy'.

PM Koirala also thought he could control the Madhes agitation by deploying the army, but the Comprehensive Peace Agreement (CPA) had bound the army to the barracks. He consulted the Maoist Chairman Prachanda. Prachanda told Koirala that he would agree to the proposal under one condition: an equal number of Maoist combatants should also be deployed for the purpose. Koirala was in no mood to accord such a concession to the guerrillas. The three subsequent Koirala–Prachanda meetings over army mobilization remained unsuccessful.

PM Koirala was also receiving information about the involvement of monarchist elements in the violence in areas such as Birgunj and Siraha. He was further alarmed by the activity shown by the former Prime Minister Surya Bahadur Thapa, who used to be close to the palace. Thapa was holding meetings with Upendra Yadav and had struck some sort of political deal. As a result, he dropped hints of support to the Madhes movement. His Rastriya Janashakti Party even threatened to boycott the Constituent Assembly election—a threat that was withdrawn just before the polls.

The source of Thapa's power was a section of the palace and army and an illiberal chunk of the Delhi establishment. Towards the second week of February, Dr Revani Thakur, secretary of the foreign cell of India's ruling Congress party, arrived in Kathmandu. Said to be close to Sonia Gandhi, she met political leaders and intellectuals. She advanced a proposal to form a 'citizen government' under Thapa's leadership. At an interaction with journalists at the Hotel Annapurna, which included me, she said the Indian government had committed a mistake in helping to forge the twelve-point understanding between the Maoists and the seven parties, under pressure from its coalition ally the CPI(M). She said that the mistake should be corrected. It could be inferred from her remarks that she favoured retaining some form of monarchy in Nepal in order to resist the 'growing communist threat'. She had come to Kathmandu carrying the monarchist line of her boss, Dr Karan Singh, as I concluded after an interaction with her.

Koirala knew where the winds were blowing and became increasingly concerned. He was under pressure from all sides: the issue of army mobilization, Thapa's politicking, the palace's attempt to fish in the troubled waters, and now the comments from Indian leaders. Koirala then declared that the Madhes issue could be resolved if only India were positive. 'If India and Nepal jointly tried, the problem of the Tarai could be resolved in one minute,' he said.[34]

Talks at the embassy: According to some high-level sources in the Indian establishment, there were two opinions in Delhi regarding Nepal affairs at this point. A section within the ruling Congress party, the opposition Bharatiya Janata Party, the Indian army and domestic intelligence agency IB thought the monarchy should be preserved in some form. But South Block, and the external intelligence agency RAW, were in favour of a republic. The Indian Ambassador Shiv Shankar Mukherjee, who had often felt disrespected during the royal regime, also favoured a republic. Pranab Mukherjee, also from Bengal, was the external affairs minister. When he too stood in favour of a republic, the embassy was given instructions to carry out policies and programmes accordingly.

Close on the heels of Revani Thakur's visit, Congress General Secretary Digvijay Singh arrived in Kathmandu in the third week of February. Though himself from a former royal dynasty in India, Singh favoured a republic as a matter of principle. He gave his advice to the Nepali parties. His political backing greatly eased the tension felt by Ambassador Mukherjee. He was already receiving requests from pro-palace elements to let the Madhes agitation intensify. The Indian embassy, as well as RAW, wanted to see the political empowerment of the Madhes, but not at the cost of impeding the election of the Constituent Assembly. So after the agitation reached a certain height, Mukherjee worked overtime to forge an understanding.

The two leaders of the forum, Upendra Yadav and Jaya Prakash Gupta, were leading the agitation in the Tarai. Ambassador Mukherjee phoned them on 15 February and called them to hold talks in Kathmandu. The leaders were not eager. Then the ambassador gave a stern warning to Yadav by phone, 'So do you guys not need India, then?'[35] Yadav and Gupta cancelled their scheduled programme in Biratnagar and headed for Kathmandu. Along with them, other Madhesi leaders such as Mahantha Thakur and Rajendra Mahato had been invited to the embassy at Lainchour on 19 February at 11 a.m. Ambassador Mukherjee told them that the 10 April elections must be held at any cost. He urged them to end the agitation through talks with the government.[36]

Under pressure, the Madhesi leaders held the first round of talks with government representatives inside the embassy the following day, which continued for a number of days. When they did not succeed, Yadav again headed for the Madhes. Ambassador Mukherjee could bring Thakur and Mahato around to favour a resolution, but had to exert full force to convince Upendra Yadav. Yadav was detained near Simara, outside Birgunj, and forcefully brought to Kathmandu on an army chopper at around a quarter past nine at night on 24 February.

Army Chief Katawal played a key role at this point. He was caught in the middle. Should he accept instructions from the palace? Or should he listen to others? The palace wanted to see the

Madhes agitation prolonged so that the election would be derailed. Delhi wanted to see the agitation end and the election take place as scheduled. All the major parties, including the NC, UML, Maoists, TMLP and NSP, wanted to strike an understanding to end the agitation. The chief saw which way the wind was blowing. So he chose the path of a resolution, as he mentioned in his memoir.[37]

Kathmandu was witnessing an acute shortage of petroleum products due to the strike in the Tarai. Katawal had dispatched three dozen army drivers in civil clothes to bring the stranded petrol tankers to Kathmandu, which gave a brief respite to the capital. Then he brought Upendra Yadav to Kathmandu. King Gyanendra was furious. It may be that from that point on, Gyanendra and Katawal never trusted one another again.

Soon after Yadav was brought to Kathmandu, an important meeting was called in the presence of Madhesi leaders, government representatives, Ambassador Mukherjee and RAW officials. The six-point list of demands put forth by the Madhesi Front were to be addressed, with some adjustments.

The same points of understanding reached during the embassy meeting on 24 February were amended to announce an eight-point understanding on the night of 28 February at the prime minister's residence in Baluwatar. The understanding included significant points envisaging the total transformation of the state structure, such as federalization of the country, ensuring Madhes province, inclusive and collective entry of Madhesi community into the Nepali Army, ensuring inclusive proportional representation of Madhesis, Adivasi–Janajatis, women and Dalits in recruitment, promotion and nomination in all organs of state, guarantee of at least 30 per cent of candidates from the Madhesi community for the Constituent Assembly election under a system of proportional representation, and so on.[38]

Army Chief Katawal publicly expressed his displeasure over the agreement for inclusive and collective entry of the Madhesi community into the Nepali Army.[39] The government had also signed the deal under double pressure. It faced pressure from Delhi on one hand and, on the other, it wanted to hold the election on time, for which it had to end the agitation.

Within half an hour of the agreement, India came up with a statement welcoming it and expressing confidence in its 'honest implementation'. In fact, India had a role in both initiating and ending the second Madhes movement. Ambassador Mukherjee had arranged the dialogue within the embassy. As Jaya Prakash Gupta later said, 'We did not want to hold talks inside the embassy. We went there when called by the ambassador. The ambassador then also called the government representatives to the embassy.'[40] In my opinion, India wanted to give two clear messages—it held the decisive rein in Nepali politics, and it wanted to allow the Constituent Assembly elections to proceed smoothly by stopping the Madhes agitation. It was a turning point from which India wanted to show its open involvement in Nepali affairs. It wanted to prove that everything happened in Nepal as per its wishes.

The understanding reached to end the sixteen days of the second Madhes agitation altered the balance of power inside Nepal. The two Madhes movements, within a span of one year, had four important results:

First, the Madhesi community won constitutional recognition. The first amendment of the interim Constitution recognized the terms 'Madhes' and 'Madhesis'. Apart from political identity, it also opened the door for inclusive representation of the Madhesi community in different organs of the state. It created a situation where leaders of Madhesi origin of national parties were compelled to either join regional Madhesi parties, or, at least, concentrate on Madhesi issues within their parties.

Second, it increased the political representation of the Madhesi community. Electoral constituencies were delineated on the basis of population. Of the total 240 constituencies set for direct election to the Constituent Assembly, 118 were in Tarai–Madhes.

A similar system was put in place for election under proportional representation, which again increased the seats for Madhesis. As a result, of the total 601 seats in the Constituent Assembly, at least 33 per cent were set aside for Madhesis. In any parliamentary exercise since 1990, Madhesis had not won more than 21 per cent in the Parliament.[41] The MJF, which led the first movement, emerged as the fourth largest party in the Constituent Assembly. The TMLP, which arose during the second movement, emerged as the fifth largest party. The two topmost positions in the Republic of Nepal—those of president and vice-president—later went to the Madhesi community. A leader of the Madhesi movement, Upendra Yadav, was established as a key political leader.

The third achievement was federalism. It could be ensured in the new Constitution due to the Madhesi movement.

Fourth, the settlement opened the way for the election of the Constituent Assembly.

These achievements were not related only to the Madhesi community; they also benefitted other communities in the country. As the writer C.K. Lal says, 'Without the political philosophy established by the Madhes uprising, we can debate whether a Madhesi (Ram Baran Yadav) who presented himself 'first as a Nepali', or a soldier (Chhatra Man Singh Gurung) who prided himself on being the son of a Janajati, would have been appointed as president and army chief, respectively.'[42]

19

Republic in Instalment

'As per the tradition of monarchy to treat people's wishes and aspirations as paramount, I have played a supporting role to ease the decision made by the Constituent Assembly election and the 28 May meeting of the CA.'

—The former king, Gyanendra Shah,
after the abolition of the monarchy[1]

A press meet at the Narayanhity Palace! Something no one could have imagined before. But 11 June 2008 was a special day. King Gyanendra was leaving the palace, in line with the decision of establishing a republic by the major political parties and as per the instruction of the Constituent Assembly. He was holding the press meet before he left for his new abode at Nagarjuna Durbar. A large crowd of journalists gathered at Kaski Sadan of the palace that day to witness the implementation of the republic. There was no one to manage the arrangements. From one of the corners of the crowd, the dethroned king came out smiling and sat on a red chair.

Most of us had thought that Gyanendra would not be able to conceal his pain and disappointment at his failure to safeguard not only his throne, but the entire institution of the monarchy. On the contrary, the manner he presented was pleasant and relaxed. Clad in a white *daura suruwal* and a blue coat, donning a *dhaka topi* and wearing spectacles with golden frames, Gyanendra also sported a red *tika* on his forehead. It seemed he was prepared; he had known that this day was coming.

After casting a glance around, Gyanendra reached inside his coat pocket and started reading from a four-page letter; he read in a focused manner and raised some specific issues.

'In whatever position or state I am in, I vow to be committed to the independence and integrity of the state of Nepal, which has remained independent and sovereign due to the blood, toil and sacrifice made by our great ancestors,' Gyanendra said, adding, 'I have not thought of leaving this country. I want to contribute to the wider interest and peace of the country by living in my motherland.'

He 'praised' the contribution of himself and his ancestors but did not delve into the reasons that brought an end to the monarchy. He also tried to defend his '1 February move' as a step taken 'in good faith to bring peace to the land of Buddha's birth'. He did admit that the step could not succeed due to various reasons, but he did not elaborate on those 'reasons'. He also claimed that he had no movable or immovable properties overseas.

For the first time, he seized the same opportunity to refute allegations levelled against him relating to the palace massacre that had taken place seven years earlier. 'We had no option other than to silently suffer from ruthless allegations and malicious aspersion levelled mercilessly and irrationally against us and our family, neither was there anyone to speak for us.'

Gyanendra, however, did not take questions. After a twenty-minute-long address, he took his leave politely and smilingly. Before his departure, his final words were: 'I have handed over responsibility for the crown and royal sceptre, used traditionally by the kings of the Shah dynasty, as a legacy of the Shah dynasty, to the government of Nepal for their preservation for eternity.'

He used an ambiguous phrase, which suggested that he had not permanently given up the ownership of the crown and sceptre, and had only transferred the responsibility of their upkeep for the time being. He tried to give a psychological message that the monarchy could return. In fact, he had tried to keep those royal items with himself but the government had refused. When he had to vacate Narayanhity palace, he asked the government for another 'palace' to live in: the Nagarjuna Durbar, located some eight kilometres to the northwest from Balaju. Despite owning a private residence, Nirmal Niwas, he asked for the palace constructed during the Rana era in the dense jungle of the Nagarjuna–Shivapuri national park. As such, he wanted to show he had shifted from one palace to another. At his request, the government also allowed the former Queen Mother Ratna, and his grandfather King Tribhuwan's concubine Sarala, to live in their usual quarters (bungalows) within the Narayanhity compound. The royal couple left Narayanhity the same evening, after the press meet.

Phase-wise implementation

The election of the Constituent Assembly on 10 April 2008 had ensured the ouster of King Gyanendra. As it shouldered the responsibility of writing a new Constitution, the CA brought about a qualitative transformation in the balance of power in Nepal. In what was seen as a continuation of Nepali voters' established pattern of giving a chance to a new force, the 2008 election propelled the Maoists, who had joined the mainstream in the 2006 movement, to become the largest party, just as voters had pushed the Nepali Congress to that position after political changes in 1951 and 1990. In the 601-member assembly, Congress and CPN–UML came a distant second and third position, respectively. The leaders of the regional MJF and TMLP were in the fourth and fifth positions.[2] Due to the introduction of a proportional representation system, the assembly was much more inclusive than the parliaments of the past.

As the strongest proponents of a republic, the Maoists had been catapulted to the leading position and the end of the monarchy had become inevitable. But the manner in which Nepali leaders carried out the republican agenda was unique. The monarchy was neither overthrown by the revolution nor was the path of referendum chosen. There was no bloodshed in the ejection of the king. Actually, King Gyanendra and the royal family were progressively stripped of their powers through a series of steps. When a complete state of powerlessness was attained, he was peacefully elbowed out. The republic was implemented in stages and not in one bloody go, which could have triggered unanticipated and unsavoury consequences.

King Gyanendra considered it a grave 'deceit'. A few years later, in an interview he gave to the News24 television channel, Gyanendra claimed there was no mention of ending monarchy in the understanding with the seven parties which led to his second address on 24 April 2006.

Gyanendra said, 'It (a republic) was nowhere in the understanding reached with us.'

'What was in it?'

'Things I mentioned before, like the restoration of Parliament, choosing a prime minister from among the parties, constitutional monarchy, and the restoration of the multiparty system. Those were the things in it, which was not difficult for me (to accept).'

'Was there constitutional monarchy and multiparty system in that understanding?"

'Definitely, there was.'

'How did things take such a turn after that?'

'I think it (turned) with the addition of the eighth party.'

'Were there other notable points in that understanding?'

'I don't have the paper (in written form). It is hard to recall. But, broadly speaking, these were the things. Basically, it was given that everything will be done in line with the 1990 Constitution.'[3]

In fact, everything *was* done based on the 1990 Constitution. Events in Nepal provide an example of how far-reaching changes can be achieved through political decisions if they have the backing of the people, international support and a hold on power. The same prime minister, Girija Prasad Koirala, to whom he had administered the oath of office, played the key role in the transformation. And Koirala's source of energy was none other than the same Parliament restored by Gyanendra. A process was put in place whereby the major parties would take certain decisions, the restored Parliament would endorse them, and the prime minister, Koirala, would carry them out. When that restored Parliament was dissolved, its responsibility was continued by the interim Parliament, with the participation of the Maoists.

The twenty-three-point understanding reached among the parties on 23 December 2007 was a decisive one, based on which the interim Constitution was amended to declare Nepal a 'federal democratic republican state'. It had also stipulated that the first meeting of the elected Constituent Assembly would implement the declaration. The sitting prime minister was also given a wide range of additional powers and made an interim head of state as well.[4] Based on the foundation of this agreement, the election of the Constituent Assembly was held on 10 April 2008, and the day of its first meeting also arrived.

This was on 28 May 2008. The leaders spent hours to reach an understanding on the language of the amendment proposal. The meeting could begin only at 9.20 p.m. The caretaker head of state, PM Koirala, addressed the assembly, quoting a famous poem by Gopal Prasad Rimal, '*Ek yugma ek din ek patak aunchha* (A day comes once in an era). That day is today. It is also the day of the fulfilment of my dream. Perhaps, it is also the day of the fulfilment of the nation's dream.'

It was around 11.22 at night when the 'dream' was fulfilled. The proposal to endorse the republic was passed by a 99.29 per cent of majority in the assembly. 'Since 560 votes have been cast

in favour of the proposal and since the number is the majority,'
declared the Congress leader K.B. Gurung, who was chairing the
first assembly meeting given his seniority, 'I declare the passage of
the proposal on implementation of the republic by majority as per
the Article 159 of the Interim Constitution of Nepal 2007.'[5]

Of the total 564 members who participated in the voting,
only four members belonging to the Rastriya Prajatantra Party
Nepal voted against the proposal. The five-point proposal on
implementation of the republic, agreed upon by top leaders of the
major parties, had been tabled at the assembly by Home Minister
Krishna Prasad Sitaula. It ended all sorts of status, power,
prerogatives, privileges and facilities accorded to the royal family.
A fourth amendment of the interim Constitution was passed, to
insert the provision for a national president.

The most important thing now was to remove Gyanendra
from Narayanhity palace. The assembly directed Home Minister
Sitaula to see that the palace was vacated within fifteen days.
The home minister went to the palace on 2 June and requested
Gyanendra to leave. Freshly dethroned, Gyanendra did not speak
much. Neither did he exhibit any sense of resentment. He only
inquired about some technical aspects, like where he would go,
what the security arrangements would be, and so on. They ended
with a gentleman's agreement by which Gyanendra agreed to shift
to Nagarjuna.[6]

Bloodshed that did not happen

In the end, Gyanendra was overthrown easily. Did that mean
the palace had not planned anything to save itself? Certainly not.
In fact, Gyanendra's ouster became possible only after a plot to
invite divisive struggle failed to take off at the last moment. The
unanticipated wave of public support for the Maoists in the election
had stunned the palace and the royalists, just like it did others. But
when the victorious former rebels demonstrated an unexpectedly

soft line towards them, the palace reposed its last hope in them.
The Maoists immediately opened up channels of communication
with Gyanendra by talking to former minister Kamal Thapa, his
son-in-law Raj Bahadur Singh, and other officials of the palace.

It was around that time that the Maoists floated the idea of a
'cultural king'. Prachanda told Kamal Thapa, 'Getting elected is
not everything. We have lost the decisiveness. The Maoists and
the monarchy must join hands to save nationalism.'[7]

In the course of his conversations with Kamal Thapa in
April and May, Prachanda told Thapa about his desire to give
continuity to the monarchy in some form. Thapa says he briefed
the king about those conversations. The king asked, 'What kind of
monarchy do they have in mind exactly?'

Thapa asked Baburam Bhattarai, and relayed the answer to
the king: 'ceremonial'. As a trial balloon, Baburam also publicly
stated, 'We are not against a cultural king.' The king asked, 'Please
seek details about the monarchy they want, in writing.'[8]

The Maoists were not willing to give it in writing. They
probably only wanted to keep the palace in confusion. There were
three thoughts behind this strategy: first, to isolate the king and
royalists so that the implementation of a republic was achieved
bloodlessly; second, to seek the backing of the army, which was
traditionally loyal to the monarchy; and third, to prevent any
cosying up between the Nepali Congress and the palace following
the Maoists' unanticipated election victory.

When PM Koirala heard the murmur about a 'cultural king'
going on between the palace and the Maoists, he went into
overdrive. He was already suspicious about the Maoists' hesitation
to elect him president. So he wanted to tame the former rebels by
getting closer to the palace himself. It was an irony that the two
republican parties were trying to outdo each other in wooing the
monarchy in the aftermath of election.

The palace was also divided as to whether they should seek the
support of the Congress or the Maoists. The king's son-in-law,

Raj Bahadur Singh, and former Prince Dhirendra's son-in-law Rajiv Shahi favoured siding with the Maoists. But others, including senior army officials, favoured siding with the Congress. It was concluded that despite their talk of a cultural king, the communists were prone to traitorousness and, therefore, the palace should side with a traditional democratic force like the Congress for a long-term alliance. The palace then slowed its contact with the Maoists while increasing its relations with Congress.

PM Koirala then proposed keeping a 'baby king' or 'minor king'. Army Chief Katawal was also making similar suggestions. Koirala indicated that he would be willing to allow a powerless monarchy if Gyanendra (and his son Paras) were willing to give up the throne in favour of Paras's infant son Hridayendra. This proposal was rejected by Gyanendra.

I met King Gyanendra in Narayanhity palace around the time Koirala was supporting this. I asked the king his view. 'A baby king is the first step towards abolition of the monarchy,' he said. 'It is possible only over my dead body.' He said all of his family would leave the palace together if they had to.[9]

Gyanendra used to make caustic comments against India, which he thought was behind the abolition of the monarchy. He felt the proposal of a 'baby king' was also an 'Indian concept'. Indian leaders like Jaswant Singh were lobbying for it in Delhi. But Gyanendra did not accept the proposal, probably because he thought he would return one day.[10] He could not understand that the days of the entire institution of the monarchy were already numbered.

Gyanendra's position pushed Koirala and the Congress further towards an outright republic. At the last moment, a proposal was made by the military secretariat of the royal palace before the army leadership, to surround the Constituent Assembly in order to foil the first meeting of the assembly, or at least influence it considerably. The proposal was studied at a meeting of the Principal Staff Officers (PSOs), the topmost policy-making body of the army. None of the generals supported it. This was the point where one could see the monarchy losing its traditional grip over the army. Most generals stood in favour of the republican transformation taking place in the country.

The palace did not give up. Based on information that a mass of Maoist supporters was planning to gherao the palace on 28 May, the day of the first CA meeting, the palace plotted to provoke the mass and turn the ensuing clash to its benefit. Before the start of the first meeting of the CA on 28 May, small bombs were set off in Ratnapark and just outside the premises of the assembly. A hitherto unheard-of group called Ranavir Sena took responsibility for the explosions. The aim was to let accusations be hurled against the palace, so that the mass would move towards the palace, creating a situation for bloody clashes, compel the mobilization of the army nationwide to control the situation, and thus prevent the first meeting of the assembly from declaring the republic.

It was rumoured that the Maoists had brought in two truckloads of its combatants armed with small weapons and positioned them inside the Khanna Garment factory in Balkumari, Lalitpur, the headquarters of its Young Communist League (YCL). As a result, Katawal dispatched a special army squad to the palace compound. They were fully briefed on how to resist if the Maoist mass attempted to enter, and in what situation they were to open fire. Microphones and video cameras were installed at several points of the palace premises, in order to defend the squad against any allegations of human rights violations.

Even though the Nepali Army stood in favour of the republic at the last moment, the palace guards located inside the palace and the generals who were posted as royal ADCs, were still loyal to the monarchy. Army Chief Katawal was concerned that these 2500 soldiers could create a problem. In fact, he had two aims in deploying an extra squad to the palace the day before the republic: to protect the king if the Maoists encircled the palace; and to bring the situation under control if the king tried to invite any confrontation using the army unit already posted there.

From the morning of 28 May, Katawal was constantly talking to leaders of the Congress, CPN–UML and Maoists and urging them to refrain from holding any demonstration in front of the palace that could lead to clashes. Due to his constant efforts, the palace's plan to incite violence and impose regression failed. However, Katawal himself was a declared monarchist. He was heard telling many people many times, 'Kathmandu will not automatically get waters from Melamchi (a long-cherished drinking water project for the parched capital); neither will the waters of Karnali turn into petrol, nor will mountains turn into gold by kicking out the king like a dog.' However, due to his official position and circumstances, he was forced to stand on the same side as the parties.

In the end, Katawal found he had a difficult choice: to choose the republic or side with the monarchy and sacrifice himself. Abandoning his life-long belief, he chose republican peace. The palace never thought he would do that. Katawal found no logic in going against the prevailing wind when he saw that the government and entire state machinery was in favour of a republic. Congress had sided with a republic, and the international community, including India, supported it. A man was cared for by the royals since his boyhood, Katawal was a darling general of the palace. When they saw him turn against them, the royalists were extremely angry with Katawal and vented their rage against him for a long time.

As for the rumours of Maoists trying to gherao the palace, they were nothing but propaganda and exaggeration. Although the Maoists held a symbolic protest in front of the palace on 28 May, their main gathering was set for the street in front of the assembly hall in New Baneshwar, aimed at pressuring the assembly members. On 27 May, the Maoists held an emergency meeting of their central secretariat, at which they decided to pass the proposal for a republic at any cost. Prachanda, who was certain to be elected the new prime minister, also harboured the ambition of taking over the role of caretaker head of state, like Prime Minister Koirala, but he did not want to take the blame for delaying the historic declaration by refusing to insert a new provision for a president in the Constitution. So at the end of the series of meetings held in Baluwatar on 28 May, Prachanda finally agreed to have separate positions of prime minister and president. When he saw the possibility of Prachanda becoming prime minister and he, himself, the founding president, Koirala quickly forgot assurances he had given to the palace, in the same manner he had chosen to forget the assurance he had given to Gyanendra on 24 April 2006, to keep a 'ceremonial monarchy'.

Race for the presidency

Gyanendra Shah had the most to lose, but Girija Prasad Koirala, who led the march towards a republic, also did not win. He had accepted the agenda without enthusiasm and under pressure from the widespread anti-monarchy sentiment. His personal battle against the king also compelled him to take a republican position. Yet he did make an effort to preserve the monarchy by floating the concept of a 'baby king'.[11] Weighing the scales in favour of his pro-republican position was his personal ambition to become the first president of Nepal. His eldest brother Matrika Prasad Koirala had the good fortune of becoming the first commoner prime minister of Nepal. Another brother, Bishweshwore Prasad Koirala, became the first elected prime minister of Nepal. So it was natural for him to harbour a desire to become the first commoner head of state of Nepal. As the chief campaigner of the anti-king agitation since the signing of the twelve-point understanding, it was also a natural progression for him. Things did not turn out as he wished.

Since the amendment of the Constitution and the suspension of monarchy, Koirala himself had borne the responsibility of a caretaker head of state, for example, in receiving the credentials of foreign ambassadors.[12] With the expectation of becoming a full-fledged president after the election, Koirala did not participate in a single election campaign rally of his party. He was assured of Maoist support in achieving his desire. But enjoying their unexpected election victory, the Maoists backed out from their earlier promise.

That was what triggered the rift between the Congress and the Maoists. As the Maoists were itching to form the government after their election victory (which had put them tantalizingly close to simple majority), the Congress, on 12 May 2008, came up with seven conditions before it would allow them to do so. Under the pretext that the former rebels had not fulfilled those conditions, Prime Minister Koirala refused to vacate his seat for three months after the election.[13] When he started telling the smaller parties that India wanted him to continue in office, Delhi intervened. During his meetings with Indian leaders, including Sonia Gandhi and Pranab Mukherjee in August (he had dropped in to Delhi during his return home from the fifteenth SAARC Summit in Colombo), he was advised to step down. Later that month, Prachanda finally became the prime minister. Koirala's utility, it seemed, had ended with the declaration of a republic.

India was the main force that had pressed Koirala to fight for a republic. He followed Delhi's advice despite many misgivings. But in my opinion, Delhi did not want to see a strong man like Koirala as head of state in the neighbourhood. His nephew Shekhar Koirala, who witnessed the machinations of the Indian establishment from close quarters, said four years later that 'India was not interested in making GP Koirala president'.[14] Shekhar had himself travelled to Delhi and lobbied with leaders like Pranab Mukherjee, but in vain.

There were some immediate reasons behind Delhi's lack of enthusiasm in seeing Koirala installed as president. For instance, Koirala had been totally negative towards the recent Madhes movement and had publicly accused India of orchestrating it.

Koirala was piqued with Delhi's efforts to dislodge old Madhes stalwarts like Mahantha Thakur from the Congress party to lead the new TMLP. Delhi was equally unhappy about his attempt to mobilize the army during the agitation. The Indians also suspected that Koirala was hobnobbing with the king and royalists behind their back. In fact, between the second people's movement and the CA election, relations between Koirala and Delhi had seen a sharp dip.

Koirala, too, felt a degree of arrogance: if he 'could tame the monarchy, why bow down to Delhi?' It was enough to infuriate Delhi. He made indirect jabs at Delhi. 'There is a danger to the independence and sovereignty of Nepal. I have told all the foreigners: Indians, Americans and even Chinese who came to meet me yesterday. I have told them that I will not compromise on these matters,' he said. Furthermore, among his confidantes in Baluwatar, he was wondering aloud, 'Are the Indians trying to make a Lhendup Dorjee out of me?'[15]

Koirala knew very well how the Indians had used Kazi Lhendup Dorjee, the last prime minister of the Himalayan kingdom of Sikkim, to merge Sikkim into the Indian Union. Koirala was so scared that he suspected the Indian embassy of leaks of information from Baluwatar, his official residence. He even ordered a thorough search of Baluwatar to detect 'bugging devices'.

Around that time, PM Koirala gave an extensive interview to *Kantipur Television* for a documentary about himself, '*Aafno Itihas, Afnai Brittanta*'. In the course of the interview, he revealed that he had received advice and other kinds of assistance from the then RAW chief, R.N. Kao, during the struggle against the Panchayat regime. The comments were construed as Koirala's indication of a continuation of similar Indian intervention. The end result of all these incidents was that India, like the Maoists, did not want to see him as the president of Nepal.

On the other hand, the Maoists had cunningly dangled the lollipop of the presidency in front of Madhav Kumar Nepal, general secretary of CPN–UML. His party also saw India's hand behind the withdrawal of Maoist support to their general secretary. According to them, following the verbal understanding between the two parties to make Nepal the president, a team of CPN–UML leaders, led by Chairman Jhalnath Khanal, had gone to the residence of Prachanda at around 8.45 p.m. on 16 July with the intention of signing a written agreement. They were asked to wait for five minutes in an outer room. Meanwhile, they saw a tall and stout man with a white moustache leaving—none other than the RAW station chief, Alok Joshi.

The meeting that then took place with Prachanda went nowhere. The following day, at the last moment for filing candidacies for the post of president, the Maoists informed the CPN–UML of their inability to support their leader. They had already chosen an old republican leader, Ram Raja Prasad Singh, as their candidate. Making the UML strongman president would have completed the communist dominance in Nepal: something totally unpalatable to the Indians. Delhi was also not in favour of the Maoist candidate Singh, who, despite having close links with India, had recently turned down a proposal to lead a campaign for an 'independent Tarai' during the Patna assembly of Madhesi leaders, since his election would have meant total Maoist domination in Nepali politics. Neither did it want to see a leader of Koirala's stature in that position.

When he understood that they would not let him become president, Koirala did not take part in the fray. Instead, he fielded his party general secretary, Dr Ram Baran Yadav, who won the election with the support of the CPN–UML, MJF and others. Although this second-rung leader of the Nepali Congress was not said to have the best of relations with them, the Indians did not raise any obstruction in his election. Instead, India chose to warm up to the new president of Nepal.[16]

Part III

The Touchdown

20

The Rise and Fall of the Maoist Government

'Your victory is a tribute to your visionary and bold decision to enter the mainstream of political life in your country through the mechanism of multiparty democracy.'

—Sonia Gandhi, in a letter congratulating
Prachanda after the election of the Constituent Assembly[1]

The results of the Constituent Assembly election were just out. The Naya Bazaar residence of Prachanda was in a celebratory mood on the afternoon of 14 April 2008. There was a long queue of people who wanted to meet him. A crowd of reporters was jostling outside the gate. When I reached there, a delegation of the European Union was just returning from a meeting with him. The Swiss ambassador had preceded them. After I spoke to him for an hour, I saw UNMIN Chief Ian Martin waiting in the outside hall.

The appeal and allure of Prachanda had increased considerably following his victory. Everybody wanted to meet this fellow. I found him sitting on a sofa with a red painting depicting a horde of marching guerrillas behind him. 'So how are you feeling about all this?' I asked.

He replied, 'Well, this is totally surprising and strange. I have never felt like this before.' He was quite excited. He kept on smiling. He could not conceal his pleasure. Perhaps he did not want to. He quickly said that they had been able to fulfil the dream of a Constituent Assembly, unfulfilled since 1951. By that time, his party had won a majority of the seats under the first-past-the-post (FPTP) system.

I asked, 'Did you think you would win these many seats?'

'I hadn't thought we would win these many, no. We were confident of winning more than 100 seats, but our win has astounded everyone,' he said, adding, 'It has crushed the egos of the Congress and the king, who consider themselves to be the vanguards of democracy.'

Out of the 601 seats of the assembly, the Maoists won 120 seats under FPTP (out of 240) and an additional 120 seats under proportional representation system (out of 335)—winning 240 seats in total, not far short of outright simple majority.

The second communist leader to become Nepal's prime minister after Manmohan Adhikari, Prachanda took over the reins of Singha Durbar on 15 August 2008.[2] The CPN–UML and MJF joined his government. The Nepali Congress stayed in opposition after the Maoists refused to part with the defence portfolio. The Maoists were already exhibiting a sense of hubris, and couldn't care less if the Congress stayed away. With the monarchy out of the picture, the Maoists even took a short-sighted decision by naming the Nepali Congress their 'principle enemy' as a representative of the 'feudal and bourgeois class'.

However, Prachanda was not as powerful a prime minister as his predecessor Koirala had been. Before Prachanda was allowed to enter Baluwatar, the interim Constitution had been amended—at the insistence of the Congress—to allow the dismissal of the prime minister by a simple majority of Parliament. The distinctive provision for consensus government, too, had been removed.

Northward steps

Less than five minutes after the appointment of the Maoist Chairman Pushpa Kamal Dahal, a.k.a. Prachanda, as the prime minister of Nepal, Nepali media houses received a congratulatory note from Indian PM Manmohan Singh. The note also included an invitation for Prachanda to visit the southern neighbour. But Prachanda went north instead.

The Chinese had invited him to take part in the closing ceremony of the Beijing Olympics. The Indians did not want him to travel to China on his maiden visit as prime minister. Nepali prime ministers have long made Delhi their customary first port of call. India is not amused by any Nepali prime minister attempting to get cosy with the Chinese. In his autobiography *Atmabrittanta*, Nepal's first elected prime minister, B.P. Koirala, recalls how the Indians had stopped him from making his first visit to Beijing in 1958.[3]

Prachanda also faced 'Prachanda' (which translates as 'fierce') pressure. In his own words, 'I was asked why the prime minister should go there instead of the sports minister. There were all kinds of pressures for weeks. I took a decision to go in the end, because I was faced with a moral question of whether we were representatives of an independent nation.'[4]

Although the Olympics provided a convenient excuse, Prachanda had previously told his party leaders that he wanted to go to China or any European country on his maiden tour, in order to break the traditional shackle. So, on 23 August 2008, he went to Beijing. His visit was not limited to attending the closing ceremony of the Olympics. The Chinese leadership also gave importance to the 'Maoist' prime minister of a strategically important neighbour. The scheduled twenty minutes of talks between Prachanda and the Chinese President Hu Jintao were extended to thirty-five minutes. President Hu expressed China's commitment to increasing economic assistance to Nepal in the changed context. China wanted to demonstrate the symbolic importance of Prachanda's visit. He was made to plant a tree sapling at a garden near the Great Wall. The sapling was, interestingly, named Pushpa Kamal Dahal 'Prachanda'. Back in 1960, B.P. Koirala had also planted a tree sapling similarly in that same garden.

In Beijing, Prachanda told a representative of the national news agency of Nepal that due to recent unrest in Tibet, China's interest in Nepal had increased. 'If Nepal is able to make positive use (of Chinese interest), we can not only create new history, but I believe it will also start a race for economic revolution in our country,' he said.[5]

Delhi was disappointed when Prachanda went to Beijing despite its goodwill towards him. Prachanda could feel that even before he returned home. So, when he faced journalists at Tribhuwan International Airport in Kathmandu after four days in China, he attempted some damage control by stating that his first 'political visit' would be to Delhi. Instead, his comments made the Chinese feel uneasy. In the end, the visit made both of Nepal's neighbours wary of him.

Prachanda went to India twice as a prime minister: first on a bilateral visit and, second, to take part in a meeting of the regional grouping BIMSTEC. On the first visit, he tried hard to shake off the image of a traditional communist. He said that his party was in favour of 'new democracy' in the place of 'formal democracy'. He presented himself as a democrat committed to multiparty competitive democracy. He also said Nepal's relationship with India could not be compared with its relationship to any other country. But the Indian leadership, particularly the bureaucracy, could not be convinced by his words.

The Kharipati extreme

Within three months of his appointment as prime minister, Prachanda's party called a plenum meeting at Kharipati,

Bhaktapur, from 21 to 26 November 2008. The plenum conducted an extensive debate on the future course of the party. Rejecting Prachanda's political paper, senior leader Mohan Baidya 'Kiran' presented a different paper at the meeting. Around 1200 participants of the plenum were divided into twelve groups that held focused discussions on the two papers, but they were not put to a vote. Rather, Prachanda chose the easier path of integrating the components of both papers. But when he amalgamated Kiran's ideas into his paper, it became so explosive that it shook establishments from Kathmandu to Delhi.

The joint paper talked about 'completing a new people's revolution through the path of people's revolt', and 'initiating ideological, organizational and technical preparations by keeping the idea of people's revolt at the centre'. It was the height of contradiction and irony that a ruling party was declaring its policy to seize power like rebels engaged in an insurgency. The Kharipati conclave also directed the party to walk out of the government if it stood in the way of organizing revolt.

In essence, the Kharipati conclave had overturned the conclusion of Chunbang meeting. It replaced the 'federal democratic republic' with the 'people's federal democratic national republic' as the party's future course. It clearly meant the party wished for a communist-modelled one-party people's republic.

The Kharipati conclave also took a hard line against India. Delhi was again termed 'expansionist'. It noted, 'In the course of the peace process since the signing of twelve-point understanding, the Indian expansionist force has brazenly interfered in economic, political, and cultural aspects of Nepal. The ambassador (Rakesh Sood by this time) has also engaged in tasks in violation of common diplomatic norms.'[6]

The conclave called for ending special relations with India, abrogating 'unequal' treaties, regaining territories unlawfully captured, and preventing India from enjoying a monopoly on Nepal's hydropower. It concluded that the issue of national independence had become the most significant. Delhi was further rattled by its decision to 'carry out joint activities' in cooperation with Indian Maoists.

The Maoists also needlessly affronted the domestic forces. The opposition Nepali Congress was declared the 'principle enemy'. The Maoists termed their own ruling ally, the CPN–UML, as 'the most opportunist rightist force'.

The resolution passed by the Kharipati conclave was the party's internal document. But the party leadership failed to comprehend that the document would, sooner or later, come out in the open and trigger a tremendous backlash. Prachanda later admitted it. In his words, 'It was a period when I had just become a prime minister. But comrades were already feeling that I was now a rightist and had surrendered before enemies. When I saw this feeling was widespread, I thought I must do something as a compromise. They were demanding that I hit everywhere at once. If I hit, they would praise me, but if I talked of compromise they would feel their chairman had sold out. As a result, I decided to go with the flow and started hitting all around.'

The 'comrades' who instigated Prachanda to become more 'revolutionary' were leaders close to Kiran. Prachanda, himself, was also buoyed by the unprecedented election result. Besides, given his weak hold on the party organization, he was compelled to join hands with Kiran. In the central committee, Prachanda and Baburam together had eighteen supporters while Kiran alone counted seventeen followers. The risk of becoming a minority in the central committee scared Prachanda, because that would mean he may have to give up the party chair and the prime minister's position. So he chose to try to win the trust of Kiran and his followers.

Baburam, on the other hand, felt Prachanda was sidelining him by moving closer to Kiran. He expressed strong dissent towards the policy adopted by the Kharipati conclave. It was a turning point that upset the unity among the Maoist leadership. Baburam, who had steadfastly stood by Prachanda since Chunbang, now started building his 'clique' inside the party. Alarmed at the rapid development of cliques by Baburam and Kiran, Prachanda gave an impetus to long-running unity talks with CPN–Unity Centre. On 13 January, 2009, the two parties united formally and the central committee was expanded to include 138 members, among whom Prachanda enjoyed a comfortable majority. The name of the party was also changed from CPN–Maoist to Unified CPN–Maoist. In his rush towards unification, Prachanda agreed to drop 'Prachandapath', which had been the guiding principle of the party since 2000. The unification would have come about sooner or later anyway, but the changing party equation after Kharipati motivated its swift conclusion.

India was not particularly against the Maoist government before the Kharipati conclave, but now Delhi concluded that it must topple Prachanda's government.[7] Indian External Affairs Minister Pranab Mukherjee, who was in Kathmandu during the Kharipati conclave, had gently warned Prachanda not to go down the extremist path, but the Maoists did not take that warning seriously. Instead, India felt the former rebels were targeting Delhi. It felt that the Maoist government had adopted a dangerous dual policy of outwardly maintaining good bilateral relations and promising they would do nothing to hurt Indian interests, but inwardly teaching their unruly cadres to engage in anti-India activities. It took serious note of the Maoist decision to dispatch its youth wing, the Young Communist League (YCL), to march to disputed land borders and mount the national flag there. At an eastern border point by Ilam district, Indian security personnel detained a team of YCL cadres. They were released only after a request from Prime Minister Prachanda.

Delhi felt that the Maoists had not resorted to such high-volume India-bashing before they came to power. Raising objections against India appeared the full-time job of ministers such as Krishna Bahadur Mahara and Dev Gurung. It might be expected to hear such bashing from party leaders known to harbour anti-India feelings, such as Kiran and C.P. Gajurel. But when sitting ministers resorted to similar tactics, Delhi felt it was the official position of the government of Nepal. It was also alleged that the government-run newspaper *Gorkhapatra* ran anti-India reports on its front page and the state-owned Radio Nepal and Nepal Television were turned into platforms for nationalist brainwashing. The Maoists attempted a number of things that caused distrust to grow: from replacing the traditional Indian priests in Pashupatinath temple with a Nepali priest, to appointing judges of their liking through the manipulation of the Judicial Council.[8]

Despite Nepal being an independent nation, India has always wished to remain a dominant force in its administration.[9] When Prachanda started advancing in all directions, India became concerned. In February 2009, visiting Indian Foreign Secretary Shiv Shankar Menon clearly presented Indian dissatisfaction before Prachanda. There were two major concerns that Menon raised: the growing proximity of the Maoist government with China, and its attempts to influence the Nepali Army.[10]

Proximity with China

The Maoists did not have relations with China for a long time. During their people's war, they were unable to build contacts with Beijing despite several attempts. One such attempt was made by the president of China Study Centre, Madan Regmi. 'I talked to the Chinese after I got a request via Padma Ratna Tuladhar. But the Chinese did not want to have anything to do with the Nepali Maoists,' Regmi recalls.

During King Gyanendra's visit to China on 11 July 2002, the Chinese foreign ministry accused the Nepali Maoists of misusing the great name and ideology of their leader Mao Tse Tung and refused to have any relation with them.[11] The Chinese President

Jiang Zemin backed the Nepal government's efforts to control the Maoist insurgency and told the king, 'China opposes all forms of violence and terrorist activities'.[12]

For the Nepali Maoists, China was not only the fountainhead of their ideology, but also an opportunity to create a strategic balance in case of a rift with India. The Chinese, on their part, suspected that the Maoists had deeper links with India. In August 2002, the Maoists dispatched Manoj Jung Thapa of Sindhuli, who worked in their foreign relations cell, to Beijing. In the course of his stay of around two weeks, he tried to explain his party's policy and win the confidence of intellectuals such as Professor Wang Hongwei, who were close to the Chinese establishment. The effort failed to develop contacts at a higher level. The Maoists then dispatched Pratap Raj Onta, who headed their intellectual cell, to Hong Kong with a similar purpose. He was not successful either.[13]

The Maoist attempt to build relations with China made progress only after the signing of twelve-point understanding with the seven political parties in December 2005. Subsequently, a Chinese diplomat travelled to Kamidanda of Kavre district to meet the man in charge of the Maoist special command, Barshaman Pun 'Ananta'. A person named Sunil Sharma had arranged the meeting. Sharma is the same fellow from Belbari, Morang, who had played a role during the initial contacts between Prachanda and Girija Prasad Koirala in 2002. Sharma had gone to China to study medicine in 2000. He became acquainted with Professor Wang Hongwei through the chief of Bishwa Bhasa Campus, Ganga Prasad Upreti. Upreti was associated with the China Study Centre.

Prof. Wang of the Chinese Academy of Social Sciences first came to Nepal in 1963 and since then, had been monitoring Nepal affairs closely. He had close relations with numerous political leaders, as well as with King Mahendra and King Birendra. Beijing considered him their resource person in Nepal matters. After the

Maoists joined the political mainstream, China dispatched a team headed by the professor, in June 2006, to study the changing politics of Nepal. The team held long discussions with Maoist leaders such as Prachanda, Baburam, Badal and Ananta. Prof. Wang then said, 'CPN–Maoist has now become a legitimate political party of Nepal. As such, the Chinese government and Chinese people want to see the peaceful resolution of problems facing Nepal by the CPN–Maoist and Nepal government.'[14]

Soon after Prof. Wang returned, Ananta went to Beijing in the first week of August. This began a series of delegations of Nepali Maoists visiting China. However, the Chinese Communist Party and the Chinese government did not immediately establish formal relations with a party that had just recently laid down arms. Relations were built via the experts of the China Institute of Contemporary International Relations (CICIR). It was only after the Maoists emerged as the largest party in the Constituent Assembly election that China sent them a congratulatory letter, according formal recognition.[15]

There were some immediate causes behind the rapid pace at which the Nepali Maoists built relations with China. First was the abolition of the monarchy. Before the second people's movement, the monarchy had been the most reliable friend of China in Nepal. After it was abolished, China wanted to promote relations with all the political parties. In this endeavour, they developed a particularly close relationship with the Maoists, mainly because of the Maoist desire to reciprocate, and their rise as the largest party following the election. Two incidents that took place before the Constituent Assembly election compelled China to increase its attention to Nepal. One was the Madhes movement, and the second was protests by Tibetans.

In Chinese eyes, there were strategic interests behind the Madhes movement. It calculated that the master plan to establish a powerful Madhes province that would be soft toward Delhi, and then set it against Kathmandu, was, ultimately, aimed against itself.

China's Nepal expert, Prof. Wang Hongwei, termed the events unfolding in the Madhes or Tarai 'unnatural and extraordinary.' He said that anarchy was being orchestrated in the region with the intention of destabilizing Nepal.[16] China was further alarmed when, a few years later, six Constituent Assembly members belonging to Madhesi parties travelled to Dharamshala in India to meet the Dalai Lama, and made comments linking Tibetan independence with the struggle for Madhesi autonomy.[17]

More importantly, China was concerned about protests in its Autonomous Region of Tibet, bordering northern Nepal. A series of riots occurred in Tibet beginning 10 March 2008. Around nineteen people were killed in the unrest in Lhasa. The Chinese considered the initiation of riots in Lhasa, just before the Beijing Olympics, when the eyes of the entire international community were focused on them, as a 'well-planned conspiracy'. They felt that pieces of the conspiracy were linked to Nepal. From 13 March, Kathmandu, too, witnessed a daily show of protests by the Tibetan refugee community, which continued even after the situation in Lhasa was brought under control. The agitation in Kathmandu saw participation by Tibetan refugees coming from India.[18]

The Chinese president, Hu Jintao, was well aware of the Nepal link with Tibetan affairs, which in turn were the number one national security challenge for China. From 1988, when he shouldered the responsibility of the Chinese Communist Party's provincial committee secretary for Tibet for four years, Hu had worked closely with the Lhasa-based Nepali Consul General's Office and the Nepali community living there. He was, therefore, personally aware of the geopolitical sensitivity of Nepal. When Tibetan protests grew in Kathmandu, President Hu's attention towards Nepal increased considerably.

The Chinese ambassador in Kathmandu, Zheng Xianglin, publicly expressed dissatisfaction over the lack of a 'strong approach' by the then interim government, which had a prime minister and home minister from the Nepali Congress party, in 'putting a stop to secessionist Tibetan demonstrations'.[19] Around that very time, the CPN–Maoist was elected as the largest party. The Chinese came forward to develop links with the new force, with the objective of neutralizing the increasing Tibetan activity in Nepal, and it worked. A tightening of the border after the Maoists came to power led to a significant reduction in the number of Tibetans who fled into Nepal. Between 2004 and 2007, more than 12,000 Tibetans had crossed the border. But after Prachanda came to power, between 2008 and 2011, only 2500 did so.[20]

Delhi did not like the growing proximity between Prachanda and Beijing. When Prachanda travelled to China on his first foreign visit as prime minister, India was extremely unhappy. 'Right from that point, they began machinations to topple my government,' says Prachanda.[21] Delhi does not like any Nepali government, prime minister or politician leaning north, according priority to China or encouraging active Chinese engagement. It considers Nepal as falling in its arc of influence. There is a dominant feeling in Delhi that dislikes the presence of any third party in Nepal.

It did not apply to Prachanda alone. Before him, Nepali leaders such as B.P. Koirala, King Birendra and King Gyanendra had to swallow the same bitter pill. When B.P. Koirala made attempts to build equal relations with Delhi and Beijing, he fell in the eyes of the Indians.[22] When King Birendra tried to raise Chinese support and even weapons to counter Indian dominance in Kathmandu, Delhi became active against him. When King Gyanendra tried to bring China into SAARC, he was not only toppled, the entire monarchy was brought down. It seemed only their father, King Mahendra, could successfully take advantage of Indo-China strategic rivalry.

When he launched the people's war, Prachanda imitated the guerrilla tactics employed by unified Nepal's founding king, Prithvi Narayan Shah. In the course of building diplomatic relations, Prachanda considered King Mahendra his undeclared ideal. He tried to follow Mahendra's formula of consolidating power and national capacity by striking a balance between India and China. But whatever concessions Mahendra could get by employing this formula in the Cold War-dominated world politics of 1960 were not available to Prachanda.

Delhi was watching closely. After Prachanda became prime minister, there had been a series of high-level visits by Chinese leaders, including Foreign Minister Yang Jiechi (2 to 4 December 2008), deputy chief of the Chinese PLA, Ma Xiaotian (6 to 10 December), Major General Ei Hujeng (20 to 23 November), Lt Gen. Yang Gyangming (10 to 16 February 2009), deputy chief of the international department of the Chinese Communist Party, Liu Hongkai (15 February), and Assistant Foreign Minister Hu Jenggui (26 February). There were dozens of delegations from China—much more than from India.[23]

A proposal for Chinese assistance in the training of Maoist combatants was presented during the visit of defence minister and Maoist leader Ram Bahadur Thapa 'Badal' to Beijing from 22 to 27 September 2008. Badal had gone to Beijing to observe the military exercise 'Warrior 2008' by the Chinese PLA. He met the vice-chair of the central military commission, the defence minister, and the PLA chief. Upon his return, Badal said the Chinese PLA was interested in expanding its relations with the Nepali Army.

The high point of Chinese proximity was the attempt by Beijing to sign a new peace and friendship treaty with Nepal. During his visit to Kathmandu from 2 to 4 December 2008, Foreign Minister Yang Jiechi proposed to replace the old treaty with a new one. He also talked about 'all kinds of Chinese assistance to help Nepal safeguard its sovereignty and territorial integrity'. Subsequently, a Chinese assistant foreign minister visited Kathmandu on 26 February and handed over a draft of the new treaty to Nepal's acting foreign secretary, Suresh Pradhan.

In 1960, Prime Minister B.P. Koirala and his Chinese counterpart Chou Enlai had signed the original treaty. The treaty had disappeared from public memory because there was no problem with it from either side. After fifty years, the Chinese wanted to update it. Prime Minister Prachanda was interested, while his Foreign Minister Upendra Yadav (head of the MJF) was equally positive. Around that time, a high-level Chinese delegation had travelled to the southern city of Birgunj to participate in the general convention of Yadav's party.

Preparations were afoot to sign the new treaty in Beijing during Prachanda's scheduled trip to China from 2 May 2009. Efforts were on to open up additional border points between the two countries, and bring Chinese railways and roads up to the border. Talks were also going on regarding Chinese aid to build a hydropower plant in a hilly district, and in opening an agricultural university in Chitwan. On the agenda was the five-point memorandum of understanding on economic and technical cooperation, a study to upgrade the ring road in Kathmandu, a dry port at Tatopani, vehicles and equipment for solid waste management, and exchange of youth delegations. But a controversy over the army chief blew up at that time, and the Maoists were forced out of the government.

The main goal was to stop Prachanda's Beijing trip, prevent the signing of a new treaty, and kick his government out. It was attained. Amid all-round pressure, Prachanda called the Chinese Ambassador Qui Guohong to Baluwatar on the afternoon of 25 April 2009 and informed the envoy of his decision to 'suspend the official visit to China in view of the development of an uneasy situation in the country'.

Army chief episode

Army Chief General Rookmangud Katawal had a strong conviction that the Maoists had not abandoned their goal of seizing power, and had seen the army as the main obstacle in their path. Therefore, he believed the Maoists would employ different tactics to weaken, destroy or take the army under control.

Soon, the Maoist government and the army headquarters headed for a confrontation. It started over the issue of opening up new recruitment into the army. Defence Minister Badal wrote to the army headquarters to stop the recruitment, saying it was against the Comprehensive Peace Agreement. The army replied that it had opened up recruitment the previous year as well, and could not stop it this year since the process had already been initiated. Badal and Katawal engaged in a public spat. Responding to a writ petition, the Supreme Court decided in favour of the army's recruitment drive.

Badal was not satisfied with the decision. When Katawal recommended to the defence ministry the extension of the terms of eight brigadier generals thought to be close to him, Badal refused. Generally, when brigadiers completed their three-year term, they were given two years' extension. Badal had approved a similar proposal with regard to other brigadiers. But in the case of these eight, he refused at the last moment. It embittered the whole army. Again, the Supreme Court intervened. Responding to a writ petition by the brigadiers in question, it gave a 'stay order' asking the government not to implement their retirement. The brigadiers were cheerful, and they went to army headquarters in official cars from the court premises directly.

Soon, there was another big incident. The 'PLA Club' of Maoist ex-combatants had applied to take part in the upcoming Fifth National Games. No decision had been taken about their application. At the last moment, Prime Minister Prachanda, in his capacity as the guardian of National Sports Council, wrote a letter to the member secretary, Jivan Ram Shrestha. Subsequently, the Council allowed the PLA Club to take part in the games. The Nepali Army raised objections. The chief ordered the army's Tribhuwan Army Club to boycott all the matches against the PLA Club.[24]

The sports row brought Prachanda and Katawal into direct confrontation. Prachanda considered it a refusal by the chief to

obey his orders. On 20 April 2009, he sought an explanation from
the chief, within twenty-four hours, on issues including his decision
to breach the government instruction by opening recruitment, to
restore the brigadier generals immediately after the court order
without waiting for a subsequent government directive, and to
boycott the National Games. The next day, Katawal gave a five-
page-long reply.

On the evening of 21 April, the meeting of the Maoist central
committee held at the PM's residence in Baluwatar concluded that
Katawal's reply was 'a rebuttal of the government position rather
than his explanation'. It recommended immediate action against
him. Prachanda could not take any immediate action, because a
section of ruling allies in the CPN–UML and MJF was already
threatening to walk out of the government. The president had
also pressured Prachanda not to take any action against Katawal
without political understanding, as per the interim Constitution.

In the end, the government decided to dismiss Katawal only
on 3 May, stating that his 'explanations were not satisfactory'. He
was replaced by the number two general, Kul Bahadur Khadka, as
acting chief.

Plan and counter-plan: The CPN–Maoists found General Kul
Bahadur Khadka to be an opportunist who fitted perfectly into
their scheme of things. He had been in contact with Baburam
Bhattarai and Prachanda through Barshaman Pun 'Ananta'. He
met Ananta via retired general Kumar Fudong, who had been
nominated as a Maoist MP in the interim Parliament. Khadka
provided a list of things he would do if he was made the chief: fix
the service term of chief at thirty-five years and others at thirty
years; integrate Maoist combatants into the army in July 2009;
appoint the Maoist Commander Pasang as a general and appoint
other commanders at ranks below general in the Nepali Army; and
deploy 50 per cent of the army in development works.[25]

Well aware of Khadka's plan, Army Chief Katawal had
prepared a counter-plan. He hoped to proceed bloodlessly by

'holding on to constitutional provisions' to the extent possible. He wanted to make the president—constitutionally, the commander-in-chief—his shield. He also considered following the model adopted by the Bangladeshi army during the coup there in 2007. In Bangladesh, the Army Chief Moeen U. Ahmed had carried out a coup and formed a civilian government, which handed over power to political parties through a general election within two years.[26]

The broad contours of the army establishment's counter-plan ran like this: carry out a 'line arrest' and block the meetings and telephone communications of the prime minister, ministers, opposition leaders, ex-king, some other leaders and officials; seize Singha Durbar (the central government secretariat), Baluwatar (the PM's official residence), ministerial quarters, Maoist party office, and YCL camps; raid the containers storing Maoist weapons; encourage Maoist combatants in cantonments across the country to vacate the camps and go home or elsewhere; and bring UNMIN monitors from the cantonments in districts to UNMIN headquarters in Kathmandu.[27]

Katawal also had access to another perfect weapon to use against Prachanda—the secret video tape of Prachanda making a provocative address to his combatants at the Shaktikhor cantonment. In that address on 2 January 2008, which was meant for internal party training, Prachanda revealed how he had hoodwinked everyone by raising the number of combatants to 20,000 from the original number of 6000–7000. He also talked about his plan to seize power by mixing his combatants into the national army.

The tape was to be used to provide political legitimacy in the event of a 'soft coup' by the army. But the Maoist prime minister himself resigned, so the coup was never staged. Later, the tape was released in order to overshadow Maoist claims made after Prachanda's resignation,. The television stations ran the tape continuously from the evening of 4 May 2009. Prachanda did not refute the authenticity of the tape. In his clarification, he said that he had made those remarks one-and-a-half years ago, when the Constituent Assembly election was shrouded in uncertainty.

Had the army establishment merely drafted a contingency plan for a 'soft coup', or did it actually want to implement it? Would the army have been able to carry out such a coup? It was not clear. Events show that the army leadership wanted to stop the Maoist penetration into the military rank and file.

Even as the controversy was brewing, the Indian Ambassador Rakesh Sood went to meet the president one morning with his own set of coup-like plans. According to top sources at Shital Niwas (the official residence of the president), the 'blueprint' handed over by Sood included imposing a state of emergency, mobilizing the army, dismissing the Prachanda-led government, the taking over of power by the president, and holding fresh elections. After the president cordially refused, the Indian proposal failed to take any shape. The president neither sacked the army chief like Prachanda wanted, nor carried out his own coup against his government. He chose to go for the middle path to manage the crisis.

The climax: On the morning of 3 May 2009, a cabinet meeting was called at Baluwatar where Prime Minister Prachanda proposed to sack Katawal and appoint Khadka as the acting army chief. The ministers belonging to CPN–UML, including Deputy Prime Minister Bamdev Gautam, walked out of the meeting as per their party's instruction. Rajendra Mahato of the Sadbhavana Party and Ganesh Shah of CPN–Samyukta also walked out. A few ministers belonging to the MJF registered their dissent. Subsequently, all the partners except for the forum announced their exit from the ruling alliance.

Katawal and Khadka had both been called to Baluwatar during the cabinet meeting. Khadka reached there at 9.55 a.m. Katawal reached an hour later. For three hours, Katawal was made to wait at a separate room. He was then handed the letter of his dismissal. He declined to accept the letter and asked that the letter be dispatched to the army headquarters instead. He was allowed to go out only after the government agreed to send the letter to the headquarters. Katawal then made his way to the headquarters, where Khadka had reached ten minutes before him, brandishing a letter of his appointment. Khadka briefed the available senior army officials about his appointment.

Katawal's letter of dismissal stated that the cabinet had dismissed him, and his dismissal would come into effect from that very day. Katawal called a meeting of the Principal Staff Officers (PSOs). The PSOs interpreted the letter to mean that the dismissal would come into effect after midnight that day. Khadka was compelled to accept the interpretation, as he found no backers among the PSOs.

With a deadline of midnight, Katawal went into overdrive to overturn the government's decision. He made an application to the president, claiming that he had been unlawfully sacked, attaching the government's letter of dismissal. He also started lobbying with political leaders and foreign contacts. The presidency appeared to be the only institution that could overturn the decision, since the president is constitutionally the commander-in-chief of the Nepali Army. The attention of all political powers was now on the president. No reply came from Shital Niwas until late at night, while Katawal and other army generals kept on inquiring. At around 9.30 p.m., the decision by Shital Niwas was faxed to the army headquarters. The instruction read that since the cabinet decision was 'constitutionally and procedurally flawed', Katawal was directed 'to continue as army chief'. Katawal used the president's instruction as his 'shield' and refused to step down. In fact, to prevent any untoward incident, he stayed put inside the headquarters for three days.

The president's decision was more political than constitutional. He overturned the decision of the cabinet because he had the backing of most of the political parties, the army establishment, and even India. The Maoists, on the other hand, had been isolated. The president based his decision on the written application by

eighteen political parties, including Nepali Congress and CPN–
UML, who had urged him to overturn the cabinet decision,
terming it unconstitutional. The parties believed that the Maoists
were trying to seize power by increasing their influence over the
national army.

The president also wanted Indian support before reinstating
Katawal. Though he got the support of Ambassador Sood, he
wanted a green signal from the Indian political leadership. After
he talked to External Affairs Minister Pranab Mukherjee at
night, he faxed his decision. Much later, a former Indian foreign
secretary revealed how India had 'interfered' to stop Prachanda in
the Katawal episode, in order to ensure that the 'professionalism'
of the army was not compromised.[28]

Actually, there was no love lost between Delhi and Katawal.
Despite being known as 'anti-India' at one point, Katawal received
Delhi's backing because of their fear of the Maoists. India did not
want to see Maoist domination in the Nepali Army following the
abolition of the monarchy. According to high-level sources, India
had promised at the height of the second people's movement that
there would be no compromise on the 'institutional interests' and
'prerogatives' of the Nepali Army. It was following this Indian
promise that the army had agreed to sever its traditional ties to the
monarchy.

According to Saran, the Maoists had promised the Indians that
they would do nothing about the Nepali Army without political
understanding.[29] Contrary to that promise, when they 'dared' to
sack Katawal, India wanted to topple Prachanda's government,
even if 'for one day'.[30]

Prachanda's two options: Prachanda did not have many options
after the president overturned his decision. First, he thought of
recognizing Khadka as army chief and ejecting Katawal from the
army headquarters. But he received an indication that there would
be bloodshed if he did that. Later, while addressing a group of
editors, he said:

There were rumours of an attack upon Baluwatar. I also thought there would be a coup! As a prime minister, I could no longer go underground. I stayed put in Baluwatar. I arranged for two machine guns to be shifted from Naya Bazaar (his private residence) and posted them at Baluwatar along with a dozen comrades. Even if there was an attack, they could resist for few hours. I wanted to establish that I had fought till the end. I remembered the Chilean Marxist President Salvadore Allende. They made him die in a coup there. I also remembered the anti-communist bloodshed in Indonesia. I recalled other world events. I was sleepless. I expected an attack at any point.[31]

In the end, Prachanda concluded it was better to vacate the front instead of fighting a losing battle. He feared there would be bloodshed, sooner or later, if he stuck to his position. He saw his position would then be like a vanquished army general. Since his allies, the CPN–UML, Sadbhavana and others had left him, his government could be toppled by a parliamentary vote as well. So he chose to resign instead. On 4 May 2009, he announced his resignation. In his resignation address, he termed the president's decision 'unconstitutional' and stated that he had chosen to step down because it was inappropriate to continue in office when a situation of 'dual regime' had been created by the president.

Prachanda's party itself was also divided over the Katawal episode. Baburam's group was in favour of taking action against the army chief whereas Kiran's group had mixed feelings. After the controversy grew, a meeting of leaders close to Kiran had met separately at the residence of politburo member Pampha Bhusal on the night of 29 April. There were nine politburo members at the meeting, including vice-chairman of the party, Kiran, Secretary Gaurav, and standing committee members Dev Gurung and Netra Bikram Chand 'Biplav'. The meeting concluded that action should not be taken against the army chief as he would carry out a coup. Leaders close to Kiran considered Katawal to be a 'patriotic' army chief. They believed Prachanda and Baburam were taking action against him according to Indian wishes. They concluded that they should prepare for resistance by the army in case of action against the chief. They later made a detailed plan.

According to the plan, they decided to ask senior leader and information minister Krishna Bahadur Mahara (who had been in the Kiran faction till then) to refrain from taking part in the cabinet meeting. Two of their ministers, Dev Gurung and Pampha Bhusal, were asked to immediately inform Biplav through SMS about the action, following which Biplav was to send pro-Kiran leaders and cadres to secured 'shelters'. The shelters of some leaders such as Kiran, Gaurav and Biplav had already been changed.[32]

On the other hand, Baburam (who was then finance minister and the right-hand man of Prachanda) wanted the government to take action against Katawal at any cost. On 20 April, when the government asked the army chief for an explanation, Baburam told journalists at Nepalgunj that the intention of seeking such a clarification was to take action against him.

Prachanda consults his wife Sita whenever he has to take important decisions. In the case of Katawal, too, he consulted her. She told him that it was a bad idea to take action against him. 'He will retire in a few months anyway. It is not appropriate to take action against him now,' she told him repeatedly. But Prachanda did not heed her advice.

Baburam used to go up to Prachanda's bedroom day and night and constantly egg him on—he used to warn that they would lose all political prestige if they backed down. In Prachanda's words, 'Badalji (defence minister) was already against Katawal. When Baburamji also started to campaign against him, I could not handle it anymore. Day and night they kept on asking me to take action against Katawal. I was, thus, compelled.'[33] The Indian Ambassador Rakesh Sood had gone to Baluwatar and warned Prachanda—there would be unimaginable consequences to any action against the army chief. It was clear that Baburam knew very well how Delhi would react to any such action. So why did he incite Prachanda?

Baburam was the only personality within the Maoist leadership who could replace Prachanda as government head. In fact, he started lobbying with Madhesi leaders immediately after Prachanda's exit to form a new government under his leadership. He continued this lobbying for a long time to come. He had been dissatisfied after he was not made deputy prime minister, and the UML's Bamdev Gautam (who had lost the CA election) was given the post. He was further irked when he was replaced in the position of deputy parliamentary party leader.

The army chief episode deeply disturbed the Nepali politics. The Maoists' relations with NC/CPN–UML soured. They were also bitter towards the president. The episode brought the Nepali Army closer to India.

India ended up with dual benefits. Prachanda had been toppled while President Ram Baran Yadav and Army Chief Katawal, known to harbour 'anti-India' feelings, were compelled to seek their blessings due to the changed context.

21

'Course Correction'

'Standing on the bloodshed by tens of thousands of patriots, we are not willing to bow down before any foreign master.'

—Prachanda, in his address to the public announcing his resignation from the prime ministership

Having walked out of Singha Durbar, Prachanda hit the streets immediately. He concluded that there was an Indian hand behind the fall of his government. He dared Delhi by openly terming it a 'foreign master'. He declared agitation, raising slogans for national self-rule and civilian supremacy over the army.

The Maoists concluded that by reinstating Katawal as army chief, President Yadav had breached the principle of civilian supremacy and violated the Constitution. They believed India backed the president in doing so, and had helped cobble together an alliance including Madhesi parties to form a government headed by the CPN–UML leader Madhav Kumar Nepal. They targeted their diatribe at Delhi.[1]

The Maoist leaders levelled grave accusations and used derogatory epithets such as 'remote-controlled' and 'puppet' against the new prime minister. The Indians also lost no time in demonstrating their diplomatic backing to Madhav Kumar Nepal. Prime Minister Manmohan Singh dispatched former Ambassador Shiv Shankar Mukherjee to Kathmandu on a special plane to convey his best wishes. PM Nepal's government felt indebted to Delhi. As such, it made a few controversial decisions. For instance, the government awarded the contract to print the Machine Readable Passports (MRPs) to an Indian government company, Security Printing and Minting Corporation, in an opaque manner, without calling for tenders. The Indian ambassador wrote a letter to Foreign Minister Sujata Koirala to bag the contract.[2] However, Prime Minister Nepal reversed the decision in the face of criticism. Likewise, he also refused to sign the extradition treaty proposed by India. He even rejected Indian advice to dissolve the CA.

PM Nepal, however, was able to end the term of the UNMIN, as India wanted. Delhi was incensed at the UNMIN after it held a collective dialogue with some Tarai groups before the CA election. It was not amused when UN officials working under a humanitarian mandate travelled across the border into Bihar to talk to Madhesi armed groups.[3] Delhi saw that its role and influence in Kathmandu would be restricted while the UNMIN was allowed to operate. The government in Kathmandu was equally unhappy with the UNMIN for its 'soft approach' toward the Maoists. With the CA election already held, and its inability to wrap up the integration and rehabilitation of Maoist combatants amid the protracted transition, the UNMIN was under pressure to prove the utility of its continued presence. It was finally wrapped up in January 2012.

Out of power, the Maoists now targeted both the governments in Kathmandu and Delhi. As a result, the peace process and Constitution-making remained stalled for a long time. The Madhav Kumar Nepal-led new government, too, could not function very well. Amid growing distrust, Delhi, however, kept its line of communication with the Maoists open. Their informal conversations with Prachanda continued via emissaries in Kathmandu, and also through those dispatched from Delhi. High-level meetings also took place: one in London and another in Singapore.

Talks with Mathur

The Indian establishment assigned its intelligence wing, RAW, to hold talks with the Maoist leadership. One of RAW's top officials has revealed that its senior officers are in direct contact with major leaders of countries such as Nepal, Bangladesh, Sri Lanka, the Maldives, Mauritius, Singapore, Iran, Egypt and so on.[4] With the Nepali Maoists, the RAW had old institutional relations.

After Ashok Chaturvedi retired as RAW chief, K.C. Verma took over the position in February 2009. He assigned his under-secretary, A.B. Mathur, to look after some South Asian countries, including Nepal. A 1975 batch officer from Manipur, Mathur had long experiences of working everywhere from Guwahati to New York, and negotiating with armed groups. Mathur was involved, as a junior officer, in the RAW team that, in the 1970s, clandestinely transported Pu Laldenga, the leader of a secessionist group active in the north-eastern state of Mizoram, from his hideout in Pakistan to Geneva for talks that ended up pulling him into mainstream politics. Delhi assigned this same Mathur to hold talks with Prachanda. They had a series of phone conversations. But neither was Prachanda able to travel to Delhi, nor was Mathur allowed to go to Kathmandu for direct talks. Delhi was keen to avoid any direct talks becoming public when its relationship with the Maoists was so bitter. So they arranged a meeting in a western capital.

Prachanda treated Mathur more as a political representative than a spy master, so he agreed to meet him even though he was organizing a fierce agitation targeting India. Accompanied by his wife Sita and son Prakash, he left for London on 8 August 2009 on a 'private visit'. The first round of talks between Prachanda and Mathur took place at the Hotel Crowne Plaza located near Buckingham Palace.

According to a source, Prachanda sought support in toppling the Madhav Kumar Nepal government, which the Indians backed. Among the three main factions within the Maoist party, the Baburam faction believed in having cordial relations with India while the Kiran faction wanted to continue its anti-India campaign. The RAW concluded that if the Kiran faction could be tamed, then it would lead to the coming together of the Baburam and Prachanda factions, resulting in a weakening of the anti-India campaign. Indian sources claim that Prachanda promised to sideline the hard-line leaders of the Kiran faction within three months. He did not keep his promise.

The London initiative got derailed when Madhav Kumar Nepal was not dislodged from the government, nor was the Kiran faction sidelined within the Maoist party. The second meeting between Prachanda and Mathur took place in Singapore on 17 November. Nepali Congress leader and former Prime Minister Girija Prasad Koirala had just been flown by air ambulance to Gleneagles hospital in Singapore. Under the pretext of visiting him in hospital and talking about a political resolution, Prachanda left for Singapore accompanied by his party's international department chief, Krishna Bahadur Mahara. In Singapore, he met Koirala and his nephew Shekhar Koirala. Prachanda had known Shekhar since the days of the twelve-point understanding. Around that time, the Indian professor, S.D. Muni, who had also played a role in that twelve-point understanding, was in Singapore as a visiting professor at the National University of Singapore. One evening, Prachanda, Mahara and Shekhar went to Muni's place. But the most important conversation Prachanda had was with the same RAW officer, Mathur.

Mathur held three rounds of talks with Prachanda, who was staying at the Four Seasons Hotel. The meeting was taking place shortly after a trip by Prachanda to Hong Kong and China, which had aroused Indian suspicions. Mathur inquired if Prachanda was trying to play the 'China card' against India. In reply, Prachanda said the Chinese were already in favour of the Maoists taking India into confidence in the days ahead. He told Mathur that he wanted to build, not damage, relations with India. 'We want to build relations with China, particularly with its communist party. It does not mean we want to go against India,' he tried to clarify.[5]

In Singapore, Prachanda had made a few suggestions to India to help mend its image in Nepal and improve relations with the Maoists. According to him, he proposed a replacement of the 1950 treaty, the handover a few hectares of disputed land in the Susta border region, the sending back of Indian security personnel across the river Kali at Kalapani and demonstrating a large heart in helping Nepal reduce its huge trade gap. He said that these matters would lead to an easing in bilateral relations. Prachanda felt that the settlement of these matters would improve the Maoists' relations with Delhi, reduce anti-India feeling in Nepal and pave the way for a long-term, strong partnership.

Importantly, Prachanda said that these things were possible only when a Maoist government was in power. Mathur did not give a concrete answer, but Delhi was in no mood to reinstate 'untrustworthy' Prachanda by displacing the friendly dispensation in Kathmandu under Prime Minister Madhav Kumar Nepal. The Maoist leadership considered it a 'betrayal'. Prachanda became further agitated and led a campaign against India.

Prachanda's reaction

In the wake of the failed Singapore talks, the Maoists intensified their anti-India rhetoric. Addressing a rally at New Baneshwar, Kathmandu, on 23 December 2009, Prachanda accused the Madhav Kumar Nepal-led government of being remote-controlled by Delhi. He said he would not talk to this puppet government and, instead, wanted direct dialogue with the 'puppet masters'.[6]

'I have held several rounds of talks with the parties. Each time, the dialogue ends at a point where they say they need to refer to Delhi. So here I am stating from this public platform—we are ready to talk to India,' he said.

He also lashed out at the Indian Army Chief Deepak Kapoor. General Kapoor had recently made a public comment against collective integration of Maoist combatants into the Nepali Army.[6] 'How dare an army chief of India speak against the Comprehensive Peace Agreement? Is he our governor?' Prachanda thundered.

Prachanda's assertion of Indian interference in Nepali affairs, and the need to stop it, was correct. But his declaration to hold talks with India to settle Nepali affairs was neither practical nor appropriate. Such comments coming from the leader of a major party, and a former prime minister at that, only exposed to what extent Nepal's dependence on others had grown. India did not pay serious attention to Prachanda's proposal, however.

Even as he stepped up his anti-India rhetoric, Prachanda started singing paeans to the erstwhile monarchy, openly praising King Birendra. On 11 January 2010, while addressing a rally in Mahendranagar of western Nepal, Prachanda raked up another controversy by implying an Indian hand behind the massacre of Birendra's family. 'Who massacred Birendra's dynasty? Why? In what circumstances?' he asked, adding, 'Here was a king with whom Maoist Chairman Prachanda was going to meet soon. He took a position of not deploying the army against the Maoists. He took a position that weapons should be imported not only from India but also from China and other countries for the army. He put forth a proposal for a Zone of Peace. Why shouldn't we deduce that these were the basic reasons that led to his killing?'[7]

It was a direct challenge to Delhi, where positions were further hardened against Prachanda. At the same rally in Mahendranagar, Prachanda said, 'Although the British have gone from Hindustan, they left behind their mentality. They want to see the Maoists run like other parties, accept their diktat and agree to be remote-controlled. I refused, my party refused.'[8] He said his party was being sidelined for these very reasons.

Separate teams of Maoist leaders held demonstrations on 12 January in disputed border regions. Prachanda himself was planning to go to the Kalapani area in Darchula district. But the plan was cancelled at the last minute. However, on 18 January, Prachanda stirred up another controversy by raising the issue of 'Greater Nepal'. He said that since the legitimacy of the Sugauli Treaty had ended, Nepal should 'lay claim on the territory from Teesta in the east to Kangra in the west' (the Sugauli Treaty of 1816, between Nepal and the British East India Company, ended the Anglo-Nepal war but is often referred to bitterly since it led to Nepal losing one-third of its territory). Prachanda said, 'The Sugauli Treaty was signed with the British and not India or the people of India. With the downfall of the British Raj, the legitimacy of the treaty has ended.'[9]

On 21 January, Prachanda again dragged Delhi into the assassination of two popular Nepali leaders. Addressing a rally in Bardiya, he implied an Indian hand in the killing of King Birendra, and in the fatal car crash of the CPN–UML General Secretary Madan Bhandari, for what he said was both men's 'patriotic stance'. Soon after he made those accusations, a mysterious murder took place in the middle of a busy Kathmandu street on 7 February. Jamim Shah, a rising media mogul who'd been accused of harbouring 'anti-India' feelings, was shot dead in broad daylight.

For a long time, Indian security agencies had been accusing Shah of working for the Pakistanis. But the way he was killed was also seen by many as intended to scare Prachanda. For instance, Dhruba Sharma, Shah's business partner, told the government investigation committee, 'There is a political reason behind this incident. The Maoists organized an anti-India agitation. Therefore, the Indians wanted to show that they could do anything they wanted. Shah ended up as a sacrificial lamb as he was killed in an area in the centre of the capital with such high security.'[10]

Prachanda did now tone down his anti-India rhetoric, but India's position against him continued to harden.

'Teaching a lesson' approach

For those in Delhi who had long considered it 'wrong-headed' giving a 'concession' to the Maoists through the twelve-point understanding found their voices with Prachanda's anti-India campaign. By that time, the two leading Indian players in the twelve-point understanding, Foreign Secretary Shyam Saran and RAW Chief Hormis Tharakan, had both retired. Those hawkish about the Maoists were now dominant in the Indian establishment: P. Chidambaram, M.K. Narayanan, K.C. Verma, Rakesh Sood and Satish Mehta.

Prime Minister Manmohan Singh, and the chief of the ruling United Progressive Alliance (UPA), Sonia Gandhi, had neither the time nor the desire to closely monitor the Nepal situation. They were engrossed in other issues, from Pakistan to China and the US, apart from internal matters. Pranab Mukherjee, an old Nepal hand, had been shifted from the external affairs ministry to the finance ministry. As the new external affairs minister, S.M. Krishna, had almost zero experience of Nepal, Home Minister Chidambaram was dominant. He was battling the activities of Indian Naxalites and, therefore, looked at Nepali Maoists through the same prism. His ministry, on 22 June 2009, put the All India Nepali Unity Society, a sister organization of the Nepali Maoists, on a list of thirty-four terrorist organizations. The society, which had also been prohibited during the insurgency, received similar treatment in peacetime—a clear indication of the hardening Indian position.

The reins of Nepal policy-making were left in the hands of the bureaucracy. The PM's NSA was at the forefront of this bureaucracy. M.K. Narayanan, a former IB chief, was known to harbour strong feelings against the Maoists. He had spent a long time in the 'B Wing' of the Intelligence Bureau, which was formed to suppress communist rebellion. Having confronted the Naxalites, and as a staunch anti-communist, Narayanan watched with contempt the growing Maoist dominance and their anti-India campaign in Nepal. Prime Minister Singh used to formulate his position on Nepal based on Narayanan's advice. The sources of Narayanan's information were the external affairs ministry and the RAW.

The RAW had made Nepal matters a priority. The formal responsibility of looking into Nepali affairs was given to Special Secretary A.B. Mathur. He was assisted by joint secretaries Prabhat Kumar and Jaya Gopal, and the chief, K.C. Verma, used to go through all major files. It goes almost without saying: they all spewed venom against the Maoists.

Reports prepared by Satish Mehta, the Nepal desk chief in South Block, were similar. Sitting in a room with a huge map of Nepal on the wall, Mehta used to monitor what comments the Maoist leaders had made and where. Tchhiring Sherpa, who had just returned to Delhi after completing his tenure as spokesperson of the Indian embassy in Kathmandu, assisted Mehta.

In Kathmandu, the ambassador was Rakesh Sood, who suited Narayanan's temperament. Unlike his predecessor Shiv Shankar Mukherjee, who had watched the peace process, the people's movement and CA election closely, and understood the intricacies, Sood was different. After he arrived in Kathmandu from India's Kabul mission, Sood invited a few journalists for an introductory meeting at his residence in Lainchour, on the evening of 7 June 2008. After downing a few pegs of whiskey, he said to us that the way the twelve-point understanding was done was not appropriate. 'How can guerrillas get the same status as a national army? That was a mistake, it should be corrected.'

Sood did not elaborate, but his illiberal road map slowly unfolded. In one interview, he opined that Maoist combatants should be 'integrated and rehabilitated into Nepali society' instead of the Nepali Army.[11] His viewpoints also influenced Nepal's political parties, whose varied opinions needlessly complicated the Constitution-making and peace process.

It was the clear conclusion of the hawkish officials dominant in the Indian establishment (Narayanan, Sood, Verma, Mehta, etc.) that the Maoists wanted to set up a one-party communist dictatorship; that they would seize power if not checked; that they would not accept India's security concerns, and would create a lot of problems if allowed to come to power. The thinking, therefore, was that the Maoists should be kept out of power, frustrated and even split, and ultimately, the CA dissolved. The assembly was the legitimate basis for the Maoists and the source of their status as the largest party of Nepal. They thought that such a 'course correction' alone would safeguard Indian interests in Nepal.[12]

The Indian establishment was bent on 'teaching a lesson' to Prachanda for his 'betrayal'. Why so much resentment? 'We welcomed Prachanda (after he became prime minister) with a red carpet. We had also assisted during the signing of the twelve-point understanding. But he betrayed us,' a top official at South Block revealed during an interaction with a visiting delegation of Nepali editors in July 2011. 'He declared India as the principle enemy, hurled a shoe at our ambassador, and targeted companies with Indian investment. How can we trust him in the wake of such incidents, one after another?'[13]

For around two years, India's Nepal policy was guided by this hawkish attitude. When he could no longer talk to Sood, and his conversations with RAW agents became fruitless, Prachanda wanted to talk to the Indian political leadership directly. But Sood and RAW worked hard to close every door leading to Delhi. Given to speaking his mind, Prachanda confided to the media at least thrice that he was going to Delhi, but each time, it had to be cancelled. A place where he was welcomed during his underground days, Delhi shut its doors on Prachanda now.

The Maoists also had themselves to blame for being unable to expand their ties at the political level in India. They were overly dependent on RAW agents and middlemen. They never could build political relations. When he visited Delhi as a prime minister, Prachanda had a long chat with Sonia Gandhi. They even talked about family matters. But he failed to give continuity to such political ties.

In the end, Prachanda called his old acquaintance in Delhi, the leftist intellectual Ananda Swaroop Verma, and the general secretary of Janata Dal (United), K.C. Tyagi, to Kathmandu. Tyagi brought a letter of invitation for an India visit from his party chief, Sharad Yadav. Prachanda replied to Yadav, 'We extend our gratitude to you for your help and support in the establishment of the people's federal democratic republic in Nepal.'

Yadav, who was then convener of the opposition National Democratic Alliance (NDA), went to visit Manmohan Singh carrying the letter, but the eyes of PM Singh fell on the words 'people's federal democratic republic'. He said: This is a plan to establish a communist state.[14]

Prachanda's India visit was again scuttled.

China, against India

After their relations with India worsened, the Maoists tried to build bridges with China. In the past, the Maoist leadership had adopted a policy of moving like a pendulum between Delhi and the Durbar: get closer to the Durbar when things went bad with Delhi, and vice versa. Prachanda wanted to do the same with Delhi and Beijing. Relations between India and China were not warm at that time. By refusing to give a visa to Lt Gen. B.S. Jaiswal of the northern command of the Indian Army (which was also posted in Jammu and Kashmir), when he wanted to travel to China on an official visit, Beijing had indirectly backed Pakistan's position on Jammu and Kashmir. The media of the two countries were also engaged in a bitter spat.[15]

Amid all this, a former Indian ambassador to China, Nirupama Rao, was appointed foreign secretary in July 2009. Within one-and-a-half months of her appointment, on 14 September, she dashed to Kathmandu, but the person whom she had come to meet had left for Hong Kong the night before. Prachanda was set to meet a Chinese security official there, who looked after Nepal matters. Rao had come with an open mind, to explore the possibility of mending ties with the Maoists. Delhi took it as an affront.

Meanwhile, Prachanda kept up his China mission. Accompanied by party Vice-Chairman Mohan Baidya 'Kiran' and the foreign cell chief, Mahara, he set out on a visit to the Chinese mainland from 10 to 19 October 2009. On the evening of 16 October, they had an extensive discussion with President Hu Jintao about their ideologies and future course. The meeting took place on the sidelines of the eleventh Chinese National Games in Jinan. Prachanda praised the economic policies formulated by President Hu's idol Deng Xiaoping, whereas Kiran criticized it. The Chinese leadership got an opportunity to observe the ideological divisions between Prachanda and Kiran.

A few months later, Prachanda again flew to Hong Kong to meet the same Chinese security official. The news of his two-hour-long conversation with Chinese security officials at a hotel in the Sino Center Plaza, 23 Jordan Road, Kowloon, became public.[16] He had also slipped across the border into the mainland and travelled to a Chinese city to meet communist party officials.

The following year, in October 2010, China invited Prachanda to the Shanghai Expo. In those meetings, the Chinese told Prachanda that he had made a mistake in exiting the government over the Katawal episode. They advised him to join the government again, and told him that he should carry out pro-people programmes and intensify development works after taking the Indians into confidence. Generally, Nepali leaders make a beeline to Delhi, but Prachanda was doing the opposite by travelling to the northern neighbour. Perhaps his goal was to scare Delhi by showing his northward inclination, so that it would end its policy of negating the Maoists and resume productive relations. In any case, getting closer to the world's second largest economy would be beneficial to his party and the country, Prachanda thought.

China was also looking for various ways to extend its influence in Nepal. When Nepal's largest political party offered itself, the Chinese were pleased. China had accorded top priority to its relations with Nepal, given the long border Nepal had with its sensitive Tibet region. China engaged through trade, industry and investment in infrastructure and, thereby, sought to increase its political and diplomatic influence. The Chinese particularly wanted to extend the railroad from Lhasa up to the Nepali border, and also expand road networks around border points. They calculated that once these projects were completed, it would trigger economic interactions and set off multidimensional social impact.[17]

China also advanced, via Prachanda, proposals for a trilateral partnership in big hydropower and other infrastructure projects. Delhi did not like the proposal. Another proposal Beijing forwarded through the Maoist leadership was for the development of Lumbini, the birthplace of Lord Buddha, which also became mired in controversy. Reuters reported news from Beijing that a Chinese NGO, formed at the behest of Beijing and called Asia Pacific Exchange and Cooperation (APEC), was to invest $3 billion in the development of Lumbini. It was said that they wanted to develop Lumbini as a sacred place for Buddhists, like Mecca or the Vatican. The plan was to build a temple, an airport, a highway, a hotel, a conference centre and a Buddhist university.[18]

The plan triggered a row within Nepal. It drew protests not only because APEC had not been registered with the Nepal government, and the plan had never been presented to the Nepali authorities, but also because Prachanda was one of the ten co-chairs of APEC. In Delhi's eyes, the Chinese had made a smart strategic move by forming APEC and backing Prachanda under the pretext of the development of Lumbini in order to enter Nepal with a strategic investment. So Delhi attempted to derail the plan at any cost, and it was largely successful.

Interestingly, along with Prachanda, former crown prince Paras was also named as co-chair of APEC. He was later removed after widespread negative comments. Prachanda had met Paras at Kuala Lumpur when they both were attending a meeting of APEC. Many also saw APEC as a Chinese bridge to connect the Maoists and the monarchists. Among the family of former royals, Paras in particular used to harbour strong views against India, and APEC was bringing him closer to the Maoists. Initially, he had a number of meetings with Krishna Bahadur Mahara. Later, Prachanda also met him. Subsequently, Indian intelligence agents got a whiff of a meeting between Prachanda and the ex-king Gyanendra in July 2010.

At the meeting of his party's central committee (21 to 24 May 2010), Prachanda presented a proposal to form a nationalist front. He then held a series of meetings with monarchists and the leaders of yesteryears, such as Tulsi Giri and Marichman Singh Shrestha. He even met the same Rookmangud Katawal whom he had tried so hard to sack.[19] Kamal Thapa's Rastriya Prajatantra Party (RPP–Nepal) even claimed that Prachanda was ready to accept 'cultural monarchy'.[20]

India was unhappy with the growing intimacy between the Maoists, China and the monarchists. In the meantime, a secretly taped telephone conversation between the Maoist leader Mahara and a Hong Kong-based Chinese contact was leaked to the media in August 2010. In the conversation, Mahara could be heard asking his contact for immediate assistance of 'NRs. 500 million, at the rate of NRs. 10 million per parliamentarian' to buy the votes of fifty parliamentarians to form a new government with a Maoist prime minister.[21]

It was not clear if the Chinese contact was a government official or not, but it was a major setback—a political one for the

Maoists, and a diplomatic one for the Chinese—whose effects would be felt for a long time.

Collapse of the general strike

The Maoists were under the impression that their anti-India campaign had paid dividends in the form of growing proximity to the Chinese, the promotion of a nationalist agenda, and strengthening their position in internal politics. Their central committee meeting of January 2010 had concluded that there were four favourable conditions for launching a revolt: first, the expansion of their political base at the cost of other parties; second, fissures and contradictions among international powers, and the possibility of one of them coming to their side; third, their ability to convince the people by raising concerns about peace and the Constitution; and fourth, the development of a refined leadership who could coordinate all these aspects.[22]

A few months after they decided to instigate revolt, the Maoists hit the streets. They launched an indefinite general strike beginning the day after May Day. Internally, they called it their 'revolt', but for external public consumption, they called it a 'third people's movement'. It was declared as being against the Madhav Kumar Nepal government. The undeclared part of the agitation was also equally clear: it was a show of force to Delhi. They calculated that the agitation would, at the very least, topple the Nepal-led government.

The Maoists summoned cadres from all over the country to the capital. Around 56,000 youth cadres were mobilized. They were put up in makeshift shelters in local schools, colleges and public places. The people of Kathmandu were, for the first time, witnessing scenes of mass Maoist mobilization: a hallmark of their war-era preparations. It instilled a sense of terror among residents, which slowly turned into expressions of resistance.

On the fifth day of the general shutdown, Baburam Bhattarai told a meeting of the Maoist standing committee that revolt was not possible and they should immediately withdraw the strike. He was overruled by the majority, which decided, instead, to pile pressure on the government by organizing human chains around the ring road the next day to surround the capital. The government was preparing to deploy the army, seeking permission from the national defence council and informing the United Nations Mission to Nepal (UNMIN). It was becoming increasingly clear that giving continuity to the general strike would amount to confronting the army head-on, and inviting bloodshed. The Maoist leadership was not prepared for that. They had only wanted to press the government to step down.

On the morning of the sixth day, a mass of people wearing white T-shirts gathered in a rally called by the business community and civil society leaders in the heart of Kathmandu, in Basantapur, to oppose the Maoists. Prachanda slammed the demonstrators by terming them 'elitists and privileged'. His use of derogatory terms against the city demonstrators turned out to be counter-productive.

The Maoist meeting in January had concluded that international powers were divided. They had calculated that in an agitation targeting India, they would attract support from the European Union, the United Nations and China. But their general shutdown attracted sympathies from none. Neither the EU nor the UN nor China came to their rescue.

The Maoist calculation that they would get support from ordinary citizens, including the foot soldiers of the army and the police and government employees, was also unfounded. They were unable to bring 6,00,000 people to the streets as planned. Their prediction that Madhav Kumar Nepal would buckle under pressure also turned out to be wrong. Their whole plan started unravelling. One reason was the lack of clarity in the goals of their agitation. They had brought in cadres from all over the country promising a revolt, but the leadership had not planned anything beyond the resignation of the government. Interestingly, amid all these events, PM Madhav Kumar Nepal appeared unfazed, compelling the Maoists to drop their indefinite agitation on just the sixth day.

On the morning of 8 May, top leaders were dispatched to each of the fifty-two makeshift camps across the capital to 'convince' their cadres. The leaders were instructed to brief the cadres that this was merely a 'rehearsal' for the actual revolt, which was coming. When they saw their leaders were stopping the agitation without any result, the cadres turned against their leaders, raising slogans against them. The Maoist leaders found it very tough to handle them.

Nine Maoist cadres had lost their lives due to road accidents and diseases during the six-day-long agitation. One of them, living in a camp at Chabahil, had died of cardiac arrest upon hearing the instruction for a sudden halt to the agitation. The collapse of the strike triggered a deep sense of frustration and disappointment among the rank and file. A week ago, they had entered into Kathmandu full of vigour. Now they were returning home with a deep sense of disenchantment and disillusion. They were also filled with a strong sense of resentment against the leadership. The failed agitation marked an important turning point for the Maoists. Gradually, Prachanda toned down the call for revolt and started talking about peace and the Constitution. He decided to make peace with India, too.

Bhatbhateni meeting

The two-year term of the Constituent Assembly was coming to an end on 28 May 2010. Since many constitutional issues had not been resolved, the term of the assembly had to be extended somehow. Till some time before that, the Maoists had not been interested in extending its term. They hoped instead for some results from their agitation. When the showdown turned into a fiasco, the Constituent Assembly was the only weapon left in their arsenal. Only the survival of the assembly could give continuity to their status as the largest party, and safeguard the path of peaceful transition. So, despite their public comments, they were trying hard to extend the assembly term. They made the resignation of Madhav Kumar Nepal's government a precondition for such an extension.

Top leaders of the NC–UML were divided over the extension of the CA's term. PM Nepal was facing the most heat. The hawkish elements of the Indian establishment, including Ambassador Rakesh Sood, wanted to see the dissolution of the assembly and implement a road map towards a new election. At this point, CPN–UML leader K.P. Oli played a decisive role. Amid the confusion, Oli—who was not even a member of the assembly, having lost the election two years ago—appeared at the Constituent Assembly building around 10.30 p.m. on 28 May. He declared that Prime Minister Nepal would resign—something Prachanda was yearning to hear, and facilitated the process for extension of the CA term.

Following Oli's proposal, the NC, UML and the Maoists reached a three-point understanding. They passed a proposal to extend the term of the CA by one more year. The third point of the understanding read: '. . . the present prime minister of the coalition government is ready to resign in order to form a government of national consensus to fulfil the appropriate responsibilities and tasks.'

'Appropriate responsibilities' mainly meant the task of management of Maoist ex-combatants. PM Nepal wanted to sacrifice his position for the sake of proceeding with the peace process, instead of risking the dissolution of the assembly. But Indian Ambassador Sood was disappointed with him for reaching the understanding. Sood was even angry at Oli, who had facilitated the whole thing. The design to tame the Maoists by dissolving the assembly had been derailed.

However, even after the understanding of 28 May, neither did the Maoists come forward to expedite the peace process, nor did

PM Nepal step down. There appeared to be no meeting point, since PM Nepal first wanted a concrete agreement on completing the reintegration of Maoist fighters, whereas the Maoists first wanted to see the back of him. The stalemate ended after a two-hour meeting between Prachanda and Nepal held on 27 June at the residence of a billionaire industrialist in Bhatbhateni. Three days later, Nepal tendered his resignation.

At the Bhabhateni meeting, the two leaders agreed on a number of issues such as integrating around 5000 ex-combatants into the army and the police; rehabilitating the rest with attractive packages; segregating ex-combatants into separate camps for integration and rehabilitation; and forming a national consensus government under Maoist leadership.[23] These agreements were never implemented. Enmeshed in complicated power politics, the country was pushed into a protracted contest over who would be the new prime minister.

Seven-month race

It took around seven months to appoint a successor to Madhav Kumar Nepal. For this period, the country was governed by a caretaker administration under him. The Parliament and the CA were left without any business to conduct. The national agenda of peace and Constitution-building remained ignored. At the first attempt to vote for a new prime minister, on 21 July 2010, there were three candidates in the fray: Prachanda, Jhalnath Khanal (chairman of the UML) and Ram Chandra Poudel (parliamentary party leader of Nepali Congress). Khanal did not enjoy the full backing of his own party, since top leaders such as PM Nepal and Oli raised a precondition—that he would get the full support of UML only if he could be assured of garnering 401 votes in his favour, to reach the two-third mark necessary for promulgating the Constitution. In the first round, Khanal was unable to gain the support of a two-thirds majority, though he got quite close. So, Khanal backed out after the first round.

The second round of voting took place on 23 July. Neither Prachanda nor Poudel garnered enough votes. Since the CPN–UML and Madhesi Front both abstained from voting, the third round, held on 2 August, also could not elect anyone. Prachanda was short by just forty-two votes of achieving a simple majority. The Indians wanted to prevent him from getting elected or, at least, to carefully weigh the chances of a 'pact' with him. In this connection, A.B. Mathur, the same RAW official whom Prachanda had met in London and Singapore the previous year, came to Kathmandu. He first met Prachanda at a private residence in Bhainsepati, and then again at Prachanda's residence in Naya Bazaar.

After the intelligence agency tested the waters, Delhi dispatched a formal envoy. Former Foreign Secretary Shyam Saran landed in Kathmandu on 4 August as an envoy of the Indian prime minister. He met a number of leaders, but his main mission was to talk to Prachanda. He had been engaging with the Maoist leadership since 2006. This time, he had been sent to learn Prachanda's calculations. When, on the morning of 5 August, he reached the residence of Prachanda in Naya Bazaar, the whole top leadership of the Maoist party was waiting for him. Prachanda was accompanied by three vice-chairmen: Mohan Baidya 'Kiran', Baburam Bhattarai and Narayan Kaji Shrestha, along with General Secretary Ram Bahadur Thapa 'Badal' and the foreign department chief, Krishna Bahadur Mahara.

Saran asked about the Maoists' commitment toward the peace process and democracy. Delhi wanted to be clear on whether the Maoists had indeed chosen the path of peaceful politics for good, or if they still harboured any plan to seize power forcefully. Saran said India wanted to see the Maoists transform into a mainstream, civilian party. The Maoist leaders replied that they wanted to conclude the integration of former fighters. But they added that they did not accept the existing parliamentary system.

The fourth round of prime ministerial voting took place on 6 August, when Saran was still in Kathmandu. In the previous round, Prachanda was short by only forty-two votes. A CA member from the TMLP, Ram Kumar Sharma, had recently left his party to join the Maoists as a central member. Sharma was actively lobbying with Madhesi members to bag votes for Prachanda. The Indian embassy was enraged by the activities of Sharma, who had once worked as their contact. Sharma then revealed that he had been receiving threatening calls from Subrat Das, a RAW official working in the embassy. He petitioned the chairman of the assembly, Subas Nembang, demanding security. The parliamentary committee on international relations and human rights instructed the government to expel Das, but the government did not carry out the instruction. Rather, Sharma's original party, the TMLP, wrote to Nembang demanding that Sharma be kicked out of the assembly, since he had switched his allegiance. In the end, Sharma himself resigned.

Amid the pressure on Sharma and the Indian drama, Prachanda lost in the fourth round too. A democracy like India had made the election of the prime minister in a neighbouring country a matter of ego. It was at this stage that the Indians, on 3 September, made public the secret recording of a telephone conversation between Mahara and his Chinese contact, in which the Maoist leader was heard asking for assistance of NRs. 500 million to 'buy off' fifty MPs. The tape was made public on the eve of the sixth round of voting, slated for 5 September. Then Prachanda understood clearly that they would not allow him to be prime minister. After the seventh round of voting on 17 September, Prachanda announced that he was withdrawing his candidacy. In this charged context, a Maoist cadre hurled a shoe at Indian Ambassador Sood in Solukhumbu on 6 October.

The Congress leader Poudel, however, kept up his lone fight till the seventeenth round of voting. He withdrew from the race only on 12 January 2011. With no candidate left in the field, the president again appealed to the political parties to form a national consensus government, as per Article 38 (1) of the interim Constitution. It was a mere formality that could not be fulfilled. So the process of electing a prime minister by majority resumed as per Article 38 (2). Apart from the three previous candidates—Prachanda, Khanal and Poudel—there was also a fourth candidate this time around: Bijaya Kumar Gachhadar, the president of the Madhesi Janadhikar Forum (Loktantrik).

At the beginning of the new round of voting, RAW's A.B. Mathur arrived in Kathmandu on 13 January. Before he returned to Delhi on 17 January, he met Prachanda twice at the New Baneshwar residence of a businessman named Ajeya Raj Sumargi. India suspected that Prachanda might support Khanal. Mathur had come with a new proposal to prevent Prachanda from supporting Khanal, because India thought that the election of Khanal could result in a coming together of communist parties, with Prachanda enjoying decisive power from behind, perhaps pushing such a government towards China and triggering a polarization against India.

Prachanda seemed to be extremely tense at his second meeting with Mathur. According to sources who were present in the meeting, he used threatening tones and said he would 'teach India a lesson by electing Khanal as prime minister if it continued to push him to the wall'. He even threatened to 'unleash anarchy'. Mathur is said to have countered him by saying that he would not be able to do 'more harm than Pakistan'.

The day Mathur returned after that bitter experience, the Indian Foreign Secretary Nirupama Rao landed in Kathmandu, on 18 January, for her second visit. She had probably already briefed by RAW and, therefore, did not talk much during the forty-minute meeting with Prachanda at his Naya Bazaar residence. But in her meeting with other parties, she pressed for the formation of a non-Maoist government.

On 22 January, the eve of the prime ministerial election, Prachanda appeared a bit 'flexible'. Holding a special ceremony

at the Shaktikhor cantonment, he declared that all the ex-
combatants staying in seven cantonments would now come under
the command of the all-party Special Committee for Army
Integration and Rehabilitation. In a situation where the UNMIN
had already left, the Maoist declaration was nothing more than
propaganda, because in a practical sense, the command of the
combatants was still with the Maoist party.

Prachanda made the declaration in order to demonstrate
his commitment towards the logical conclusion of the peace
process. But it had no impact on the political negotiations on
the election of prime minister. Prachanda was convinced that
he would not be allowed to become prime minister. So, in the
very first round of the election on 3 February, he withdrew
from the race and backed Khanal instead. As a result, Khanal
was elected as the fourth communist prime minister of Nepal.
And Prachanda declared in Parliament, 'Today we are making
history, a norm that Nepali parties and Nepali leaders are
capable of deciding on their own. We are capable of writing our
fate and future ourselves, and not under someone else's direction
and command.'

Mathur had come from Delhi again to influence Prachanda
in the run-up to that election. He was staying at the Yak and
Yeti Hotel, where he received information from a senior Maoist
leader that Prachanda was preparing to back Khanal in the prime
ministerial election. Mathur consulted with Shivshankar Menon,
who was now the national security advisor, over the telephone,
and then encouraged Prachanda to 'wait for two more days and
then form government under your own leadership'. But Prachanda
had already made up his mind. Khanal was elected. It was a bitter
moment for Mathur, who had been in extensive negotiations
with Prachanda for the last one-and-a-half years. Just recently, he
had been defeated in the race to become RAW chief by Sanjeev
Tripathy. After the election of Khanal, Mathur was shunted
out from the special secretary (neighbourhood) desk as well,

and transferred to the Aviation Research Centre with technical responsibilities.

The Maoist–UML alliance was not only unanticipated, but a setback for Delhi's strategic calculations. The first point of the seven-point understanding, reached between the two parties to elect Khanal, stated that they would 'firmly safeguard national independence, integrity and sovereignty'. Soon after Prachanda backed Khanal, the 'democratic alliance' between the UML and the NC collapsed, and the two communist parties began a leftist alliance—which was worse for India than Prachanda becoming prime minister. After the second people's movement, for the first time, an alliance critical of India, and even oriented towards China, had come to power.

Self-course correction

A few weeks after Khanal became prime minister, the chief of the Chinese People's Liberation Army, General Chen Wengde, came on a three-day visit to Nepal. China also sent a delegation under Qiu Yongkang, one of the nine supreme leaders on the standing committee of the Chinese Communist Party. Beijing also dispatched a draft of an agreement on expanding assistance and information sharing between the security agencies of the two countries.

India's one-point agenda of sidelining the Maoists had brought about unintended consequences, such as the reduction in its diplomatic dominance and expansion of the influence of its strategic rival China in the country.[24] In a report prepared for the Institute for Defence Studies and Analyses (IDSA), a joint secretary of the Indian defence ministry, Arvind Gupta, had noted, in July 2010, that the Indian policy of sidelining Maoists was damaging its image in Nepal. 'It appears that it would be difficult to prevent the Maoists from coming to power by forging opportunistic alliances against them,' Gupta's report stated. 'The

Maoists will need to be engaged and locked into agreements and arrangements common in democratic set-ups. They will be exposed if they do not play by the rules of democracy. There is no realistic way of keeping them away from power given their obvious strengths.'[25]

Writers who regularly wrote about Nepal affairs in the Indian media, such as Siddhartha Varadarajan, Prof. S.D. Muni and Prashant Jha, were constantly questioning India's intolerant policy towards the Maoists. Then the editor of *The Hindu* and a member of a high-level board formed to formulate foreign and strategic policy, Varadarajan even wrote, 'India is playing (in Nepal) a dangerous game that will eventually boomerang.'[26]

That was what ultimately happened, and India started changing its position. Incidentally, there had also been a big change in the Delhi bureaucracy by then. The hawkish NSA M.K. Narayanan had been appointed as governor of West Bengal, replaced, as mentioned earlier, by Shivshankar Menon, a former foreign secretary who had experience of overseeing the Nepal desk in the past. Sanjeev Tripathi had replaced K.C. Verma as the chief of RAW. Nirupama Rao was replaced by Ranjan Mathai as the foreign secretary. In Kathmandu, Jayanta Prasad had come in place of Ambassador Sood. The changes in this set-up helped in changing India's policy towards Nepal, particularly towards the Maoists.[27]

Indian External Affairs Minister S.M. Krishna came to Kathmandu for a visit from 19 to 22 April 2011. In his meeting with Prachanda, Krishna drew his attention towards the widening rift due to the Maoists' campaign against India. He also expressed concern about China's increasing strategic presence in Nepal.[28]

In order to address those concerns, India did not adopt an offensive policy against the Maoists like in the past. Rather, it weighed how it could play into the internal dynamics of the Maoist party. It found Baburam Bhattarai most useful, since Bhattarai was nursing discontent against his chairman, Prachanda, for picking

Khanal as prime minister over him, whom he considered the better choice. He had not concealed his disappointment. He clearly said, 'Elements within the party prevented me from becoming prime minister.'

Prachanda had reached a truce in his diatribe against Delhi, but there was a tempest brewing within his own party.

22

The Tempest Within

'India has done a wise thing to let Baburam sail through in the
PM election with the support of Madhes groups.'

—Professor S.D. Muni, reacting to
Bhattarai's election as prime minister[1]

Among the camps of the Young Communist League (YCL) in
Kathmandu, Khanna Garment in Balkumari was particularly
notorious. The garment factory had been abandoned after its
proprietor failed to pay bank loans. The Maoists held most of their
secret meetings and training sessions there. On 3 January 2010, a
training session had been scheduled there for the central office-
bearers of All Nepal People's Cultural Federation. It was there
that Prachanda made an explosive remark: India was pressing him
to make Baburam the prime minister.

This was before Jhalnath Khanal became prime minister.
'I was seriously taken aback when they directly and indirectly said
that they would help if we were to make Baburam Bhattarai the
prime minister,' Prachanda told his close confidantes. With Kiran
sitting at his side, Prachanda said, 'The Indian expansionism is

playing here. To say that they would immediately help make Baburam the prime minister, but not the chairman (himself).'

The training session at the Khanna garment factory was a secret one, but someone there recorded it. It was splashed across the front page of *Nagarik* the following day, along with the audiotape attached on its website.[2] This episode sent huge ripples through the Maoist party. Baburam was not present in that training programme. He had probably not been invited. After listening to the audiotape, Baburam fumed with anger. He shot back, 'This is disinformation. This is an attempt at character assassination. There should be debates and discussions if someone is not happy about something. To portray somebody as a foreign agent is not a good political culture.'[3]

The dispute between Prachanda and Baburam now resumed. At the crux of it was the clash of personalities, but the external factor of India added fuel to the fire. Prachanda believed that India was behind the situation that led to his exit as prime minister. He found it strange that the same India wanted to make his deputy the prime minister. Baburam, on the other hand, was unhappy that Prachanda kept on stopping him from becoming prime minister, even though he was acceptable to India. In order to give an ideological garb to their dispute, they advanced the traditional debate on what should come first: 'nationalism' or 'democracy'.

Baburam's logic was, 'Nationalism is important but for the time being, it would be more important to give priority to internal democracy in order to safeguard progress. Projecting external contradictions as the chief priority would weaken the nation and lead to regression.'[4]

Prachanda, on the other hand, believed that democracy and nationalism could not be separated. 'In the past, when internal contradictions were dominant, we used to engage in agitation by sometimes giving priority to nationalism and sometimes to democracy. But the situation has changed now,' he said, adding, 'In the past, the Narayanhity palace or the monarchy was the seat of all conspiracies and repression against revolutionary movements of Nepal. Now that seat has shifted to the Delhi Durbar. A situation has emerged where Delhi is decisive on who should lead the government here, who should be toppled, and who should command the Nepali Army.'[5]

Baburam was also not in favour of the party's policy of hitting out at India. He concluded that such a policy would end up being suicidal. As such, within the Maoist party equation, Prachanda and Kiran were on one side while Baburam was on the other. The subsequent central committee meeting decided to name Prachanda as the party's candidate for prime minister. This further enraged Baburam Bhattarai.

Before and after Palungtar

The Maoist party was witnessing differences over the party's future course. The differences were not limited to Prachanda and Baburam alone. Mohan Baidya 'Kiran' led a third faction in the party.

At the central committee and politburo meetings in July 2009, differences emerged between the Prachanda and Kiran factions as well. But when the meeting, after long deliberations, declared organizing a 'people's movement for civilian supremacy, national independence, peace and new Constitution and the formation of a national unity government' as the party's immediate policy, the Kiran faction calculated that their plan of revolt would be incorporated by the 'people's movement'.

The Kiran faction was also pleased by the decision to transform the organization of the party by creating a structure with multiple positions at key levels. In a party that had been single-handedly run by Chairman Prachanda, they were pleased to introduce the multi-position structure akin to 'bourgeois' parties. Subsequently, Kiran, Prakash and Baburam were made vice-chairmen while Ram Bahadur Thapa 'Badal' became general secretary and

C.P. Gajurel 'Gaurav' and Post Bahadur Bogati 'Diwakar' were made secretaries. The restructuring slightly weakened Prachanda, but he had no other way to deal with burgeoning conflicts.

Prachanda could breathe a little easier after he transformed the party's top structure and made Kiran the number two leader at the position of senior vice-chairman. Baburam was not pleased. This also triggered a new phase of proximity between Prachanda and Kiran. The central committee meeting of January 2010 decided to launch revolt. The disastrous indefinite strike of May 2010 was the result of the extremist decision of this meeting. The strike had neither the support of Baburam nor his expected participation. In the subsequent central committee meeting, held from 21 to 24 May, Prachanda appeared a bit confused. At the meeting, he presented a political paper full of ambiguities over the impending deadline of the Constituent Assembly's term, the policy of revolt and chief contradictions. The paper was slammed by both Baburam and Kiran.

Kiran was unhappy with the abandonment of the May agitation and the extension of the CA term. Baburam wanted to take advantage of Kiran's displeasure to become prime minister himself. That proximity further developed during the central committee meeting in July. Kiran and Baburam presented separate papers at the meeting, rejecting the one presented by Prachanda. The internal differences that had been festering for the past year could not be resolved by the central committee, compelling the chairman to call a plenum. The sixth plenum was organized at Palungtar, Gorkha, from 21 to 27 November 2010.

All three papers were presented at the Palungtar plenum, where around 5500 party cadres had gathered. Prachanda's paper talked about 'struggling for peace and Constitution' and 'creating a base for launching revolt by prioritizing the issue of national independence'. Baburam stated that the 'domestic reactionaries protected by Indian expansionism' should be treated as the principle enemy. Kiran advanced the policy of 'launching a revolt to establish a people's federal republic'.

With three papers by three leaders, the plenum could not pass a single paper. The plenum ended with a decision that the party's future course would be set by subsequent central committee meetings. Within the next three weeks, before the central committee meeting, Prachanda considerably strengthened his position. At the meeting, held on 17 December, Prachanda's paper was endorsed with the backing of Kiran. Around 113 members out of a total of 148 stood in favour of Prachanda–Kiran.

The document passed by the majority incorporated aspects such as the necessity and justification of revolt, along with a description of its preparation. As the party endorsed the line of 'people's revolt', Baburam was left with only eight CC members on his side, and they wrote a note of dissent.[6]

The subsequent central committee meeting, in January 2011, concluded that Baburam had breached party discipline. Baburam again refused, and wrote another note of dissent. The 'cold war' ended only after the party decided, through extensive deliberations, to dispatch both the party's decision (that he breached discipline) and his note of dissent for discussion by the cell committees at the local level of party organization.

The outward aspect of the dispute was ideological, but at its core the dispute was about competition for the position of prime minister. Soon after he got Kiran to endorse his document, which gave priority to the agenda of nationalism, Prachanda revealed that he was under pressure from the Indians to make Baburam the prime minister (this episode was mentioned earlier in this chapter).

Dhobighat alliance

From the very day of its formation, exercises were on to topple the government of Jhalnath Khanal and terminate the Maoist–UML alliance. The lobbying started in Delhi, making the case that the only way to replace Khanal was by electing Baburam as the next prime minister. Baburam was ready, but he disagreed with the plan of dislodging Prachanda from the party leadership, which, he thought, would mess up the agendas of peace and the Constitution. There was a need to corner Prachanda by weaning Kiran away from him and forcing him to withdraw support from the Khanal government. So a master plan was hatched to manufacture the appropriate context.

The Kiran faction was also frustrated by the constant switching of ideological positions by Prachanda and his ceaseless dominance over the party. They believed that siding with 'rightist' Baburam was a better and more durable option than backing 'untrustworthy' Prachanda.

Amid the growing dispute, the party called a central committee meeting from 24 June 2011. On the first day of the meeting, the Kiran–Baburam group presented the chairman with the signatures of 159 Maoist Constituent Assembly members, criticizing the lack of representation from the party in the Khanal cabinet. This meant 159 out of 237 CA members of the party had questioned the chairman's decision. Prachanda understood this as an attempt to displace him from the position of parliamentary party leader. About three ministers close to the Kiran faction refused to take the oath of office, raising the same demand. Actually, the issue of representation was merely a pretext; their main aim was to hit Prachanda.

As the differences could not be narrowed down, the central committee meeting was suspended. This, however, did not arrest the series of factional meetings that were taking place. The climax of these meetings was seen on 12 July 2011 in Dhobighat, Lalitpur. Even leaders considered close to Prachanda, such as Vice-Chairman Prakash and his followers, General Secretary Badal, Secretary Gaurav, and the coordinator of central advisory committee (and one of the founders of the party) Nara Bahadur Karmacharya, stood against him. The gathering amounted to a direct challenge to Prachanda's leadership.

Kiran and Baburam could never see eye to eye regarding the party's course, but their common opposition to the chairman made the impossible alliance possible. Seven top leaders present in Dhobighat (Kiran, Baburam, Prakash, Badal, Nara Bahadur Karmacharya and Sonam Saathi) signed a five-point commitment paper stating that Prachanda was the source of the 'anarchy' and 'factionalism' rife in the party and promising a 'joint initiative to transform the party towards a collective leadership system in practice'.

Their demand was that a single person (Prachanda) should not be chairman, parliamentary party leader and commander of the PLA, all in one. They wanted these positions to be divided. Since 1989, when he took over the reins of the party leadership, Prachanda had been in command without any interruption. And whoever had felt dissatisfaction against him at whatever point during that period had gathered in Dhobighat. They were all clamouring for justice. In the past, Prachanda had taken action against Badal on the charge of exhibiting a 'Lin Biao tendency', and against Baburam on the charge of being rightist. Kiran had been accused of dogmatism.

The unprecedented alliance of his comrades against him caused Prachanda serious tension. He decided to make Baburam, who had played a relatively 'balancing role' even when engaged in opposing him, the prime minister. There was no other option to break the Baburam–Kiran Dhobighat alliance.

Mission Malaysia

Prachanda suddenly left for Malaysia on 7 August, 2011 to meet the newly appointed RAW chief, Sanjeev Tripathi. RAW Special Secretary Alok Joshi, who looks after the south Asia desk, including Nepal, was also with Tripathi. Joshi was an old acquaintance of Prachanda. He was the RAW's station chief in Kathmandu till early 2010.

The Malaysia meeting was aimed mainly at improving relations between Delhi and the Maoists. In the course of his anti-India agitation, Prachanda had helped form the Khanal government and 'nationalist-leftist' alliance in order to 'teach India a lesson'. But when there was a real possibility of 'teaching him a lesson' instead, through the Dhobighat alliance, Prachanda relented. After two years of confrontation with Delhi, he was compelled to correct his course amid growing disputes within and outside his party. After the Malaysia talks, Prachanda agreed to topple Khanal's government.

Prime Minister Khanal, meanwhile, was unaware of what was cooking. When he received 'credible assurances' from the Maoists regarding the handover of their arms to the state, and the group classification of ex-combatants into those who opted for integration and those who opted for rehabilitation, Khanal announced he would step down if he could not take 'the peace process to its logical conclusion' by 13 August 2011. He was under tremendous pressure from his own party over his inability to complete the management of ex-combatants. But, despite the assurances, the Maoists did nothing. Consequently, he quietly resigned on 14 August. He had been caught in the Maoist ambush without knowing it.

The day after Khanal's resignation, RAW Special Secretary Alok Joshi came to Kathmandu and stayed in the Radisson Hotel in Lazimpat for three days. He held further talks with Prachanda, who had recently shifted to a new residence in Lazimpat, on making Baburam the prime minister. Then he convinced the Madhesi leaders. As a consequence, the Madhesi parties, who had refused to support Prachanda's bid for the premiership seven times, were now ready to support Baburam. On 28 August 2011, Baburam was elected by a simple majority.

The Madhesi front signed a four-point understanding to support Baburam Bhattarai. One of the points read, 'High priority will be accorded to the improvement of relations with both neighbours of Nepal. Taking into consideration the bilateral respect and interests of Nepal and relevant friendly countries, efforts will be made to reach understanding on matters that warrant understanding.' Of the two neighbours, Nepal did not have any serious differences with China. So the point clearly meant improving relations with India.

Some of the steps taken by Baburam, as a transitional prime minister, had far-reaching consequences. One was the issue of integration and rehabilitation of Maoist combatants. Second was the dissolution of the Constituent Assembly on his watch. The 'ultra-revolutionary' faction within the Maoists, led by Kiran, walked out and formed a separate party. The two-year-long 'cold war' with the Indian establishment ended, and his party transformed into a friendly force for India.

The end of the peace process

Tenth April 2012. All of a sudden, the national army was sent into all of the seven major cantonments of Maoist ex-combatants across the country. The government was led by the Maoist party, but it made an unusual decision of mobilizing the army to take the combatants and their weapons under control.

Amid rumours that the disgruntled Kiran faction was planning to seize weapons from the cantonments, military patrols were dispatched around midnight the day before. The same army teams entered the cantonments at 6.30 in the evening, and within one hour, took control of the Shaktikhor cantonment, known as the headquarters of the Maoist camps. The army reached the other six cantonments by 9.30 p.m., and the twenty-one satellite camps were brought under control by midnight. The operation was conducted under the command of Maj. Gen. Daman Bahadur Ghale, head of the Directorate of Military Operations of the Nepali Army. In the words of Maj. Gen. Ghale, 'Such a breakthrough in the peace process was achieved without firing a single bullet. The combatants and their weapons came under the control of the state.'[7]

The 'People's Liberation Army, Nepal', formed in August 2001, was dismantled when the Maoist government was in power. The combatants who had fought against the state army came under their chain of command. What happened on one day, 10 April, almost concluded the peace process, which had been dragged on for five years under various pretexts. The only thing remaining was the selection of combatants who wanted to join the army and their subsequent training. Earlier, within three days of his election as prime minister, Baburam Bhattarai had decided to hand over the keys of the containers that stored the weapons of combatants to the all-party Special Committee for Army Integration and Rehabilitation.

As distance grew between Baburam and Prachanda and the Kiran faction in the party, it was gradually reflected in the cantonments as well. Previously, there had been reports of camp commanders confiscating paycheques, or demanding certain portions of their amount, that were provided by the government to those who chose rehabilitation. In some instances, combatants were found to have rushed to the police for protection from their own commanders. Some were detained within the camps and many others fled.

When the Kiran faction tried to take advantage of the brewing discontent, there were instances of combatants turning against their commanders in some camps. At the fourth division camp in Nawalparasi, Division Commander Tej Bahadur Oli was attacked. There was a heated exchange of words, with some combatants accusing leaders of seizing their money. Company Assistant Commander 'Yuganta' had to open 'blank fire' to disperse the crowd. Oli, who was trying to flee the scene, was forced to step down from his jeep. The enraged combatants torched the vehicle. At the camp of the first division in Ilam, combatants raised regional slogans. Division Commander Yam Bahadur Adhikari

'Pratikshya' fled the camp at 3 a.m. when ex-combatants started seizing his weapon and shouting, 'This is Limbuwan. We don't want a commander from the west.'[8]

After this serious turn of events, Prachanda proposed handing over the command of the cantonments to the army. The Maoist–UML–NC parties gave their agreement, in principle, to his proposal. Soon after, Baburam passed the proposal through the cabinet, and the army started the operation in the evening.

According to top sources in the Maoists, they also handed over 1100 unregistered weapons to the army. In 2006, the Maoists had declared they had only 3428 weapons and handed over the list to the government. That was apparently not true. Five years later, the Maoists handed over the additional 1100 weapons. The leaders of other parties were informed, but it was not made public.

Meanwhile, the Kiran faction was able to lay its hands on around 200 modern weapons. According to a top Maoist leader, sixteen weapons were seized from the second division cantonment, forty-six from the fourth division, sixty-one from the sixth division, and twenty-six from the seventh division. The seized weapons included eight LMG (Light Machine Guns)—four each from the fourth and seventh divisions. They also had a few more weapons that had been given earlier for the security of leaders. No attempts were made to return or confiscate those weapons, which could be used in any future armed struggle, such as they had promised to launch.

The Kiran faction reacted strongly to the decision of its own party's government to hand over the cantonments to the army. Prachanda–Baburam responded by saying that they had handed over the camps 'not to the old royal army but the new republican army'. They said the move was necessary in order to complete the peace process.

Although the government and the Maoists had signed the Comprehensive Peace Agreement on 21 November 2006, and declared the cessation of armed insurgency, the disarmament issue in the peace process could not be resolved for a long time. Instead, the integration and rehabilitation of the ex-combatants triggered several disputes. Where to integrate the combatants? In the army, police or elsewhere? Should the integration be carried out on an individual basis or collectively? In what number? What amount of money should be given to those who chose rehabilitation? What positions should be offered to those integrated? Leaders skirted these questions for years. When the United Nations Mission to Nepal, after four years in the country, left the country in January 2011, the process of integration had not even begun.

When they failed to arrive at an understanding, despite several attempts, the political parties gave the responsibility of preparing a framework of integration to the Nepali Army. Army Chief Chhatraman Singh Gurung 'briefed' the government and the party leaders about the framework the army had prepared.[9] The army concluded that rather than integrating the ex-combatants into separate security agencies, it would be appropriate to bring them under one single agency, the army. He floated the idea of forming a separate 'National Security and Development Directorate' within the army for the purpose. On 1 November 2011, leaders of the Maoists, NC, UML and Madhesi Front signed a decisive agreement prepared on the basis of the army's proposal.

The seven-point agreement stated that there would be maximum 6500 troops in the proposed directorate: 65 per cent from security agencies (35 from army, 15 each from police and armed police) and 35 per cent Maoist ex-combatants. The directorate was given a mandate to carry out development works, forest security, industrial security and disaster management. Meanwhile, those combatants who opted for rehabilitation were to be given between NRs. 6 and 9 lakh based on the duration of their involvement. And those choosing voluntary retirement were offered a cash package of between NRs. 5 and 8 lakh.

The process of classification of ex-combatants was begun. Initially, 9705 out of 19,601 combatants wanted to be integrated into the Nepali Army. The number gradually reduced. In the end, only 1463 chose integration, while the rest went home accepting voluntary retirement. Around seventy-one ex-combatants began the army's officer training course in November 2012 at the Kharipati Army Academy. There was a political understanding to award the position of colonel to one ex-combatant, and lieutenant colonel to two. The rest were assimilated in positions between second lieutenant and major.

In the early phase, the Maoist leaders made ambitious statements, such as that they wanted to merge the Nepali Army and their PLA to form a new national army. It never happened. Of the 32,000 'combatants' they assembled, the United Nation Mission to Nepal (UNMIN) registered only 19,601. When the integration finally happened, there were only around 1400 combatants integrated. That number was further reduced in the course of training. This marked a victory for the strategy of integrating only a handful of combatants by prolonging the process, making them languish in the camps for a long period of time and frustrating them in the end. The trickiest part of the peace process, which could not be completed during the terms of Girija Prasad Koirala, Prachanda, Madhav Kumar Nepal and Jhalnath Khanal, was done on Baburam's watch.

Another major incident during Baburam's tenure was the dissolution of the Constituent Assembly (CA).

Death of a dream

Bugles and a Tiger, the memoir of his Second World War experiences by Lt Col. John Masters of the British Army, gives its name to a bar in Kathmandu's five-star Hotel Everest. Decorated in the style of an old-fashioned Gorkha officers' mess, the bar is a well-known watering hole for Kathmandu's elite and expatriates.

It was 13 May 2012, 5 p.m. As we came out of the lift on the seventh floor, there was an air of unusual security activity. The glass door of the bar was shut. Inside, we saw three to four people huddled in a corner. There was the leader of the CPN–UML, K.P. Oli. Our eyes met. As a courtesy, I approached him.

'Hello, Sudheerji. How are you?' Another man rose from the group with hands extended towards me. He was Peter J.P. Hanaman, Minister (Consular) at the Indian embassy in Kathmandu.

My companion was Vijay Kumar and Oli introduced us both to the unknown guest he was talking to. 'This is Vijay Kumar, a very famous television personality in Nepal. And this is Sudheer Sharma, Nepal's reputed journalist . . . editor of the *Kantipur* daily.'

Peter added, '*Kantipur* is Nepal's leading daily, sir!'

The 'sir' rose from the chair and shook our hands. He did not say a word, visibly uncomfortable at our sudden presence.

'And who is he?' Vijay Kumar asked Oli.

Oli replied, 'Friend from Delhi.'

The stranger was forced to introduce himself, 'I am Mr Sharma.'

Obviously a 'big shot' had flown in. We didn't want to disturb them and moved away but Peter followed.

The deadline for the CA to complete the Constitution was coming closer. Indian diplomats were openly active. They were in favour of the identity-based federalism pushed by the Maoist–Madhesi Morcha, and were exerting all-round pressure on leaders like Oli, who were against the idea.

Right then, the *Kathmandu Post*'s editor Akhilesh Upadhyay, the chairman of Kantipur Media Group Kailash Sirohiya, and the chairman of Image Television R.K. Manandhar arrived. Just as he sat down, Kailash asked the usual question, 'So, how is the country?'

Pointing at the number three man at the Indian embassy in Kathmandu, I replied, 'Why don't we ask him? He knows all things!'

Peter did not want to divulge much. But he indicated that the main political parties were making efforts and could strike a deal soon. 'The form of federalism and the number of states has been agreed. Their names have not been (decided),' he said.

In fact, as we well knew, Peter J.P. Hanaman was the Nepal station chief of RAW. He was from Meghalaya, went to school in Kurseong, West Bengal, which has a Nepali-speaking majority, and was married to a lady of Nepali origin; he was a fluent Nepali speaker. Just as we started our conversation, the team from the other table rose.

Peter also stood up and rushed to take the notepad and diary of the person who had introduced himself as 'Mr Sharma'. When an officer of the rank of joint secretary did that, one could fairly surmise that Mr Sharma, clad in trousers and a T-shirt, must be quite a senior officer.

Oli got up to leave, indicating the CA building through the window. The meeting of the leaders of the largest political parties—the Maoists, Nepali Congress, UML and Madhesi Morcha—had just begun at the nearby International Convention Centre, which housed the assembly. Oli rushed towards the assembly.

Just then, my cell phone rang. A ruling party leader wanted to hurriedly share some 'breaking news' with me. 'Do you know? A big shot has arrived from Delhi.'

'Who?'

'Chief of RAW!'

I understood then that the person who had introduced himself as 'Mr Sharma' to us just moments ago was none other than RAW Chief Sanjeev Tripathi.

Tripathy had met Maoist Chairman Pushpa Kamal Dahal 'Prachanda,' the then Prime Minister Baburam Bhattarai, Madhesi Morcha coordinator Bijaya Gachhadar, the chairman of the TMLP Mahantha Thakur, and several other top-ranking leaders. Those meetings were all secret. Oli chose to meet him at a public place and that's why we were able to see him.

As only days remained before the deadline of the CA expired (27 May 2012), RAW was aggressively active at the centre stage of Nepali politics. Tripathi had come to Kathmandu to drive the parties to an agreement, even as the parties remained bitterly divided, especially on the basis and number of federal states in the new Constitution. The Madhesis and the Maoists were in favour of single ethnic identity-based federalism. The Madhesi Morcha was adamant that there should be, at most, two provinces in the Tarai, the southern plains of Nepal bordering India. The Nepali Congress and CPN–UML, on the other hand, were in favour of multi-ethnicity-based federalism. They wanted more than two provinces in the Tarai, like in the hills.

Nepali leaders who had been bickering among themselves suddenly started talking about a deal following their meetings with Tripathi. On 15 May 2012, a decisive meeting was held at the prime minister's official residence in Baluwatar, Kathmandu. The meeting announced that the Maoists, Congress, UML and Madhesi Morcha had reached a deal, not only on the issue of federal restructuring but also other thorny issues such as the form of governance, judiciary, etc. It said there would be eleven provinces in Nepal, including five in the Tarai; and their demarcation and names would be recommended by a proposed Federal Commission. Based on its recommendation, the final decision would be ratified by Parliament.

On the very day when we had run into RAW Chief Tripathi at the bar, he had held a meeting with the Madhesi leaders Mahantha Thakur and Bijaya Gachhadar at the residence of the RAW Station Chief Peter J.P. Hanaman in Bishalnagar, Kathmandu. The leaders were pressed to sign a 'deal'.[10]

The deal triggered a fierce response among Madhesi intellectuals. The executive director of Nepal Madhes Foundation, Tula Narayan Shah, along with the lawyer Dipendra Jha and former Ambassador Vijay Kanta Karna, got together and decided they must do something. 'We felt that dividing the Tarai into five provinces without any basis was not appropriate. We wanted to give some reaction,' Shah remembers. 'We pressed the Madhesi leaders to reject the deal.'

At Shah's initiative, an interaction was called at Madhes Media House, located at Anamnagar in Kathmandu, on 17 May. For the first time, intellectuals, Constituent Assembly members belonging to the Madhesi and Adivasi-Janajati (indigenous nationalities) communities deplored the eleven-province deal in a single voice. Madhesi members were angry that the deal spoke of more than two provinces in the Tarai, while the Janajatis concluded that any deal that did not finalize the demarcation and nomenclature of federal provinces would never be implemented.

The Sadbhavana Party Chairman Rajendra Mahato threatened to walk out from the government unless the deal was corrected. Other Madhesi parties, led by Upendra Yadav and Sharat Singh Bhandari, who were outside the government, joined in the protests. They termed Gachhadar and Thakur 'traitors' and made efforts to woo the larger Madhesi public.

Finally, the Madhesi Morcha backed out from the deal, which was never to its liking in the first place. It made a new demand—that the federal restructuring be done on the basis of either the fourteen-province model passed by a majority of the CA's State Restructuring Committee, or the ten-province model proposed by the State Restructuring Commission. Both these proposals provided two provinces for the Tarai. The Morcha thought that if there were only two provinces in the Tarai, then they would be politically powerful, be able to control the crucial roads linking Kathmandu to the rest of the country and the outside world, enjoy high Madhesi representation in the central legislature and, consequently, greater access to central power.[11]

When it became clear that the deal had come undone, the Indian agencies looking after Nepali affairs changed gears overnight.[12] They backed the position of Madhesi leaders. As far as intelligence agencies are concerned, most of the time, it is difficult to divine which is their actual position and which is not.

With the Madhesis going back on the deal, the Maoists, too, started saying that they could not implement every aspect of the deal. They did not want to lose the support of their allies. After two of the four main forces withdrew, the deal, which had raised hopes that the Constitution would be promulgated within the 27 May deadline, suddenly unravelled.

On 24 May, the Supreme Court issued an interim order asking the government and the assembly chairman to refrain from extending the term of the CA. Chief Justice Khila Raj Regmi's single bench issued that order a day after a writ was filed against the government's proposal for a three-month term extension. Now it became clear—whether a Constitution was promulgated or not, the CA would be no more after 27 May.

So why did Chief Justice Regmi show such urgency to issue the interim order just three days before the expiry of the assembly? Although it was said that the order was only a reiteration of what the apex court had already stated in a previous order, many suspected a political motive behind it. After an interesting turn of events, and amid an extraordinary political situation, the following year, Regmi himself was invited to head the government.

On the last day of the CA, 27 May, a meeting of the top leaders of the major parties started early, at 9 a.m. But their discussions went nowhere. The Maoist–Madhesi combine were in no mood to compromise on their federalism model. The Congress–UML now wanted to promulgate a brief (incomplete) Constitution by passing the issues that had already been agreed upon and leaving the outstanding parts for the Parliament to decide. But the Maoist–Madhesis refused the proposal to promulgate a Constitution that did not address the thorniest issue of federal restructuring.

PM Bhattarai dissolved the assembly and announced fresh polls. Following the decision of the cabinet, he went to the president's office at close to midnight, accompanied by a team of his ministers to inform him about the decision. From there, he went straight to his Baluwatar residence and held a press meet at 11.50 p.m., at which he announced that he had dissolved the CA and called fresh elections 'in line with the decision of the Supreme Court'.

The Supreme Court, on 25 November 2011, had delivered a verdict ordering the assembly chairman and the government of Nepal, Office of the Prime Minister and Council of Ministers, to hold either a referendum or a new election of the assembly, or to arrange for 'any other appropriate constitutional alternative', in case the assembly was unable to promulgate the statute even within the latest extension of its term. However, the prime minister had not explored the option of seeking a solution from within the CA first, nor had he consulted with the CA chairman when he announced the new election.

The unnatural death of the CA was not directed by a single cause. It symbolized a collective failure of the major parties. A look at the immediate events would suggest federalism as the root cause of its demise. The Maoists not wanting to climb down from single-identity-based province model; the Madhesis remaining adamant about two provinces at most in the Tarai; and Congress–UML refusing to entertain it—were the primary reasons for the dissolution of the CA. Despite their different agendas, all of them thought that letting the CA dissolve would be a safer option for them. However, looking at it from a wider perspective would reveal many more causes for what happened.

The traditional thinking, that federalism would ultimately lead to the disintegration of the country, was strongly prevalent. Particularly, there were many within Congress and the UML who held that view. They wanted the CA to be dissolved, if only to stop federalism. The fundamental flaw of the major parties was to treat the CA more as a regular Parliament. They were engaged in the seating and unseating of governments, rather than focusing on Constitution-making.

Much-needed coordination among these parties was never explored. They never even tried to first write a common preamble to initiate Constitution-making in the right spirit. Neither did they try to forge a common understanding on fundamental issues. Instead of dealing with the most contentious issues, such as the form of governance and federalism, they postponed them to the very end. They also failed to document areas of agreement. And they never attempted to settle the dispute by putting contentious issues to a vote in the CA.

The blunder on the part of the top leaders was to ignore the CA as a forum where contentious issues could be discussed and settled. There were over two dozen parties represented at the assembly. It was impressively inclusive. All ideologies and classes, castes, regions, genders and different social segments were represented there. Unfortunately, the major parties did not permit the assembly to become decisive. In their bid to forge a political consensus, they instead opted for back-room dealings in a hush-hush manner.

The parties, who had limited the discussion of national importance to a narrow strait, were themselves a divided lot. And the nation lacked a leader of high stature who could provide much-needed guidance to Constitution-making. One of the signatories of the peace accord, the Congress President Girija Prasad Koirala, had already passed away, while Prachanda was fast losing the grip he seemed to have had on his party and others. Prime Minister Baburam Bhattarai had made his mind to hold fresh elections. So no one could play any role to save the Constituent Assembly at the eleventh hour.

Division of the party

The dissolution of the PLA and the CA triggered profound changes within the Maoist party—and precipitated a third important development. The Maoist party split. The Kiran faction was already unhappy over the abandonment of the line of 'people's war' by the party. After these two significant dissolutions, they broke up the party.

Kiran, who had been arrested in India during the insurgency, had been released only after the start of the peace process. He had been the party's general secretary till 1989. When he returned to Kathmandu, he found two things that greatly disturbed him. He was not pleased with the decision of the party to abandon the 'people's war' in favour of a Constituent Assembly. After the election of the assembly, the party nominated him under the proportional representation system. On the first day of the assembly, he sat towards the far end of the hall. Soon after, he resigned. He was opposed to the assembly forever after.

The second thing that disturbed him equally was the increasing interventionism of the Indians. Kiran was alarmed to see his comrades surrendering before Delhi's diktat. He considered Indian intervention to have peaked during the election of his comrade Baburam Bhattarai as prime minister. He demanded that Baburam be sacked from the government, accusing him of 'treason' and indulging in 'anti-people' behaviour.[13]

Prachanda shrugged off Kiran's accusations by saying that Kiran himself had forced his hand through the Dhobighat alliance with Baburam. Kiran did not have a satisfactory reply to that, but he never stopped demanding the removal of Baburam. The Kiran faction alleged that while Baburam had always belonged to the Indian camp, Chairman Prachanda, too, was going that way. When Prachanda started firmly backing the agenda of peace and Constitution as the party's future course, the Kiran faction was further agitated.

Prachanda was caught in the middle. He did try hard to prevent the split at the last moment. He even expressed his willingness to have formal correspondence and talks, and offered to step down from the chair. But he could not reignite the confrontation with India by forcing Baburam down from the government. Besides, he also had differences with Kiran on the basic party line. Prachanda was in favour of peace and a Constitution, whereas Kiran wanted to go for immediate revolt. In the end, the Kiran faction called a national gathering of around 2500 of its representatives. The gathering, held at the hall of Sherpa Sewa Samaj in Boudha from 16 to 18 June 2012, announced the formation of a new 'Communist Party of Nepal–Maoists'.

Prime Minister Bhattarai appeared totally unfazed by the division of his party. On 18 June, he left for Brazil, where he was scheduled to meet Indian PM Manmohan Singh. It seemed that he had known a long time ago that the division was inevitable.

23

Constitution on Fast Track

'Others are saying fast track. But I say mere fast track is not enough, let's go to double fast track (to write the Constitution).'

—Sushil Koirala, then prime minister of Nepal[1]

On 12 December 2012, RAW Chief Sanjeev Tripathi made a sudden dash to Kathmandu. He was accompanied by Shashi Bhushan Singh Tomar, who had recently been appointed special secretary (N) to handle the Nepal desk at the agency. That very day, they went to Baluwatar to meet Prime Minister Baburam Bhattarai. Although Baburam did not have a long acquaintance with Tripathi, he knew Tomar from the days of the twelve-point negotiations. The meeting that evening was not very cordial. The Tripathi–Tomar team told Baburam that he needed to go in order to form an elected government. They advised forming an 'Advisory Council' as an elected government, including retired bureaucrats, army and police officials.

Baburam became restless after getting this advice to step down.

PM-in-waiting

Not only opposition parties Nepali Congress and the CPN–UML, even his party Chairman Prachanda wanted to pull Baburam's government down. President Ram Baran Yadav had been nursing a 'deep resentment' against Baburam from the day of the dissolution of the Constituent Assembly. He had declared the Baburam government a 'caretaker'.

Baburam failed to hold an election on the day he had announced. Only he was not to blame. When opposition parties refused to accept his government leadership, the ruling alliance alone could not go ahead with the polls. Baburam went to his chairman, Prachanda, with a proposal to make the opposition NC's President Sushil Koirala the prime minister, instead of the 'advisory council' proposed by RAW. Prachanda was pleased with Baburam's proposal. Prachanda feared that Baburam would continue to grow his political power if allowed to continue in office.

Prachanda started deliberations with leaders of the NC–UML. The Congress made a formal decision to field its President Sushil Koirala as a candidate for prime minister. As a former NC general secretary, President Ram Baran Yadav also looked forward to seeing Koirala as the prime minister. The three parties drafted an understanding. It stated that the Baburam government would forward an Order to Remove Constitutional Obstacles (a presidential order was required in order to amend the Constitution to hold a second election of a Constituent Assembly at a time when there was no Parliament to do so), leading to the formation of a consensus government under Koirala.

The final decision had not yet been made. A new game was played then and there. The RAW's road map did not include the formation of a Koirala government to replace Baburam's. It wanted a non-political advisory council. The RAW started machinations to foil the three parties' plan. Koirala was still in India's bad books, following his strong reaction during the Mehta episode in May, and his subsequent outbursts at the Indian ambassador.

For these reasons, Koirala was 'unacceptable' as prime minister of Nepal. Baburam started singing a different tune within a couple of days. He sent a clear signal to Prachanda that he would not step down since he had the support of the army and India.[2] In public, he raised a precondition that the NC should first join his government before he stepped down.

It was at this point that initiatives were taken to form a non-political government under the leadership of chief justice of the supreme court, Khila Raj Regmi. It was a refinement of RAW's earlier proposal of forming an advisory council. On 13 March 2013, the four major political parties reached an eleven-point understanding to form an apolitical government. The 'interim election Council of Ministers', headed by Regmi, had ten former secretaries as ministers, who were chosen on the basis of division among the parties, the president, and Regmi himself.

Giving power to the chief justice became possible because the NC–UML were unwilling to go to election under the Baburam government, while the Maoists–Madhesi front was unwilling to accept Sushil Koirala as prime minister. It was a clear signal of the collective failure of the political parties. Ironically, the leaders were so engrossed in their self-serving power game that they could not prevent the transfer of executive power from their hands to a non-political leadership. And the force that compelled them to become silent witnesses was not even domestic. In the third week of January, the special secretary of RAW, Shashi Bhushan Singh Tomar, came to Kathmandu and met the president, the prime minister, Prachanda, and other leaders to discuss the framework of the non-political government.

Was it not possible to form an all-party government under Baburam's leadership, as the force that could install Regmi in Singha Durbar really wanted? Questions like these were left hanging in the air. Baburam, with his 'pro-India' image, was shown the exit and a non-political government was, forcefully, put in place. Retired bureaucrats found themselves in unanticipated roles, as they were dramatically named ministers overnight. Political parties stood witness. They even helped to amend the interim Constitution to remove constitutional obstacles to form such a government—in the hope of second Constituent Assembly election.

Ordinarily, it required a two-thirds majority of the Parliament to amend the Constitution. But when the plan for a non-political government was enforced, with the acquiescence of both external and internal forces, such an impossible matter was made possible in the name of the 'doctrine of necessity'. The president gave his endorsement to the deal. The Bar Association, intellectuals, smaller parties, and some leaders of major parties made some noises in protest, but in vain.

With the chief justice as the head of the government, the judiciary ended up as a tail of the executive. An order delivered by the supreme court asked Regmi not to describe himself as chief justice while he headed the executive. But since he did not resign as chief justice, the shadow of Singha Durbar continued to envelop the judiciary.

The move to form the Regmi government was a carefully calculated one. Previously, Regmi's order as chief justice had blocked the possibility of extending the Constituent Assembly beyond 27 May 2012. It had prompted its dissolution. The Maoist leaders tried to convince their cadres that making Regmi the government head would reduce the chances of such an intervention by the court in the future. But this was not the only reason.

The declared goal of the government, led by Chief Justice Khila Raj Regmi, was holding the second Constituent Assembly election. The election took place on 13 November 2013. The Regmi government was able to successfully carry out its primary duty, which would lay down Nepal's future constitutional-political road map.

Second Constituent Assembly

The second election of the Constituent Assembly altered the political power balance. The Nepali Congress (NC) became the largest party by winning 196 out of 601 seats. The Communist Party of Nepal–Unified Marxist Leninist (CPN–UML) bagged 175 seats to come out second. The Maoists, who were the largest party in the first CA, were a distant third with just eighty seats.[3]

The election results startled the Maoists. Their initial reaction was filled with aggression and immaturity. As reports of their poor performance started pouring in from constituency after constituency across the country, the Maoist leadership made a midnight announcement of withdrawal of their representatives from counting centres, claiming 'institutional and policy fraud'. Their claim of vote-rigging and irregularity in the transport of ballot boxes under the security of the army had no strong basis, but the possible complication of a major party—that, too, a part of the peace process—refusing to accept election results was huge. The Maoists also received support from some of the Madhesi parties in this matter. It led to continuation of political confusion for a couple of months. The process of the new Constituent Assembly could not proceed.

Once they cooled down and started reviewing their electoral defeat, the Maoist leaders gradually began to admit that the main cause was internal. The UCPN–Maoist party also found itself under huge domestic as well as international pressure to accept the results of the election. Neither was it in a position to just walk out of the Constituent Assembly and take up revolt. Consequently, on 24 December 2013, the parties forged a four-point agreement to bring on board the Maoists and the Madhesi parties. The agreement included conducting a parliamentary inquiry on possible vote-rigging, formation of a political committee, preparing the first draft of the Constitution in six months and full Constitution in a year.[4]

The Maoists then returned to the process of the Constituent Assembly. The first meeting of the second CA was held on 26 January 2014. It opened the door for handover of the reins of government back to political parties. In keeping with the changed power equation, an alliance between the NC–UML was struck. They signed a pact on 9 February 2014. It stated that the Constitution would be promulgated within a year; the second CA would take up the ownership of the achievements of the first one; the Parliament would endorse the incumbent president and vice-president; and the CPN–UML would support the NC president, Sushil Koirala, as prime minister. What was left unwritten in the pact but was presented as a 'gentleman's agreement' was that upon the promulgation of the Constitution in a year, Koirala would hand over the reins of prime ministership to UML Chairman K.P. Oli. Based on this new agreement, NC President Koirala became the thirty-seventh prime minister of Nepal on 11 February 2014.

The sixteen-point road map

In fact, the parties had tried hard to write the Constitution through consensus during the first CA as well. It was not possible at that point. But then the parties did not try to write the Constitution through majority, which ultimately led to the dissolution of the first CA. Possibly, having learnt their lessons from the first CA, the two largest parties, NC and CPN–UML, adopted a path of trying to converge, at least, their positions and on 7 November 2014, they made public their seven-point proposal. The aim of their joint proposal was to force the Maoists and the Madhesi parties to come on board, and if not, then complete the Constitution-writing by adopting the process of majority.

Between them, the NC and UML had 371 seats, which were only a few seats short of the two-third majority of 401 seats— necessary for passing the Constitution. The shortfall could be overcome by winning the support of smaller parties besides the Maoists.

The NC–UML joint proposal had common positions on contentious issues such as federalism, form of governance and judiciary. It included the seven-province model of federalism, parliamentary system of governance, House of Representatives with 165 members elected directly and a National Assembly with seventy-five members elected through a proportional representation system.

When the first and second largest parties of the assembly suddenly presented a joint front without so much as consulting with them, the Maoists and Madhesi Morcha were taken aback. This precipitated the formation of a thirty-party opposition alliance including the Maoists and Madhesi parties. The alliance launched agitations in the streets and also called bandhs and shutdowns. There were even clashes within the Constituent Assembly. As a culmination of these protests, a public rally was organized on 28 February 2015 in the Khula Manch of Kathmandu. But the rally did not attract a huge number of participants, nor could it lead to a decisive movement as had been promised by the opposition.

The Maoist leadership now started laying emphasis on dialogue with the NC–UML. Prachanda–Baburam in particular were beginning to return to the fold of the Constituent Assembly from the streets with the intention of completing the Constitution-writing. And then a devastating earthquake struck on 25 April 2015. According to government figures, at least 8700 died and over 22,000 were injured in that earthquake, which destroyed over 6,00,000 houses. The incident triggered a national calamity. It shook the general psyche of all Nepalis. Like the general public, the political leaders also spoke about their feelings—the impermanence of life. This 'ultimate truth' also affected national politics.

The political parties had committed to writing the new Constitution through the second CA within two years. But the progress had not been encouraging. The sudden earthquake shook the political parties enough to encourage them to conclude their national duty. The sixteen-point agreement was the result of this circumstance, which proved to be the entry-point for the Constitution-writing as well as the hill–Madhes divide.

The sixteen-point pact, in fact, was a refinement of a renewed partnership between the two largest communist parties. It would not have been possible had UML Chairman Oli and Maoist Chairman Prachanda—hitherto leaders of two opposing communist camps—not reached an understanding.

The period had also marked the failure of one of the major points of the previous NC–UML pact, which was to complete Constitution-writing by February 2015. For this very reason, PM Koirala continued to remain in office, to Oli's dismay. One of the main reasons for the failure in Constitution-writing was the opposition and obstruction by the Maoists. Oli saw that keeping the Maoists in good humour could not only lead to early writing of the Constitution but also accelerate his journey to power.

Prachanda had his own compulsions. Having abandoned the agitation, he had to join hands with one of the two large ruling parties. He found the UML more suitable than the NC. Besides, the agendas of the two communist parties were closer in some of the fundamental constitutional issues. Maoist leader Baburam Bhattarai and UML leader Bishnu Poudel started informal negotiations in this regard. Once these talks matured, Oli and Prachanda came to the scene.

Having built an environment of trust between them, they then took forward the discussions by involving the NC as well as Madhesi parties. PM Koirala was happy that an agitating party was returning to the path of Constitution-making. Following several rounds of negotiations, the NC, CPN–UML, UCPN–Maoists and Madhesi Janadhikar Forum (Loktantrik) signed an agreement. The agreement signed on 8 June 2015 had sixteen points, settling contentious issues in the Constitution.

The agreement stated that there would be eight provinces formed on the five bases of identity and four bases of capacity (these bases had been identified by the first Constituent Assembly). It was also stated that the government should form a federal commission to settle their demarcations whereas their names would be decided by the respective provincial assemblies in the future. This was interpreted by some as an attempt to dilute federalism by putting off demarcation and naming of provinces. It became highly controversial. Madhesi parties were the most vocal against it. Apart from the Bijaya Kumar Gachhadar-led Madhesi Janadhikar Forum (Loktantrik), none of the other Madhes-centred parties stood in its favour.

The agreement also stated that there would be 165 parliamentary constituencies based on geography and population. A total of 165 members would be elected directly from the constituencies, apart from 110 who would be elected through the proportional representation election system—275 members altogether. The National Assembly was to have a total of forty-five members, including forty elected by provinces and five nominated by the cabinet. In the first CA election, the proportion was 60–40 between members elected through proportional representation (PR) and first-past-the-post (FPTP) systems. The sixteen-point pact, on the other hand, proposed to alter this proportion to 40–60. Madhesi parties claimed that it would lead to a reduction in the representation of smaller parties and would deal a setback to the principle of inclusion.

The agreement also stated that there would be a 'multiparty competitive federal democratic republican parliamentary system of governance'. Since the UML abandoned its earlier position of directly elected prime ministerial system and since the Maoists, too, did not pursue their position of directly elected presidential system, the NC could take solace in the symbolic victory of its principle of parliamentary system of governance. The new Constitution was to have a similar system of governance, with few refinements, that the country had practised since the political change of 1990.

The agreement expressed a commitment to elect president, vice president, prime minister, speaker and deputy speaker through the transformed legislative-Parliament following the promulgation of the new Constitution. The idea was that once the Constituent Assembly promulgated the new Constitution, it would automatically dissolve, but would be active in its second avatar as a transformed Parliament. The parties also agreed to form a separate constitutional court to look into issues related to constitutional conflict.

Out of these various points, the most contentious was the one related to what was portrayed as incomplete federalism. It was criticized by a large section of intellectuals as well as the Madhesi parties. President Ram Baran Yadav urged parties not to promulgate the Constitution without clear demarcation of provinces. In the meantime, a petition was filed in the Supreme Court on 19 June 2015. In response to the petition, the Supreme Court reminded the Constituent Assembly of its obligation as per the interim Constitution to promulgate the Constitution only by completing the demarcation of provinces. This verdict made it mandatory for the parties to do so.

On 7 July, the Constituent Assembly passed a preliminary draft of the Constitution based on the sixteen-point pact. The members were then dispatched to the districts to get public feedback on the draft. They came back largely with suggestions that the Constitution should not be promulgated without the demarcation of provinces. In fact, the Madhesi parties obstructed the process of public opinion collection in the Tarai. They used this opportunity to vent their discontent over the draft.

It was around this time that Maoist Chairman Prachanda and leader of the NC, Sher Bahadur Deuba, dashed to Delhi, separately, at the invitation of the Indian government. During their discussions with the Indian political leadership, including

PM Narendra Modi, they were advised to promulgate the Constitution only after resolving the issue of demarcation of provinces. In an interview with this author, Prachanda said, 'I had always thought that the issue of demarcation would be used as a weapon to stop Constitution-writing. That was what happened in Delhi. I came back after telling the Indians that demarcation would be carried out. Subsequently, we came up with a framework of six provinces along with their demarcations. But then other issues were raised.'

The parties found themselves being cornered—in the face of public opinion, court verdict, president's appeal, opposition by Madhesi parties and Indian pressure—and could see no alternative to demarcating the provinces. On 8 August, a framework of six provinces was made public. The names of the provinces were not given but their borders were determined. The framework included a fully Tarai-centric province number 2, from Saptari in the east to Parsa in the west. It seemed like an attempt to address the demands of the Madhesi community. Other provinces were either a mixture of hill–Tarai or covered only hilly regions. In the case of three districts of the east (Jhapa, Morang and Sunsari) and two of the west (Kailali and Kanchanpur), which had been contentious since the first Constituent Assembly, the new framework suggested that the position of NC–UML had prevailed.

The most impractical one was province number 6, which appeared too large and included regions from the current midwestern and far western districts. The hilly residents of Seti and Mahakali zones of the region had been vocal about their demand for 'undivided far west'. The residents of Surkhet and Karnali hills of the midwestern region, too, did not want to be joined to the far west. As such, protests started in Surkhet, Jumla, Mugu, Humla, Dolpa and Kalikot. The Tharu community of the western plain region also launched their agitation, demanding a separate province for themselves. Faced with rising dissent, the senior leaders of the parties promised to amend the demarcation of provinces. Everyone thought that their demand would be addressed. The Tharu community was looking forward to the fulfilment of their demand. But Kathmandu was seen to give importance only to the demand of the hilly residents calling for an 'undivided region'.

The interests of many influential leaders with access to Kathmandu's political power are attached to the mid and far western hills. Therefore, it might be that Kathmandu's leadership only heard them. A new decision was suddenly made public on 21 August. It lumped together all districts of Seti and Mahakali zones of the far west, forming the seventh province.

Why did the sixteen-point pact propose to form eight provinces? Why was it then changed to a six-province model? And what prompted the final adoption of seven provinces? There was no clear logic in all this gerrymandering of provincial demarcations. It kept fuelling dissent for a long time to come.

The formation of province number 7 did address the demands of those calling for an 'undivided far west', but the indigenous Tharu communities felt betrayed. They exploded with anger against the 'division of their identities' across provinces number 5, 6 and 7.

Tharu rage

The stories of injustice and discrimination faced by the Tharu community abound in the history of this country. The community, which had been the country's shield in the western Tarai, makes up 7 per cent of the total population. So when the country decided to go for a total restructuring of the state and adopt federalism, the Tharus harboured the fair expectation of getting a province reflecting their political inclusion and representation. The community had freed itself from the shackles of serfdom that it had been subjected to in the past in the name of *kamaiya* (bonded labourers). They now understood their rights. But the community was pained to see that Kathmandu was still indifferent to their concerns.

When the Tharus were overlooked during the seven-province model, the Bijaya Kumar Gachhadar-led Madhesi Janadhikar Forum (Loktantrik) walked out of the four-party alliance. The party had a large Tharu constituency and had even swallowed a bitter pill in the past to accept the sixteen-point pact with the three parties (NC, UML and Maoists). But when they saw that the latest decision to form the seventh province totally disregarded Tharu demands, they did not want to further antagonize the community and announced a departure from the Constitution-writing process.

Credit must go to the Maoists for politically empowering Tharus in the recent years. Youths from the Tharu community were second only to Magars in terms of strength within the combat structure of the Maoists during their insurgency years. But the community found itself 'betrayed' by the same party that was now 'kowtowing' to the NC and the UML in denying them their demands. It naturally led them to feel enraged. On the top of that, several interest groups were active in fuelling the fire. The result of this deadly mixture was seen in the form of a violent incident in Tikapur of Kailali district, 16 km to the south of Lamki on the east–west highway.

King Mahendra had set up the settlement of Tikapur along the bank of Karnali river and near the border with India. It has a mixture of the hill and Tharu communities. The hill residents of Tikapur were in favour of the recently announced seventh province of the undivided far west, whereas the Tharu community wanted their own separate province. The situation was building up to a clash of the communities.

The Tharus began to lose their trust in major parties such as the NC, UML and the Maoists. Instead, the Madhesi parties, hitherto active in central and eastern Tarai only, were now keenly courting the community. These Madhesi parties kept themselves outside the process of Constitution-writing and looked for opportunities to increase their strength. Thus, they concluded that they could not only make inroads into the western Tarai by riding on Tharu distrust, but could actually intensify the agitation with immediate effect.

It was probably with these objectives in mind that president of the Madhesi Forum, Upendra Yadav, Sadbhavana Party President Rajendra Mahato and NC lawmaker Amaresh Kumar Singh descended on Tikapur on 13 August to address a public rally. Yadav made a political remark in the rally, but Mahato and Singh gave highly provocative speeches, which further enraged the already angry community. When the Madhesis had raised the demand for 'one Madhes, one province' a decade ago, the Tharus were the most vocal against it, presenting themselves as a separate community from the Madhesis. However, the latest incidents showed that the Tharus were being pushed towards the Madhesi umbrella.

The Tharu agitation was led by Tharu Kalyankarini Sabha, which itself is not a political organization but had Tharu workers belonging to all political parties. They planned to hold a decisive agitation in Tikapur. Defying the prohibitory orders clamped by the local administration, they planned to replace signboards of government offices with ones stating 'Tharuhat autonomous province'. In fact, they had already been doing so in rural regions.

There is a traditional practice of *badghar* in the Tharu community—a sort of local leaders who are selected during the festival of Maghi every year. These local leaders can issue orders to the community. At the heat of the agitation, the badghars ordered all members of the community to participate in the public rally. Any household found absent would be charged a fine of one thousand rupees. On 24 August, a huge rally was held in which thousands participated, including elders and women.

When the huge crowd tried to cross the line set by the police, tension erupted in several places. All of a sudden, a section of rioters started attacking police with domestic weapons. In the subsequent clashes, eight policemen, including Senior Superintendent of Police Laxman Neupane, were killed. An eighteen-month-old infant was also killed in the ensuing clashes.

It is not clear whether the incident was the result of a calculated plot. But its consequence was terrible for ordinary Tharus. Dozens of incidents of beating, setting fire to houses and shops, and assault were reported. In the immediate aftermath of that incident, some of us journalists reached the curfew-clamped Tikapur. We found it enveloped in a deathly silence. We confronted deep distrust replacing the age-old harmony between Tharus and Pahadis. The police was enraged following the killing of their comrades. Their fury could be seen in the subsequent Madhes agitation, where they used excessive force. The Tikapur incident, which occurred before the Constitution promulgation, was a forewarning that the government failed to read correctly.

In order to bring the situation under control, the government deployed the Nepali Army in the Tikapur area. For almost a week, the region was under dawn-to-dusk curfew. The Tharu community found itself on the defensive following the incident. Their agitation lost its intensity. In fact, the agitation itself shifted to central and eastern Tarai after that incident—in the form of the Madhes movement.

Climax of Constitution

One major message of the sixteen-point pact was that the unity among the three main parties (NC, UML, and Maoists) could not only ensure the requisite two-third majority to pass the Constitution but also thwart any untoward foreign pressure. But their inability to bring the Madhesi parties on board and their decision to push the Constitution through proved to be myopic.

It seemed the three parties wanted to rush through the Constitution-making process and take the fast-track route. They even shortened the process of the Constituent Assembly for this purpose.

On 28 June 2015, the first draft of the Bill of Constitution was presented at the assembly. Subsequently, the Civic Relations and Constitution Suggestion Committee started the process of gathering public opinion from the districts by mobilizing the members of the assembly. However, the process was limited mostly to a formality and in many places, the Madhesi parties obstructed it. The draft along with the report on public opinion was then submitted to the Baburam Bhattarai-led dialogue committee. With some changes, it was forwarded to the drafting committee led by Krishna Prasad Sitaula. The drafting committee presented the revised draft of the Constitution Bill to the assembly on 23 August. Madhesi parties boycotted the meeting of the assembly in protest.

On 11 September, Indian Ambassador Ranjit Rae was visibly active. He met with top leaders and urged them to suspend the process for a few days and initiate dialogue with Madhesi parties. There also was huge domestic pressure on the parties to talk to agitating Madhesis and promulgate the Constitution only after accommodating all. From media to civil society, everyone called for a brief halt to the process. In the end, the parties suspended the process of the Constituent Assembly for two days. But no decisive meeting could take place in that period with the Madhesi parties.

Prime Minister Koirala wanted to suspend the process for few more days. He even called an all-party meeting to discuss this idea on the morning of 13 September. However, his major allies, including Oli and Prachanda, did not even turn up at the meeting called at his official residence in Baluwatar.

That day, the meeting of the Constituent Assembly started a bit late, at around 1 p.m., only because the PM arrived late after the failed Baluwatar meeting. The assembly was addressed by top leaders of the NC, UML, the Maoists and RPP. Sitaula then presented a proposal requesting article-wise voting on the

Constitution bills. Although fifty-four amendments had been filed, most were withdrawn. It set off the process of passing the articles of the Constitution by a two-thirds majority.

In accordance with the pre-scheduled timeline, the Constituent Assembly endorsed the new Constitution on 16 September. There was a presence of 532 out of 598 assembly members. Of them, 507, or 89 per cent, members voted in favour of the Constitution bill whereas twenty-five members, belonging to the monarchist party RPP–Nepal, voted against it. Sixty-two members belonging to Madhesi parties were absent from the assembly. The nation had received a Constitution, finally, after a protracted political flux. It was indeed a historic achievement. The pleasure of having finally been able to deliver a Constitution—in the background of the dissolution of the first CA and continued complexities in the second one—was clearly visible on the faces of the members, whose delight knew no bounds. The members were seen busy taking selfies and sharing compliments.

Moreover, the top leaders must have felt as if they had conquered a mighty mountain. They spent the few days that remained before the formal promulgation of the Constitution in trying to hold dialogue with the Madhesi parties. At the very least, they wanted to bring back on board the signatory of the sixteen-point pact, the Bijaya Kumar Gachhadar-led Madhesi Janadhikar Forum (Loktantrik). They held talks till late at night on 19 September at the prime minister's residence in Baluwatar; they even drafted a three-point agreement, but they could not sign it. Gachhadar wanted the draft to include a phrase that the issue of federalism would be settled by federal commission and the problems of Tarai–Madhes would be resolved through a constitutional amendment. But the rest of the three parties did not want to insert the word Tarai–Madhes in the phrase. The talks broke down. Gachhadar and some leaders from his party actually wept when talks failed. Unwillingly, they were compelled to remain outside the process of Constitution-making.

The D-day finally arrived. The very last meeting of the Constituent Assembly began at 5.30 p.m. on 20 September 2015. Leaders were still unsure whether the chief guest, President Ram Baran Yadav, would arrive at the ceremony. Yadav was not only dissatisfied over the way the ceremony was being held, he was equally apprehensive about promulgating the Constitution without accommodating the Madhesis—a fact he had publicly stated. But he eventually joined the ceremony. And the chairman of the assembly, Nembang, requested the president to sign the five copies of the Constitution. After signing the five copies, written on traditional Nepali *lokta* paper, President Yadav made a significant gesture by repeatedly picking up the copies to touch them with his forehead: the customary sign of paying respect. His body language indicated that although he might have had some dissatisfaction over the process, he did not want to shirk his constitutional duty. Perhaps, the sense of duty overrode his personal preference.

Following the promulgation of the Constitution, Deepawali was organized at several places in the capital at the initiative of major political parties. But darkness descended in the Tarai. The promulgation had further deepened the cloud of frustration and despondency in the Tarai—which was a lull before the storm.

Third Madhes movement

Was it not possible to promulgate Constitution by accommodating the Madhesi parties? This question still echoes in the public sphere. In informal talks, top leaders of major parties reveal that they would never have been able to promulgate the Constitution had they not done it this time and in this manner. When asked to clarify who would have made it impossible, their fingers pointed towards India. They also claimed that Indian interests were intertwined in the demands and agitation of the Madhesi parties. They had deep suspicions that India would either allow a Constitution of its liking or not allow it at all. They recalled their belief that the Indian role was decisive even in the dissolution of the first Constituent Assembly. Such 'fear' of India was evident not only among known India-sceptics, but also among those thought to be close to Delhi in the past. That single fear was enough to bring together leaders such as Sushil Koirala, K.P. Oli, Prachanda, Sher Bahadur Deuba, Madhav Nepal and Ram Chandra Poudel to a common point on the Constitution despite so many other differences and the suspicions they harboured against each other.

They were also scared about former King Gyanendra's intention. There were unconfirmed reports swirling around in Kathmandu that Gyanendra had gone to Bangkok–Singapore for an unknown reason and had then travelled directly to Delhi to meet the Indian leadership, possibly to plot the restoration of a Hindu state and the monarchy in some form. Against this backdrop, the leaders were united that there should be no more delay.[5]

Besides, they themselves were not confident that their unity could endure for a longer period. So they wanted to get it done and over with before the unity collapsed in the face of domestic–foreign pressure.

The resolute focus of the leaders to deliver the Constitution was a correct one. But their strategy to overlook the agitating parties that were launching a major movement in one part of the country triggered political, social and regional division in Nepali society. Although the Tharu agitation in western Tarai cooled down in the wake of the Tikapur incident, Madhesi parties continued their protests in central and eastern Tarai. The four Madhesi parties—Sanghiya Samajbadi Forum, Tarai Madhes Loktrantik Party, Sadbhavana Party and Tarai Madhes Sadbhavana Party—reactivated the Samyukta Loktantrik Madhesi Morcha. The Morcha spearheaded the agitation. Besides, a Sanghiya Samabeshi Morcha that had eleven smaller parties and Tharuhat–Tharuwan parties was also part of the agitation. Pressing for provincial demarcation, proportional inclusion, population-based electoral constituencies and a change in citizenship-related matters, they declared a general shutdown in the Tarai from 17 July 2015.

Before the promulgation of the Constitution, and in the course of the two-month-long movement in Tarai–Madhes, forty-nine Nepali nationals lost their lives. Out of those, thirty-two were killed at the hands of security personnel and nine at the hands of agitators. Three were killed in accidents that occurred during the agitation. The deaths of the other five seemed to have occurred at the hands of agitators, even though the latter denied any responsibility. The death toll increased once the promulgation of the Constitution further provoked the agitation.

The report of the National Human Rights Commission states that the police used excessive force in the name of riot control.[6] It said that most agitators died of bullet wounds to their chest, head and upper body parts. It even seemed that the police were avenging the deaths of their eight colleagues, including an SSP, who were killed by agitators in Tikapur. As the Nepal Police and Armed Police Force could not bring the situation under control, the government deployed the Nepali Army as per the local administration act, 2028 BS, in some districts.

In fact, the government had wanted to fully mobilize the army when the Madhes agitation intensified. But the Army Secretariat issued a statement on 15 September 2015 that said, 'The Army urges all concerned to understand that the Nepali Army has been deployed to carry out its duty as per the Aid to Civil Authority and not as military mobilization.' The army also expressed its commitment to return to the barracks soon after completing its duty, and in a few weeks, it did.

The level of atrocities declined with the presence of the army on the streets, but it created an environment of fear. On their part, the agitators also exhibited violent behaviour by using domestic weapons during demonstrations, killing police officials in Kailali and pulling an injured policeman out of an ambulance and killing him. Incidents of hurling petrol bombs at security personnel became commonplace.

As the date of the promulgation of the Constitution approached, the government and the parties found themselves under intense pressure to initiate dialogue with the Madhesi Morcha. Prime Minister Koirala wrote letters twice, calling the Morcha for dialogue. A three-member talks team was formed, headed by his trusted aide, Forest Minister Mahesh Acharya. A resolution was also filed in the Parliament to amend the Constitution once it was promulgated to ensure that election constituencies were based on population. However, the agitating parties did not accept the government's invitation, claiming the lack of a proper environment. Furthermore, the big parties also failed to take any institutional initiative to bring them to talks.

In fact, Kathmandu believed that it had addressed the Madhesi demands to a large extent by forming province number 2, including the Tarai region from Saptari to Parsa districts. One major demand of the agitators was to add the eastern Tarai districts of Jhapa, Morang and Sunsari to province number 2. Interestingly, there was no significant agitation in these three districts, neither did the major parties want to put these districts, where they enjoyed dominance, inside the Madhes province. Similarly, the agitations in province number 5 to remove few hilly districts from it had also not been strong. The eye of the storm was in the border town of Birgunj, which itself, more interestingly, had no specific demarcation demand. The demand for allowing naturalized citizens to hold important state positions was taken up by a few Madhesi leaders and intellectuals, but it was never a demand of the mainstream indigenous Madhesis.

Certainly, the Constitution had some weaknesses, but it still had a lot of progressive provisions. But the top leaders failed to explain them, nor could they justify their several decisions. They did not travel outside the valley of Kathmandu to explain the Constitution—instead, they seemed content at taking part in a series of meaningless meetings in Singha Durbar. It did not help the cause of building ownership of the Constitution. Since the Madhesi parties were outside the process of Constitution-writing, they could not be expected to take up ownership of the document before extracting some political gains. In such a situation, it was not unnatural for the general Madhesi population and intellectuals to feel snubbed by Kathmandu, once again. It was one of the chief reasons the Madhesi movement went on for so long and which resulted, ultimately, in a situation of blockade and obstruction of Indo-Nepal supply lines.

It was at this point that Indian interests made a blatant entry and, on the back of the Madhesi movement, India imposed a lengthy blockade against Nepal for the third time in history.

24

The Blockade

'. . . The foreign secretary was sent to convey a hard message to the Nepali government only a couple or so days before that. I think this is not a very good way of tackling a very difficult problem.'

—Manmohan Singh, former Indian prime minister[1]

The Constituent Assembly had already formally adopted the new Constitution. It was to be officially proclaimed on 20 September 2015 in a special ceremony. Just two days before the ceremony, Indian Foreign Secretary S. Jaishankar rushed to Kathmandu as a special envoy of Prime Minister Narendra Modi. In all the subsequent meetings he had with top Nepali leaders, the foreign secretary was unrestrained in pressing the leaders to stop the process of Constitution promulgation.

Jaishankar was accompanied by Ambassador Ranjit Rae and the MEA's northern division chief, Abhay Thakur, in these meetings. The most notable meetings occurred in Lazimpat, at the residence of Maoist Chairman Prachanda. In his ground floor living room, Prachanda was waiting for Jaishankar along with his two senior leaders, Baburam Bhattarai and Narayan Kaji Shrestha. Soon after they sat down, Jaishankar minced no words in asking them to stop the Constitution promulgation for a few days.

When Prachanda drew his attention towards the 'wrong timing' of his visit and replied that the promulgation ceremony could not be stopped when the Constitution had already been adopted by the assembly, Jaishankar was visibly upset. According to Prachanda, in an apparent reference to the Maoists using India as a hideout during their insurgency days, Jaishankar said, 'Had we not supported you, had we not given shelter, you would still be in the jungles. The king's regime would have continued. Now you are doing this?'[2]

He also asked the leaders how they could issue the Constitution in the midst of a curfew when people were agitating everywhere. He warned them that India would not support the new Constitution and added that support from the rest of the world would have no meaning.[3]

Following the bitter exchange with Prachanda, Jaishankar left for the Budhanilkantha residence of senior Congress leader Sher Bahadur Deuba. There, too, he repeated the concerns of his political leadership and asked for suspension of Constitution promulgation for at least fifteen days. Once again, Deuba replied that the timing of his visit was wrong and he could do nothing to stop the process at this point. The reply he got from CPN–UML President K.P. Oli was also similar. Prime Minister Sushil Koirala didn't even want to meet with the Indian foreign secretary, who had landed in Kathmandu without an invitation. However, since a refusal to meet the envoy of neighbouring country's prime minister would have sent the wrong diplomatic message, he called the Indian team to Baluwatar. But that meeting, too, was futile.

In fact, the suddenly scheduled two-day visit of Jaishankar ended in total failure.

He had delivered a 'blunt message' to Nepali leaders: 'India is unhappy about the manner in which they have gone about adopting the country's new Constitution.'[4] Possibly, Delhi thought that the direct message from the prime minister's envoy would convince Nepali leaders to suspend the Constitution promulgation process. But the leaders were helpless even if they wanted to suspend the process, since the assembly had already adopted the Constitution.

The tension of a failed mission was apparent on Jaishankar's face when he spoke to reporters at Tribhuwan International Airport on his way back. 'India has been strongly supportive of Constitution-making in Nepal. We would like its completion to be an occasion for joy and satisfaction, not agitation and violence.' The Indian foreign secretary also issued a veiled warning: 'We hope that Nepal's political leaders will display the necessary flexibility and maturity at this crucial time to ensure a durable and resilient Constitution that has broad-based acceptance.'[5]

The son of a well-known strategic affairs analyst, K. Subrahmanyam, Jaishankar was a close confidante of Prime Minister Modi. Just over eight months ago, Modi had called Jaishankar, then Indian ambassador to the US, to take up the reins at the MEA, replacing Sujatha Singh. Known as an expert on nuclear diplomacy and US affairs, Jaishankar, however, had had no experience in Nepal affairs ever since he had joined the foreign service in 1977. After the 2019 general election, Prime Minister Modi appointed him as the new minister of external affairs.

A day after Jaishankar returned from Kathmandu, on 20 September, President Ram Baran Yadav officially proclaimed the Constitution adopted by the assembly. The northern neighbour China had given its best wishes to Prime Minister Sushil Koirala through its Ambassador Wu Chuntai on the same day the assembly adopted the Constitution, 17 September. 'As a friendly neighbour, the Chinese side notes with pleasure the Nepal Constitution Assembly endorsed the new Constitution. China hopes that Nepal will have a new path of political stability and economic development.'

Unlike China, the Americans pointed at some of the weaknesses of the Constitution but nonetheless termed it a milestone in Nepal's democratic journey.[6] However, India's reaction was uncharacteristically cold. On the evening of 20 September, it issued a terse statement on Nepal's Constitution. 'We note the promulgation in Nepal today of a Constitution.' Other lines of the statement had further ominous tones. 'We are concerned that the situation in several parts of the country bordering India continues to be violent.' India also asserted that the Constitution lacked broad-based ownership and acceptance.[7]

In my opinion, India had already committed two mistakes. First, by sending a special envoy to stop Constitution proclamation at the eleventh hour and, second, by simply 'noting' the promulgation of Nepal's new Constitution, without welcoming it. This was now prompting India to commit the third historic blunder—a blockade against Nepal. But before delving into this episode, it would be appropriate to return to events in the wake of Modi's rise in India and his attempts to improve relations with Nepal at the political level—and their ultimate failure.

Modi's first visit

The most unequal aspect of present day Nepal–India relations is the lack of equal relations at the political level. The passing of the first-generation leaders of both countries who knew each other well since the 1950s has resulted in a vacuum. Consequently, the access of the latter generation leaders of Nepal is now limited to Delhi's administrative-intelligence apparatus. This was because of Indian leadership handing over the management of Nepal affairs mainly to the security establishment. Things have come to such a pass that the main point of contact in Delhi for the Nepali leadership nowadays is their national security advisor (NSA). The extent to which Modi's predecessor, Manmohan Singh, had involved his NSA during his first term (2004–2009) can be gauged from the snippets available in the memoir of his media advisor, Sanjaya Baru.[8]

Despite his ten-year-long prime ministership, Manmohan Singh did not wish to visit the neighbouring country Nepal even once. The Nepali leadership, too, knowingly or unknowingly, alienated themselves from Indian political leaders. The ground was left open for the Delhi security establishment to advance their 'micromanagement' of Nepal's internal affairs. Thus, India's image in Nepal suffered and the bilateral relationship was burdened by constant distrust.

It was against this backdrop that BJP leader Narendra Modi swept to power, winning absolute majority in the parliamentary elections of 2014. The election manifesto of BJP stated that the 'Congress-led UPA (government) has failed to establish enduring friendly and cooperative relations with India's neighbours. India's relations with traditional allies have turned cold.' It added that instead of being guided by the interests of big powers, the party would pursue friendly relations with the neighbourhood and periphery.[9]

It reflected Modi's ambition to become a world leader by winning the hearts and minds of the neighbourhood. The BJP's 'neighbourhood first' policy was quickly reflected in his oath-taking ceremony on 26 May 2014 where he invited SAARC leaders as guests. Modi started his foreign tour from Bhutan. When addressing the Bhutanese Parliament, he inadvertently uttered the word 'Nepal'.[10] Perhaps Nepal was on his mind. It could be because of his old ties with Nepal. Modi seemed to have a deep spiritual attachment with the erstwhile Hindu state. He had not only visited many religious sites of Nepal in the past as a pilgrim, but also spent a long time here.

After Bhutan, he embarked upon a Nepal visit on 3 and 4 August 2014. While addressing the Nepali Parliament, he said, 'I had come here many years ago as a pilgrim. There is a saying that if you visit Nepal once, you will have a lifelong attachment.' He became the first Indian prime minister to visit Nepal after seventeen long years. He was a game changer in altering the Indo-Nepal relations, which had been passing through a long phase of distrust. In fact, Modi himself raised many issues close to Nepal, showed a liberal attitude and won over the majority of Nepalis without too much diplomatic investment. As a result, there was a dramatic improvement in bilateral relations for some time. Particularly, many festering water resource issues started getting resolved. A Power Trade Agreement (PTA) was signed. Project Development Agreements (PDA), too, were signed on the Upper Karnali and Arun III mega hydro power projects. Transport connectivity between the two countries was eased and telephone tariffs were brought down.

Modi's fair disposition towards Nepal was evident in the address he gave to the Nepali Parliament. The first point he raised was about the close religious-spiritual ties that existed between the two countries. He gave an account of his personal journey—being born in the land of Lord Somnath (Gujarat), having politically blossomed in the land of Kashi Vishwanath and now, coming to the land of Lord Pashupatinath. He fondly recalled the age-old tradition of Nepali priests in the temples of Kashi and Indian priests in Pashupatinath. He said his relations with Nepal had deepened after being elected from Kashi. He also mentioned Nepal as the birthplace of Sita and Gautam Buddha. Nepal took this statement of his most favourably, in view of past propaganda by a section of Indians that the Buddha was born in India.

The second part of his statement dealt with the famed bravery of Nepali. 'There is no war that India has won in which Nepali blood has not been spilt,' Modi praised the Nepalis, adding, 'I salute the brave Nepalis who have died for India.'

The third important statement he made was on Constitution-making. 'I can say now that the attention of not only the citizens of Nepal but the whole world is focused on Nepal's Constituent Assembly. You have been granted this rare opportunity as drafters of the Constitution,' he addressed the assembly members. 'It is necessary to have hearts of sages (*rishi mann*) to write a Constitution—ones who can see far, estimate the problems of the future and take the society hundred years forward.'

It was not clear what Modi meant exactly by rishi mann, but it was understood as his advice to take a long view in Constitution-writing and was, thus, favourably accepted. During his address, Modi said a 'federal democratic republic' was the 'best course', indicating his support for federalism and republic—and, interestingly, leaving out 'secularism', the third tenet of the colossal political change that Nepal had recently adopted.

Modi affirmed Nepal as a sovereign nation and vowed not to interfere in any of its affairs, but rather support the path it decided to take—which proved to be a false assurance, with a blockade imposed a year later. But for the time being, his visit was considered a milestone in the improvement of bilateral relations. The thirty-five-point joint statement issued at the end of the visit included many important aspects. It stated that the bilateral agreements, including the 1950 Treaty of Peace and Friendship, would be reviewed, adjusted and updated; pending border disputes would be resolved; an eminent persons' group would be formed to further expand and consolidate the close and multifaceted bilateral relations; the texts of Extradition Treaty and Mutual Legal Assistance would be finalized; a soft credit line of $1 billion would be made available to Nepal; implementation of Pancheshwore project would begin and so on.

The Janakpur trap

Modi's visit had, to a great extent, improved the image of India in Nepal and had brought about visible changes in the Nepali perspective towards its southern neighbour. It was possible because of the attempt by India's prime minister to give a fillip to the relations from the top political level. Had the attempt been allowed to continue, it would have taken Indo-Nepal relations to a new height. But the permanent establishment of India (bureaucracy, security agencies, etc.) didn't seem particularly excited by the attempts by their own prime minister.

To be fair, Delhi's establishment was new for Modi himself. Having steered the state of Gujarat for twelve years before he was catapulted to prime ministership, he was not immediately able to grasp the various dimensions of the Delhi establishment. Particularly, in the case of India's Nepal policy, the security establishment had been enjoying a decisive role.[11] Modi's initial approach was different from the policy of micromanagement practised in Nepal by his security establishment. In the end, such circumstances evolved, or were created, in which Modi found himself unable or unwilling to overstep the line drawn by India's permanent security establishment. During his tenure, the security establishment became more dominant in India's foreign affairs.[12] In the Indo-Nepal context, the turning point was his proposed Janakpur visit.

The land of Sita and King Janak, the city of Janakpur on the southern fringe of Nepal is a famous religious site as well as the heartland of the Maithili–Madhesi identity. Three months after his successful first visit, Modi was once again coming to Nepal to take part in the eighteenth SAARC Summit. This time, he professed his desire to come via the land route and enter Janakpur from the Indian state of Bihar. In preparations, the roads across the border in Bihar started to be black-topped overnight. Other preparations were also put in place. But the Janakpur visit fell into controversy from the very start. He was supposed to address the public and distribute a large number of bicycles to the local people. Seemingly, the idea was to not only expand India's influence among the local Madhesi community but also, by extension, to influence the election scheduled a few months later in the state of Bihar, which had a close sociocultural affinity with the Madhesis.

It was not clear what Modi had in mind and what statement he would have made following the darshan of the Janaki temple, located in the heart of Janakpur, but his mere presence there would have been associated with the issues of Madhesis and Hindutva when the Constitution-making process was going on. Besides, it was not

Modi alone who would be reaching Janakpur. A huge procession of over 200 Indian sadhus was travelling there from Ayodhya under the leadership of a vice-president of the Vishwa Hindu Parishad, ostensibly to carry out the marriage procession of Ram–Sita.

Modi's proposed religious undertaking in Janakpur could not be openly welcomed by Nepal's secular government. Furthermore, the proposed public address and plans to distribute bicycles in a region that was considered sensitive due to the ongoing dispute over federalism was also not to Kathmandu's liking. Initially, the plan was to felicitate Modi in the big ground of Barha Bigha, where he would also address the public. But the Nepali government limited his itinerary to the Janaki temple. The first signs of doubts emerged from that very point.

The responsibility of preparing for Modi's visit to Janakpur had been entrusted to the Physical Planning and Construction Minister Bimalendra Nidhi, who hailed from the same region. All of a sudden, he announced the cancellation of Modi's Janakpur visit. He issued the statement in his personal capacity without waiting for the official decision of his own government. It was not clear why he did that. He later clarified that he issued the statement after he received a call from a diplomat in the Indian embassy who informed him of the cancellation. Strangely, the Indian side then called off the visit, citing the announcement from the organizer.

It was apparent that the Indian bureaucracy had fired its shot from Nepal's shoulder. With the cancellation of the Janakpur visit, Modi stayed away from Lumbini as well. His visit was limited to Kathmandu. Following that episode, Modi's tone and temperament towards Nepal changed markedly. Perhaps he took the Janakpur fiasco as a personal affront. It encouraged the elements that were already displeased with his efforts to improve relations with Nepal from the political level. The Nepali leadership, too, failed to demonstrate the diplomatic skill necessary to arrest the slide in Modi's trust. Once again, Indo-Nepal relations turned frosty.

The same Modi who had earlier upheld Nepal's right to self-determination during his first visit now wantonly interfered in Nepal's internal affairs. The unexpected speech he made in Hindi on the very day he landed in Kathmandu at a function held to inaugurate a trauma centre, built with Indian assistance, triggered political ripples far and wide. Flanked by the Nepali prime minister and chairman of the Constituent Assembly on 25 November 2014, Modi advised them to write the Constitution on consensus, not on numerical strength.[13]

The arrogant advice they received from the prime minister of a neighbouring country at the crucial juncture of Constitution-making generated mixed reactions from the Nepali parties. The ruling parties Nepali Congress and CPN–UML who were trying to complete the process by majority, found themselves under pressure. But the advice was music to the ears of Maoists and Madhesis, who were in the opposition. For India itself, the advice turned out to be counterproductive as it pushed India to a narrow plank vis-à-vis its policies with Nepal. In principle, the advice for a consensus was a reasonable one, but clearly, it was up to the Nepalis to decide which course to take. It was one mistake that upset everything else. Modi's remarks became a policy decision for India—and in the name of enforcing it, the permanent establishment tried to drag the Nepali political leadership towards the agenda. The question here arises—who suggested that Modi say what he said that day? Who drafted his speech? Whoever it was, it ultimately led India on the path that would take it to the point of committing the historic blunder of imposing the extreme diplomatic measure of a blockade.

'Promises' they made

In fact, following his second visit, Modi's advice for consensus was slowly cooling off. The UCPN–Maoists and one constituent of the Madhesi Morcha, the Madhesi Forum Loktantrik, also gravitated towards the NC–UML position of Constitution by majority. The result was the sixteen-point pact signed to write the Constitution. This agreement was carried out by the Nepali parties on their own volition—and it made the leaders suspect, rightly, that India would be enraged and would try to derail it. Therefore Prachanda, K.P. Oli, Baburam Bhattarai and other leaders tried to explain their decision to the Indian ambassador and other Indian channels.

Other countries and the United Nations welcomed the sixteen-point pact. A meeting, called by the UN, of Kathmandu-based diplomats including Indian Ambassador Ranjit Rae, supported the pact. While India did not issue any statement about it, unlike its customary practice, it also did not react sharply. Perhaps it was in recognition of the evolving situation. In the words of a former prime minister, it was after Nepali leaders started publicly declaring that they reached the agreement without any foreign involvement, that India smelt a rat. They were further startled that along with the sixteen-point pact, the leaders had even decided, tacitly, upon the future power-sharing formula by electing K.P. Oli as prime minister and Sushil Koirala as president after the promulgation of the Constitution.

This then led to the visit to Delhi by Maoist Chairman Prachanda and NC leader Sher Bahadur Deuba, one after another. Both of them undertook the visit at the Indian invitation with twin objectives—to assuage Indian apprehensions over the sixteen-point pact and enhance their personal relations with the Indian leadership. But both the visits turned out to be counterproductive.

Prachanda reached Delhi in mid-July. Deuba followed in his footsteps and reached there towards the end of the month. Both of them held discussions with the top Indian leadership, including the president, the prime minister, the external affairs minister and the home minister. In Nepal, the process was on to collect public feedback over the first draft of the Constitution. The visiting Nepali leaders were pressed on mainly two matters. One, that the

Constitution should be issued only after accommodating Madhesi parties and by clarifying federal provinces; and two, the provision of secularism should be removed. The first issue appeared to be the priority of the bureaucracy while the political leadership was keen on the second one.

While he was in India, Prachanda travelled to Modi's state of Gujarat and revealed his discontent over what he called 'increasing Christianity' in Nepal—an indication that he, too, was not in favour of secularism. Likewise, in an interview, Deuba said, 'I did inform them (India) that we parties were ourselves moving towards an agreement to replace secularism with a phrase indicating religious freedom.'[14] Both the leaders also expressed their commitment to issuing the Constitution only after accommodating Madhesi parties and clarifying the demarcations of provincial boundaries.

Back in Kathmandu, the leaders then came up with the Constitution draft, which first had six and then seven provinces. They supposed that this decision would satisfy India and also address the demands of Madhesi parties. But they were wrong. There were intense debates on secularism as well. There was a tug-of-war went on whether to remove secularism and replace it with a phrase indicating religious freedom. In fact, the top leaders of all three major parties, the NC, UML and the Maoists, were ready to drop secularism. But it was blocked by Baburam Bhattarai, who headed the crucial dialogue and consensus committee of the Constituent Assembly. In the end, a compromise was struck. Article 4 of the Constitution stated Nepal was a secular state, but with a caveat (in the form of an explanation) that this secularism would mean religious and cultural freedoms, including protection of religion, culture handed down from the time immemorial (*sanatan dharma*).

In fact, the leadership of the BJP, including Modi, wished to see the restoration of Hindutva in Nepal. But India's permanent establishment had a different goal—to perpetuate its decisive role in Nepal affairs. Surprisingly, the Indian bureaucracy did not even want to be seen as being anywhere close to Hindutva. Take, for instance, how it reacted to the remarks made by a visiting BJP vice-president, Renu Devi. When she said, 'Nepal should be a Hindu state,' at a public programme, the Indian embassy in Kathmandu issued a prompt rebuttal: 'The remarks attributed to Mrs Renu Devi in the media are her personal opinion and do not reflect the policy of the Indian government.'[15]

Kamal Thapa is a seasoned politician and knowledgeable about the dynamics of Delhi. On one occasion, the Deputy Prime Minister and Foreign Minister Thapa wondered, 'Nepal needs to be very cautious about different Indian agencies working for different goals. Our leaders ask "which India?" when we ask about their talks with India, as the different Indian agencies have their own set of relations with different quarters of Nepal. Perhaps their goal is the same, but the difference in the manner they reach out should startle us.'[16]

When the two former Prime Ministers Deuba and Prachanda talked to top Delhi leadership, they failed to keep with them any note-taker. The promises they made or the commitments they expressed were not registered in Nepal's official record. Even if they had made any kind of commitments, they were made without the knowledge of the 'system'. In fact, there is no record of even that so-called significant telephone call made by Modi to his Nepali counterpart Sushil Koirala on 25 August 2015. The Indian side leaked to the press that Modi had repeated his assertion for a consensus Constitution, to which Koirala had apparently acquiesced. But neither the Madhesis were taken on board nor was secularism removed. The Indian leadership took this as a grave 'affront'.

Height of distrust

As the date of Constitution promulgation approached, Kathmandu and Delhi drifted further apart. Madhes, too, was spiralling into violence. Nepali leaders were under domestic pressure to refrain from promulgating the Constitution without addressing Madhesi issues. Cornered, they announced the suspension of the process of Constituent Assembly for two days, till 13 September. But the Madhesi leaders did not return to talks; instead, Jaishankar showed up as India's special envoy.

Just before Jaishankar's arrival, the 'prime minister-in-waiting', Oli, had dispatched his party secretary, Pradeep Gyawali, to Delhi to 'convince' the Indian political leadership. Oli was certain to become prime minister once the Constitution was promulgated in accordance with the previous deal he had struck with the Nepali Congress. In Delhi, Gyawali met the leaders of the ruling party, senior bureaucrats and security officials. In one of those meetings, BJP's General Secretary Ram Madhav said to him, 'The monarchy is gone from Nepal due to its own reasons. We do not think it should be restored. For the past six months, emissaries of the king have been asking for time to meet us, but we have refused. However, we are displeased by Nepal's decision to abandon a Hindu state.'[17] In India, the political leadership's fondness for the religion and the bureaucracy's obsession with Madhes, thus, continued.

The most important of Gyawali's Delhi deliberations took place on 16 September 2015 at the office of NSA Ajit Doval. Foreign Secretary Jaishankar, MEA's Nepal desk head Abhay Thakur and some other officials were present. Around forty-five minutes into the discussions, Jaishankar received a call from somewhere. He jotted something down in a note, passed it to Doval and said, 'What is the use of talking anymore?'

He had received information from Kathmandu that the Constituent Assembly had passed the Constitution. But Doval did not give too much importance to the note and continued the discussions. Therefore, Gyawali thought that Delhi would coolly welcome the Constitution. He did not guess that their reaction would be the blockade.[18]

After the afternoon meeting, Doval had told Gyawali to expect his call in the evening. The call did not come. Instead, Jaishankar was flown to Kathmandu the following day with the express objective of stopping the Constitution promulgation. It has already been discussed earlier in this chapter how Jaishankar's mission failed. On 20 September, Indian Ambassador Ranjit Rae belatedly reached the ceremony to proclaim the Constitution. Immediately, the MEA issued a harsh statement that did not welcome the new Nepali Constitution. It merely 'noted' its promulgation.

The three major parties of Nepal, the NC, the UML and Maoists, had reached a broad agreement—that if they again followed India's advice, this time, they might as well forget about ever completing the Constitution. So they took a conscious and collective decision to first issue the Constitution and then look into possibilities of resolving outstanding issues within that framework. This further aggravated Delhi. Although the main concern of India's political leadership was secularism, they were not able to officially voice this. Therefore, they began pointing at the continued dissatisfaction of the Madhesi–Tharu, increasing tension on the border and its likely spillover onto the Indian side.

The calls for a single Madhes province (*ek Madhes ek pradesh*) in the southern belt of Nepal had first been made towards the final phase of the Maoist insurgency. During the first Constituent Assembly, this call got further traction. But when it was not heeded, its proponents started calling for two provinces in Madhes. In fact, it was mainly due to differences over the Madhes province that the first assembly was unceremoniously dissolved. In the second assembly, the Madhesi parties made two provinces their bottom line. But they lacked the numbers to actually press their positions effectively within the assembly. NC–UML were never in favour of those calls and when the Maoists, too, abandoned them, the Madhesi parties' agenda was further weakened.

In the new Constitution, a separate Madhes province was formed, spanning the area from the Saptari district in the east to Parsa in the west. But it left out the second Madhes province in the western plains—against the expectations of the Madhesi parties. The most contentious five Tarai districts (Jhapa, Morang and Sunsari in the east and Kailali and Kanchanpur in the west), too, were included in the hill provinces. Madhesi parties continued their agitation over these concerns. India supported them. India seemed to have its own geopolitical interest in seeing a province covering only the plains.

Border crisis

After it refused to entertain India's counsel and coercion, many in Nepal thought India decided it was time to teach a lesson to its small neighbour. And to teach such a lesson, it had in its arsenal the ultimate weapon of a border blockade. However, since the international community could come out against it and since it could be difficult to justify such a move, India never did officially announce the blockade. The crippling blockade was enforced unofficially. India found it convenient to pass the buck to the Nepali agitators and declared that its cargo truck drivers were refusing to cross the border due to insecurity.[19] In practice, the Nepali people saw that the blockade was already in force and India was actively stopping supplies to Nepal even before the agitators had gathered at the border points. Nepali tankers were being turned back empty from the refineries of Indian Oil Corporation. Indian authorities were stopping cargo movement from even those border points where there were no agitations.

The initial justification, that the movement of trucks and containers was stopped due to the situation in Nepal, could not be sustained for more than a few days. And that was the point when the Samyukta Loktantrik Madhesi Morcha came to India's rescue by formally taking responsibility for the border blockade. In fact, it had already been three days since India had imposed the blockade when, on 24 September 2015, the Morcha meeting held in Rajbiraj took the decision formally to hold a sit-in agitation on the borders. India started increasing its active support to the Morcha's agitation.[20] A local trader of Raxaul, Mahesh Kumar Agrawal, who also happened to be a BJP worker, arranged regular meals at his residence for agitators in Birgunj. It was not clear whether Agrawal had decided to incur the expenses to feed the agitators from across the border of his own volition or whether he was encouraged to do so by the Indian government.[21]

India found its space to play in Nepal shrinking rapidly due to the unity among the major Nepali parties, the NC, UML and the Maoists. Although it could not stop the promulgation of the Constitution, India wanted to break this alliance in the course of subsequent power-sharing.[22] Prime Minister Koirala went back on his promise to hand over the reins to K.P. Oli. He himself stood as a candidate for the election of prime minister. There was strong opposition for his move from within his own party. NC General Secretary Krishna Sitaula publicly criticized him for breaching the gentlemen's agreement. His co-General Secretary Purna Bahadur Khadka resigned from his position.

It was only a night before the scheduled election that Koirala made the decision to contest. On the night of 10 October, RAW's former Special Secretary, Mathur, visited Baluwatar to convince him. In a surprising move, the MPs belonging to the agitating Madhesi Morcha also returned to the Parliament to vote in favour of Koirala. In any case, Koirala lost. He not only lost the post of prime minister but also lost the chance of becoming the president, as had been agreed in the now defunct gentlemen's agreement. The president of the CPN–UML, K.P. Oli, was elected the prime minister and his party's Vice-President Bidya Devi Bhandari was elected the first female president of Nepal. In reality, it was on Koirala's watch that Indo-Nepal relations had dipped so low. But eventually, he ended up being used by the Indians and got thoroughly discredited in domestic politics.[23]

Anyway, the change in guard presented a new opportunity to improve bilateral relations. In a congratulatory call he made to the newly elected Prime Minister Oli, Modi said, 'We are confident that the Government of Nepal will address the remaining political issues confronting the country in a spirit of dialogue and reconciliation.'[24] Subsequently, Oli wrote a letter on 16 October calling on the Madhesi Morcha to abandon its agitation and initiate dialogue. In response, the Morcha said it was willing to hold talks but could not stop the agitation.

It was then that the government concluded that it would try to find a solution by talking to Delhi instead of the Madhesi Morcha. Deputy Prime Minister and Foreign Minister Kamal Thapa was sent to Delhi for the purpose. Thapa met Indian External Affairs Minister Sushma Swaraj, Home Minister Rajnath Singh, and NSA Ajit Doval. On 19 October, he also met PM Modi. Thapa requested the lifting of the blockade, but the Indians were indifferent. They did not even keep their promise of opening border points other than Birgunj and re-routing the trucks and containers lined up in Birgunj.

In Kathmandu, the government formed a dialogue team led by Thapa to hold talks with the Madhesis and Tharus. But it went nowhere. On 2 November, India issued another warning: 'Since the problems facing Nepal are of a political nature, use of force will not give any solution. The government of Nepal must effectively and trustfully address the issues leading to the situation of violence.'[25]

That led to a daily issuance of statement and counter-statement between the Nepal government and the Indian embassy. When, on 2 November, minister without portfolio Satya Narayan Mandal accused India of sending plainclothes security personnel, the embassy termed the statement 'provocative, baseless and filled with mala fide intention.'[26] It also took strong exception to public utterances by Deputy Prime Ministers Chitra Bahadur K.C. and C.P. Mainali and responded with a strongly worded statement.[27]

Despite huge difficulties caused by the Indian blockade, Nepal did not wish to internationalize the issue. It thought that such a move would further widen the rift and narrow the possibility of a resolution. It, instead, opted for patience. On the contrary, India engaged in active lobbying against its smaller neighbour. On 5 November 2015, India levelled grave charges against Nepal at a meeting of the United Nations Human Rights Council in Geneva. India remarked that 'violence, extrajudicial killings and ethnic discrimination' continued in Nepal and expressed its strong apprehensions. Countering the Indian statement, the visibly upset Nepali Deputy Prime Minister and Foreign Minister Kamal Thapa asked the floor, 'Can Nepal not issue its own Constitution?'

A week later, when Indian PM Modi visited Britain, the joint statement they issued unnecessarily included a Nepal-related point. 'The two prime ministers stressed the importance of a lasting and inclusive constitutional settlement in Nepal that will address the remaining areas of concern and promote political stability and economic growth.'[28]

Again on 30 March 2015, the joint statement issued after the thirteenth EU–India summit in Brussels dragged Nepal into the discussion. It stated, 'They also agreed on the need for a lasting and inclusive constitutional settlement in Nepal that will address the remaining constitutional issues in a time-bound manner.' Seemingly, India wanted to prove its point that Nepal's Constitution was flawed. Nepali, too, strongly reacted to these Indian moves.

Search for a middle ground

India was persistent about both the blockade and international lobbying against Nepal. In Nepal, the population that had not even fully recovered from the impact of the devastating earthquakes, and found itself grappling with severe fuel shortages and many other difficulties as consequences of the Indian blockade. The situation demanded decisive action. The Nepali leaders agreed to send Deputy Prime Minister Thapa to Delhi, once again, for decisive talks. 'It was also agreed that in case this mission too failed, Nepal would then internationalize the issue of the blockade, raise its voice on international platforms and file a case against India for violating the rights of a land-locked country. I told both PM Oli and Prachanda that personally, I was not fond of the new Constitution because my own ideology was vastly different (Thapa heads a party that believes in a Hindu monarchical state), but I would take ownership for it since I had accepted the process. So I asked them to tell me how far I could go if I were to have a decisive dialogue with the Indians. Give me the bottom line, I asked,' Thapa said.

Subsequently, the three major parties agreed on some common points: to pass the Constitution amendment bill registered by the previous Koirala government with some changes; to resolve issues related to citizenship through mutual consent; to revise provincial demarcation to address the demands of agitating Madhesi parties; and to form a political committee to look into the issues of demarcation and further amend the Constitution based on the suggestion of experts within three months. Armed with this four-point non-paper, DPM Thapa flew to India on 1 December 2015. He first reached Bangalore and visited the ashram of Sri Sri Ravi Shankar, whom he knew well. Industrialist Binod Chaudhary, with PM Oli's consent, also reached the Art of Living Centre. Thapa and Chaudhary both had cordial relations with Ravi Shankar who, on his part, had access to the Delhi establishment. Ravi Shankar lobbied positively during the subsequent meetings in Delhi.

DPM Thapa met External Affairs Minister Sushma Swaraj on 2 December. Thapa presented the non-paper to her and sought her cooperation. Swaraj did not say anything at the outset. She said the matter would need approval from Prime Minister Modi himself. 'Perhaps they then went over it and appeared willing to some degree. But they were not fully convinced about me and wanted to talk to our PM,' Thapa recalls. 'The following morning, I again met Swaraj and I dialled the number of our prime minister. Our prime minister talked to her and they appeared convinced. We were confident that the blockade would now be lifted.'

After that visit, India relaxed other border points except Birgunj. The Madhesi Morcha's agitation became centred on the Birgunj border point. With the intention of apprising the Madhesi leadership of these developments, Swaraj invited the Morcha leaders to Delhi. Mahantha Thakur, Upendra Yadav, Rajendra Mahato and Mahendra Raya Yadav went to Delhi but could not be convinced. Meanwhile, in January, the major parties passed the first amendment of the Constitution unilaterally. It was welcomed by India. The amendment basically gave more priority to population in the determination of election constituencies and also guaranteed proportional representation in state apparatus. Although formally, the Morcha stayed away from the process, some of their demands were addressed by the amendment. As their demands were partially met, the intensity of their agitation, too, subsided.

Compulsion to lift the blockade

People in the know say that India's initial plan was to impose the blockade for a maximum of ten days. But it got extended to five months. Nepalis were naturally at the receiving end but India, too, was not in a position to prolong it. It was assumed that Nepal, being wholly dependent on India for its imports, would be thrown into disarray by the blockade and its political leadership would be forced to acquiesce. In fact, India had made a successful test of such punishment back in 1989. Back then, the blockade had led to people resorting to a movement against the government and the uprooting of the Panchayati regime. But times had changed. In 1989, Nepal had an autocratic regime. In 2015, the Indian punishment was against the democratically elected government.

Therefore, the public outrage was expressed not against the government in Kathmandu but against India.

In what was a dramatic development, a whole generation of Nepali youths was turned anti-India by the blockade. The Indian intelligence bureau seriously alerted their political leadership about the changing environment in Nepal.[29] The platforms of social media such as Twitter and Facebook were replete with criticisms levelled at India. In addition to that, Prime Minister Modi himself got to see the Nepali people's mood first-hand when he visited London. Due to noisy demonstrations by the Nepali community, they had to change the route when Modi went to meet the British prime minister. Surprised at the level of criticism, the Indian PMO ordered an inquiry into the incident.[30] Given the increased volume of the Nepali diaspora, similar protests were held elsewhere, too.

For India, the biggest headache was the expanding role of China in Nepal, even though it was natural for Nepal to turn to another neighbour for succour and support when one neighbour had become so bitter. The signing of an understanding on import of petroleum products from China, on 28 October 2015, and the subsequent supply of Chinese petrol—more symbolic than substantive—sent shockwaves through Delhi. If nothing else, the agreement showed the possibility of Nepal and China moving on a course towards a strategic and political relationship—something that India simply did not want to see.[31]

Gradually, other countries, including the United States, pressed India to end the blockade as it was leading to a humanitarian crisis in Nepal. In an interview given to Akhilesh Upadhyay and me, the US ambassador to Nepal, Alaina Teplitz, commented, 'This Constitution, looking at this in a historical context, is a huge milestone for Nepal.'[32]

The worst criticism of Modi, in fact, was seen inside India. Generally, one does not see much variance among domestic Indian actors such as government, opposition and media on issues of foreign policy. But in the case of the blockade against

Nepal, a large section of Indian intellectuals turned against their government.[33] On 7 December 2015, the Upper House, Rajya Sabha, held a debate on the 'Situation in Nepal and the State of Indo-Nepal relations'. There was a long discussion and much criticism against Modi's policy. During the three-hour-long discussion, fourteen MPs, including Mani Shankar Aiyar, Karan Singh, Pawan Verma, Sharad Yadav and D.P. Tripathi spoke on the issue. Most of them were critical of the government. Even the usually laconic former Prime Minister Manmohan Singh, in an interview, said the Modi government was committing a strategic blunder by irritating a close neighbour like Nepal.[34]

In the eyes of the ruling BJP, one factor related to the Madhes agitation was the impending state elections in Bihar. The election had become a prestige issue for Modi. A section of the party thought that the support lent to Madhesis across the border—who had close *roti-beti* relations with their voters—could help it at the hustings. It turned out to be untrue. The BJP was routed in the election, and the Mahagathbandhan (grand alliance) of Lalu Prasad Yadav and Nitish Kumar posted a victory. Subsequently, a team of Madhesi leaders—Upendra Yadav, Rajendra Mahato and Mahendra Raya Yadav—reached Patna and met the Rashtriya Janata Dal Chief Lalu Yadav. The meeting of 1 February 2016 proved counterproductive to the Madhesi leaders for two obvious reasons. The BJP leadership was not at all amused to see the Madhesi leaders hobnobbing with their rival. And when the picture of the meeting—which showed the Nepali Madhesi leaders sitting on plastic chairs on lower ground, listening attentively to Lalu sermonizing from a sofa—was made public, it led to further castigation of the Madhesi leaders for kowtowing to India.

The Madhesi Morcha was slow in realizing that their continuous agitation was witnessing declining participation by party workers, and alienating a large section of the local population and traders irritated by the border-centred agitation. They also could not comprehend India's gradual withdrawal. Kathmandu had not experienced much pressure from the Madhes movement. The network of cross-border smugglers had ensured a minimum level of supplies to the hills despite the blockade. People were certainly down but not out. The worst impact of the blockade was felt in Madhes itself. When the risk of Madhes' business capital Birgunj turning into a dead city became real, the agitators not only lost the support of locals from both sides of the border, but had to face their rage.

As the Madhesi parties could not sustain their movement for long, Delhi's weapon of the blockade was blunted. On its part, the Nepali government had carried out some reforms, including an amendment to the Constitution. All this meant that Delhi wanted to end the blockade. For this purpose, Delhi invited Prime Minister Oli. But Oli was adamant that he would not visit India till the latter lifted the blockade first. His public posture and the fear among Indians that Oli would choose to visit Beijing instead and develop closer relations with the north was building up. At that very point, the roles played by the defence establishments of the two countries proved to be effective.

Nepali Army Chief General Rajendra Chhetri was in India on a customary tour. There is a unique tradition between the two countries, whereby the chief of one country's army is made the honorary general of the other. But General Chhetri's visit was not limited to this formality. His informal role was catalytic in restoring normal bilateral ties. Consequently, when he left for Delhi, Nepal was suffering a blockade, but when he came back, it had been dramatically lifted.

Not all quarters in India had liked equally the imposition of a blockade against Nepal. Particularly, its defence establishment was sending signals of displeasure. The reason for their displeasure was connected to their institutional interest as well, what with the presence of a large contingent of Gorkha soldiers in their rank and file.[35] Besides, then Indian Army Chief General Dalbir Singh himself was once attached to the Fifth Gorkha Rifles.[36] While in Delhi, General Chhetri cautioned them about the security implications of the blockade. He pointed at the risks of insecurity for both countries due to the obstructions in no man's land. His counterpart General Singh and Indian Defence Minister Manohar Parrikar both lent a sympathetic ear to his concerns.[37]

A day before General Chhetri returned to Kathmandu, on 6 February 2016, the Birgunj blockade was cleared after 135 days. The agitators who wanted to resume the sit-in at the border were evicted by Indian police in plainclothes. Delhi, it seemed, had changed its colours when its interests with Kathmandu converged. This does not mean that General Chhetri alone was instrumental in the lifting of the blockade. Rather, his was the visit that took place at a time when Delhi's leadership was already under pressure to review its Nepal policy due to continuous criticism from the media.[38] Incidentally, Chhetri got the opportunity to communicate Nepal's concern at a crucial time.

Oli's Chinese sojourn

The Madhesi Morcha was in no position to continue its border agitation after India withdrew its hand. However, Prime Minister Oli could not demonstrate the required political insight to bring the Madhesi parties into the mainstream: he appeared wholly focused on winning over, if not forcing, Delhi into ending the blockade. The months-long Madhes agitation, which saw the deaths of dozens of citizens, came to an abrupt halt without any solution—and the rift between the hills and the plains was stark. The gross inability to arrest that social polarization appeared to be the worst weakness of the Oli government.

There was nothing that stopped Oli from making the trip to Delhi once the blockade ended. He was invited on a state visit. India rolled out the red carpet in his welcome and he was lodged as a state guest in the Rashtrapati Bhawan. During his February visit to India, a number of agreements were inked, such as allowing

Nepal to use the Vishakhapatnam port in Andhra Pradesh; a new route permit to use Kakarvitta–Banglabandh; operationalization of the Dhalkebar–Muzaffarpur transmission line; and forming of an eminent persons' group to review past agreements. But the political and diplomatic warmth of yore could not be wholly restored.

Even before his visit ended, Oli was quick to claim that clouds of distrust between the two countries had been cleared. But the Indian side was not so forthcoming. Foreign Secretary S. Jaishankar, at a press briefing, said that though PM Oli had said he had come to Delhi to end the misunderstandings, apart from two points of constitutional amendment, India expected that the remaining constitutional issues were resolved in the spirit of consensus and dialogue and in a time-bound manner.[39]

As a result, the two countries could not issue even a joint statement at the end of the visit. The joint statement could not be agreed upon after India refused to include a phrase welcoming Nepal's Constitution. The Indians did not take kindly to some of the voices hurled at them in the presence of PM Oli himself. At a programme held to felicitate Oli at the Nepali embassy's premises, a political representative was heard saying, 'Without firing a single shot, Comrade Oli has won the battle against India.' Slogans were also raised hailing Comrade K.P. Oli, which reminded one of the 'hail Modi' slogans that were once heard in Kathmandu.[40]

There was no marked improvement in bilateral ties even after Oli's visit. Instead, immediately upon his return, there appeared reports in the Indian media of India slashing its grants to Nepal by 40 per cent.[41] On top of that, attempts were made to break the ruling alliance between Oli's CPN–UML and the Maoists, which would have pulled the rug from underneath Oli. The PM's officials accused India of having a hand in these attempts.[42] The alliance was saved by a nine-point deal between the two parties. But the visit to India of Nepal's first female president, Bidya Devi Bhandari, was cancelled at the eleventh hour. Oli also recalled Nepali Ambassador Deep Kumar Upadhyaya, who was also a leader of the opposition Nepali Congress party. It was said that PM Oli felt Upadhyaya was involved in the attempts to derail his government. These two events again led to the deterioration of Indo-Nepal relations.

Clearly, PM Oli had visited Delhi with great expectations in the wake of the recently lifted blockade. When he did not find relations improving accordingly, he started looking north at China. Even at the height of the blockade, Nepal had not requested much help from China, because Oli was still looking expectantly to Delhi. It was also natural to feel easier dealing with India than with the other trans-Himalayan neighbour, China. Even at a personal level, till before he was elected Nepal's PM, Oli was considered a leader with close ties to Delhi. Why and how the trust between him and India broke down is a matter for inquiry. But its result was apparent. As PM, his policy started gradually tilting towards China.[43]

Within a few weeks of his failed visit to India, in March 2016, Oli went on a formal visit to China. A number of agreements with long-term significance were signed during the visit—until then, such agreements with China had not been reached due to either unwillingness or inability on Nepal's part. The agreements included obtaining Chinese assistance in building an international airport in Pokhara; upgrading of roads linking Nepal with China; and building border bridges and other infrastructural projects. Likewise, exploration works for gas and fossil fuel started with Chinese involvement. Nepal was made a dialogue partner in the Shanghai Cooperation Organization. China also agreed to build a fuel reserve depot, proceed with the Arun–Kimathanka hydropower project and undertake a study of inter-country transmission lines.

The most important among the deals was the one related to transport and transit rights. China gave Nepal the right to use its ports: a move that could, in the long run, balance the total dependence on Indian ports. Land-locked Nepal is currently wholly dependent on India for transit and access to sea trade. Soon after the agreement, a freight train carrying eighty-six cargo containers left for Nepal from the north-western Chinese city of Lanzhou. The train reached Xigatse city of Tibet, from where the containers were transported by road to the bordering town of Keyrung and then all the way to Kathmandu—and it was accomplished in only ten days, a fact that was highlighted by the Chinese.[44]

It was a merely symbolic supply: substantive implementation of the transport and transit agreement can be possible only after the completion of the ongoing project to expand the Lhasa–Xigatse railway network up to the Nepali border in Keyrung. It will connect mainland China and its ports with Nepal. China is aiming to complete the railway network up to Keyrung in 2020. The two countries have agreed, in principle, to further extend that network all the way up to Kathmandu, Pokhara and Lumbini. In fact, China wants to extend it eventually to northern India—in case India gives its consent to this Chinese ambition, Nepal could one day become a bridge linking these two huge economies. It could also then lead to the realization of the Chinese proposal for a tripartite partnership with Nepal and India.

China is not going to immediately replace India in the close relations and contact Nepal has had with its southern neighbour. But it is clear that China will gradually be a factor in reducing Nepal's overdependence on India. And its influence is bound to increase in Nepal. The rising status of China as a global power, the priority it has given to improving relations with its neighbours, and Nepal's contiguous long border with its sensitive region of Tibet will ensure this. In the wake of the painful Indian blockade, the Nepali political leadership, too, was desirous of advancing economic and diplomatic proximity with China. Oli's willpower was decisive at this point. Consequently, unprecedented fronts were opened with China during his prime ministership.

The grip of India on Nepal's domestic politics, which started tightening with the resolution of the Maoist insurgency and the second people's movement, loosened with Oli's rise to power. And he became the person who, unexpectedly, took fundamental steps to reduce Nepal's dependence on India and advanced ties with China—moves that could alter the geopolitics of Nepal. The endgame of these moves, however, lies in the realm of the future.

Part IV

Destiny

25

Realm of Republic

'The exercise of democracy around the world has proven that
monarchy is not an essential condition for a democracy. If they
are found existing side by side in some countries, those are
exceptions, not a rule.'

—Prof. Krishna Pokharel, predicting
the coming of republic in the country[1]

In the trilateral covert and overt confrontation among the three
forces—the Maoists, Delhi and the monarchy—the first defeat
was handed to the monarchy. There were several reasons for it:
the ambition of King Gyanendra to directly exercise executive
power, the growing gap between him and the mainstream parties,
the republican campaign by the Maoists, the changing socio-
economic context of Nepal, and India's anti-monarchy strategy.

In the analysis of the sociologist Professor Chaitanya Mishra,
in the latest phase, the Shah dynasty had been losing its grip
on its major political, cultural and economic bases, and become
overly dependent on its military strength. Meanwhile, the political
dominance of the seven parliamentary political parties, including

the Nepali Congress and the CPN–UML, pushed the monarchy onto the back foot. The political role played by the seven parties, and the military role played by the Maoists, were crucial in the creation of the republic.[2]

Lost opportunity

Although communists in Nepal had been raising the issue of a republic for a long time, this was mainly limited to academic debates. In fact, many communist leaders had ended up joining hands with the monarchy in the name of advancing nationalism. Therefore, King Gyanendra did not expect that the seven parties and the Maoists would gang up against him. It was his misadventure into active politics that created the situation in which this could occur.

The Maoists had adopted a soft approach towards the monarchy till 2001 in order to ensure that the military was not mobilized against them. The durbar was misled into sympathizing with the Maoists, whom it believed had raised arms only against the parliamentary system. When, later on, the Maoists confronted the military and the monarchy, they sought support from Delhi. After the 1 February 2005 coup by King Gyanendra, the distance between Delhi and the Durbar grew. The new situation put the king on one side and the parties, the Maoists, and Delhi on the other. The king couldn't win.

The Maoists wanted to topple the monarchy with Indian help. India gradually made up its mind to work with the parties and the Maoists to bring down the monarchy. The fourth pole of this equation, the monarchy, failed to demonstrate any tactical or strategic thinking—it could not build favourable relations with the parties, the Maoists or Delhi, nor maintain the support of the people at large. Had it known how the Maoist insurgency would develop, the Durbar would certainly have allowed the deployment of the military to nip it in the bud. Instead, it committed a blunder by calculating that it could take advantage of the Maoist movement. Within five years of his coronation, King Gyanendra led the 250-year-old Shah dynasty to destruction.

The Maoist theory of utilitarianism had started from the time of King Birendra, who also tried to take advantage of the instability triggered by the insurgency to get back to power. Gyanendra did three additional things which his elder brother Birendra had not: he held formal dialogue with the Maoists; he mobilized the army against them; and he carried out a coup. But Gyanendra failed on all three counts.

Actually, the palace massacre of 1 June 2001 did severe damage to the palace, from which it could never really recover. In a majority Hindu society, with deep religious beliefs, people considered the king an incarnation of God Vishnu. The news of the assassination of the king, the massacre of his entire family, and the accusations levelled at the crown prince, these things were deeply disturbing and shook every Nepali to their core. The massacre ended up destroying their long-held beliefs, their veneration and the awe with which they looked up to the Shah dynasty. The monarchy during the subsequent reign of King Gyanendra lacked its previous charisma and magnetism.

The Maoists were not the type to miss such an opportunity. They seized the moment and carried out extensive propaganda, claiming that the republic had already arrived. King Gyanendra, on the other hand, was always 'haunted' by the accusations that he was responsible for the massacre. Due to the lack of a credible investigation and conclusive evidence, the massacre was always shrouded in mystery. From day one, Gyanendra found himself the object of suspicion. He could never satisfactorily defend himself.

It was a blunder on his part to carry out a coup before successfully defending his reputation. The king calculated that the people were frustrated with the political parties and scared of the Maoists. If he could control the Maoists, he thought, he would get popular support. Initially, people were indeed hopeful, because they yearned for peace and stability. So there were no street protests against the coup. Later, when the king was unable to deliver peace, the people grew restless. Perhaps society would have accepted him if he had been able to bring the Maoists into the mainstream.

Erroneous calculation

The king was also mistaken in underestimating the strength of the political parties. He once declared, 'There are now only two sides in Nepal—terrorists on one side and those who want peace, on the other.'[3]

This remark, which reeked of arrogance towards the political parties, was similar to the slogan of American President George W. Bush who, after the terrorist attack of 9/11, declared, 'Either you are with us or you are with the terrorists.'

It so happened that early in King Gyanendra's reign, the two major parties, the NC and the CPN–UML, were unpopular and weak. Perhaps this made him feel that there were only two forces left in the country, the Maoists and the monarchy. This was a mistake. The unpopularity of the parliamentary parties did not mean that they had lost their voter base at the local level. When the king failed to deliver good governance, the people flocked back to the parties, and the king could no longer face the challenge posed by the parties.

King Gyanendra seized power, but he had neither any plan to make it durable, nor any exit plan in case of adversity. He had not even calculated his own strengths, and how far the army would be willing to go with him. He also failed in choosing his team. There was no teamwork. His ministers were engaged only in pulling each other down.

Gyanendra, in fact, repeated what his father had done back in 1960. Kirti Nidhi Bista and Tulsi Giri, whom King Mahendra had

used decades earlier, were given the positions of vice-chairmen of
the council of ministers by Gyanendra. Perhaps Giri and Bista had
been useful in the past. But four decades later, there had been a
sea change. Gyanendra could not grasp that such crude imitation
would not work.

At the time of Mahendra's coup, the public was poorly
informed. There was no mass media. When Gyanendra repeated
the act, the media was available throughout Nepal. And none of
the influential media backed him. He, therefore, dispatched army
officers to the media houses to censor media content—which
backfired. The newspapers, TV stations and radio made a joint
attack against his autocratic rule. Their relentless opposition shook
the throne. His attempt to curtail communication by blocking
mobile services could not be continued after a few days.

Another blunder was the formation of a Royal Commission
on Corruption Control. In view of the widespread corruption
of leaders, he thought he could pick and choose his culprits by
creating a commission that bypassed the existing Commission
for Investigation of Abuse of Authority (CIAA). The royal
commission was empowered to accuse, investigate and adjudicate,
which drew criticism normally reserved for the kangaroo courts
created by the Maoists in their base areas. At the height of his
executive power, on 13 February 2006, the Supreme Court declared
the royal commission null and void. This helped to shorten the life
of the monarchy.

In 2003, King Gyanendra had removed Sher Bahadur Deuba
from the premiership, charging him with the inability to hold
elections. But he himself failed to hold that election. There was
only 20.8 per cent voter participation—the lowest in Nepal's
history—in the municipal elections he organized on 8 February
2006. This showed the lack of public support for him. Alienating
the political parties was turning out to be his gravest mistake. The
Maoists were waiting to ally with them instead. The king handed
them to the insurgents on a silver platter.

The Shah dynasty deserves credit for giving Nepal its present shape by organizing the unification campaign from the small Gorkha kingdom. For 104 years, the Shah kings were made mere puppets of the Rana oligarchy, who became powerful hereditary prime ministers. The Nepali Congress played a key role in breaking the shackles of the Shah kings, and ushering in democracy in 1950. But the leaders of Congress were seething with anger at what they considered the Shah's betrayal, not once or twice, but thrice—in 1960, 2002 and 2005, when the monarchy dismissed Congress governments. It pushed them to join hands with the Maoists against the monarchy.

'Overturning of circumstances'

Having played an active role in restoring Shah kingship in 1950, Delhi was growing gradually disenchanted with the Nepali monarchy. Therefore, it nudged the Maoists and the seven parties to sign the twelve-point understanding. The second people's movement was unleashed on the basis of this. At the climax of the people's movement, on 21 April 2006, King Gyanendra agreed to relent when Dr Karan Singh, a close confidante of Sonia Gandhi, arrived in Kathmandu with assurances from Indian PM Manmohan Singh. He thought that the Indian assurances carried by Dr Singh, who also happened to be his distant relative, would be the basis for the continuation of the monarchy in Nepal.

Is the restoration of monarchy now possible? The possibility cannot be rejected outright, given the continuing instability. But a restoration is not going to be as easy as some monarchists would like to believe. If the new Constitution is not widely accepted and enforced, or if the country is embroiled in another big civil war or conflict, the monarchy may have an outside chance of coming back. The former king might be hoping that following some crisis in the future, he might earn back the sympathies of domestic and international powers, especially India, and get them to review their policy toward monarchy. Otherwise, monarchy cannot return to Nepal.

Few men get to be kings. Fewer still get to be king twice in their lifetime. Fate had it that Gyanendra wore the crown twice, even though he was not in the line of natural successors. The first time was in 1950, when his grandfather King Tribhuwan left with all his family members—except him—for India to pressure the Ranas to give up power. The Ranas enthroned the young Gyanendra for a short period, before his grandfather returned home. The second time was in 2001, after the palace massacre. What an irony that both times Gyanendra was dethroned. The second time it was the entire monarchy that came down with him.

A few years later, when the TV channel News24 interviewed him, Gyanendra was asked, 'Did you feel there was any mistake on your part in the elimination of the monarchy?'

'Well, I have not felt it completely. But sometimes I do feel that had I done things differently, perhaps things would not have gone this far. But the circumstances overturned so wildly that it became tough to handle them.'[4]

26

Changed Rebels

'... *said he would change the world,*
But ended up changing himself.'

—Avash[1]

The village of Madi in Chitwan is not too far from Hetauda, but it took the Maoists twenty-odd years to travel from Madi to Hetauda. They organized the sixth national convention of the party in 1992 in Madi, which laid down the course of armed insurrection. Based on that, the party engaged in a decade-long insurgency. Two decades later, they held their seventh national convention in Hetauda, which formally endorsed the abandonment of armed insurgency and the adoption of a peaceful political path.

In 1992, their aim was to establish a 'new people's republic'. They declared, 'The central task of the new people's revolution will be to demolish the reactionary regime of constitutional monarchy and a parliamentary system through the force of long-term people's war and to replace it with a regime under the dictatorship of the proletariat covering all the revolutionary classes of people.'[2]

Two decades later, in 2013, they expressed satisfaction at the establishment of a 'federal democratic republic'. They said, 'In the present Nepali context, the party should give immediate priority to ensuring the consolidation of federal democratic republic in the new Constitution through the Constituent Assembly.'[3]

There had been a sea change in the aim, ideology and attitude of the Maoists in these twenty years. Despite their vow to complete the revolution, they could not seize power by themselves. Therefore, they chose compromise and tried to give an ideological garb to whatever they could gain. They wanted to set up a communist republic. They couldn't do it. They had to be content with a democratic republic. They had aimed to seize power in Kathmandu through people's war and people's revolt. But they were forced to choose the path of Constituent Assembly. They had promised not to give up arms midway. But they ended up summarily dismantling their People's Liberation Army. They had wanted to establish a dictatorship of the proletariat. But they were forced to join multiparty competition. Even during the course of negotiations, the Maoists claimed they would not be joining the mainstream; rather, they would be creating a new mainstream. That also turned out to be a farce.

It appeared that Prachanda's comrades were no longer the staunch Maoists of previous years. It appeared that the party wanted to turn itself into a socialist party incorporating all classes of people. The Hetauda convention made socialist revolution its goal and stressed economic prosperity. More importantly, it discarded the notion upheld by Nepali communist parties since 1949 that Nepali society is semi-feudal and semi-colonial in nature. Following the abolition of the monarchy, the Maoists may have been correct up to a point in saying that there had been a fundamental shift, and declaring Nepali society as no longer 'semi-feudal'. But how could they declare overnight that Nepali society was no longer 'semi-colonial' when unequal relations with India remained intact? Rather than being based on objective reasons, the Maoists reached this conclusion because of their improved relations with India. Therefore, the Hetauda convention not only refrained from naming India as the 'principle enemy', as the party had always done in the past, it also stopped short of calling it 'expansionist'.

With the passage of time, the Maoists joined the same state against which they had earlier raised arms. The living standards of the general populace, and of their own cadres, remained stagnant. But most Maoist leaders ended up not as leaders of the proletariat but as members of the elite. They embraced capitalism with such zeal that a large number of Maoist leaders became nouveau riche, amassing everything from plush bungalows to glittering vehicles and other valuable assets. They were seen hobnobbing with middlemen and financiers of questionable integrity. But this was not a totally new trend. In 1950 and 1990, too, revolutionaries had quickly transformed into new elites. After the movement of 2006, it was the turn of the Maoists to undergo such a transformation. When they saw they could not complete the revolution or change society, they started changing themselves.

Gradual transformation

When the Maoists raised arms against the state, the flame quickly spread across the country due to several factors such as poverty, rampant unemployment, ethno-regional repression, untouchability, state repression, and the energetic motivation of their leaders for revolt. The root of these problems lay inside the country, which provided the foundation for them. However, the inherent contradictions between the palace and Delhi helped to fan the fire.

Upon seeing that it was not going to be possible to change the Kathmandu regime by Mao's strategy of rural people's war, the Maoists started exploring options to expand their war. In 2000, their second national gathering concluded that change was not possible through a protracted people's war alone. Prachanda proposed forging a 'fusion' between people's war and urban insurrection in an apparent imitation of Russian revolt. His propositions were called 'Prachandapath'.[4]

After they confronted the military in 2001, they quickly reached the conclusion that they would not be able to achieve military victory. So they took initiatives to ensure a safe landing for their insurgency. The Maoists presented with a political proposal for an all-party conference, and making a new Constitution through the Constituent Assembly as a means of ending the war. They held two rounds of negotiations with the government, but in vain.

The Maoists then began to identify the weaknesses of the international communist movement. Around 2003, they started asking themselves, 'Why did the revolutionary parties around the world that demonstrate earth-shattering bravery and willingly embrace the ultimate sacrifice when fighting the class war against enemies, so easily transform into bureaucratic, revisionist, reactionary forces and become alienated from people in a short period after capturing state power?'[5]

They came up with the answer—that it is because communist regimes lack political competition. The Maoists had reached this conclusion even before they signed the twelve-point understanding with the seven parties. At the central committee meeting of May 2003, they passed a document entitled 'Development of democracy (janabad) in the 21st century', and decided to 'engage in political competition in a political system that is constitutionally bound to be anti-feudalist and anti-imperialist'. It was not easy to change overnight their cadres, who had been fed the communist dream. Therefore, they imposed a condition: that the parties would compete within a system that must be anti-feudalist and anti-imperialist. This decision was a milestone in the transformation of the Maoists. Within three years, they joined the mainstream multiparty system.

The Maoists went a step further at their Chunbang meeting of September 2005. They stated, 'Today's objective reality has overtaken the analyses of imperialism by Lenin and Mao, and several of the norms they put forth regarding the proletarian strategy based on those analyses.'[6] They decided in favour of a Constituent Assembly and democratic republic at this meeting.

In 2008, the Maoists became the largest party following the Constituent Assembly election, and their Chairman Prachanda became the head of the government. That was the point when it became evident that Prachanda was still in two minds. While he continued to back the agenda of a Constituent Assembly, republic and peace process in the public, he also continued to talk to his cadres about a people's republic, power capture and revolution. There was a significant contradiction within his party. Baburam Bhattarai was clear on the idea of landing the revolution through the Constituent Assembly, and engaging in economic transformation. The faction led by Mohan Baidya 'Kiran' treated the Constituent Assembly, democratic republic and peace process merely as a means and not the end of the revolution. They were looking for ways to capture power through any means. Prachanda also wanted to explore this option. But when he found he could no nothing, Prachanda abandoned the path of revolt around 2011. It was only after he reached this conclusion that the peace process (i.e., the dissolution of the PLA) could be completed.

There were also a few immediate reasons behind the Maoists' transformation. For instance, during their first term in government, they made an unsuccessful attempt to remove Army Chief Katawal and restructure the military. They tried to change the geopolitical picture by inviting China as a parallel to India, which contributed to their exit from power. Despite leading the government thrice, they were unable to change the structure of the military, bureaucracy or judiciary. This compelled them to agree to a series of compromises, one after another.

The hard-line faction within the party, led by Kiran, considered this a surrender. Looking from their classical communist point of view, they found Prachanda engaged in a serious digression, and saw their party was moving towards the 'rightist' swamp by following Baburam's line. Prachanda was rich in the political flexibility of making an immediate decision based on an objective analysis. But he was unable to get his whole party behind his decision. Various power centres jumped in to exploit these internal contradictions of the Maoists. In the end, the party split into several groups.

One party was now led by Prachanda and another by Kiran. The Maoist split was not limited to that. Further divisions appeared in both the factions led by Prachanda and Kiran. Netra Bikram Chand 'Biplav', a leader well-liked in the Maoist heartland of Rolpa, walked out from Kiran's party and vowed to traverse the same old path by declaring his intent to capture power through armed revolt. A sizeable section of urban trade union members, and the Maoist workers who had felt cheated, joined his party.

Prachanda shared a similar fate when Baburam Bhattarai deserted him soon after the promulgation of the Constitution by the second Constituent Assembly. In 2016, Baburam formed a party named 'New Force Nepal' by including leaders and cadres from the faction he led in the Maoists plus non-communist personalities. His was a move quite different from earlier splits in that he not only left the party but declared a departure from communist ideology altogether. He seemed to be embracing a leftist-democratic-socialist path. In 2019, Baburam became the convener of Samajbadi Party Nepal after the unification with Upendra Yadav-led Sanghiya Samajbadi Forum. Around the same time, a sizeable section of Kiran's party—its General Secretary Ram Bahadur Thapa 'Badal', Dev Gurung and Pampha Bhusal—as well as other leaders such as Matrika Yadav and Mani Thapa, who had parted ways in the past, came back and re-joined Prachanda's party. These events pointed to the polarization in Maoist politics, in which splits were commonplace and unity rare.

Other events were also not what the Maoists had previously imagined. The party was forced to dismantle its People's Liberation

Army and the first Constituent Assembly was dissolved without promulgating a new Constitution. They had talked of establishing a new national army by merging their PLA into the Nepali Army. But they ended up sending only a few combatants into the army, while packing off the majority with rehab packages. So what did the Maoists get?

Their most important achievement is the manner in which Nepali society accepted their political agenda. Another achievement is the tremendous improvement in the level of political consciousness among the general public. The Maoists helped instil a sense of ethnic identity among indigenous nationalities or Janajatis; the sense of regional identity among Madhesis; and the sense of marginalization among women and Dalits. The Maoists must get the credit for bringing the agendas of republicanism, secularism and federalism into the mainstream discourse. Among these agendas, federalism was announced in the context of the Madhesi uprising while secularism attracted interest from non-Hindu groups.

The most visible achievement of the Maoists, through the people's war and the Constituent Assembly, was the establishment of a republic. Another achievement is the promulgation of a new Constitution through a Constituent Assembly. Although the Nepali Congress had called for a Constituent Assembly back in the 1950s, the credit for bringing this issue back to the centre stage of Nepali politics goes to the Maoists. It is not clear what the future of the Constitution written by the Constituent Assembly is, and how well it will be implemented. But the fact that the political road map of writing a Constitution through elected representatives was made possible only due to the Maoist movement will be registered in history.

Strategic shift

Although there were objective factors present in Nepali society favourable to launching a revolt, the Maoists were able to multiply their strength by sometimes allying with the monarchy against India, and sometimes vice versa. They defined it as playing into contradictions. But they themselves were used by others in the process.

When they started their people's war, the Maoists termed 'domestic reactionaries' and 'Indian expansionism' their principle enemies. The first nine points of the forty-point list of demands, which they presented just before they raised arms, were related to the re-interpretation of Indo-Nepal relations. The Maoists never tried to address these demands when they got the chance, thrice, to lead the government. Neither did they ever accept that those demands were wrong. Instead, through the Hetauda general convention, they declared an end to the 'semi-colonial' state of the country.

In their own words, the Maoists entered into 'undeclared unity in action' with King Birendra on the common agenda of 'nationalism' or India-bashing. This continued till the palace massacre of 2001 and the subsequent mobilization of the military against them. Then the Maoists made a policy decision in favour of a republic, and became aggressive towards the monarchy and the military. They opened institutional contacts with Delhi. The way the Maoists developed contacts and built relations with Indian intelligence agencies, and worked with them against national forces, is certain to draw constant questions in the future. They do not seem to have any satisfactory answers to those questions.

Though they initiated institutional relations with Delhi in 2002, Prachanda then returned to Nepal talking about waging a 'tunnel war' against India, following the arrest there of key Maoist leaders including Gaurav and Kiran. He made an attempt to forge a partnership with the palace. When his attempts failed, and when King Gyanendra seized power, Prachanda decided to side with the parliamentary parties under Indian facilitation. The palace was totally defeated in this phase. Consequently, the Constituent Assembly process took off, and Prachanda headed the government after winning the assembly election. However, when he tried to come out of the Indian encirclement, and tried to develop strategic relations with China, his government was pulled down under various pretexts. For the next two years, Prachanda engaged in an anti-India campaign. But when Prachanda felt double pressure within the party, with the alliance between the 'pro-India' Baburam faction and 'anti-India' Kiran faction, he 'compromised'. As a result, a government was formed under the leadership of Baburam, with support from Madhesi parties. Prachanda had another phase of contention with India when, later in 2015, the new Constitution was promulgated and he joined K.P. Oli's government. But India was pleased when Prachanda built an alliance with the Nepali Congress to dislodge Oli and make his second bid for prime ministership.

Prachanda's relationship with India was based on tactical machinations, going through hot and cold phases. He repeated the weakness of raising nationalist agendas but failing to see them through. His relationship with India was shaped mainly by the internal equation in his party and by national politics. In fact, not only the Maoists, the entire political leadership of Nepal exhibited the same weakness in dragging India into domestic politics.

India already nursed the ambition of playing an active role in Nepal's domestic affairs. The issue of the reduction of external influence, and boosting national capability, became a central concern. However, the Maoists' Hetauda convention took the exactly opposite position. The document it passed portrayed 'feudalists, brokers and comprador capitalists' as the main obstacles to progress, as it tried to close its eyes to the external challenges that had grown considerably when compared to the past.[7]

Before the Hetauda general convention in early 2013, Prachanda had adopted the policy of forging tactical relations with India and strategic relations with China. After the convention, he decided to have close relations with India, while not going too far away from China.

Their conclusion at the Hetauda convention that the Nepali communist movement faces two risks—one from forces that want to turn Marxism into a weapon for class coordination, and another from extremists like the Kiran faction with their mechanical, narrow-minded and dogmatic interpretation of communist ideology—shows where they are headed. They want to wedge their party between those two lines: the space that was captured by the CPN–UML after the 1990 political change. The Maoists took the same path. The party unification with the CPN–UML was the result of that mindset. Will the Maoist movement be seen as successful in history?

It is too early to call. For instance, the Maoists said at their Hetauda convention, 'Will the nationalist and pro-people forces be able to institutionalize the change brought about in the traditional power balance? Or will the status-quoist and reactionary forces from within and outside the country be able to block the change? The final answer to these questions and processes has not come yet.'[8]

27

Unchanged Neighbour

'Within the Asian theatre, no region is more vital for India than South Asia. India cannot hope to arrive as a great power if it is unable to manage relationships within South Asia.'

—'Non-alignment 2.0', a report by a task force
set up to advise on India's foreign and
strategic policy in the twenty-first century[1]

At a press meet held in Kathmandu on 21 October 1992 by the visiting Indian Prime Minister P.V. Narasimha Rao, a journalist from the Kolkata-based magazine *Sunday*, Avirook Sen, asked, 'India is generally perceived as a big brother in the subcontinent. Do you think your visit is trying to change that perception?'

Rao smiled and answered, 'There is no way that I can change my size. Please understand.'[2]

Though he said it in a light-hearted manner, it clarified the Indian perception. In fact, you can neither change your neighbour nor its shape. But the problem arises when your neighbour never comes out of its 'big brotherly' approach, which leads to an unnecessarily high level of interest in your domestic affairs.

Just as the question of why the Maoists sought the backing of a foreign nation in the course of a domestic conflict will continue to be asked, there will also be questions as to why a democratic India encouraged rebels that had raised arms against the democratic system of a neighbouring country. Actually, India finds its 'national interest' much more important than democracy or the maintenance of cordial relations with a neighbour, and this leads India to adopt whichever means are necessary. From sending the army to control Tamil rebels in Sri Lanka, to splitting east Pakistan to establish Bangladesh, from mobilizing its intelligence agency to annex Sikkim, to turning Bhutan into a protectorate—there are several examples of the enforcement of India's adventurous foreign policy in south Asia.

Despite the language used in formal diplomacy, democracy, Constitution-making, or backing any particular individual or party are not India's priority. The main thing is they do whatever is required to safeguard their interest. India once backed the Panchayat regime, then encouraged the people's movement against it. Backing Congress's armed revolt against the party-less Panchayat system, and backing the Maoists' insurgency against the multiparty system, were guided alike by the same Indian strategy. On one hand, they sent mixed signals to King Gyanendra, and on the other, they helped forge an alliance between the Maoists and the seven parties to overthrow the monarchy. At first glance, India's policy toward Nepal appears incoherent. They are seen backing one or the other forces or individuals at different times. It is said there are no permanent foes or friends in international relations. The only thing permanent is national interest. Delhi seems to be following this approach by the book.

Besides, there is no single India. There are many smaller Indias, whose understanding about Nepal are different. The external affairs and home ministries, IB and RAW, the army and the defence ministry, former royals and business houses, provinces bordering Nepal, the PMO and the national security advisor, all have different stakes in Nepal. But at the top is India's 'national interest', which generally brings all of them together. So despite their proximity with different parties and leaders at different times, these actors have not shifted from their main goal. And that goal is not letting smaller neighbours like Nepal drift away from India's sphere of influence.

Nepal has been at the receiving end of this attitude for a long time. Although it was never directly colonized, Nepal fell under the influence of British India after the Sugauli Treaty of 1816. After 1947, India replaced the departing British in that role. India was directly or indirectly linked with all of the important political events of Nepal after 1950. Certainly, the political movements of 1950–51, which ended the Rana regime, the people's movement of 1990 which ended the Panchayat regime, and the movement of 2006 that ended the royal regime of King Gyanendra, were the result of Nepali consciousness. But Delhi's direct or indirect role was also a factor in all of these changes.

However, the changes brought about by these movements have not been durable. Each time, the blame was placed on the political parties, their leaders, and the Constitution at that time. Despite changing Constitution five times in the past sixty years, Nepal did not achieve stability. One of the main reasons was that after every change, Delhi tried to exact its pound of flesh, and, sooner or later, it was construed as Indian interference. Consequently, this resulted in growing internal contradictions, and ultimately dealt a setback to the achievement of the previous movement itself.

Actually, Nepal was never able to proceed independently. It was not allowed to. Neither did the Nepali leaders make honest efforts to abandon the tendency of dependence. Whoever made such efforts found themselves kicked out, under this or that pretext, and was 'black-listed'. Therefore, the Nepali goals of peace, stability and prosperity were never achieved. The country has been trapped in a series of unending political transitions since 1950.

Changed palace

Even during the term of the first prime minister of independent India, Jawaharlal Nehru, there were several instances of India trying to extend its influence in the neighbourhood. However, having championed the cause of independence and democracy, Nehru generally did not encourage anti-democratic steps. When King Mahendra carried out his coup in 1960, Nehru emerged as its fierce critic. India had helped reinstall his father King Tribhuwan on the throne of Nepal. But with Mahendra's step, distance grew between Delhi and the Durbar.

Nehru's successor, Lal Bahadur Shastri (1964–65), did not harbour much animosity towards Mahendra. He travelled to Kathmandu, indicating his desire to improve bilateral relations. He dispatched Shreeman Narayan, a Gandhian leader who was previously general secretary of the Indian National Congress, as the Indian envoy to Nepal. Narayan played a crucial role in bringing Delhi and the Durbar closer.[3]

In the words of the eminent Nepali diplomat, Professor Yadunath Khanal, Lal Bahadur Shastri 'brought bilateral relations, that had been straying, onto the right track'.[4] It was during his tenure that King Mahendra entered into the controversial military pact of 1965 to improve bilateral relations. Relations between the two countries might have developed differently had Shastri continued in office. He died in mysterious circumstances in Tashkent. The emergence of Indira Gandhi coincided with an environment of tension and suspicion in the entire region. The smaller neighbours of India watched with growing alarm how Indira Gandhi helped in the birth of Bangladesh in 1971 and the merger of Sikkim in 1975. The newly formed Research & Analysis Wing (RAW) swiftly extended its influence across the region.[5] 'Security interests' and 'Indian dominance' began to gain a central position in Indian foreign policy. There were even fears that Nepal could be targeted next, after Sikkim. Perhaps due to these apprehensions, the Nepali democratic leader B.P. Koirala, who was launching an armed struggle from Indian soil, returned to Nepal appealing for 'national reconciliation'.[6]

After the assassination of Indira Gandhi, her son Rajeev replaced her in 1984. He adopted an even more aggressive posture towards Nepal. Due to his bitter rivalry with King Birendra, Nepal suffered an economic blockade at Delhi's hands in 1989.[7] The growth of disenchantment built on this foundation quickly led to the first people's movement in Nepal, which overthrew the Panchayat system. During the climax of the people's movement, India's Foreign Secretary S.K. Singh had arrived in Kathmandu with an eighty-three-page draft of an agreement. The Indians gave assurances that the movement would fizzle out if Kathmandu signed the pact. King Birendra did not want to sign an agreement that was likely to undermine his country's independence. Instead, he chose to negotiate with national forces and handed power over to them.[8]

The Durbar's bitterness with the Gandhi family started to dissipate once P.V. Narasimha Rao became the Indian prime minister in 1991. Like Shastri, Rao looked at relations with Nepal from a constructive perspective. On one hand, he started mending ties with the monarchy and, on the other, he thought that smaller neighbours should not be looked at from a security perspective alone.[9] He believed in strengthening economic ties as well. His national priority, too, was economic reforms. Rao's foreign minister, Inder Kumar Gujral, adopted a policy of non-reciprocity in helping neighbours. In 1997, Gujral became prime minister and his policy became widely known as the 'Gujral doctrine'.[10] He did not enjoy a long stint in power, though.

In 1998, when the Hindu nationalist Bharatiya Janata Party, which was said to be close to the Nepali monarchy, came to power and its leader, Atal Behari Vajpayee, became prime minister for six years (he had earlier been elected to the post of prime minister for thirteen days in 1996), Indo-Nepal relations took an unanticipated turn. As Nepal endured a Maoist conflict, Delhi started engagement with the Maoists through its external intelligence agency, the RAW.[11] The RAW built covert relations with the Maoists, because it calculated the strategic gains it could make in the years ahead. In the meantime, Indian Naxalites were drawing encouragement from Nepal's growing Maoist insurgency. India was also feared that the insurgency could spill over from the Nepali hills into the subcontinental plains and destabilize the entire region.[12] It could be managed only through the mainstreaming of Nepali Maoists.

After the ghastly murder of King Birendra's family in the palace massacre of 2001, King Gyanendra sought Delhi's help in expanding his executive powers, first through the removal of Sher Bahadur Deuba in October 2002. But when he carried out a second coup in 2005, he set off a series of events that led to the dissolution of the entire institution of monarchy. Delhi used all its levers to bring the seven parties and the Maoists together to topple the monarchy. Forced on the back foot owing to his several mistakes, King Gyanendra was unable to confront the combined strength of political parties, insurgents and Delhi.

Since Nepali society was advancing rapidly and embracing modern institutions and ideologies such as democracy and progress, the traditional support base of the monarchy was already crumbling. Sooner or later, the institution was bound to transform or go, but the pace picked up with Delhi's active encouragement. Despite all its weaknesses, the monarchy was the pillar of Nepali nationalism and, often, had become an obstacle in Delhi's desire to increase its influence in Nepal.[13] It turned out to be true. Those who used to look up to and 'worship' Narayanhity palace as the final bastion of Nepali power in the past are now found paying the same homage to what they call the 'Delhi durbar'.

Micromanagement

There used to be a time when Indian prime ministers, from Jawaharlal Nehru to Indira Gandhi, looked after Nepal affairs.

They had direct correspondence with Nepali prime ministers and kings.[14] Inder Kumar Gujral and Chandra Shekhar, too, had a direct interest in Nepal. Kathmandu still believes that the whole of Delhi's establishment is watching it. But that, alas, is no longer true.

The previous generation of Nepali leaders, such as B.P. Koirala, Subarna Shumsher Rana, Ganesh Man Singh, Krishna Prasad Bhattarai, Manmohan Adhikari, Mahendra Narayan Nidhi and Girija Prasad Koirala, had respectable access to Delhi's political circles. Girija Prasad Koirala enjoyed cordial relations with Atal Behari Vajpayee, Inder Kumar Gujral, Chandra Shekhar and Lal Krishna Advani. However, the recent generations of Nepali leaders do not have such a luxury. Their relations are limited to the bureaucracy of South Block, the Indian embassy, security officials or, at the most, the National Security Advisor. They either did not want to or could not develop relations at the highest political level. When one has direct contact with leaders, ministers and prime ministers, it gives one a parallel status. It could also help in controlling any mischief by the bureaucracy. Nepali leaders failed to understand this, and it led to the gradual rollback in relations.

Since 2002, the responsibility for formulating and monitoring Nepal policy has been handed over to the prime minister's National Security Advisor. Simply put, this meant that India saw Nepal through a security lens. The regular briefs by RAW and IB help the NSA in building his opinion. A political leader wishes to conduct bilateral relations on the basis of politics and diplomacy. But an intelligence agency does not have such limitations. They put the stress on adventurous and thrilling operations. They are not challenged by any resource constraint. According to a former RAW official, retired Maj. Gen. V.K. Singh, India's finance ministry does know about the budget allocated to RAW, but there is no audit on how the budget is spent.[15]

Some Indian officials are seemingly obsessed that all actors in Nepal accept their 'supremacy' in Nepali affairs. They do not bat an eyelid before 'teaching a lesson' to anyone who does not fall in line. The feeling of hegemony is all too apparent. Piqued at what they saw as 'crossing a red line', the Indians forced Prachanda out of the government, and prevented Girija Prasad Koirala from becoming the first president of republican Nepal.[16] With sixty years of politics behind him, Girija Prasad Koirala would have carried great weight and prestige to the presidency. But the Indians, perhaps, did not want to see strong status and decisiveness in that institution. In 2012, Girija's successor as Nepali Congress party president, Sushil Koirala, was similarly prevented from becoming prime minister. When he did not heed India's direction, Upendra Yadav's Madhesi Janadhikar Forum was split numerous times. The RAW was used to splitting parties that fell out of favour and planting leaders of their choice.[17]

Mainly after 2007, Delhi started to delve into 'micro-management' in every important sector. Not only did it immerse itself in the game of forming and toppling governments, it also started taking a keen interest in who should be appointed where. From attempting to prevent the appointment of a certain person it disliked (Lilamani Poudel in 2012) as chief secretary to lobbying to ensure the appointment of a controversial former chief secretary (Lokman Singh Karki in 2013) as the chief of the anti-corruption watchdog, Indian officials started intervening overtly.[18] Its eyes started twinkling at everything, from the form of federalism to foreign investment from other countries, activities of political parties to internal promotions in the army, police and bureaucracy, and other key appointments. The tendency to check independent decision-making became dominant. The biggest example of this could be seen during the time of the Constitution promulgation by the Constituent Assembly in 2015. When it felt that the Constitution was promulgated against its counsel, India imposed a five-month-long blockade against Nepal.

Pre-2015, the perception among Nepalis that nothing happens here without India's signal ended up being the strongest weapon in Delhi's arsenal, because at the end of the day, diplomacy is as much about perception as it is about reality. In fact, it has already been proved that things do not happen in Nepal just because India or some other foreign country wants them to happen. During the peak of the second people's movement, Delhi's envoy Dr Karan Singh came with an Indian prescription for a deal with the king, but it did not work. Later, Nepal invited the United Nations Mission to Nepal (UNMIN) to monitor the peace process, despite Indian unwillingness. Likewise, the Jhalnath Khanal-led government was formed despite India's attempts to prevent it. There are many other examples. The most remarkable instance is the promulgation of the Constitution against India's wishes. Subsequently, the Maoists–UML unification was forged and K.P. Oli became prime minister despite India attempting to prevent it.

These examples notwithstanding, the story of excessive dependency is true. The major share of the blame must go to the Nepali leadership, who always looked up to Delhi and failed to show their boldness and stature. It is topical here to recall a remark made by one Indian foreign ministry official: 'All the leaders or senior government officials who come here (from Nepal), come with their individual or partisan concerns rather than a national one.'[19]

The penchant for seeking Indian blessings to become a minister, prime minister, or for seeking financial support, or seeking scholarships for kith and kin, has certainly undermined Nepal's integrity. None of the top leaders of any of the major parties is an exception in displaying this propensity. Alarmingly, such a penchant for Delhi's blessings is now being felt even in other organs of the state. Correction is urgent if we are to reduce Nepal's excessive dependence.

Secondly, we must elevate Nepal's relationship with India from the current level of bureaucrats and spies to that of high diplomatic and political leadership. Thirdly, Nepal must be clear about its India policy, and should proceed with reviewing and refining the past agreements and treaties where necessary. Fourthly, the political leadership of Nepal must rise to the occasion, and address the legitimate security concerns of India while not being afraid to cast aside the illegitimate pressures.

Goal

Regarding India's Nepal policy, there are some vital questions that remain unanswered. What does India actually want from Nepal? What type of relationship does it want to maintain? Does it want to turn Nepal into another Sikkim? Or does it want to see Nepal as a dependent state, like Bhutan? Or is it we Nepali people who always see 'conspiracy' behind every legitimate policy action by India?

There definitely is a degree of inferiority complex in Nepal, given our size and the feeling of disrespect. So whenever any issue related to India emerges, we either get unnecessarily sensitive and resort to ultra-nationalist sloganeering, or we become unnecessarily servile. But, in the end, the major reason behind the unending chill in the bilateral relations is not Kathmandu's hot and cold perception, but Delhi's neo-colonialist approach.[20]

Although the approach is hegemonic, it does not appear to be guided by the ancient thinking of usurping territories. That is not possible in the present context of a conscious citizenry and twenty-first century political awareness. Nepal's unique identity, peculiar geopolitical location, and international contacts will not allow such a tragedy to hit this oldest nation-state of the entire south Asian region. So, logically speaking, although Sikkimization may be on somebody's agenda, it is not going to be possible.[21] But the thinking of Bhutanization does appear in some instances. It is pertinent to ponder a comment made by a participant during an interaction with Nepali journalists in Delhi, organized by India's external affairs ministry in April 2013. He had said, 'In terms of mutual assistance and partnership, Bhutan is a role model for India. And, Bhutan is our friendliest neighbour, not Nepal.'[22]

A few years later, India's ruling BJP's leader Bhagat Singh Koshiyari reiterated a similar opinion when he said in July 2016, 'We want to see Nepalis happy like the Bhutanese.'[23] Such frequent utterances from the Indian side do reflect their wish to see Nepal as subservient as Bhutan.

However, in June 2013, there was a fierce reaction in Delhi when Bhutan accepted twenty buses from China as assistance, and gave consent, in principle, to open their embassy in Thimphu. Enraged, Delhi responded by cutting subsidies it had been providing Bhutan on kerosene and cooking gas, and manufactured an environment in which a pro-India party won the subsequent election.[24] Delhi was not amused by Bhutan's attempts at independent diplomacy in recent years. Bhutan was the only country in South Asia with which India did not have any problem, but when Bhutan made even a slight attempt to push the envelope, Delhi saw red.

If we examine the series of political events since 1950, my conclusion is that India wants to see Nepal as just a loyal neighbour or a kind of client state, which follows its diktat without question, does not breach any instruction, supports it in international forums, and plays the role of an ally.

As far as India's other interests are concerned, enjoying preferential access to Nepal's huge water resources is one of them. India is especially concerned about preventing the entry of other countries or their companies in the construction of mega hydropower projects in Nepal. After 2006, a few Indian companies did bag a couple of mega hydro projects. But these companies have not started construction yet, pointing to various hurdles.[25] Experts believe that India is more interested in cementing its dominance in the utilization of water than the development of hydropower in Nepal.[26] They say India sees Nepal's huge water resources as the key to resolving its problem of water scarcity—the thinking being that while energy has other replacement sources, there is no alternative to drinking water. In fact, India needs access to Nepal's water resource to complete its ambitious 'river linking' project. Proposals for constructing high dams in Nepal are also guided by the objective of water use.

Another major Indian interest in Nepal is linked to its security concerns. These are growing, as one can see by the manner in which India has handed over the responsibility for Nepal policy to its National Security Advisor. The periodic outbursts of anti-Indian sentiment, real or perceived Pakistan-sponsored activities inside Nepal, and the growing Chinese footprint in the country are all matters of 'security concern' for India.[27]

One of the major headaches for India is the possibility of the exploitation of Nepali soil by anti-India terrorists. There is an instance of hijacking an Indian plane from Kathmandu. There are also incidents of fake Indian currencies into being brought into India through Nepal. Such incidents are not only against India, but also against Nepal's vital interests. Nobody can be given any concession for such activities. The problem arises when Indian security agencies try to take the initiative themselves, within Nepal, to control such activities, whereas the job should be left to Nepali security bodies. Since these activities mostly take advantage of the open border, perhaps the time has come to regulate the cross-border movement of people using identity cards.

India's greatest concern in Nepal, and all over south Asia, in terms of its strategic, economic and political interests, is the growing presence of China.[28] The second largest economy in the world, China has adopted a policy of maintaining good relations and contacts in the neighbourhood. Besides, given Nepal's contiguous border with its soft underbelly, Tibet, China does have its own concerns in Nepal. Therefore, it is attempting to expand its relations through increasing economic investment, trade and people-to-people contact. This, ultimately, leads to an increase in Chinese influence in Nepal's politics and diplomacy. As it currently enjoys singular dominance on everyday politics and other affairs of Nepal, India is displeased at the possibility of China's entry into its sphere. So the Indians discourage any kind of Chinese investment in Nepal. Instances of such discouragement can be heard regularly from political party leaders, government officials, businessmen and industrialists.[29]

In south Asia, China has had a traditional camaraderie with Pakistan. It is increasing its presence in Sri Lanka, the Maldives, Afghanistan and Bangladesh. It has initiated efforts to establish bilateral diplomatic ties with Bhutan and open an embassy there. One can sympathize with India's concern that Nepal may drift away from its sphere of influence. However, despite those concerns, the fact of the matter is that China is certain to expand its economic diplomacy in the region, given its huge and growing trade with India, its increasing stature in world politics, and the construction of rail and road networks that will link China with trans-Himalayan neighbours like Nepal.

Sino-India relations are moving on parallel tracks of cooperation and competition. However much they cooperate in economic and technical aspects, they compete equally fiercely in security and strategic matters. In 2009, the Indian ministry of defence concluded that China, instead of Pakistan, posed its main security challenge.[30] Therefore, Nepal will need to identify the point to which it can benefit from the Chinese economic empire without hurting India's security concerns. The proposal for a trilateral partnership in the construction of mega infrastructure projects could be one option. Though this proposal is coming from the Chinese side, it might be a win-win formula for India too, as it gives equal space to all.[31]

In the wake of the Indian blockade against Nepal, both the countries appeared to have reached a conclusion that they ought to redefine their relationship. An Eminent Person's Group (EPG) has been formed, with four members each from both sides, to review the 1950 peace and friendship treaty and other bilateral agreements. It prepared a joint report in June 2018.[32] The EPG itself is not a decisive entity, it can only give suggestions to the political leadership. The final decision on changing bilateral pacts rests with the respective governments.

Though Nepal faces tremendous Indian influence, it has never tried to study the internal dimensions of India, identify India's changing priorities, and engage in academic research to shape its India policy accordingly. In comparison, Indian policymakers appear much more focused. There is a system of institutional memory in India. But still, in my opinion, there is also the same predisposition for looking at things from a short-term perspective, jumping the gun, and, sometimes, undermining Nepal's status as an independent country. Perhaps such a tendency has been etched into the mindset of Indian diplomats due to the open border between Nepal and India; the existence of 'special relations' at the people's level; the employment opportunities enjoyed by hundreds of thousands of Nepalis in various parts of India; the excessive economic dependence of Nepal on India; and the periodic attempts by Nepali leaders to seek India's blessings.

In my opinion, the same tendency encourages India to indulge in one experiment after another in Nepal, at the heart of which lies its desire to have a state of 'controlled instability', where no single force is decisive, so that Nepal's dependence on its neighbour persists and it can guide the country where it sees fit. Such a tendency, though not overtly exhibited, can be felt strongly through its attitudes and behaviour. India's role in such diverse events from the Maoist revolt to the Madhesi uprising and during the promulgation of the new Constitution are all guided by the same experimental desire for 'controlled instability'.

Yet the reality is that India itself has not gained much from its all-round interventions, breaching diplomatic frontiers and encroaching into affairs related to politics, bureaucracy, economics and social affairs. Instead, in its attempt to micro-manage Nepal, India is losing its natural soft power dominance in the country, leading to unprecedented levels of anti-India sentiment. For instance, an Indian think tank has expressed its concerns thus: 'The greatest change has to be seen in the behaviour of our diplomats and officials who deal with the officials and people of Nepal on a regular basis.' For that to happen, India must first stop itself from 'micro-managing' Nepal. Otherwise, it will continue to face the consequences, the same report states.[33]

If Delhi, indeed, wants to review its Nepal policy, this is the main point it would need to refine.

Acknowledgements

This book would not have been possible without the Nepali book *Prayogshala*. Therefore, I am grateful to all those who contributed to the birth of *Prayogshala*. I am also grateful to my friend and fellow journalist Sanjaya Dhakal whose role is important in the release of this version. He translated the Nepali piece into English with much enthusiasm. I also received help from another friend and writer, Thomas Bell, during its preliminary editing.

I would also like to thank Ranjana Sengupta and Aditya Mani Jha of Penguin Random House India (PRHI) for the long discussions and feedbacks. I am equally indebted to Meru Gokhale, editor-in-chief of PRHI, and Alkesh Biswal, for showing interest in its publication.

I have received a lot of suggestions and help from friends in the course of publishing this book. I would particularly like to thank my friends Akhilesh Upadhyay, Jugal Bhurtel, Yangesh, Akhanda Bhandari and Kalpana Dhakal for their invaluable input that helped sharpen the presentation and correct my mistakes. Thanks to Niraj Bhari, Ajit Baral and all the FinePrint members.

Likewise, I am grateful for suggestions, advices and help extended by Anand Swaroop Verma, Mumaram Khanal, Hari

474   Acknowledgements

Roka, Sitaram Baral, Jhalak Subedi, Rajendra Dahal, Kanak Mani
Dixit, Bharat Dahal, Prashant Jha, Prashant Aryal, Tula Narayan
Shah, Govinda Neupane and many others. I am grateful to all
those who gave me interviews. I am also thankful to all the sources,
who did not wish to disclose their identity but gave me access to
important information and analysis.

Finally, I cannot forget the encouragement I received from
my mother, sister and brother for writing this book. I am also
truly indebted to my wife Kalpana and son Saumik. I did great
'injustice' to them by using the little time I got after my daily
office work to write this book. But they continued to encourage
me through continuous suggestions and advice.

Notes

Part I: The Beginning

Chapter 1: The Revolt

1. Mao Tse Tung, *Antarbirodh Bare* (Pragati Prakashan, Kathmandu, BS 2047), p. 6. English version is available at www.marxists.org/reference/archive/mao/selected-works/volume-1/mswv1_17.htm.
2. Read more on Prachanda: Deepak Adhikari, 'The Fierce One', *The Caravan*, February 2013, pp. 42–47; Anirban Roy, *Prachanda: The Unknown Revolutionary* (Mandala Book Point, Kathmandu, 2008); and Rajendra Maharjan, ed., *Janayuddhaka Nayak* (Mulyankan Prakashan Griha, Kathmandu, BS 2063).
3. Read about the history of the Nepali communist movement in Dr Surendra KC's books: *Nepalma Communist Andolanko Itihas (first part)* (Vidyarthi Pustak Bhandar, Kathmandu, BS 2056); *Nepalma Communist Andolanko Itihas (second part)* (Vidyarthi Pustak Bhandar, Kathmandu, BS 2060); and *Nepali Communist Andolanko Bigat Ra Bartaman* (Pairavi Prakashan, Kathmandu, BS 2064).
4. Prachanda, *Nepali Krantika Samasyaharu (Part 2)* (CPN–Maoist, Central Publication Department, BS 2057), pp. Kha-Ga (Introduction).

5. Lekhnath Neupane, *Akhil Gyan* (Vision Prakashan, Kathmandu, BS 2063), p. 9.
6. Rajendra Maharjan, ed., op. cit., p. 40.
7. *Nekapa Maobadika Aitihasik Dastawejharu (Part 1)* (CPN–Maoist, Central Publication Department, BS 2054), p. 27.
8. The forty-point demands on 'nationalism', 'democracy' and 'livelihood' became a sort of manifesto for the Maoist movement. They included demands for a new Constitution, end of privileges for the royal family, declaration of secularism, establishment of an ethnic state, revocation of the 1950 Indo-Nepal Treaty, land for the tiller and so on. Of these, thirty demands were such that they could be immediately resolved or, at least, efforts initiated to resolve them.
9. Krishna V. Rajan (Ed.), *The Ambassadors' Club* (Harper Collins Publishers, New Delhi, 2012), pp. 48–49.
10. *'Kehi Jaroori Saiddhantik Ebam Rajnitik Prashna'*, *Maobadi* (ideological mouthpiece of CPN–Maoist) (BS 2053 Magh), p. 5.

* My interviews/conversations with Mohan Bikram Singh, Prachanda, Baburam Bhattarai, Barshaman Pun 'Ananta', Janardan Sharma 'Prabhakar', Netra Bikram Chand 'Biplav', Haribol Gajurel, Narendra Jung Peter and other Maoist leaders.

Chapter 2: Police a Foe, but Army a Friend!

1. Shyam Kumar Tamang, *Janamukti Sena: Euta Nalekhiyeko Itihas* (Ekata Prakashan, Kathmandu, BS 2057), p. 244 and p. 248.
2. Sudheer Sharma, *'Maobadi Gadhma Senako Sakriyata'*, *Himal Khabarpatrika*, July 16–30, 2000, pp. 38–39.
3. Interview with Prachanda, *Nepal Samacharpatra*, April 22, 1999.
4. In formal government records, the campaign was called 'Police Special Mobilization,' but it was better known by its radio codename, 'Operation Kilo Sierra-2'.
5. In 1996, when the 'people's war' started, there were 1968 police posts across the country. Their number had shrunk to 750 by 2005.
6. Nepali Army and Nepal Police have published books tracing their history: Shiva Prasad Sharma, Tulasi Ram Vaidya and Tri Ratna Manandhar, ed., *Nepalko Sainik Itihas* (Royal Nepali Army

Headquarters, BS 2049); Tulasi Ram Vaidya, Tri Ratna Manandhar and Bhadra Ratna Bajracharya, ed., *Nepal Prahariko Itihas* (Police Headquarters, Kathmandu, BS 2052).

7. Interview with Krishna Prasad Bhattarai, *Himalaya Times*, May 22, 1999.

8. Ram Chandra Poudel, '*Maobadile Angaleko Anishtakari Bato*', *Kantipur*, December 5, 2001.

9. '*Abakash Prapta Maharathi Shree Dharmapal Barsingh Thapako Baktabya*', *Antarastriya Manch*, June, 1999.

10. Shiva Gaunle, '*Rajako Chithi*', *Himal Khabarpatrika*, March 14–31, 2000.

11. Bhojraj Bhat, '*Bidrohako Bharat Connection*', *Nepal*, March 10, 2013.

12. There were three preconditions in the letter Prachanda wrote to Home Minister Purna Bahadur Khadka on 25 February 2005: (1) Make the whereabouts of missing citizens, including Dinesh Sharma, public immediately, and start the process of releasing them; (2) Initiate the process of releasing arrested cadres and sympathizers; and (3) Stop state terrorism, investigate the recent grave arson and killings in Rukum by government forces, initiate action against the perpetrators and provide compensation to victims.

13. Interview with Prachanda, *Chhalphal*, June 18, 2000.

14. Durga Subedi, *Biman Bidroha* (Kitab Publishers, Kathmandu, 2018), pp. 242–43.

15. Kishor Nepal, *Mero Samaya* (Fine Print, Kathmandu, 2014), pp. 452–53. Nepal was the press advisor to then Prime Minister Bhattarai.

16. Sudheer Sharma, '*Police Marda Sena Kina Ayena?*', *Himal Khabarpatrika*, October 2–31, 2000.

17. The army had trained 374 policemen on guerrilla warfare, for the first time, at the Police Training Academy in Kakani, Nuwakot, in 1996. Those trainees made up a 'special task force', and it later became known as 'elite force' within the police.

18. Till 1999, the police had 17,000 .303 rifles, 1800 shotguns, 2000 magnum rifles, 5100 pistols, 32,000 revolvers, etc.: altogether 29,000 weapons. Of the total, around 1000 were seized/looted by the Maoists.

19. Nanda Kishor Pun 'Pasang', *Itihaska Raktim Paila* (Sambad Prakashan Abhiyan, Kathmandu, 2064 BS), p. 89.

20. A similar incident had occurred in May 2000. The government obtained an 'intelligence report' that said Maoists were heading towards Panchkatiya of Jajarkot district with donkeys carrying loads of their weapons. The army was requested to provide support to check them, but in vain. Consequently, thirteen policemen, including an inspector, were killed. The forty-seven weapons the insurgents looted from those policemen were used to attack Dunai, the district headquarters of Dolpa, four months later.

21. According to a report by a task force formed to study the violence and terror unleashed by the Maoists and the government, CPN–UML, central office (Kathmandu, BS 2058), p. 9–10, Schedule 2(a).

22. Prime Minister Girija Prasad Koirala had decided to appoint Achyut Krishna Kharel as the ambassador to Myanmar in October 2000, but the king refused to endorse it.

23. Rana had made such comments on 12 April 2001, before the Maoist study task force constituted by the CPN–UML. According to the report by the task force formed to study the violence and terror unleashed by the Maoists and the government, p. 12, Schedule 2(b).

24. On 31 January 2000, the government had formed a seven-member task force headed by former Home Secretary Khemraj Regmi to recommend the formation of the Armed Police Service. The task force came up with a 105-page-long report after two-and-a-half months.

* My interviews/conversations with then Lt Col. Jaga Bahadur Gurung, Lt Gen. (Retd) CB Gurung, IGP (Retd) Achyut Krishna Kharel, Bam Kumari Budha, Girija Prasad Koirala, Durga Subedi, Purna Bahadur Khadka, Mumaram Khanal, Lt Gen. (Retd) Bibek Kumar Shah, army, police and palace officials.

Chapter 3: Royal Cooperation

1. Mohan Bahadur Karki 'Jibanta', *Dhirendra Shah Sanga Rajnitik Sambad*, *Mahima*, June 12, 2008.

2. Interview with Sharad Chandra Shah, *Jana Aastha*, December 17, 1997.

3. Interview with Tej Bikram Shah, *Janadesh*, April 9, 1996.

4. Keshar Jung Rayamajhi, *Kehi Samjhana Kehi Chintan* (Banita Pandey, Kathmandu, BS 2059), p. 49.

5. Jayaraj Acharya, *Yadunath Khanal: Jibani Ra Bichar* (Sajha Prakashan, Lalitpur, BS 2059), p. 61.

6. Interview with Baburam Bhattarai, *Ghatana Ra Bichar*, July 12, 2000.

7. Girija Prasad Koirala himself revealed this in his memoir: G.P. Koirala, *Afnai Kura* (Jagadamba Prakashan, Lalitpur, BS 2067).

8. Baburam Bhattarai, 'Bela Bakhatka Kura', *Janadesh*, February 22, 2000.

9. Sudheer Sharma, 'Jasusiko Jalo', *Himal Khabarpatrika*, June 15–30, 2000, pp. 30–35.

10. Narayan Wagle, 'Bharatiya Chasoko Chabi', *Nagarik*, October 4, 2012.

11. 'Statement of the Indian Minister of State for External Affairs Ajit Kumar Panja in the Lok Sabha on Indo-Nepal ties, as cited in Avatar Singh Bhasin', *Nepal-India, Nepal-China Relations (Part 1)* (Gitika Publishers, New Delhi, 2005), p. 1115.

12. Girija Prasad Koirala, *Afnai Kura* (Jagadamba Prakashan, Lalitpur, BS 2067), p. 154.

13. Interview with Ramesh Nath Pandey, *Janadesh*, August 22, 2001.

14. Interview with Dhirendra Shah, *Ghatana Ra Bichar*, May 31, 2000.

15. Baburam Bhattarai, 'Dhirendra Shahko Bhutle Aatankit Bhayeko Sansad', *Janadesh*, July 18, 2000.

16. Mohan Bahadur Karki 'Jibanta,' op. cit.

17. Ibid.

18. Although the Maoists sympathized with King Birendra during the period of the palace massacre, they changed their analysis subsequently. For example, Baburam wrote, 'It is not true that we would be in favour of continuing the monarchy had King Birendra lived on . . . We would have been compelled to change our analysis at the point where army would have been mobilized and when Indian intervention would have been invited.' See: Baburam Bhattarai, *Barta Ra Tatkalin Rajnitik Nikasko Prashna*, CPN–Maoist, Special Central Command, BS 2059, p. 27.

19. The team included Deputy Prime Minister Ram Chandra Poudel, Defence Minister Mahesh Acharya, Finance Minister Ram Sharan

Mahat, Chief Secretary Tirtha Man Shakya, Army Chief Prajwalla Shumsher Rana, Chief of Armed Police Force Krishna Mohan Shrestha, NID Chief Devi Ram Sharma, Home Secretary Shrikanta Regmi, the defence secretary, the finance secretary and others from the army and the police.

20. Girija Prasad Koirala, op. cit. p. 153.

21. Jaya Prakash Ananda, *Akhtiyarko Thuna, Mero Samjhana*, Madhesi Human Rights Protection Centre, Kathmandu, BS 2061, p. 78.

22. Written statement by Army Chief Prajwalla Shumsher Rana, delivered at the graduation ceremony at Nepali Army Staff College, on April 20, 2001.

23. A report by a task force formed by the CPN–UML to study the violence and the terror unleashed by the Maoists and the government, p. 11, Schedule 2(a).

24. Interview with Girija Prasad Koirala broadcast in the *Dwandako Dashak* programme of the BBC Nepali Service on April 18, 2005. See Suman Kharel, *Radio Yatra*, Fineprint, Kathmandu, BS 2068, p. 59.

* My interviews/conversations with Sharad Chandra Shah, Brig. Gen. (Retd) Dilip Jung Rayamajhi, Lokendra Bahadur Shah, Bibek Kumar Shah, Ramesh Nath Pande, Hari Bhakta Kandel, Prachanda, Krishna Dhwaj Khadka, Bharat Dahal, Dhruba Kumar, Girija Prasad Koirala, Rabindra Shrestha, palace and government officials.

Chapter 4: A 'Coup' That Never Happened

1. Krishna V. Rajan, ed., *The Ambassadors' Club* (Harper Collins Publishers, New Delhi, 2012), pp. 53–54.

2. Girija Prasad Koirala, *Afnai Kura* (Jagadamba Prakashan, Lalitpur, BS 2067), p. 163.

3. Bibek Kumar Shah, *Maile Dekheko Durbar* (Yeti Publications, Kathmandu, BS 2067), pp. 57–58.

4. Ibid.

5. Ten members of royal family, including King Birendra, Queen Aishwarya, Crown Prince Dipendra, Prince Nirajan, Princess Shruti, Dhirendra, Shanti Singh, Sharda, Jayanti and Khadga Bikram Shah were killed in the palace massacre.

6. Girija Prasad Koirala, op. cit. p. 156.
7. Ibid, p. 158.
8. Ibid.
9. Khuman Singh Tamang, 'Rajako Kriyakalaple Durbar Hatyakanda Rahasya Tarfa', Kantipur, February 20, 2004.
10. K. Shankaran Nair, Inside IB and RAW: The Rolling Stone That Gathered Moss (Manas Publications, New Delhi, 2008), p. 169; and V. Raman, The Kao Boys of RAW: Down Memory Lane (Lancer Publishers, New Delhi, 2007), p. 54.
11. Sanjay Upadhya, The Raj Lives: India in Nepal (Vitasta Publishing, New Delhi, 2008), pp. 85–89.
12. Krishna V. Rajan, ed., op. cit., p. 38 and p. 42.
13. Ibid, p. 54.
14. Bibek Kumar Shah, op.cit. p. 53.
15. Ibid.
16. Sudheer Sharma, 'Jasusi ko jalo', Himal Khabarpatrika, June 15–29, 2000, p. 30–35.
17. J.N. Dixit, ed., External Affairs: Cross Border Relations (Roli Books, New Delhi, 2003), p. 99.
18. Interview with former crown prince Paras, The New Paper on Sunday, March 29 and 30, 2009.
19. Wang Chung, Nepal's National Security Strategy and Nepal–China Relations (China Study Centre, Kathmandu, 2005), p. 19.
20. Krishna V. Rajan, ed., op. cit., pp. 59–60.
21. Baburam Bhattarai, 'Naya Kot Parvalai Manyata Dinu Hudaina', Kantipur, June 6, 2001. Then editor of Kantipur daily Yubaraj Ghimire, managing director Kailash Sirohiya and director Binod Gyawali were arrested and a case lodged against them for publishing this article.
22. Baburam Bhattarai, 'Naya Kot Parvalai Manyata Dinu Hudaina', Kantipur, June 6, 2001.
23. Interview with Baburam Bhattarai, Nepali Times, July 13–19, 2001.
24. Wayne Madsen, 'Comparison Between Recent US-Backed Coups', Monthly Review, http://monthlyreview.org/commentary/comparisons-between-recent-u-s-backed-coups, accessed on May 19, 2013.
25. Ibid.

26. Press statement issued by Prachanda, June 11, 2001.
27. Interview with Prachanda, *Janayuddha*, February 2002, p. 6.

* My interviews/conversations with Col. (Retd) Sundar Pratap Rana, Prachanda, Baburam Bhattarai, Bibek Kumar Shah, Mumaram Khanal, Maoist leaders and palace officials.

Part II: The Climax

Chapter 5: Gyanendra on the Throne—War and Jaw

1. Ram Chandra Poudel, *'Ajako Rajneeti Ra Bahudaliya Morchako Awashyakta'*, *Himalaya Times*, June 19, 2001.
2. *'The Aviation Aspect of Holeri Operation'*, an internal report prepared by the Nepali Army, 2001.
3. The letters exchanged by the Nepali Army and the People's Liberation Army were published in the Maoist mouthpiece *Janadesh* on July 22, 2001.
4. Girija Prasad Koirala, *Afnai Kura* (Jagadamba Prakashan, Lalitpur, BS 2067), p. 162.
5. Ibid.
6. Interview with Girija Prasad Koirala, *Kantipur*, April 2, 2006.
7. Sher Bahadur Deuba, *'Girijababuko Abhavma Hami Badhi Jimmewar Hunechhau'*, *Nagarik*, March 24, 2010.
8. Statement issued by CPN–UML, August 20, 2001.
9. Interview with Madhav Kumar Nepal, *Jana Aastha*, September 7, 2005.
10. *'Madhav Nepal Dosro Rayamajhi Banne'*, *Janadesh*, August 28, 2001.
11. *Nepal Communist Party (Maobadi) ka Aitihasik Dastawejharu* (CPN–Maoist, Mechi–Koshi Regional Bureau, BS 2063), pp. 225–26.
12. Ibid.

* My interviews/conversations with Girija Prasad Koirala, Bhesh Bahadur Thapa, Barshaman Pun 'Ananta', Mukti Pradhan, Dilip Jung Rayamajhi, Brig. Gen. (Retd) Deepak Gurung, Krishna Bahadur Mahara, Narayan Kazi Shrestha, Padma Ratna Tuladhar, Ratan Aire,

Sachhit Shumsher Rana, palace officials, army sources and Maoist leaders.

Chapter 6: Indian Abode

1. Avatar Singh Bhasin, *Nepal–India, Nepal–China Relations (Part 1)* (Gitika Publishers, New Delhi, 2005), p. 1186.
2. Prachanda, *'Barga Sangharsha Ra Vidyarthi Aandolan'*, *Yoddha*, BS 2062, Shrawan, p. 31.
3. For example, politburo meetings in Lucknow (December 1996, May and November 1998), Sonepat (June 2001), Jalpaiguri (July 2001), Faridabad (March 1997 and October 2001), Talwada (October 2003), Delhi (standing committee meeting in December 2003), Goa (standing committee meeting in March 2004), Mysore (April 2004). Central committee meetings in Siliguri (June 1996), Faridabad (June 1997), Gurgaon (August 1998), Ropad (August 1999), Jalandhar (December 1999), Jalpaiguri (April 2000), Goa (May 2002). See *Maobadi Bhitra Baicharik-Rajnitik Sangharsha* (Jhilko Prakashan, BS 2068), pp. 18–27.
4. The first serious academic attempt to explore the Indian connection with the Nepali Maoists was made by Rabindra Mishra. See 'India's role in Nepal's Maoist insurgency', *Asian Survey*, September–October 2004, pp. 627–46.
5. For instance, Indian left writer Anand Swaroop Verma had undertaken a month-long 'speaking tour' in January 2006 to fifteen European cities to campaign in favour of the Nepali Maoists. He has also written a book, *Rolpa Se Dolpa Tak*, on Nepali Maoists.
6. Press conference of the Indian external affairs minister, Jaswant Singh, as cited in Avatar Singh Bhasin, *Nepal–India, Nepal–China Relations (Part 1)* (Gitika Publishers, New Delhi, 2005), p. 1024.
7. Interview with Ram Sharan Mahat, then foreign minister, *Gorkhapatra*, September 19, 1999.
8. Achyut Krishna Kharel, *Aatma Katha* (Publication Nepalaya, Kathmandu, 2018), pp. 348–350.
9. Interview with Bhesh Bahadur Thapa, then Nepali ambassador to India, April 25, 2013, Kathmandu.
10. Ibid.
11. Ibid.

12. Ibid.

13. Sharad Adhikari, *'Maobadi durbar ra Bharat bat sangrakchit: Koirala'*, *Kantipur,* August 27, 2001.

14. Ibid.

15. Singh had said, 'Wherever there is terrorism, we oppose it. In Nepal, we openly opposed Maoists. We support the king of Nepal and the Nepal government of Sher Bahadur Deuba. We are with them in their fight against Maoists.' Transcript of press briefing by Jaswant Singh on September 21, 2001, http://www.mea.gov.in/outoging-visit-detail.htm?6280/ Transcript+of+Press+Briefing+by+the+Official+Spokesperson.

16. The force was later renamed 'Sashastra Seema Bal'.

17. The extremist al-Qaeda, led by Osama Bin Laden, killed almost 3000 people by attacking the World Trade Center and the Pentagon in the US on September 11, 2001.

18. S.D. Muni, *Maoist Insurgency in Nepal: The Challenges and the Response* (Rupa, New Delhi, 2003), pp. 56– 57.

19. A written report presented by Director of Military Operations, Major General Kul Bahadur Khadka, before the visiting US Assistant Secretary of State Christina Rocca, on December 17, 2003.

20. Col. Prem Singh Basnyat, *New Paradigm in Global Security: Civil-Military Relations in Nepal* (Bhrikuti Academic Publications, Kathmandu, 2004), p. 149.

21. Statement issued by Kumar Dahal 'Bijaya,' Kathmandu Valley Regional Bureau in-charge of Maoists, November 15, 2002.

22. Nepali Maoists were classified Specially Designated Global Terrorist under Executive Order 13224 and were included in the Terrorism Exclusion List, pursuant to the Immigration and Nationality Act of the United States. They were taken off the list after nine years on September 7, 2012.

23. Sarojraj Adhikari, *Jasusiko Jalo* (Sunita Bhattarai, Kathmandu, BS 2065), pp. 149–68.

24. The London meeting was attended by the joint secretary (north) of the Indian external affairs ministry, Mira Shankar, and the Chinese ambassador to the UK. There were representatives from the UK, the US, Russia, Japan, France, Germany, Norway, Switzerland, Finland, Denmark, Australia, the World Bank,

UNDP and DPA. The five-member Nepali team was led by vice-chairman of the National Planning Commission, Dr Shankar Sharma, and included Rookmangud Katawal, then a major general in the Nepali army.

25. The Indian displeasure was apparent during the opening of a training centre for peacekeeping forces at Panchkhal in Kavre district. In the two-week 'multinational army exercise' held there in January 2000 were army generals from seventeen different countries, including General Denise Blair of the US Pacific Command. But the Indians expressed their displeasure by sending a small team led by two majors.

26. The written statement by Sibal given at the French Institute of International Relations on December 17, 2001, was published in *The Indian Express* on January 3, 2002.

27. Interview with Shyam Saran, *Nepali Times*, March 15–21, 2003.

28. Diplomatic cable sent by US Ambassador Malinowski to the American state department on February 14, 2003, as leaked by Wikileaks, 03KATHMANDU280.

29. Diplomatic cable sent by US Ambassador Moriarty to the state department on September 22, 2006, as leaked by Wikileaks, 06KATHMANDU2587.

30. Pranav Dhal Samant, 'Spy Cooled His Heels in Nepal For One Week, Then Left for US', *Sunday Express*, December 19, 2004; and V. Raman, 'Escape To Nowhere: A Mix of Facts and Fiction', South Asia Analysis Group, paper no. 5137, July 28, 2012, www.southasia-analysis.org/papers52/papers5137.html.

31. *Nepal Communist Party (Maobadi) ka Aitihasik Dastawejharu,* op. cit., p. 272.

* My interviews/conversations with Ram Karki, Bhesh Bahadur Thapa, Ananda Swarup Verma, Achyut Krishna Kharel, Indian diplomats, Nepal government ministers and army sources.

Chapter 7: Midnight at Narayanhity

1. Bibek Kumar Shah, *Maile Dekheko Durbar* (Yeti Publications, Kathmandu, BS 2067), p. 106.

2. This conclusion is based on my interview with Koirala and his political secretary, Puranjan Acharya, April 27, 2013, Kathmandu.

3. Interview with Baburam Bhattarai, *Janadesh*, June 30, 1998.

4. Govinda Neupane, *Nepalma Jatiya Prashna: Samajik Banot Ra Sajhedariko Sambhawana* (Centre for Development Studies, Kathmandu, 2000), p. 152.

5. Girija Prasad Koirala, *Afnai Kura* (Jagadamba Prakashan, Lalitpur, BS 2067).

6. *Jana Pratirodhka Gauravshali Char Saya Dinharu* (CPN–Maoist, Special Central Command, BS 2059), p. 46.

7. Girija Prasad Koirala, op. cit., p. 26.

8. 'Bharatiya Raksha Mantri Fernandesdwara Koirala Ra Maobadibich Bartako Pahal', *Kantipur*, June 8, 2002.

9. Ajith Pillai, 'By George, He's Still An Activist', *Outlook*, April 6, 1998.

10. Interview with Girija Prasad Koirala, April 6, 2004, and July 2005, Kathmandu.

11. Ibid.

12. Ibid.

13. The government had announced a cash prize of NRs. 5 million to anyone handing over, dead or alive, the top three leaders of the Maoists: Prachanda, Baburam and Kiran. Likewise, it announced prizes between NRs. 1 and 3.5 million to anyone handing over other Maoist leaders, according to their importance.

14. Written statement delivered by Army Chief Prajwalla Shumsher Rana at Army Staff College, March 27, 2002.

15. The initial state of emergency imposed for three months from November 26, 2001 onwards, following the Maoist attack on military barracks, was extended by three more months with the permission of the Parliament on February 21, 2002.

16. Bibek Kumar Shah, op. cit., pp. 105–6.

17. Jaya Prakash Anand, *Akhtiyarko Thuna, Mero Samjhana*, Madhesi Human Rights Protection Centre, Kathmandu, BS 2061, pp. 41–42.

18. For more information on Krishna Sen, see Ishwor Prasad Gyawali et al, ed., *Ichhuk Smriti Grantha* (Akhil Nepal Jana Sanskritik Mahasangh, Kathmandu, BS 2065).

* My interviews/conversations with Girija Prasad Koirala, Govinda Neupane, Krishna Khanal, Narahari Acharya, Puranjan Acharya, Mumaram Khanal, Prachanda, Bharat Bhusan, Baburam Bhattarai, Chakra Banstola, Sher Bahadur Deuba, Narayan Kazi Shrestha and palace sources.

Chapter 8: Dual Diplomacy

1. Col. Bijaya Thapa, *'Nepalko Maobadi Andolanko Swarup, Bartaman Abastha Ra Bhabisya'*, *Shivapuri Journal* (mouthpiece of the Nepali Army Command and Staff College, Kathmandu), BS 2060 (Vol. 10), p. 20.
2. As communicated by Rana to US Ambassador Malinowski. See diplomatic cable sent by US embassy to the State Department on July 5, 2002, as leaked by Wikileaks, 02KATHMANDU1216.
3. This description is based on several anonymous sources.
4. See interviews with King Gyanendra, *Nepal Samacharpatra*, August 19, 2001, and *Nepal*, August 18– September 1, 2003, pp. 18–20.
5. Jaya Prakash Anand, *Akhtiyarko Thuna, Mero Samjhana*, Madhesi Human Rights Protection Centre, Kathmandu, BS 2061, p. 113.
6. Article 127 of the Constitution of the Kingdom of Nepal, 1990, stated, 'If any difficulty arises in connection with the implementation of this Constitution, His Majesty may issue necessary Orders to remove such difficulty and such Orders shall be laid before the Parliament'.
7. Maharajkrishna Rasgotra, *A Life in Diplomacy* (Penguin/Viking, New Delhi, 2016), pp. 94–123 and pp. 297–311.
8. Jaya Prakash Anand, op. cit, p. 41.
9. Kishor Shrestha, *Magh-19 ko Mahabharat* (Aastha Prakashan, Kathmandu, BS 2062), pp. 19–20.
10. Press statement issued by Indian embassy, Kathmandu, October 5, 2002.
11. Saurabh Shukla, 'King's Ransom', *India Today*, June 5, 2006.
12. Interview with Prachanda, March 16, 2006, New Delhi and August 24, 2011, Kathmandu.
13. S.D. Muni, *Maoist Insurgency in Nepal: The Challenge and the Response* (Rupa & Co., New Delhi, 2003), pp. 66–67.

14. Interview with Prachanda, March 16, 2006, New Delhi.

15. Interview with S.D. Muni, November 25, 2010, Kathmandu.

16. Baburam Bhattarai, *Monarchy Versus Democracy: The Epic Fight in Nepal* (Samakalin Teesri Duniya, New Delhi, 2005), pp. 165–169.

17. Interview with Prachanda, March 16, 2006, New Delhi.

18. Sebastian von Einsiedel, David Malone and Suman Pradhan, ed., *Nepal in Transition: From People's War to Fragile Peace* (Cambridge University Press, New York, 2002), pp. 321.

19. Prashant Jha, *Battles of the New Republic* (Aleph Book Company, New Delhi, 2014), pp. 89–90.

20. K. Sankaran Nair, *Inside IB and RAW: The Rolling Stone That Gathered Moss* (Manas Publications, New Delhi, 2008), pp. 101–103.

21. Sebastian von Einsiedel, David Malone and Suman Pradhan, ed., *Nepal in Transition: From People's War to Fragile Peace* (Cambridge University Press, New York, 2002), pp. 321.

22. Bibek Kumar Shah, *Maile Dekheko Durbar* (Yeti Publications, Kathmandu, BS 2067), pp. 80–81.

23. For example, see Rohan Gunaratna, *Indian Intervention in Sri Lanka: The Role of India's Intelligence Agencies* (South Asian Network on Conflict Research, Colombo, 1994), p. 39.

24. Diplomatic cable sent by US Ambassador Malinowski to the state department on December 4, 2003, as leaked by Wikileaks, 03KATHMANDU2366.

25. Girija Prasad Koirala, *Afnai Kura* (Jagadamba Prakashan, Lalitpur, BS 2067), pp. 104–5.

26. Diplomatic cable sent by US Ambassador Malinowski to the state department on December 4, 2003, as leaked by Wikileaks, 03KATHMANDU2366.

27. This recorded conversation is compiled in a book. See, Avatar Singh Bhasin, *Nepal-India, Nepal–China Relations (Part 1)* (Gitika Publishers, New Delhi, 2005), pp. 1141–42.

* My interviews/conversations with Sher Bahadur Deuba, Bhesh Bahadur Thapa, Baburam Bhattarai, Prachanda, S.D. Muni, Indian officials and Maoist leaders.

Chapter 9: No Meeting with the King

1. Ganesh Raj Sharma, compiled by, *BP Koiralako Atmabrittanta* (Jagadamba Prakashan, Lalitpur, BS 2055), p. 305.
2. Interview with Mumaram Khanal, November 6, 2012, Lalitpur.
3. Sudheer Sharma, 'Barta Ra Shantiko Bhabisya', *Mulyankan*, March 2003.
4. In order to assist the negotiator Pun, a group was formed in March 2003 that included the former army chief, Dharmapal Barsingh Thapa, the former police chief, Dhruba Bahadur Pradhan, the former chief secretary, Karna Dhwaj Adhikari and advocate Bal Krishna Neupane.
5. The preconditions of the Maoists were: (1) To limit the movement of the Royal Nepali Army to within 5 km of barracks, to release central leaders of the Maoists, to make public the whereabouts of those disappeared and to implement decisions made in the second phase; (2) The king should either directly take part in negotiations, or should publicly state that the government negotiating team is fully empowered; (3) The Royal Nepali Army should publicly state its willingness to abide by the code of conduct and to implement decisions reached by the negotiating teams; (4) Revoke the counter-terrorism agreement with the United States and remove American military advisors from the country; and (5) The Government should make public its agenda for a forward-looking political resolution.
6. See this for the report by the National Human Rights Commission on the Doramba killings: www.nhrcnepal.org/nhrc_new/doc/newsletter/Reprot_Doramba_R.pdf, accessed on June 4, 2013.
7. There was continuous tension between the Maoists and the army in the course of the seven-month-long truce. The twenty-two-point code of conduct was limited to paper. There were fifty incidents of ambush, clashes, killings and explosions in which eighty-three people lost their lives. Of these, fifty were killed at the hands of the security forces and thirty-three at the hands of the Maoists.
8. Baburam Bhattarai, 'Naya Kot Parvalai Manyata Dinu Hudaina', *Kantipur*, June 6, 2001.
9. Bibek Kumar Shah, *Maile Dekheko Durbar* (Yeti Publications, Kathmandu, BS 2067), p. 114.
10. Interview with Shyam Saran, *Kantipur*, June 11, 2003.

11. Jit Man Basnet, *258 Dark Days* (Advocacy Forum, Kathmandu/ Asian Human Rights Commission, Hong Kong, 2007), p.30–31.

* My interviews/conversations with Prachanda, Baburam Bhattarai, Lokendra Bahadur Chand, Kamal Thapa, Ramesh Nath Pande, Bibek Kumar Shah, Narayan Singh Pun, Krishna Bahadur Mahara, Padma Ratna Tuladhar, Mumaram Khanal and palace officials.

Chapter 10: Startling Raids

1. Anil Sharma, *Samjhanama Bharatiya Jail* (Vision Publications, Kathmandu, BS 2065), p. 36.
2. The minister was not the well-known Congress leader Digvijay Singh, but a leader of the Samata Party elected from Bihar who goes by the same name. See Avatar Singh Bhasin, *Nepal-India, Nepal-China Relations (Part 1)* (Gitika Publishers, New Delhi, 2005), pp. 1177–78.
3. They were arrested on the information leaked by one of their district leaders when they were heading from Siliguri via Janakpur–Jayanagar to Sindhuli to attend training for the eastern command by Kiran.
4. Sitaram Baral, *Ram Raja Prasad Singh: Ganatantraka Lagi Sangharsha* (Pragya Foundation/Ultimate Marketing, Kathmandu, BS 2066), pp. 237–39.
5. Kiran, 'Party Kunai Halatma Nafutaunu Hola', *Naya Patrika*, August 10, 2011.
6. Bhattarai says that in his capacity as chief of the party's foreign department, he made every possible diplomatic and other effort to have Kiran and Gaurav released. See statement issued by Baburam Bhattarai, May 24, 2005.
7. Anil Sharma, op. cit., p. 39.
8. 'PM's Speech at the Chief Ministers' Meet on Naxalism', April 13, 2006, http://pmindia.gov.in/speech-details.php?nodeid=302, accessed on December 23, 2012.
9. According to the Union Home Ministry of India, in 2002, there were 1465 Naxalism-related incidents, 138 per cent more than in the previous year. Around 623 people were killed, including those from the police, the Maoists and the general public. In 2003, there

were 1597 such incidents in which 731 were killed. These numbers went on increasing.

10. The People's War group had been formed in 1980 by Kondapalli Seetharamaiah of Andhra Pradesh. The MCC had been formed in 1975 by a group led by Amulya Sen and Kanhai Chatterjee. See Abhaya Kumar Dubey, *Krantika Atmasangharsha: Naxalbadi Andolanka Badalte Chehreka Adhyayan* (Vinay Prakashan, Delhi, 1994), pp. 201–3.

11. There were nine founding parties of CCOMPOSA: People's War group, MCC, Revolutionary Communist Centre of India (Maoist), Revolutionary Communist Centre of India (MLM), Bangladesh Communist Party (ML), Purvo Bangla Sarbahara Party (CC), Purvo Bangla Sarbahara Party (MPK), Ceylon Communist Party (Maoists), and CPN–Maoists. Later, the Bhutan Communist Party (Marxist–Leninist–Maoist) also joined the network.

12. Annual Report 2004–05 of the Indian Home Ministry, p. 43. See http://mha.nic.in/sites/upload_files/mha/files/pdf/ar0405-Eng.pdf.

13. The Maoists had good contacts with the group of Kanu Sanyal, known as the number two leader, after Charu Mazumdar, in the Naxalite movement. He had severely criticized the arrest of Kiran. Born in Kurseong, Sanyal had good relations with the Nepali community. His chief aide, Krishna Bhakta Poudel of Kalimpong, was the first Naxalite to travel to China via Nepal. See Keshav Pradhan, *'Samyabadi Biruddha Samyabadi'*, *Samay*, June 24, 2004, p. 23.

14. The slogan of Nepali identity had been raised in Darjeeling since 1947. When India achieved independence, communist leaders of the region, such as Ratan Lal Brahmin and Ganesh Lal Subba, had demanded that a separate 'Gorkhastan' nation be established by merging Darjeeling, Sikkim and Nepal, and that demand had been endorsed by the Indian Communist Party (CPI). Delhi gets agitated whenever similar sounding slogans of 'Greater Nepal' are raised.

15. Rajendra Maharjan, ed., *Janayuddha ka Nayak* (Mulyankan Prakashan Griha, Kathmandu, BS 2063), p. 41.

16. The organization formed on November 3, 2001, under the coordination of Indian journalist Anand Swaroop Verma, which was hardly active, was represented by Krishna Sen from Nepal. See

Sudheer Sharma, *'Deep Red in the Heartland'*, *Himal South Asian*, January, 2002, p. 35.

17. 'In the smuggling route, East is best', *The Times of India*, September 7, 2003, https://timesofindia.indiatimes.com/city/kolkata/In-the-smuggling-route-East-is-best/articleshow/170111.cms.

* My interviews/conversations with C.P. Gajurel, Bamdev Chhetry, Upendra Yadav, Mohan Baidhya 'Kiran', Ram Karki, Barshaman Pun 'Ananta', Prachanda, Dilip Jung Rayamajhi, Devi Ram Sharma, intelligence sources and army officials.

Chapter 11: Struggle between the Comrades

1. Amit Dhakal/Kiran Bhandari, *'Hisilale Prachandalai Aunlyaudai Bhanin – Yiniharule Sidhyaune Bhaye'*, www.setopati.com/blog/350/ accessed on April 24, 2013.

2. Narayan Sharma, *'Shikchhak Hudai Patrakaritabata Netritwa Samma'*, *Pahal*, May 6, 2007.

3. Statement issued by Maoist central committee, September 1, 2004.

4. *'Adhyakchya Prachandale Pahilo Patak Sarbajanik Rupma Garnu Bhayako Sambodhan'*, *Udgam*, April–July 2005, p. 6.

5. Interview with Prachanda, *Janadesh*, August 21, 2004.

6. Sachin Roka, *'Nepalma Sambhavit Bharatiya Hastachhep: Maobadi Tayari, Yasko Asar Ra Parinam'*, *Janadesh*, November 3, 2004.

7. Aditi Phadnis, 'India Plans Air Supplies To Nepal', *Business Standard*, August 22, 2004.

8. Sachin Roka, op. cit.

9. Ibid.

10. Ibid.

11. *Maobadi Bhitra Baicharik-Rajnitik Sangharsha* (Jhilko Prakashan, Kathmandu, BS 2068), p. 27.

12. Baburam Bhattarai, *Rajnitik Arthashastrako Ankhijhyalbata* (Utprerak Prakashan, Kathmandu, BS 2055), pp. 26–29.

13. Baburam Bhattarai, *'Naya Sansad Ra Sikkimikaranko Khatara'*, *Kantipur*, June 25, 1999.

14. Baburam Bhattarai, *'Naya Panchayatko Ek Barsha'*, *Janadesh*, October 28, 2003.

15. The thirteen-point *'Antarparty Chhalfalka Mulbhut Bishayaharu'* presented on November 30, 2004, by Baburam Bhattarai to the party leadership.
16. Ibid.
17. *Maobadi Bhitra Baicharik-Rajnitik Sangharsha*, p. 2.
18. Baburam Bhattarai's thirteen-point proposal.
19. Out of fifteen full members of the politburo, the majority of ten included Prachanda, Badal, Diwakar, Mahara, Ananta, Biplav, Dev Gurung, Agni Sapkota, Hitman Shakya and Rabindra Shrestha, whereas the minority of four included Baburam Bhattarai, Dinanath Sharma, Hisila Yami and Mani Thapa. Haribol Gajurel stood neutral.
20. Shubha Shankar Kandel, *Maobadi: Bidroha, Bibad Ra Rupantaran* (Pairavi Prakashan, Kathmandu, BS 2067), pp. 127–28.
21. See Baburam Bhattarai, *'Atma Samarpan Garne Dharko Aguwa Hoina, Ma'*, *Samay*, January 6, 2005, p. 9 and Baburam Bhattarai, *'Raja Rajauta Prabritti Ra Loktantra'*, *Kantipur*, January 19, 2005.
22. Subas Devkota, *'Swabhabai Janda'*, *Himal Khabarpatrika*, January 29–February 11, 2013, p. 30.

* My interviews/conversations with Prachanda, Barshaman Pun 'Ananta', Baburam Bhattarai, Dinanath Sharma and Maoist leaders.

Chapter 12: The Royalist Turn

1. An excerpt from a three-page-long letter written by Maoist politburo member Matrika Yadav, on February 12, 2004, from the detention camp of Yuddha Bhairav Gana, Shivapuri. The letter was addressed to King Gyanendra, seeking a meeting.
2. Dinanath Sharma, *Jiban Yatra Ra Jiban* (Sajha Prakashan, Lalitpur, BS 2066), pp. 54–55.
3. Ibid, p. 56.
4. *Pratikrantikari Bhagauda Prabritti Biruddha Sangharsha*, Janadisha Prakashan, p. 44.
5. Ram Karki, *'Antarsangharshako Sansmaran'*, *Naya Patrika*, March 22, 2011.
6. Sudheer Sharma, *'Baburamko Bisthapan'*, *Nepal*, March 20–27, 2005, pp. 24–26.

7. Statement issued by Baburam Bhattarai and Hisila Yami, March 24, 2005.

8. Baburam Bhattarai, 'Krantikari Andolan Ra Netritwako Prashna', Kantipur, August 27, 1999.

9. For further information on Alok, see Arun Baral, Alok: Shahid Ki Gaddar? (Pragyan Prakashan, Kathmandu, BS 2064).

10. Baburam Bhattarai, 'Pheri Ekpatak Netritwakai Kura', Janadesh, June 13, 2000.

11. The political and organizational proposal presented by Prachanda and endorsed by the central committee of CPN–Maoist, October 2005, p. 8.

12. Ibid.

13. Interview with Prakash Dahal, Profile, January 2007, p. 22.

14. Interview with Prachanda, March 16, 2006, New Delhi.

15. Statement issued by Prachanda, May 26, 2005.

16. Interview with Prachanda, Janadesh, June 21, 2005.

17. Interview with Ananta, Janadesh, June 28, 2005.

18. Prachanda's address to the meeting of the United Revolutionary People's Council, Naya Disabodh, November 2005, p. 3.

* My interviews/conversations with Matrika Yadav, Mumaram Khanal, Baburam Bhattarai, Prachanda, Devi Ram Sharma, Pradeep Giri, Durga Subedi, army officials and palace sources.

Chapter 13: Decisive Drift

1. Rabindra Mishra, Bhumadhyarekha (Fine Print, Kathmandu, BS 2067), p. 116.

2. Avatar Singh Bhasin, Nepal-India, Nepal–China Relations (Part 1) (Gitika Publishers, New Delhi, 2005), p. 1260.

3. Statement issued by Indian external affairs ministry, New Delhi, February 1, 2005.

4. Avatar Singh Bhasin, Nepal-India, Nepal-China Relations (Part 1) (Gitika Publishers, New Delhi, 2005), p. 1268.

5. Surendra Phuyal, 'Bharat, America ra belayatdwara Thap Chaso', Kantipur, March 17, 2005.

6. Khim Ghale, *'Sahayata Roknu Durbhagyapurna'*, *Kantipur*, February 24, 2005.

7. Ramesh Nath Pandey, *Kutniti ra Rajniti* (Sangrila Books, Kathmandu, BS 2072), p. 553.

8. *'Shree Panch Tatha Pakistani PM Bich Telephone Barta'*, *Gorkhapatra*, February 9, 2005.

9. These passages are based on some anonymous sources.

10. Interview with Prabhakar Shumsher Rana, *Himal*, September 1–16, 2005, p. 53.

11. Narayan Wagle, *'Shantiko Karyasuchima Nepal Prabesh'*, *Kantipur*, February 25, 2005.

12. *'Chiniya Sahayog Ramro Lakchhyan Hoina'*, *Rajdhani*, October 27, 2005.

13. *'Afna Samasya Samadhan Garna Nepal Sakchhyam: Chiniya Rajdoot'*, *Kantipur*, April 7, 2005.

14. Roshan Thapa, *'Sinocitis'*, *Outlook*, December 12, 2005, p. 58.

15. *'Chinabata Hatiyar Payekoma Bharatko Chinta'*, *Kantipur*, December 21, 2005.

* Interviews/conversations with Minendra Rijal, Ramesh Nath Pande, palace sources and Indian officials.

Chapter 14: Delhi Agreement–II

1. Leo E. Rose, *Nepal: Strategy for Survival* (Mandala Book Point, Kathmandu, 2010), p. 194.

2. Kishor Shrestha, *Magh-19 ko Mahabharat* (Aastha Prakashan, Kathmandu, BS 2062), pp. 42–44.

3. Surendra Phuyal, *'Why Nepal's leaders prefer Indian Docs?'*, rediff.com, June 24, 2005, http://www.rediff.com/news/2005/jun/24spec.htm.

4. Interview with Prachanda, August 24, 2011, Kathmandu.

5. Subas Devkota, *Shantibarta Antarkatha* (Yugantar Prakashan, Kathmandu, BS 2064), pp. 84–87.

6. Ibid.

7. Ibid.

8. Narahari Acharya, *Nepalko Rajsanstha* (Sambatsar Prakashan, Kathmandu, BS 2062).

9. *Nepal Communist Party (Maobadi) Ka Aitihasik Dastawejharu* (CPN–Maoist, Mechi–Koshi regional bureau, BS 2063), p. 309.

10. Netra Panthi, *Maobadibhitra Antarsangharsha* (Bishwa Nepali Publications, Kathmandu, BS 2069), pp. 177–79.

11. Ibid, pp. 186–87.

12. Anil Thapa, *Abiram Baburam* (Sangrila Books, Kathmandu, BS 2073), p. 161.

13. *Nepal Communist Party (Maobadi) Ka Aitihasik Dastawejharu*, p. 312.

14. Prachanda, *Nepali Krantika Samasyaharu (Part 4)* (Bibek Sirjanshil Prakashan, Kathmandu, BS 2064), p. 61.

15. Interview with Amaresh Kumar Singh, who had assisted Koirala in New Delhi, May 6, 2006, Kathmandu.

16. Interview with Narayan Kaji Shrestha 'Prakash', September 14, 2012, Lalitpur. Also see, Subas Devkota, *Shantibarta Antarkatha* (Yugantar Prakashan, Kathmandu, BS 2064), pp. 108–9.

17. The twelve-point understanding was signed by Prachanda on behalf of the Maoists, and Girija Prasad Koirala (NC), Madhav Kumar Nepal (UML), Sher Bahadur Deuba (NC–Democratic), Amik Sherchan (People's Front), Bharat Bimal Yadav (NSP), Krishna Das Shrestha (Leftist Front), and Prem Suwal (Nepal Workers and Peasants Party) on behalf of the seven parties.

18. Rajesh Gautam, *Nepalka Prajatantraka Prabartak Rastrapita Shree Panch Tribhuwan* (Department of Printing and Publications, Kathmandu, BS 2045), p. 63–64.

19. The tenth point of the forty-point demands put forth by the Maoists stated, 'New Constitution should be written by selected people's representatives in order to establish people's republic.' It did not expressly mention a Constituent Assembly.

* My interviews/conversations with Girija Prasad Koirala, Sher Bahadur Deuba, Amaresh Kumar Singh, Prachanda, Baburam Bhattarai, Barshaman Pun 'Ananta', Narayan Kazi Shrestha, Krishna Prasad Sitaula, palace insiders and Indian sources.

Chapter 15: Seen and Unseen Actors

1. V.K. Singh, *India's External Intelligence: Secrets of Research and Analysis Wing* (Manas Publications, New Delhi, 2007), p. 12.

2. Sebastian von Einsiedel, David Malone and Suman Pradhan, ed., *Nepal in Transition: From People's War to Fragile Peace* (Cambridge University Press, New York, 2002), p. 327.

3. Ibid.

4. P.K. Hormis Tharakan, 'Best of All Uncertainties', *The Indian Express*, April 22, 2008).

5. Avatar Singh Bhasin, *Nepal-India, Nepal-China Relations (Part 1)* Gitika Publishers, New Delhi, 2005, p. 1226.

6. 'Parties' Concern Over Nepal Situation', *The Hindu*, August 4, 2005.

7. Interview with Indian Ambassador Mukherjee, *Kantipur Television*, aired on January 8, 2006.

8. Deepak Adhikari, *'Kina Aye Saran?'*, *Nepal*, December 25, 2005, pp. 28–29.

9. Interview with Shyam Saran, *Kantipur*, January 15, 2013.

10. Vice-chairman of the council of ministers, Kirti Nidhi Bista, had said, 'S.D. Muni makes mean and tactless remarks against His Majesty. Is it proper for the Indian government to turn a blind eye towards it?' See *'Shree Panch Biruddha Ashista Tippani Garne Bharatiya Biruddha Ankha Nachimlina Ahwan'*, *Gorkhapatra*, May 25, 2005.

11. S.D. Muni, *Maoist Insurgency in Nepal: The Challenge and Response* (Rupa & Co., New Delhi, 2003), pp. 66–67.

12. In the 2004 general election, sixty-five leftist members were elected out of total 545-member Lok Sabha of India. Forty-three seats were won by the CPI(M). It was the largest number of seats won by the leftist parties since the independence of India.

13. 'King Gyanendra Will Be Last Monarch In Nepal: Karat', *Hindustan Times*, September 5, 2005.

14. Interview with D.P. Tripathi, *rediff.com*, July 10, 2006, http://in.rediff.com/news/2006/jul/10inter1.htm.

15. Akshay Mukul, 'Indian Spies Host Nepal's Top Maoists', *The Times of India*, May 26, 2005.

16. Interview with Ashok Mehta, *BBC Nepali Service*, May 24, 2005.

17. *Nepal Communist Party (Maobadi) Ka Aitihasik Dastawejharu* (CPN–Maoist, Mechi–Koshi regional bureau, BS 2063), p. 271.

18. Interview with Rabindra Shrestha, *Drishti*, September 12, 2006.

19. Interview with Jayanta Prasad, *Nagarik*, May 24, 2013.

20. Sebastian von Einsiedel, David Malone and Suman Pradhan, ed., op. cit., p. 328.

21. Ibid.
22. J.K. Sinha, op. cit.
23. Interview with Pranab Mukherjee, *Al Jazeera*, aired on January 28, 2009, www.english.aljazeera.net/news/asia/2009/01/200912718176587252.html accessed on December 25, 2011.
24. Ashok Raina, *Inside RAW: The Story of India's Secret Service* (Vikas Publishing House, New Delhi, 1981), p. 68.

* My interviews/conversations with Prakash Karat, P.K. Hormis Tharakan, D.P. Tripathy, Prachanda, Baburam Bhattarai, Girija Prasad Koirala, S.D. Muni, Amaresh Kumar Singh and Indian officials.

Chapter 16: Spring Revolt

1. International Crisis Group, *Nepal: From People Power To Peace?*, May 10, 2006, Kathmandu/Brussels, p. 2.
2. The other three deputy commanders included Barshaman Pun 'Ananta', Nanda Kishor Pun 'Pasang' and Chakrapani Khanal 'Baldev'.
3. Pyar Jung Thapa, *'Hamile Madhavjilai Pradhanmantri Bhanyau, Shyam Saranle Girija Prasad'*, www.setopati.com/raajneeti/373/ accessed on April 25, 2013.
4. Ibid.
5. Statement issued by Indian external affairs ministry, April 22, 2006.
6. 'India cannot afford to see Nepal becoming a failed state: PM', www.hindustantimes.com/news/181_1681168,001300980002.htm, accessed on April 24, 2006.
7. Ibid.
8. Pyar Jung Thapa, op. cit.
9. Shyam Saran, *How India Sees the World* (Juggernaut Books, New Delhi, 2017), pp. 159–60.
10. Ibid.
11. *'Shantima Sabai Swikarya'*, *Kantipur*, April 27, 2006.
12. *'Damanma Afno Ra Senako Kunai Bhumika Naraheko Dabi'*, *Gorkhapatra*, August 4, 2006.
13. 'Delhi Twice Shy On Nepal,' *The Telegraph*, April 26, 2006.
14. Jagat Nepal, *'2063 Baisakh 11: Ek Dinko Katha'*, *Kantipur*, April 24, 2015.

15. Interview with former minister Radhakrishna Mainali, *BBC Nepali Service*, January 21, 2008.
16. *'America Sambidhansabha Prati Ashabadi'*, *Kantipur*, April 28, 2006.
17. Prachanda, *'Bartaman Janasangharsha Bare Kehi Kura'*, *Janadesh*, May 2, 2006.
18. Girija Prasad Koirala, *Afnai Kura* (Jagadamba Prakashan, Lalitpur, BS 2067), p. 149.

* My interviews/conversations with Netra Bikram Chand 'Biplav', Janardan Sharma 'Prabhakar', Barshaman Pun 'Ananta', Prachanda, Baburam Bhattarai, Girija Prasad Koirala and palace insiders.

Chapter 17: Treacherous Transition

1. Interview with Girija Prasad Koirala, *Nepal*, December 9, 2007, pp. 14–15.
2. *'Itihasko Naya Adhyaya Koriyeko Chha'*, *Janadesh*, June 6, 2006.
3. The first document clipping the wings of British monarchy, issued in 1215, is known as the Magna Carta or 'The Great Chapter of the Liberties of England'.
4. *'Pradhanmantri-Pradhansenapati Bartalap'*, *Agenda*, May 24, 2006.
5. *'Itihasko Naya Adhyaya Koriyeko Chha,'* op. cit.
6. *Nepal Communist Party (Maobadi) Ka Aitihasik Dastawejharu* (CPN–Maoist, Mechi–Koshi regional bureau, BS 2063), p. 332.
7. Saroj Raj Adhikari, *Jasusiko Jalo* (Sunita Bhattarai, Kathmandu, 2008), pp. 53–54.
8. In the deal signed on November 8, 2006, the UML had inserted a note of dissent stating that it favoured holding a referendum to decide on the monarchy, and the implementation of fully proportional representation system for the election of a Constituent Assembly.
9. S.D. Muni, *India's Foreign Policy: The Democracy Dimension* (Foundation Books, New Delhi, 2009), p. 95.
10. UN Secretary General Kofi Annan had mentioned in the annual report he presented to the General Assembly in 2002 that the UN could support the exploration of a peaceful resolution to the Nepal conflict.
11. The weapons registered by the UNMIN included ninety-one mortars, sixty-one machine guns, 2403 rifles, sixty-one automatic

weapons, 114 side arms, 212 shot guns, 253 miscellaneous items, and 233 country-made weapons.

12. *'ISI ko Sahayog Aswikar Garyau'*, *Kantipur*, November 20, 2006.

13. Interview with Nirmala Deshpande, www.headlinesindia.com, accessed on April 16, 2008. She passed away in New Delhi on May 1, 2008, at the age of seventy-nine when she was preparing to visit Kathmandu at Prachanda's invitation.

14. Biplav, *'Naya Karyanitilai Dridhtapurbak Karyanwayan Garau'*, *Janadesh*, April 17, 2007.

15. Diplomatic cable sent by US Ambassador Moriarty to the State Department on June 18, 2007, as leaked by Wikileaks, 07KATHMANDU1197.

16. *'Naya Baicharik Spashtata Ra Naya Krantikari Andolan Srishti Garna Ekjut Haun'*, the political report presented by Prachanda at the fifth plenum of the central committee of CPN–Maoist, held at Balaju, Kathmandu, July, 2007, p. 8.

17. *'Maobadi Sarkarbata Hatyo'*, *Kantipur*, September 19, 2007.

18. Interview with Prachanda, *Janadesh*, December 18, 2007.

19. Rookmangud Katawal, *My Story* (Publication Nepalaya, Kathmandu, 2016).

20. Prachanda, *'Karyadisha ra Karyayojana Bare Prastab'*, *Nagarik online*, September 12, 2010, http://www.nagariknews.com/maoist-dastabed.html.

21. Kiran Bhandari/Yubaraj Ghimire, *'Sambidhansabha Bhanddai Rajasanga Milera Satta Hatyauna Chahanthe Prachanda-Baburam'*, www.setopati.com/raajneeti/650/, accessed on May 9, 2013.

22. Saroj Raj Adhikari, *Jasusiko Jalo* (Sunita Bhattarai, Kathmandu, 2008), pp. 56–58.

23. Ibid.

* My interviews/conversations with Prachanda, Girija Prasad Koirala, Baburam Bhattarai and Maoist leaders.

Chapter 18: Madhes Explodes

1. Pradeep Giri, *Nepali Congress, Maobad Ra Madhes* (Vidyarthi Pustak Bhandar, Kathmandu, BS 2066), p. 170.

2. Frederick H. Gaige, *Regionalism and National Unity in Nepal* (Himal Books, Lalitpur, 2009), p. 193.

3. There are twenty districts in the Tarai region: Jhapa, Morang, Sunsari, Saptari, Siraha, Dhanusha, Mahottari, Sarlahi, Rautahat, Bara, Parsa, Chitwan, Nawalparasi, Rupandehi, Kapilvastu, Dang, Banke, Bardiya, Kailali and Kanchanpur.

4. For various dimensions of Madhes discontent, see Basant Thapa and Mohan Mainali, ed., *Madhes: Samasya Ra Samadhan* (Social Science Baha, Lalitpur, 2006).

5. Govinda Neupane, *Nepali Samajko Rupantaran* (Center for Development Studies, Kathmandu, 2001), p. 21.

6. In the general elections of 1991, 1994 and 1999, NSP won six, three and five seats, respectively.

7. *Nepal Communist Party Maobadika Aitihasik Dastawejharu* (Central Department of Publication, CPN–Maoist, BS 2054), p. 58.

8. The remaining eight autonomous provinces included Seti–Mahakali, Bheri–Karnali, Tharuwan, Magarat, Tamuwan, Tamsaling, Newa and Kirat. See Statute of United Revolutionary People's Council, Nepal, central ad hoc committee, BS 2058, pp. 14–15.

9. Baburam Bhattarai, *'Madhesi Prashnalai Herne Dristikon Bare'*, *Lal Madhes*, February 2006, p. 10.

10. Maoist leader Ajab Lal Yadav was killed on March 22, 2002 in Saptari; Sherman Kunwar and Mohan Chandra Gautam on September 5, 2004 in Siraha; and Dev Narayan Yadav on June 14, 2005 in Siraha.

11. *'Swatantrata Ra Mukti Sangramma Aghi Badhna Madhesi Mukti Morchako Appeal'*, *Janadesh*, October 3, 2000.

12. Prachanda, *'Barga Sangharsha Ra Vidyarthi Andolan'*, *Yoddha*, BS 2062 Shrawan, p. 23.

13. Shyam Saran, *How India Sees the World* (Juggernaut Books, New Delhi, 2017), pp.169–70.

14. 'Nepal's Troubled Tarai Region', International Crisis Group, Kathmandu/Brussels, Asia Report No. 136, July 9, 2007, p. 22.

15. Ibid.

16. Interview with Matrika Yadav.

17. Kalyan Bhakta Mathema, *Madheshi Uprising: The Resurgence of Ethnicity* (Mandala Book Point, Kathmandu, 2011), p. 74.

18. *'Swatantrata Ra Mukti Sangramma Aghi Badhna Madhesi Mukti Morchako Appeal'*, op. cit.

19. Prachanda, op. cit., p. 22.

20. Exploring the bases for launching a movement in Madhes, Upendra Yadav had written a book in Hindi, *Nepali Jana Andolan Aur Madhesi Mukti ka Sawal* (Madhesi Janadhikar Forum, 2003).

21. Rajendra Maharjan, ed., *Janayuddha Ka Nayak* (Mulyankan Prakashan Griha, Kathmandu, BS 2063), p. 116.

22. For analysis of the reasons behind the Madhesi uprising, see Kalyan Bhakta Mathema, *Madhesi Uprising: The Resurgence of Ethnicity* (Mandala Book Point, Kathmandu, 2011), pp. 39–68, and Rajendra Maharjan, ed., *Madhes Adhyayan*, BS 2069 Falgun, pp. 35–60.

23. An MLA from Sitamarhi, India, Shahid Ali Khan had supported the Madhesi movement, terming it 'in favour of honour'; Anil Sinha of the Bharatiya Janata Party had resorted to a demonstration in Raxaul to support the movement. See *'Nepal's Troubled Tarai Region'*, p. 14.

24. Dhirendra Premarshi and Tula Narayan Shah, *Madhes Bidrohaka Paanch Barsha: Upalabdhi Ra Chunauti* (Nepal Madhes Foundation, Lalitpur, BS 2068), p. 15.

25. According to one report, between January 1, 2008 and May 13, 2011, 149 people were killed by armed groups in the Tarai whereas 132 lost their lives at the hand of state forces. See Deependra Jha/ Sanjay Aryal, *'Taraima Byapta Hatyako Shrinkhala'* (Democratic Freedom and Human Rights Institution, Lalitpur, BS 2068), p. 3.

26. *'Naya Baicharik Spashtata Ra Naya Krantikari Andolan Srishti Garna Ekjut Haun'*, the political report presented by Prachanda at the fifth plenum of the central committee of CPN–Maoist, held at Balaju, Kathmandu, July 2007, p. 17.

27. Indian Ambassador Shiv Shankar Mukherjee had claimed that Indian criminal elements had no hand in criminal activities in the Tarai. See *'Bharatiya Samlagnata Chhaina'*, *Kantipur*, November 24, 2007.

28. Tilak Pathak, *'Patna Baithakko Antar Katha,'* *Nepal*, July 8, 2007, pp. 22–25.

29. Ibid.

30. These passages cite anonymous sources.

31. Prashant Jha, *'South of the Border'*, *Nepali Times*, May 2–8, 2008.

32. *'Nepal's Troubled Tarai Region,'* op. cit., p. 28.

33. 'Birodh ka majh tarai dashau din pani ashanta', BBC Nepali Service, February 22, 2008, https://www.bbc.com/nepali/news/ story/2008/02/printable/080222_terai_update.shtml, accessed on May 17, 2018.

34. Interview with Girija Prasad Koirala, BBC Nepali Service, aired on November 18, 2007.

35. Tilak Pathak/Jitendra Khadga, 'Bharatiya Dutawasma Nepali Rajniti', Nepal, March 2, 2008, pp. 22–25.

36. Ibid.

37. Rookmangud Katawal, Aatmakatha (Publication Nepalaya, Kathmandu, BS 2014), p. 386.

38. The deal was signed by PM Girija Prasad Koirala on behalf of the government, and by Mahantha Thakur, Upendra Yadav and Rajendra Mahato on behalf of the UDMF. On federalism, the deal stated, 'Accepting the aspirations for federal structure including autonomous Madhes province for the people of Madhes, and other autonomous regions for the people of other regions, Nepal shall be a federal democratic republic.'

39. On the military, the deal stated, 'In order to ensure that the Nepali Army is inclusive and reflects national outlook, proportionally inclusive and collective entry of Madhesis and other communities shall be ascertained.' In an indirect indication of dissatisfaction over the deal, Army Chief Rookmangud Katawal had said, on March 8, 2008, at the anniversary programme of NCC in the presence of PM Koirala: 'We have decentralized our recruitment process in order to ascertain easy access into the army for all Nepalis. When entry is already easy and accessible, it is equally important to prove oneself in the competition, as is the international norm.'

40. Tilak Pathak/Jitendra Khadga, op. cit.

41. Dhirendra Premarshi and Tula Narayan Shah, op. cit., pp. 41–42.

42. C.K. Lal, 'Nepaliya Hunalai . . . ' (Martin Chautari, Kathmandu, BS 2067), p. 32.

* My interviews/conversations with Pradeep Giri, Tula Narayan Sah, Matrika Yadav, Prachanda, Upendra Yadav, Jaya Prakash Gupta, Ram Raja Prasad Singh, Chandra Kishor, Dilip Jung Rayamajhi, Revani Thakur, Indian officials and Madhesi politicians.

Chapter 19: Republic in Instalment

1. Press statement issued by former King Gyanendra when he left Narayanhity palace and moved to Nagarjuna Palace, June 11, 2008.
2. In the Constituent Assembly election, 240 members were elected under the first-past-the-post system; 335 were elected under the proportional representation system; and twenty-six were nominated by the cabinet. As such, the Maoists bagged 239 seats (including People's Front, which merged into it); Nepali Congress won 114 seats, CPN–UML won 108 seats; MJF won fifty-two seats and TMLP won twenty seats.
3. Interview with former King Gyanendra, aired on News24 Television on July 8, 2012.
4. The seven parties that expressed a commitment to abolishing the monarchy included the Nepali Congress, the CPN–UML, the Maoists, the People's Front, the Nepal Workers and Peasants Party, the Sadbhavana Party (Anandi Devi) and the United Leftist Front.
5. Madhav Dhungel, *'Ek Dinko Ek Jug'*, *Nepal*, June 8, 2008, pp. 26–27.
6. Krishna Prasad Sitaula, *'General Pani Jangiye'*, *Annapurna Post*, May 29, 2013.
7. Kiran Bhandari/Yubaraj Ghimire, *'Sambidhan Sabha Bhanddai Raja Sanga Milera Satta Hatyauna Chahanthe Prachanda-Baburam,'* www.setopati.com/raajneeti/650/ accessed on May 9, 2013.
8. Ibid.
9. My conversation with then King Gyanendra, September 7, 2007, Narayanhity Palace, Kathmandu.
10. Ibid.
11. Interview with Girija Prasad Koirala, August 15, 2009, Kathmandu.
12. With the fourth amendment in the interim Constitution on May 28, 2008, the president replaced the king as head of the state.
13. The seven conditions laid down by the Nepali Congress were: full implementation of peace agreement; dissolution of YCL and ending their anarchic behaviour; return of seized properties; environment conducive for return of displaced persons; integration of combatants; and handover or destruction of weapons.
14. Interview with Shekhar Koirala, *Nagarik*, March 29, 2013.
15. Tilak Pathak, *'Maobaditira Dhalkiyo Delhi'*, *Nepal*, June 22, 2008.

16. For the election of president and vice-president, the Nepali Congress fielded Ram Baran Yadav and Man Bahadur Bishwakarma; the UML fielded Ramprit Paswan and Ashta Laxmi Shakya; and the Maoists fielded Ram Raja Prasad Singh and Shanta Shrestha, respectively. The MJF fielded former judge Parmananda Jha as a candidate for vice-president. In the first phase of election on July 19, 2008, Jha was elected vice-president. But none of the candidates for president were able to garner the required majority. In the second phase of the election, held two days later, Congress candidate Yadav was elected the president with support from the UML and the MJF. Yadav bagged 308 votes against his competitor Ram Raja Prasad Singh, who got 282 votes.

* My interviews/conversations with then King Gyanendra Shah, Girija Prasad Koirala, Krishna Prasad Sitaula, Prachanda, Maoist sources, palace officials and army brigadiers.

Part III: The Touchdown

Chapter 20: The Rise and Fall of the Maoist Government

1. A portion of the letter written by India's Congress President Sonia Gandhi to Prachanda on April 16, 2008. A copy is available with the author.
2. In the voting conducted by the Parliament to elect prime minister, Prachanda, who was backed by twenty-one parties, including the CPN–UML and the MJF, bagged 464 votes, whereas Congress leader Sher Bahadur Deuba obtained only 113 votes.
3. Ganesh Raj Sharma, compiled by, *BP Koiralako Atmabrittanta* (Jagadamba Prakashan, Lalitpur, BS 2055), p. 230.
4. Interview with Prachanda, *BBC Nepali Service*, aired on December 23, 2009.
5. 'China Bhraman Safal: PM', *Gorkhapatra*, August 27, 2008.
6. 'Krantikari Karyadisha Tatha Karyanitiko Thap Bikas Gardai, Naya Baicharik Ekrupta Ra Sangathanatmak Ekata Hasil Garna Ekjut Houn', the political report endorsed by Kharipati conclave of the Maoists, BS 2065 Mangsir, p. 5.

7. As I confirmed from multiple sources including Indian officials, Prachanda, and Nepali Congress leaders.

8. Aditya Adhikari, *The Bullet and the Ballot Box: The Story of Nepal's Maoist Revolution* (Aleph Book Company, New Delhi, 2014), p. 214.

9. As a think tank report comments, 'New Delhi does not view Nepal as a fully foreign or fully sovereign country.' See *Nepal's Future : In Whose Hands?*, International Crisis Group Policy Report No. 173, Kathmandu/Brussels, August 13, 2009, p. 22.

10. Interview with Prachanda, August 24, 2011, Kathmandu.

11. *'Maobadile Maoko Naam Durupayog Garyo: China'*, *Kantipur*, July 12, 2002.

12. *'Chinadwara Maobadi Biruddhako Karbahiko Samarthan'*, *Kantipur*, July 11, 2002. During the period of insurgency, Maoists had smuggled in NRs. 7 million worth of AK-7 rifles, gelatins, ammunitions and combat dresses from Tibetan region. On October 27, 2003, Chinese police arrested four Nepalis, including Maoist worker Hiralal Shrestha 'Ananda', from Khasa bazaar in a bordering Tibetan city. They were taken to Lhasa, where they were sentenced to death. However, due to intervention from a higher level, the sentence was suspended. Of them, Shrestha was released much later, after the peace process began in Nepal, in March 2009. See *'Hiralal Shrestha Ananda: Jo Mrityudandako Sajaya Jitera Banchiraheko Chha'*, *Naya Patrika*, November 30, 2011.

13. Deepak Sapkota, *Uthalputhalka Dus Barsha* (Krantikari Patrakar Sangh, Kathmandu, BS 2066), p. 46.

14. Interview with Prof. Wang Hongwei, *Janadesh*, July 11, 2006.

15. Wang Jiarui, minister of the international department of the central committee, Chinese Communist Party, had written a letter on April 18, 2008 to congratulate Prachanda. The letter said, 'The success of the Constituent Assembly election represents a milestone in the country's peace process.'

16. Interview with Wang Hongwei, *Nepal*, November 4, 2007, p. 30.

17. Suresh Karki, *Badlindo Sandarvama Nepal-China Sambandha Ra Bharat*, Nepal China People's Forum, Kathmandu, pp. 68–70.

18. According to official figures with the home ministry, there are 25,000 Tibetan refugees living in Nepal.

19. Talking to journalists, the Chinese ambassador lambasted the 'arrest and release' of Tibetan demonstrators by the Nepali government as a 'drama' and said it was staged at the direction of foreigners. See *'Bikhandankari Gatibidhi Rokna China Ko Agraha'*, *Kantipur*, May 13, 2008.

20. Saransh Sehgal, 'Nepal bends to China over Tibet', *Asia Times online*, December 6, 2011.

21. *'Beijing Janasath Sarkar Dhalne Khel Shuru Bhayo: Dahal'*, *Nagarik*, June 22, 2009.

22. Kamal Prakash Malla, ed., *Nepal: Perspective on Continuity and Chang*, (Center for Nepal and Asian Studies, Kathmandu, 1989), p. 349.

23. Hiranya Lal Shrestha, *Sixty Years of Dynamic Partnership, Nepal-China Society*, Kathmandu, 2015, pp. 65–68.

24. Sudheer Sharma, ed., *Nepali Sena: Nagarik Niyantran ka Chunauti* (Martin Chautari, Kathmandu, 2010), pp. 52–53.

25. Sudheer Sharma, *'Jhandai Durghatana'*, *Kantipur*, April 25, 2009.

26. Ibid

27. Ibid.

28. Saran made the revelation at a programme in New Delhi held on July 27, 2012. See Mahesh Acharya, *'India intervened in Katawal case: Saran'*, *The Kathmandu Post*, July 29, 2012.

29. Interview with Shyam Saran, *Kantipur*, January 14, 2013.

30. As told by a Kathmandu-based Indian diplomat.

31. Prachanda had said this during an interaction with select editors and writers at his Naya Bazaar residence on August 24, 2011.

32. Gopal Kirati, *'Baidyaka Saat Bikalpa'*, *Kantipur*, July 5, 2013.

33. Interaction of editors with Prachanda, Naya Bazaar residence, August 24, 2011.

* My interviews/conversations with Ram Baran Yadav, Prachanda, Baburam Bhattarai, Mohan Baidhya 'Kiran', Netra Bikram Chand 'Biplav', Barshaman Pun 'Ananta', Majoj Jung Thapa, Prof. Hu Sheshing, Prof. Wang Hongwei, Ai Peng, Madan Regmi, Sunil Sharma, Amaresh Kumar Singh, NC leaders, Maoist sources, staff of President's office, Chinese diplomats, Indian officials, my interaction with Indian and Chinese experts/officials in Delhi and Beijing, army officers, UNMIN officials and Nepali Congress leaders.

Chapter 21: 'Course Correction'

1. Prachanda himself revealed that he had tried to talk to senior Indian officials before taking action against Katawal. He had urged Indian Ambassador Sood to relay the message that he wanted to invite the foreign secretary or another high-ranking official. Sood, however, replied that was not going to be possible since India was already in election mode. See interview with Prachanda, *The Hindu*, May 11, 2009.

2. Letter by Indian ambassador to Nepali foreign minister on December 4, 2009. See *'MRP Nirnaya Radda'*, *Kantipur*, April 2, 2010.

3. Sebastian von Einsiedel, David Malone and Suman Pradhan, ed., *Nepal in Transition: From People's War to Fragile Peace* (Cambridge University Press, New York, 2002), p. 217.

4. V. Raman, *The Kao Boys of RAW: Down Memory Lane* (Lancer Publishers, New Delhi, 2007), pp. 245–46.

5. The deputy chief of mission at the US embassy, Randy Berry, had mentioned in his cable sent to Washington DC quoting sources that Prachanda had met not only Indian but also Chinese officials in the course of his Singapore visit. See cable leaked by Wikileaks, 09KATHMANDU1094.

6. Dinesh Wagle, *'Samuhik Samayojan Nagarna Sujhab'*, *Kantipur*, December 20, 2009.

7. Prachanda, *'Bideshi Haikam Ra Hastachhep Biruddha'*, *Naya Patrika*, January 12, 2010.

8. Ibid.

9. Gajendra Bohora, *'Teesta-Kangra Dabi Garnuparchha'*, *Nagarik*, January 19, 2010.

10. Saroj Raj Adhikari, *Chakrabyuhama Chandra Surya* (Shangrila books, Kathmandu, BS 2069), p. 51. After the assassination of Jamim Shah, general secretary of Islamic Sangh Faizan Ahmed was killed similarly and Yunus Ansari, director of National Television, was shot at inside the prison. Earlier, so-called anti-Indians such as then MP Mirja Dilsad Baig, Majid Manihar, Saukat Baig had also been killed. See Saroj Raj Adhikari, *Chakrabyuhama Chandra Surya*; and K.P. Dhungana, *Open Secret* (Fineprint, Kathmandu, BS 2069).

11. Interview with Rakesh Sood, *Kantipur*, June 14, 2009.

12. Prashant Jha, 'Re-engagement', *Nepali Times*, March 11–17, 2011.

13. Sudheer Sharma, 'Delhika Tin Chaso', *Kantipur*, July 27, 2011.

14. Ananda Swaroop Verma, 'Bharat Sarkar Chahadaina Prachanda', *Samachar*, July 17–August 1, 2011.

15. 'Denial of China visa to top general angers India, defence ties on hold', *The Indian Express*, August 28, 2010.

16. The report was published in a paper edited by Kishor Shrestha, who is the president of the Nepal–China Media Forum. See 'Hong Kongko Hotelma Prachandale Kosita Haat Milaya?', *Jana Aastha*, January 13, 2010.

17. In the words of the head of the Tibetan government-in-exile, Lobsang Sangay, 'Although rest of the world is not paying attention, Nepal is falling under Chinese influence.' See his interview, *Time*, October 10, 2011.

18. Benjamin Kang Lim/Reuters, 'China to invest 4 billion US dollars for Lumbini development', *Republica*, June 20, 2011.

19. Admitting that he met Katawal, Biplav had said in one interview, 'Yes, it is true that (I met) with few army generals including Katawal.' See *Janadesh*, September 21, 2010.

20. According to Chandra Bahadur Gurung, parliamentary party leader of RPP–Nepal, 'Prachanda has talked about the possibility of keeping cultural or religious monarchy. Our main agenda on national unity and independence is also similar.' See *Himal Khabarpatrika*, August 1–16, 2010, p. 27.

21. See details of Mahara–Chinese dialogue: 'Maobadidwara Sabhasad Kinna China Sanga 50 Crore Maag', *Annapurna Post*, September 4, 2010. The Chinese embassy in Kathmandu claimed that the news report was totally wrong and malicious.

22. Saroj Dahal, 'Asafal Bidroha,' *Himal Khabarpatrika*, May 15–29, 2010, p. 23.

23. 'Nepal-Dahal Gopya Sahamati Alpatra', *Nagarik*, July 5, 2010.

24. Sanjay Upadhya, *Nepal and the Geo-Strategic Rivalry between China and India* (Routledge, New York, 2014), pp. 155–58.

25. Arvind Gupta, 'India needs a new paradigm in its Nepal policy', IDSA comment, August 18, 2010, www.idsa.in/idsacomments/IndianeedsanewparadigminitsNepalpolicy_agupta_180810 accesses on April 23, 2013.

26. Siddhartha Varadarajan, 'The danger in India's Nepal policy', *The Hindu*, August 16, 2010.

27. After he took over as India's foreign secretary in August 2011, Ranjan Mathai said that his main challenge would be to maintain constructive cooperation with close neighbours and he would emphasize the same during his tenure.

28. S.D. Muni, 'Chinese influence in Nepal: A major challenge for India', *The Tribune*, April 30, 2011.

* My interviews/conversations with Madhav Kumar Nepal, Prachanda, Baburam Bhattarai, Jaswant Sinha, P. Chidambaram, Rakesh Sood, UNMIN officials, MEA officers and Chinese academics.

Chapter 22: The Tempest Within

1. Soon after Baburam was elected as prime minister, Prof. Muni tweeted this. See www.twitter.com/SDMUNI/status/108059094316883968, accessed on August 29, 2011.

2. Bhojraj Bhat, *'Bhattarailai Pradhan Mantri Banauna Bharatko Dabab'*, *Nagarik*, January 5, 2010; and *'Sarkarma Gaye Pani Bidroha, Nagaye Pani Bidroha,'* *Nagarik*, January 6, 2010.

3. Interview with Baburam Bhattarai, *BBC Nepali Service*, aired on January 5, 2010.

4. Interview with Baburam Bhattarai, *Nagarik*, December 16, 2010.

5. *'Sarkarma Gaye Pani Bidroha, Nagaye Pani Bidroha'*, *Nagarik*, January 6, 2010.

6. Those who wrote the 'note of dissent' against the party's decision included Baburam Bhattarai, Dinanath Sharma, Bhim Prasad Gautam, Nabaraj Subedi, Prabhu Sah, Ramrijhan Yadav, Khagaraj Bhatta and Sabina Aryal.

7. Daman Bahadur Ghale, *'Chaitra 28 Ko Breakthrough Ra Pachhillo Almal'*, *Annapurna Post*, June 28, 2012

8. *'Tyas Din Kasari Kura Ultiyo?'*, *Jana Aastha*, April 18, 2012.

9. The army had prepared at least two proposals on this. One was the *'Maobadi Ladakuharuko Samayojanko Bikalpa (BS 2067)'* which the brigadier general Mahesh Bikram Karki 'briefed' the political leaders about. The second was the concept paper tilted *'Rastriya Bikas Tatha Surakchhya Mahanirdeshanalayako Gathan Prakriya (BS 2068).'*

10. Prashant Jha, *Battles of the New Republic* (Aleph Book Company, New Delhi, 2014), p. 320.
11. Interview with Rajendra Mahato, May 29, 2013, Kathmandu.
12. Prashant Jha, *Battles of the New Republic* (Aleph Book Company, New Delhi, 2014), p. 320.
13. Letter written by Kiran and Badal with conditions for party unity, on June 14, 2012.

* My interviews/conversations with Prachanda, Baburam Bhattarai, Mohan Baidhya 'Kiran', Narayan Kazi Shrestha, Rajendra Mahato, Indian diplomats, Maoist leaders, army officers and PLA commanders.

Chapter 23: Constitution on Fast Track

1. 'New Constitution through double fast track: PM', *The Kathmandu Post,* June 18, 2015.
2. Interview with Prachanda, September 26, 2015, Kathmandu.
3. In the second CA, RPP–N had twenty-three seats, MJF–D fourteen, RPP thirteen, TMLP eleven, MJF–N ten and the other twenty-four smaller parties, seventy-nine.
4. The Parliament had formed an inquiry committee under NSP leader Laxman Lal Karna, which didn't find any evidence of vote-rigging.
5. These information and analyses are based on multiple anonymous sources related to Nepali political parties.
6. 'Human Rights Situation During the Agitation Before and After Promulgation of the Constitution of Nepal', November 2015, National Human Rights Commission Nepal, p. 17.

* My interviews/conversations with Ram Baran Yadav, Prachanda, Baburam Bhattarai, Sushil Koirala, K.P. Sharma Oli, Rajendra Mahato, Ranjit Rae and other Indian diplomats.

Chapter 24: The Blockade

1. Jyoti Malhotra, 'Modi should know that he is PM of all of India, says Manmohan Singh', *India Today,* February 11, 2016, http://indiatoday.intoday.in/story/manmohan-singh-narendra-modi-politics-gandhis/1/592973.html.

2. Interview with Prachanda, September 26, 2015, Kathmandu.

3. Ibid.

4. Prashant Jha, 'How India was both right and wrong on Nepal', *Hindustan Times*, September 20, 2015, www.hindustantimes. com/analysis/how-india-was-right-and-wrong-on-nepal/ article1-1391810.aspx.

5. Press statement, Embassy of India, Kathmandu, September 19, 2015.

6. 'Statement on the Promulgation of Nepal's Constitution', American Embassy, Kathmandu, September 22, 2015.

7. 'Statement on the situation in Nepal', press statement issued by the Indian Embassy, Kathmandu, September 20, 2015.

8. Sanjaya Baru, *The Accidental Prime Minister: The Making and Unmaking of Manmohan Singh* (Penguin Books, New Delhi, 2014), pp. 38–40.

9. *Ek Bharat Shreshtha Bharat*, BJP election manifesto 2014, pp. 39–40.

10. 'Modi's oops moment: Calls Bhutan, "Nepal" during Parliament address', timesofindia.indiatimes.com, June 16, 2014.

11. Jaya Raj Acharya, *Yadunath Khanal: Jiwani ra Bichar* Sajha Prakashan, Lalitpur, BS 2059), p. 85.

12. Suhasini Haidar, 'South Block in the Shade', *The Hindu*, May 13, 2016.

13. 'Text of the PM's speech at the official handover and inaugural ceremony of National Trauma Centre in Kathmandu', November 25, 2014. For the full text, see goo.gl/L25iTX.

14. Interview with Sher Bahadur Deuba, *Kantipur*, August 2, 2015.

15. Press statement, Embassy of India, Kathmandu, February 18, 2015.

16. Kamal Thapa, 'Bharatka pharak-pharak nikayko pharak-pharak udeshya', *Kantipur*, February 19, 2016.

17. Interview with Pradip Gyawali, November 23, 2015, Kathmandu.

18. Interview with Pradip Gyawali, November 23, 2015, Kathmandu.

19. 'Statement on the situation in Nepal', Embassy of India, Kathmandu, September 21, 2015.

20. Ibid.

21. Muzamil Jaleel, 'Why Bihar is tracking a group of protesters on a border bridge', *The Indian Express*, October 4, 2015.

22. '*Sushil Koirala pradhanmantri ummedwar banda Dahal dukhi*', setopati.com, October 11, 2015.

23. Dhanraj Gurung, '*Shdayantrako bhumarima Sushil*', *Kantipur*, October 27, 2015.

24. 'Statement on the election of the new Prime Minister of Nepal', Embassy of India, October 11, 2015.

25. Press Statement, Embassy of India, Kathmandu, November 2, 2015.

26. Press Statement, Embassy of India, Kathmandu, November 3, 2015.

27. Press Statement, Embassy of India, Kathmandu, November 7 and 8, 2015.

28. 'Joint Statement on the United Kingdom–India Summit 2015', November 12, 2015, https://www.gov.uk/government/news/joint-statement-on-the-united-kingdom-india-summit-2015.

29. 'Intelligence Bureau alerts Modi govt over growing anti-India anger in Nepal', *Mail Today Daily*, October 7, 2015, http://indiatoday.intoday.in/story/ib-spooks-modi-govt-over-anti-india-anger-in-nepal/1/492286.html.

30. 'PMO asks High Commission for report on Nepalese protesters in London', *The Indian Express*, November 14, 2015.

31. Sumit Ganguly and Brandon Miliate, 'India Pushes Nepal into China's Arms', *Foreign Policy*, October 23, 2015, http://foreignpolicy.com/2015/10/23/india-pushes-nepal-into-chinas-arms/.

32. 'This Constitution is a huge milestone for Nepal', *The Kathmandu Post*, November 23, 2015, http://bit.ly/1I5lkNG.

33. For example: Prem Shankar Jha, 'India's Big Brother Approach Will Not Work With Nepal Anymore', *The Wire*, April 14, 2016; Mani Shankar Aiyar, 'Well Done, Modi, For Driving Nepal Into China's Arms', *ndtv.com*, March 28, 2016; Harish Khare, 'How Nepal was lost', *The Tribune*, October 9, 2015; Rajiv Kumar, 'Big brother's blockade', *The Indian Express*, October 10, 2015.

34. Jyoti Malhotra, 'Modi should know that he is PM of all of India, says Manmohan Singh', *India Today*, February 11, 2016, http://indiatoday.intoday.in/story/manmohan-singh-narendra-modi-politics-gandhis/1/592973.html.

35. '*Bharatiya nakabandi hatauna sena ko bhumika thiyo*', setopati.com, February 11, 2017.

36. Ibid.

37. Sudheer Sharma, *'Sthai sattatarpha pharkando sambandha'*, *Kantipur*, February 9, 2016.

38. Bharat Bhushan, 'India's spectacular policy failure in Nepal', *Catchnews.com*, September 29, 2015. See http://www.catchnews. com/india-news/india-s-spectacular-policy-failure-in-nepal-1443031577.html.

39. Devendra Bhattarai, *'Oliko parantu bhraman'*, *Kantipur*, February 24, 2016.

40. Ibid.

41. Shubhajit Roy, 'Days after Oli visit, 40% cut in aid to Nepal', *The Indian Express*, March 1, 2016.

42. 'Kathmandu accuses Delhi of backing plot to topple government', *The Hindu*, May 8, 2016.

43. Sumit Ganguly and Brandon Miliate, 'India Pushes Nepal into China's Arms', *Foreign Policy*, October 23, 2015. See https://foreignpolicy.com/2015/10/23/india-pushes-nepal-into-chinas-arms/.

44. 'China opens its first combined transport service to Nepal', *People's Daily Online*, May 12, 2016, http://en.people.cn/n3/2016/0512/c90000-9056831.html.

* My interviews/conversations with Sher Bahadur Deuba, Prachanda, Kamal Thapa, K.P. Sharma Oli, Pradeep Gyawali, Gen. Rajendra Chettry, Mahesh Maske, Ranjit Rae, Congress, UML and Maoist leaders, Indian officials, Madhesi leaders and army officers.

Part IV: Destiny

Chapter 25: Realm of Republic

1. Surya Thapa, *Nepalma Rajtantra Ra Dalharu Bichko Sangharsha* (Navayug Prakashan, Kathmandu, BS 2062).

2. Chaitanya Mishra, *Rajtantra Antyaka Karan: Khukuliyeko Samajik Sambandha, Nepal,* June 8, 2008, pp. 34–36.

3. Narayan Wagle, *'Shantiko Karyasuchima Nepal Prabesh,'* *Kantipur*, February 15, 2005.

4. Interview with ex-king Gyanendra, aired on News24 channel, July 8, 2012.

* My interviews/conversations with then King Gyanendra Shah, army sources and palace officials.

Chapter 26: Changed Rebels

1. Aavas, *Palapala,* Event Nepalaya, Kathmandu, 2004.
2. *Nepal Communist Party Maobadika Aitihasik Dastawejharu* (Central Department of Publications, CPN–Maoists, BS 2054), p. 19.
3. 'Nepali *Krantiko Naya Samsleshan: Ek Aitihasik Awashyakta,'* political paper presented at the seventh general convention, BS 2069, p. 36.
4. *Mahan Agragami Chhalang: Itihasko Apariharya Awashyakta* (CPN–Maoist, Central Department of Publications, BS 2057), pp. 78–79.
5. *Nepal Communist Party (Maobadi) ka Aitihasik Dastawejharu* (CPN–Maoist, Mechi–Koshi regional bureau, BS 2063), p. 254.
6. Ibid, p. 309.
7. 'Nepali *Krantiko Naya Samsleshan: Ek Aitihasik Awashyakta,'* op. cit., p. 38.
8. Ibid, p. 35

* My interviews/conversations with Prachanda, Baburam Bhattarai and other Maoist leaders.

Chapter 27: Unchanged Neighbour

1. *Non Alignment 2.0: A Foreign and Strategic Policy for India in the Twenty-first Century,* a report prepared for India's National Defence College and Centre for Policy Research, by eight experts (Sunil Khilnani, Rajiv Kumar, Pratap Bhanu Mehta, Prakash Menon, Nandan Nilekani, Shrinath Raghavan, Shyam Saran and Siddhartha Varadarajan), 2012, p. 15.
2. Avatar Singh Bhasin, *Nepal-India, Nepal-China Relations (Part 1)* (Gitika Publishers, New Delhi, 2005), p. 871.
3. Shreeman Narayan wrote a memoir about his efforts to improve ties with the monarchy. See Shreeman Narayan, *India and Nepal: An Exercise in Open Diplomacy* (Hind Pocket Books, Delhi, 1971).

4. Jayaraj Acharya, *Yadunath Khanal: Jibani Ra Bichar* (Sajha Prakashan, Lalitpur, BS 2059), p. 78.

5. To understand the role of RAW during Sikkim's merger, read GBS Sidhu, *Sikkim: Dawn of Democracy* (Penguin Random House, Gurgaon, India), 2018.

6. Jagat Nepal, *BP ko Bidroha* (Barhakhari Books, Kathmandu, BS 2075), p. 273.

7. S.D. Muni, *India's Foreign Policy: The Democracy Dimension* (Cambridge University Press, New Delhi, 2009), pp. 61–62.

8. Dhruba Kumar, ed., *Nepal's India Policy* (Center for Nepal and Asian Studies, Kathmandu, 1992), pp. 5–33. A draft of proposed agreement is also included in the book.

9. Krishna V. Rajan, ed., *The Ambassadors' Club* (Harper Collins Publishers, New Delhi, 2012), pp. 38–42.

10. V.G. Verghese, 'Give the Gujral doctrine a chance,' www.rediff.com/news/oct/30diplo1.htm accessed on December 16, 2012.

11. Prashant Jha, *Battles of the New Republic* (Aleph Book Company, New Delhi, 2014), pp. 89–90.

12. Hari Sharma, *'Nepalko Bhurajniti ra Maobaadi Janayuddha'*, *Himal Khabarpatrika*, BS 2061 Bhadra, Year 14, Vol. 10.

13. India's former Foreign Secretary Shyam Saran has analysed the Nepali monarchy's 'nationalist card' from the Indian perspective. See Shyam Saran, *How India Sees the World*, (Juggernaut Books, New Delhi, 2017), p. 166.

14. Such letters are available in documents compiled in *Part 1-5 of Nepal-India, Nepal-China Relations* by Avatar Singh Bhasin (Gitika Publishers, New Delhi, 2005).

15. V.K. Singh, *India's External Intelligence: Secrets of Research and Analysis Wing* (Manas Publications, New Delhi, 2007), p. 50.

16. Interview with Shekhar Koirala, *Nagarik*, March 29, 2013.

17. 'Ad hoc Country', *The Economist*, June 22, 2013, p. 27.

18. Rameshwore Bohora, *'Lajjaspad Nirnaya'*, *Himal Khbarpatrika*, May 19, 2013, p. 30.

19. Devendra Bhattarai, *'South Blockko Nepal Drishti'*, *Kantipur*, April 27, 2013.

20. Sanjay Upadhya, *The Raj Lives: India in Nepal* (Vitasta Publishing, New Delhi, 2008), p. 232.

21. Ibid., p. 246.

22. Ibid.

23. Chandra Shekhar Adhikari, *'Sandhi-samjhauta punarawalokan'*, *Kantipur*, July 5, 2016.

24. Sachin Parashar/Sanjay Dutt, 'Ties strained as India cuts fuel subsidy to Bhutan', *The Times of India*, July 6, 2013; and C. Rajamohan, 'The Faraway Neighbor', *The Indian Express*, July 17, 2013.

25. Although India's GMR bagged Upper Karnali (900 MW) and Upper Marshyangdi (800 MW) and Sutlej bagged Arun Third (900 MW) hydropower projects, the process of their construction had not taken off for a long time.

26. Kanak Mani Dixit and Shastri Ramachandran, ed., *State of Nepal* (Himal Books, Lalitpur, 2002), pp. 235–52.

27. Dhruba Kumar, 'Reconsidering Nepal-India Bilateral Relations', *Contributions to Nepalese Studies*, Vol. 21, No.1, January 1994, pp.73–89.

28. Anja Manuel, *This Brave New World: India, China, and the United States* (Simon & Schuster, New York, 2016), p. 227.

29. As I heard from Nepali government officials, businessmen and industrialists during my conversations with them.

30. 'Know Your Own Strength', *The Economist*, March 30, 2013, pp. 20–22.

31. 'Wang Yi Talks about the Trilateral Relations Among China, Nepal and India', Chinese foreign ministry press note, April 18, 2018. See www.fmprc.gov.cn/mfa_eng/zxxx_662805/t1552708.shtml accessed on December 13, 2018.

32. The EPG has former foreign minister Bhekh Bahadur Thapa, former minister Nilambar Acharya, former Chief of CIAA Surya Nath Upadhyaya and NCP leader Rajan Bhattarai from the Nepali side; and BJP leader Bhagat Singh Koshiyari, former Ambassador Jayanta Prasad, Prof. Mahendra P. Lama and Prof. B.C. Upreti from the Indian side.

33. Rumel Dahiya and Ashok Behuria, ed., *India's Neighborhood: Challenges in the Next Two Decades* (IDSA/Pentagon Security International, New Delhi, 2012), p. 156.

* My interviews/conversations with Nepali and Indian officials.

List of Interviews/Conversations

1. Achyut Krishna Kharel, former IGP of Nepal Police: November 15, 2005, Kathmandu
2. Ai Peng, then vice minister of International Department of Communist Party of China: September 9, 2011, Beijing
3. Amaresh Kumar Singh, NC leader: May 6, 2006, Kirtipur
4. Ananda Swaroop Verma, Indian writer: January 24, 2011, New Delhi
5. Amod Gurung, former SSP of Nepal Police: December 8, 2005, Kathmandu
6. Baburam Bhattarai, former prime minister: April 24, 2011, Lalitpur and August 31, 2005 (via email)
7. Bam Kumari Budha, former member of Parliament: July 3, 2003, Rolpa
8. Bamdev Chhetri, former Maoist leader: June 2, 2006, Kathmandu
9. Barsha Man Pun 'Ananta', NCP leader and former Maoist commander: June 7, 2006, Lalitpur
10. Bharat Bhushan, Indian journalist: April 7, 2005, Kathmandu
11. Bharat Dahal, former Maoist leader: July 7, 2003, Dang
12. Bhesh Bahadur Thapa, former foreign minister: April 25, 2013, Kathmandu
13. Bibek Kumar Shah, Lt Gen. (Retd) of Nepali Army and former military secretary to the king: December 18, 2007, Kathmandu

14. C.B. Gurung, Lt Gen. (Retd) of Nepali Army: August 28, 2006, Kathmandu
15. Devi Ram Sharma, former chief of National Investigation Department: June 5, 2013, Lalitpur
16. Deepak Gurung, Brig. Gen. (Retd) of Nepali Army: October 9, 2005, Kathmandu
17. Dhruba Kumar, professor of political science: July 25, 2003, Kathmandu
18. Dilip Jung Rayamajhi, Brig. Gen. (Retd) of Nepali Army and former chief of Military Intelligence: May 5, 2012, Kathmandu
19. Dinanath Sharma, former Maoist leader: June 3, 2006, Kathmandu
20. Deep Kumar Upadhyay, NC leader and former Nepali ambassador to India: September 26, 2015, Kathmandu
21. Durga Subedi, former leader of NC: November 5, 2012, Kathmandu
22. Gyanendra Shah, former king: September 7, 2007, Kathmandu
23. Girija Prasad Koirala, former prime minister and NC president: April 6, 2004, July, 2005 and August 15, 2009, Kathmandu
24. Govinda Neupane, writer: October 5, 2005, Kathmandu
25. Haribol Gajurel, former Maoist leader: July 11, 2013, Kathmandu
26. Hu Sheshing, professor of China Institutes of Contemporary International Relations: September 9, 2011 and October 12, 2015, Beijing
27. Janardan Sharma 'Prabhakar', NCP leader and former Maoist commander: June 3, 2005, Kathmandu
28. Jaya Prakash Gupta, former minister: November 5, 2005, Kathmandu
29. Sir Jeffrey James, then British special envoy to Nepal: June 14, 2003, Kathmandu
30. Kamal Thapa, RPP–N president and former deputy-prime minister: May 15, 2008 and December 9, 2015, Kathmandu
31. Krishna Bahadur Mahara, speaker of the Parliament and former Maoist leader: May 21, 2003, Kathmandu
32. Krishna Dhoj Khadka, former Maoist leader: June 18, 2006, Kathmandu
33. Krishna Khanal, professor of political science: August 24, 2005, Kathmandu
34. Krishna Prasad Sitaula, NC leader: June 10, 2012, Kathmandu

35. Lokendra Bahadur Shah, former president of Rukum District Development Committee: July 22, 2003, Kathmandu
36. Madan Regmi, founder of China Study Center, Nepal: April 25, 2012, Kathmandu
37. Mahantha Thakur, Madhesi leader: November 18, 2015, Kathmandu
38. Mahesh Kumar Maskey, former Nepali Ambassador to China: September 12, 2015, Beijing
39. Masta Bahadur Shrestha, former Maoist leader: July 6, 2003, Dang
40. Matrika Yadav, former Maoist leader: December 5, 2005, Nakkhu jail
41. Minendra Rijal, NC leader: June 11, 2005, Kathmandu
42. Mohan Baidya 'Kiran', Maoist leader: January 5, 2013, Kathmandu
43. Mohan Bikram Singh, CPN–Masal leader: November 16, 2003, Kathmandu
44. Mumaram Khanal, former Maoist leader: November 6, 2012, Lalitpur
45. Narayan Kaji Shrestha 'Prakash', NCP leader and former deputy prime minister: September 14, 2012, Lalitpur
46. Narendra Jung Peter, former Maoist leader: July 9, 2003, Nepalgunj
47. Netra Bikram Chand 'Biplav', Maoist leader: December 15, 2005, Rukumkot and July 17, 2016, Kathmandu
48. P. Chidambaram, then Indian home minister: July 27, 2011, New Delhi
49. Padma Ratna Tuladhar, human rights activist: July 22, 2005, Kathmandu
50. P.K. Hormis Tharakan, former chief of RAW: August 17, 2009, New Delhi
51. Pradip Gyawali, NCP leader: November 23, 2015, Kathmandu
52. Prakash Karat, then general secretary of CPI–M: January 7, 2010, New Delhi
53. Puranjan Acharya, former secretary to Girija Prasad Koirala: April 27, 2013, Kathmandu
54. Pushpa Kamal Dahal 'Prachanda', former prime minister: March 16, 2006, New Delhi, August 24, 2011 and September 26, 2015, Kathmandu.
55. Rabindra Shrestha, former Maoist leader: June 6, 2006, Kathmandu
56. Rajendra Mahato, Madhesi leader: May 29, 2013, Kathmandu
57. Ram Baran Yadav, former President of Nepal: November 26, 2015, Lalitpur

58. Ram Karki, NCP leader: November 30, 2012, Kathmandu
59. Ravi Karki, former Maoist leader: November 1, 2005, Kathmandu
60. Sachhit Shamsher Rana, former chief of Nepali Army: August 25, 2002, Kathmandu
61. Santosh Buda Magar, Maoist leader: December 11, 2005, Rolpa
62. S.D. Muni, professor and former ambassador of India: November 25, 2010, Kathmandu
63. Shakti Lamsal, former Maoist leader: October 19, 2005, Kathmandu
64. Sher Bahadur Deuba, NC president and former prime minister: April 25, 2003 and October 13, 2015, Kathmandu
65. Sushil Koirala, former prime minister and former president of NC: January 24, 2013, Kathmandu
66. Thomas A. Marks, US researcher: January 23, 2004, Kathmandu
67. Tula Narayan Shah, executive director of Nepal Madhes Foundation: November 22–23, 2012, Lalitpur
68. Wang Hongwei, professor of Institute of Asia-Pacific Studies, Beijing: September 8, 2011, Beijing and October 26, 2007, Kathmandu
69. Yashwant Sinha, former Indian Minister: January 5, 2010, New Delhi